2nd Edition

Integrated **Business Projects**

Olinzock, Arney, & Skean

Dr. Anthony A. Olinzock
Professor and Chair
Department of Instructional Systems, Leadership,
and Workforce Development
Mississippi State University

Dr. Janna B. Arney
Assistant Professor, School of Business
University of Texas at Brownsville

Wylma Skean
Associate Professor
Marshall University

Contributing Authors
Tinukwa C. Okojie
Graduate Teaching Assistant
Mississippi State University

Tommy Newland, Jr.
Director, Advanced Digital Resource Center
Mississippi State University

THOMSON
★
SOUTH-WESTERN

Australia · Canada · Mexico · Singapore · Spain · United Kingdom · United States

Integrated Business Projects, 2nd Edition

Olinzock, Arney, & Skean

VP/Editorial Director:
Jack W. Calhoun

VP/Editor-in-Chief:
Dave Shaut

Senior Publisher:
Karen Schmohe

Acquisitions Editor:
Jane Phelan

Project Manager:
Dave Lafferty

Director Educational Marketing:
Carol Volz

Marketing Manager:
Michael Cloran

Marketing Coordinator:
Georgianna Wright

Consulting Editor:
Dianne S. Rankin

Editor:
Kim Kusnerak

Copyeditor:
Marianne Miller

Production Manager:
Tricia Matthews Boies

Sr. Print Buyer:
Charlene Taylor

Production House:
GGS Information Services

Printer:
Quebecor World
Dubuque, Iowa

Design Project Manager:
Stacy Jenkins Shirley

Cover/Internal Design:
Joseph Pagliaro Graphic Design

Cover Images:
Courtesy of ©Getty Images

Opener Photos:
Joseph Pagliaro Graphic Design

Permissions Editor:
Linda Ellis

Photo Researcher:
Deanna Ettinger

For more information, contact
South-Western
5191 Natorp Boulevard
Mason, Ohio 45040.
Or you can visit our Internet site at:
http://www.swlearning.com

For permission to use material from this text or product, submit a request online at http://www.thomsonrights.com. Any additional questions about permissions can be submitted by email to thomsonrights@thomson.com.

Internet Office Projects 2E is a project-based approach to teaching about the Internet as a research tool. Each project requires students to use the Internet to accomplish realistic tasks, such as searching for jobs, planning vacation and business travel, retrieving investment information, marketing a business, and designing Web pages.

Text *(softcover, side spiral, 4-color, 128 pages)* . . . . **ISBN 0-538-72747-0**

Business Applications with Microsoft Word: Advanced Document Processing offers realistic workplace projects that integrate business vocabulary, critical-thinking strategies, and Web-research skills into the instruction of document processing. The project-based applications reinforce the full range of word-processing features and provide over 150 assignments.

Text/CD Package *(softcover, side spiral, 4-color, 240 pages)* . . . . **ISBN 0-538-72549-4**
Text *(hardcover, side spiral, 4-color, 240 pages)*. . . . . **ISBN 0-538-72756-X**

Integrated Applications combines all the Microsoft Office XP tools and integrates them with Word 2002. The text covers all core MOS competencies of *Excel*, *PowerPoint*, *Access*, *FrontPage*, and *Outlook* as well as speech recognition basics. The basics of the Office applications are organized into specific modules giving the flexibility to pick and choose lessons to cover based on student needs.

Text/CD Package *(softcover, top spiral, 4-color, 392 pages)* . . . . **ISBN 0-538-72548-6**

DigiTools: Technology Application Tools is a comprehensive text that gives detailed instruction on input technologies, such as word processing and speech and voice recognition. Keyboarding and career and job-search information are also covered.

Text *(hardcover, top bound, 4-color, 512 pages)* . . . . **ISBN 0-538-43486-4**

Multimedia and Image Management prepares students for a business world in which they will be expected to use business-standard software applications to complete projects. The concept-based book covers such applications as presentation, digital photography, image manipulation, Web design, and more. Also available is a software specific **Multimedia and Image Management Activities** book.

Text *(hardcover, side bound, 4-color, 384 pages)*. . . . . **ISBN 0-538-43463-5**
Activities Text/CD Package *(softcover, side bound, 2-color, 496 pages)* **ISBN 0-538-43464-3**

Preface

To the Student

Integrated Business Projects, Second Edition, is a business simulation designed to help you reinforce and build software skills, improve Internet skills, and develop teamwork and critical-thinking skills. You will work as an administrative assistant at Star River Adventures, a company that provides whitewater rafting excursions and other outdoor adventures. You will learn about the operation of a small business as you work in various departments and for the owner of the company.

Organization of the Text

Integrated Business Projects is organized into an Introduction, four parts, and five appendices. The parts of the text are described in the following sections.

Introduction

The Introduction provides information about the Star River Adventures company, staff, and services. You will meet the people with whom you will be working and learn about the exciting excursions offered in this section of the textbook. You will need to refer to the company organization chart and the company's contact information frequently as you complete your work.

Parts

Integrated Business Projects contains four parts, which are divided into projects. Part 1, Marketing and Sales, emphasizes word processing applications. Part 2, Finance and Accounting, emphasizes spreadsheet applications. Part 3, Operations, emphasizes database applications, media development, and Web page development. Presentation applications are included in all parts. Although each part has a primary software application focus, the projects are integrated and require use of various programs. Part 4, Capstone Project, requires use of all of the software applications mentioned and builds on knowledge and skills learned in earlier projects.

Projects and Jobs

Each project begins with a list of objectives and a summary of software skills that are covered in the project. Projects contain up to seven related jobs of varying difficulty. Each job begins with a list of software skills that you will apply when completing the job. Some jobs are further divided into related tasks. General information and step-by-step directions are provided for completing jobs. You will work from source documents provided in the text and use data files to complete jobs. Some jobs require research using the Internet or other sources.

Special Features

Elements that appear at the left of the page provide information to help you complete a job or to emphasize skills used. *Software Reviews* contain step-by-step directions for software procedures that should be applied in the job. *Success Tips* provide general information related to the job that can be helpful to you. *Help Keywords* provide terms that you can use with the software Help feature to learn more about a software task or feature. *Vocabulary words* define terms with which you may not be familiar. *Internet* and *Teamwork icons* emphasize use of these skills in a job. The *Disc icon* alerts you that a data file is needed to complete the job.

Internet Icon

Teamwork Icon

Disc Icon

Thinking Critically activities appear as part of each project. These questions are designed to help you think through an aspect of the project or a related topic.

Challenge activities are also provided throughout the text. These activities give you the opportunity to complete a more advanced or complicated task related to a job. They allow you to expand your understanding or to complete a challenging software task.

Appendices

The text contains five appendices. *Appendix A, Reference Guide,* contains sample documents and formatting guidelines that you will use to prepare documents. Proofreaders' marks are also included. Reviewing these marks before you key rough-draft documents will be helpful.

Appendix B, Computer Concepts, provides a basic review of computers, file management, and use of the *Microsoft Windows®* environment. You will need to create folders in which to store the files you create for this course. You also will need to copy and rename files as you complete your work. Review the appropriate sections of Appendix B for help with these tasks.

Appendix C, Keyboarding Skill Building, contains keyboarding drills and timed writings. Use this material to help improve your keyboarding skill and speed.

Appendix D, Directory of Jobs and Files, lists the data files that are provided for use with each job. The names of files you will create as you complete jobs are also listed. Use this information to help you keep track of your files.

Appendix E, Microsoft Office *Certification Correlation,* lists the correlations of the skills covered in this text for *Microsoft Office XP* and 2003 for *Word, Excel, PowerPoint,* and *Access.*

Teamwork

Teamwork skills will be important to your success, now while you are in school and later when you are on the job. You will participate in real and simulated teamwork as you complete projects. Working with classmates to do research, compose reports, evaluate presentations or Web sites, and verify work provides real opportunities to build teamwork skills. Completing tasks that have been begun by other employees at Star River Adventures lets you experience teamwork as part of the simulated work environment.

Data Files

Data files for you to use in completing the activities found in the textbook are provided on the *Instructor's Resource CD-ROM* and on a *Data CD-ROM*. Your instructor may need to make the data files available to you on disk or on your local area network. You will revise or complete some data files. You will use other files as source documents and still others to enhance presentations or documents. Files in HTML format (Web pages) are used as reference sources.

Software Certification

The *Microsoft Office* Specialist certification program recognizes individuals who have achieved a certain level of mastery with *Microsoft Office* products. The program provides a framework for measuring end-user proficiency with the *Microsoft Office* applications. By passing one or more *Microsoft Office* Specialist program certification exams, you demonstrate to employers your proficiency in a given *Office* application. Individuals who pass one or more exams can gain a competitive edge in the job marketplace. Completing the projects in *Integrated Business Projects* can help you prepare to pass a *Microsoft Office* Specialist certification exam. For more information about the *Microsoft Office* Specialist certification program, visit Microsoft's Web site at http://www.microsoft.com/traincert/mcp/default.asp.

To the Instructor

Integrated Business Projects, Second Edition, is completely new and is designed as a complete course. However, the text can also complement and enhance technology classes such as Information Processing and Computer Applications. Students will be challenged to apply basic to advanced software skills in realistic business situations.

Completion Time and Software

Integrated Business Projects provides about 120 hours of work. You can omit some jobs to reduce the completion time. If time is short, you might also choose to provide solution files to students for some jobs rather than have students create the files. You can use Challenge activities to extend the completion time.

The actual completion time for the course will vary depending on students' skills. Software Reviews are provided in the text to help students with some software procedures. However, students need basic proficiency with *Word, Excel, PowerPoint,* and *Access* to complete the projects. Project 18 requires basic knowledge of *Fireworks MX* or a similar program for creating graphics. Project 19 requires basic knowledge of *FrontPage* or a similar program for creating Web pages. Projects 18 and 19 can be omitted if the appropriate software is not available.

Instructor's Resource CD-ROM

An *Instructor's Resource CD-ROM* (ISBN: 0-538-72764-0) is available to instructors who adopt *Integrated Business Projects* for class use. The CD-ROM includes:

- Teaching notes for each project.
- Data files for use by students in completing activities for the textbook.
- Sample solution files.
- Electronic slides (in *Microsoft PowerPoint* format) for Parts 1–4.
- Application tests.

See the Web site for additional resources for both the instructor and the student: www.ibp.swlearning.com.

Teaching Notes

Teaching notes for each project are provided on the *Instructor's Resource CD-ROM.* Each Teaching Notes file includes objectives for the project, an overview of the project, and teaching suggestions for each job.

Data Files

Data files are provided on the *Instructor's Resource CD-ROM.* These files should be made available to students on local computer hard drives or on a local area network if students do not have a *Data CD-ROM.* Some files will fit on a floppy disk, but many files will not. These files are required for students to complete projects in the text. See *Appendix D, Directory of Jobs and Files,* for a list of data files and the format of the files.

Solution Files

Solutions files for most jobs are provided on the *Instructor's Resource CD-ROM.* These files are provided for your use in evaluating student work or for demonstrating sample solutions. For many jobs, students' work should match the solution file closely. For some jobs that require students to compose, do research, or make decisions on formatting or content, the solution files serves as examples of the completed jobs.

Electronic Slides

Electronic slide shows for Parts 1–4 are provided on the *Instructor's Resource CD-ROM.* The slide shows include objectives for each part, Success Tips, and illustrated Software Reviews. You can use these slides to introduce each part and to review software procedures that students will use in completing projects.

Application Tests

Application tests for Parts 1–3 are provided on the *Instructor's Resource CD-ROM*. You can print and distribute these tests to students. Each of the seven tests is divided into two or more tasks to facilitate administering the test in more than one class period if desired. Evaluation guidelines and sample solution files are provided for each test.

Some tests require students to use data files. Data files and solution files for tests are in a different folder on the *Instructor's CD-ROM* than the folders that contain data files and solutions for projects.

Two or three tests per part are provided as listed below. No tests are provided for Projects 18 and 19 because they are considered optional projects. Skills covered in Project 20 are evaluated in the tests for Parts 1–3. You may wish to use this capstone project as an evaluation instrument along with the tests.

Test 1 Projects 1–3

Test 2 Projects 4–6

Test 3 Projects 7–9

Test 4 Projects 10–12

Test 5 Project 13

Test 6 Projects 14–15

Test 7 Projects 16–17

Acknowledgments

The authors extend their thanks to the following people and organizations for providing inspiration and images used in *Integrated Business Projects*:

Doug Proctor and Rita Jeffries at Class VI River Runners
Angie Gray and Erik Bledsoe at Ace River Center
David Fattaleh and Matt Turner at WV Division of Tourism

Thanks, also, to our consulting editor Dianne S. Rankin and to contributing authors Tommy Newland and Tinukwa C. Okojie for their contributions to this textbook.

Table of Contents

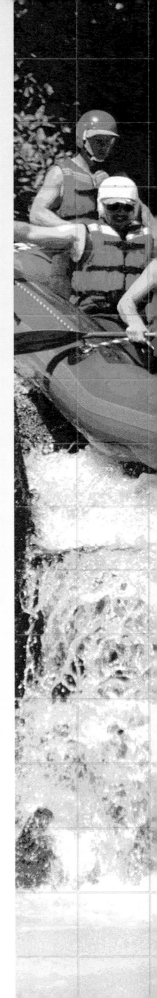

Directory of Applications

Job Nos.	Word Processing	Spreadsheet	Database	Presentations	Desktop Publishing	Web Page Creation	Multimedia	Graphics	Email	Internet Use
1-1 to 1-7	X				X			X		X
2-1 to 2-6	X				X					X
3-1 to 3-6	X	X			X	X		X		
4-1 to 4-5	X	X	X	X	X	X	X	X	X	X
5-1 to 5-5	X	X	X		X	X		X		
6-1 to 6-5	X			X	X	X	X	X		X
7-1 to 7-6	X	X	X							X
8-1 to 8-6	X	X						X		
9-1 to 9-6	X	X		X	X	X	X	X	X	X
10-1 to 10-6	X	X		X			X	X		X
11-1 to 11-6	X	X								
12-1 to 12-6	X	X				X		X	X	X
13-1 to 13-6	X	X		X		X	X	X		X
14-1 to 14-5	X		X							X
15-1 to 15-5	X		X					X	X	X
16-1 to 16-5	X	X	X	X		X	X	X		X
17-1 to 17-5	X		X			X				X
18-1 to 18-6	X			X	X	X	X	X		X
19-1 to 19-6	X					X	X	X	X	X
20-1 to 20-6	X	X	X	X		X	X	X	X	X

How to Use This Book

Projects involve jobs to create business documents.

Objectives are for the business skills and documents that students create in this project.

Microsoft Office **Skills** are software features covered in this project from *Word, Excel, PowerPoint, Access,* and *FrontPage.*

Jobs consist of tasks to create specific business documents.

Disk icon shows that a data file is needed to complete the job.

Skills Applied are the *Microsoft Office* features covered in a job.

Success Tips provide general information related to the job.

A **task** is part of a job and lists the steps to perform.

Help Keywords provide terms you can use to learn more about a software task or feature.

Software Reviews contain step-by-step directions for software procedures related to the job.

Project 1

Preparing Marketing and Administrative Documents

Objectives

☐ Create and format letters, envelopes, and labels
☐ Produce documents from rough-draft copy
☐ Produce documents with hanging indents and automatic numbering
☐ Work with tables, including inserting formulas
☐ Use desktop publishing skills to design documents
☐ Input and format reports
☐ Insert a file into a document
☐ Print documents, envelopes, and labels

Summary of Microsoft Office Skills

✔ Correct spelling and grammar usage
✔ Enter and format date and time
✔ Apply character styles
✔ Modify paragraph formats
✔ Set and modify tabs
✔ Apply bullet, outline, and numbering format to paragraphs
✔ Apply paragraph styles
✔ Create and modify a document style
✔ Modify document layout and Page Setup options
✔ Create and modify tables
✔ Preview and print documents, en...
✔ Save documents and folders
✔ Manage files and folders
✔ Insert images and graphics
✔ Sort paragraphs in lists and t...
✔ Perform calculations in Word
✔ Control pagination

---

18   Project 1: Preparing Marketing and Administrative Documents

Job 1-4 Use Desktop Publishing for Stickers and Thank-You Note

Skills Applied
- Applying paragraph formats and character styles
- Printing labels
- Adding images to documents
- Modifying and positioning graphics
- Modifying page margins and page orientation

When customers book their trips early in the season, scheduling employees and equipment is much easier for the Operations Department. For this reason, the company offers discounts for early-bird bookers.

Task 1 Format Labels for Stickers

Star River Adventures regularly sends out brochures advertising its services. You will create stickers to be placed on the covers of all brochures mailed in January and February.

1. Create a full page of Avery 3111 labels. Enter the text shown on the label below.
2. Format the first line of text for Garamond, 20-point, bold font. The remaining lines of text should be in Times New Roman, 14-point font. Use center alignment for all lines. Create the labels as a new document.
3. Your sticker should appear similar to Figure 1-2. Save the document as **1-4 Stickers.** Print the stickers.

Success Tips

- If you do not have labels, print on plain paper.
- The company phone number can be found on page 7.

Help Keywords

Labels
Customize labels
Symbol
Insert a symbol

Software Review

To create labels:
- Select *Letters and Mailings* from the Tools menu.
- Select *Envelopes and Labels.*
- On the Labels tab, select *Options.*
- Select the desired label product and product number.
- Key text and apply formatting. (Select text and right-click to change font or paragraph alignment settings.)
- Select *New Document.*

> **Early-Bird Bookers!**
>
> Save 10% on all trips booked before February 28.
>
> Call (number) today. Mention code F28Y04.

Figure 1-2 Sample Sticker

Vocabulary words define terms with which students may not be familiar.

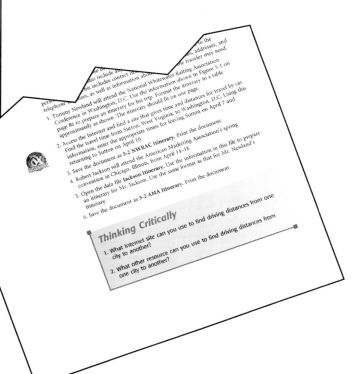

Other Taxes and Deductions

In addition to income tax, employers are also required to deduct payroll taxes from each employee's gross income. The two basic payroll taxes are Social Security, also called FICA (Federal Insurance Contribution Act) tax, and Medicare tax.

The current Social Security tax (in 2003) is 6.20 percent of gross income earned up to an income of $87,000. Gross income over that amount is not taxed for Social Security. Currently all employees at Star River Adventures earn less than $87,000 per year. The current Medicare tax rate is 1.45 percent. There is no limit on the amount of wages subject to Medicare tax.

In addition to income taxes and payroll taxes, employees can request that their employer take additional deductions for retirement accounts or other benefits available, such as dental or eye care insurance. At this time, no employee of the company has requested additional deductions.

Most states require employers to deduct state income taxes. The state tax rate for West Virginia is currently (in 2003) 6.5 percent of gross earnings. The yearly salaries for the current fiscal year for the full-time employees of Star River Adventures are shown in Figure 7-3 on page 118.

gross income: income before deductions

Social Security tax: provides retirement benefits to employees and their dependents

Medicare tax: provides medical benefits to individuals when they reach the age of 65

Prepare Marketing Brochure   99

16. See Figure 5-5 on page 98 for an example of how page 3 should look. Save the file using the same name. Print the brochure.

Challenge: Prepare Brochure Page 4

1. Open the file **5-5 Brochure** that you created earlier. At the end of the document, insert a section break *Next page* to create page 4. Create a table on page 4 with the same layout and format as the one on page 2.

2. In Column 2 (right column) on page 4, insert a graphic. Search the Internet or use clip art to find an image related to rafting, West Virginia, or mountain scenery. Adjust the height of the image to about 2" and center it horizontally within the column. Readjust the size later, if needed, to fit the image and the following article on the page.

3. Below the image, enter the main heading *Raft in the Newest Duckies on the Oldest River in the World.* Apply the Title 1 style. Insert the appropriate text from the data file **April Articles.**

4. In Column 1, enter the main heading *Distances.* Apply the Title 1 style. Insert the paragraph and list of cities from the data file **Distances.** Apply the Paragraph style to the text. For the list of cities, change the paragraph spacing for *After* to 0 point.

5. Work with two or three classmates to find the driving distance in miles from Sutton to the cities listed. Use the Internet or other resources to find mileage numbers.

6. Enter the mileage numbers into the brochure. Use a right tab to align the numbers at the right edge of the column.

7. Near the bottom of Column 2, insert an appropriate image, such as a map of West Virginia.

8. Save the document as **5-5 Challenge Brochure.** Print the last page of the brochure.

Challenge activities give the opportunity to complete a more advanced task related to the job.

Teamwork icons emphasize that this task should be performed with others.

also include an ... to the ... is includes contact in ... addresses, and ... , as well as information about ... the traveler may need.

1. Tommy Newland will attend the National Whitewater Rafting Association Conference in Washington, D.C. Use the information shown in Figure 5-1 on page 86 to prepare an itinerary for his trip. Format the itinerary in a table approximately as shown. The itinerary should fit on one page.

2. Access the Internet and find a site that gives time and distances for travel by car. Find the travel time from Sutton, West Virginia, to Washington, D.C. Using this information, enter the appropriate times for leaving Sutton on April 7 and returning to Sutton on April 10.

3. Save the document as **5-2 NWRAC Itinerary.** Print the document.

4. Robert Jackson will attend the American Marketing Association's spring convention in Chicago, Illinois, from April 14–18.

5. Open the data file **Jackson Itinerary.** Use the information in this file to prepare an itinerary for Mr. Jackson. Use the same format as that for Mr. Newland's itinerary.

6. Save the document as **5-2 AMA Itinerary.** Print the document.

Thinking Critically

1. What Internet site can you use to find driving distances from one city to another?

2. What other resource can you use to find driving distances from one city to another?

Internet icons emphasize the use of the Internet in a job.

Thinking Critically questions are designed to help students think through an aspect of the project.

Introduction

Welcome to Star River Adventures, your gateway to a premier rafting experience. For more than twenty years, Star River Adventures has provided our customers with safe and exciting adventures in West Virginia's awe-inspiring wilderness. Our trips allow you to raft gently down one of our rippling streams or to conquer our explosive rapids. You choose your event, and we will make it come true. All trips are supervised by expert guides. Our staff will help you plan your entire adventure whether it is for an individual, a family, or a group.

Star River Adventures is located in Sutton, West Virginia. We plan and conduct events throughout the state. You choose an adventure on one of our many rivers and streams, including the Big Sandy Creek, Bluestone River, Cheat River, Gauley River, Lower Meadow, Meadow River, New River, Potomac River, Tygart River, or Shenandoah River. We take care of everything else.

STAR
River
Adventures

About Our Company

Star River Adventures is focused on you. We plan professionally guided whitewater events that range from gentle, tranquil raft day trips down one of our scenic streams to wild and wet excursions that challenge even the expert rafter. Whatever the adventure, your safety is our number one concern.

Many amenities are available with our trips, such as sleepovers at various sites, camping, bicycle tours, hiking, food services, and a variety of other special events.

Our Mission

Our mission at Star River Adventures is to:

- Offer you the adventure you envision in a safe and exciting environment.
- Provide you with the best value for your dollar.
- Make you feel as though you are a member of the Star River family.
- Have you come back to Star River again and again because we provide the service you expect at a fair price.

Our Headquarters

Our headquarters is located in Sutton, West Virginia. We plan adventures throughout the state of West Virginia. The rivers and streams we raft and the bike trails, camping sites, overnight accommodations at lodges, and parks we use are located throughout the state. Your trip is planned here, but your adventure will take you into West Virginia's scenic wilderness.

COURTESY OF ACE RIVER ADVENTURE CENTER

Figure 1 Star River Adventures' trips allow guests to enjoy West Virginia's scenic wilderness.

Tommy Newland

Our Staff

Star River Adventures is owned by Tommy Newland, a former river guide. Mr. Newland has run commercial rafting excursions throughout the United States, Australia, and South America. He is a member of the International Rafting Federation (IRF) and has over 15 years of experience handling the logistical and operational duties related to rafting excursions.

Mr. Newland is assisted in running the company by employees in the Operations, Accounting, and Marketing and Sales departments. The organization chart in Figure 2 shows the structure of Star River Adventures.

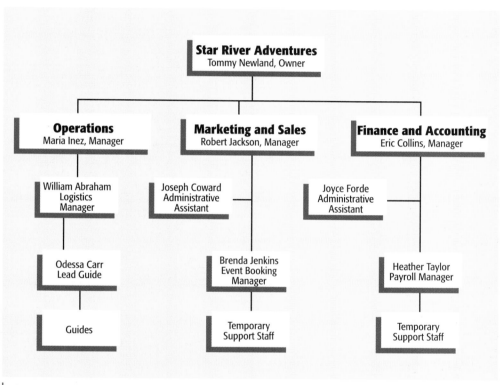

Figure 2 Star River Adventures Organization Chart

Maria Inez

Operations Department

The Operations Department is headed by Maria Inez. Maria has managed rafting trips and events throughout the United States, including numerous regional, state, and national championships. She is also an experienced rafter. Maria earned a bachelor of science degree in Fitness Management from Mississippi State University and an M.B.A. from California State University.

William (Willie) Abraham is manager of logistics. A native of New York and a sports enthusiast, Willie has been involved in challenging sports activities during most of his life. He played high school football and attended numerous summer sports camps during his high school years. During this time, he developed a passion for river rafting. He continued this passion throughout his collegiate career by rafting more than 100 rivers throughout the world. Willie is a licensed guide and oversees the additional training required of all licensed guides who seek employment with Star River Adventures. Willie's experience in course design for numerous national competitive events ensures that each Star River excursion is awe-inspiring—whether you are enjoying the scenic view of West Virginia as you gently raft down one of our rivers or the excitement of battling the rapids on one of our more challenging adventures.

Odessa Carr is our lead guide. Odessa is a licensed guide and a licensed guide instructor. She has over ten years of rafting experience. Odessa has worked for whitewater rafting businesses throughout the United States and has completed thousands of rafting excursions. Odessa is a graduate of West Virginia University and has extensive experience navigating the rivers and streams of West Virginia. Her education in the area of sports teaching/coaching and sports communications, along with her professional experience in whitewater rafting, make her an ideal lead guide.

Marketing and Sales Department

Robert Jackson is the manager of the Marketing and Sales Department. Robert has a B.S. in Marketing from the University of Nebraska and has extensive experience in marketing a variety of events and in developing marketing strategies. He has been responsible for marketing a number of national whitewater rafting competitive events.

Robert Jackson

Brenda Jenkins is the manager of Event Booking. Brenda is an accounting graduate from Robert Morris College, Pittsburgh, Pennsylvania. Brenda is a detail-oriented individual and will make booking your adventure an ease.

Joseph Coward is an administrative assistant to Robert Jackson in the Marketing and Sales Department. Joe is a graduate of Itawamba Community College in Mississippi. Once you book an event with Star River Adventures, Joe will keep you informed and up to date as your adventure date approaches. Joe is a real "people person" and is available to handle any inquiries you might make. If Joe cannot answer your questions, he will locate the person who can.

Eric Collins

Finance and Accounting Department

Eric Collins is the manager of the Finance and Accounting Department. He has 12 years of experience in financial management at various organizations throughout the country. He earned a bachelor of science degree in Computer Science and Accounting from the University of Georgia. Eric is a whitewater rafting enthusiast and joins many of our excursions when time permits.

Heather Taylor is the Payroll Manager. Heather earned an associate degree in Accounting from Allegheny Community College in Pennsylvania and has worked in the accounting field for over five years. Heather recently joined the Star River Adventures family.

Joyce Forde is an administrative assistant to Eric Collins in the Finance and Accounting Department. Joyce is a recent graduate from Southeast College of Technology in Memphis, Tennessee. This is her second year as part of the Star River family.

About Our Trips

Each of our adventures begins at one of fifteen different sites throughout West Virginia. Once you plan your excursion with one of our expert staff, you will be given a detailed map that highlights each exciting step of your fantastic adventure. Besides an awesome raft trip, you will enjoy the scenic beauty of West Virginia's forests, canyons, and wildlife. At the conclusion of your trip, your vehicle will be waiting for you or you will be transported back to the point of origin in a luxury motor coach.

Quality

Our rafting equipment (boats, life vests, wet suits, and splash jackets) is top of the line and state of the art. If you choose an adventure that includes camping, we will supply clean, high-quality sleeping bags, pads, and tents. After you select your supplies, we will have the campsite set up and waiting for you. If you want to include hiking or biking as part of your adventure, we contract these services from vendors in each area who provide quality equipment and supplies, as well as qualified guides when needed. Any activity you request is included in the price of your Star River adventure.

Safety

Your safety is our number one concern here at Star River Adventures. The equipment you use is inspected and certified prior to all excursions, and we replace our equipment on a regular schedule. All of our guides are highly skilled, licensed oarsman. They receive additional training here at Star River and must pass our own competency exam prior to employment. In addition, our guides have studied the rivers they raft and are highly skilled at navigation. Star Rivers has not had a serious boating accident in its 20-year history.

Dress for Your Adventure

Star Rivers Adventures is open year round, but our excursions are seasonal. Trips are scheduled during March through October based on weather conditions and water currents and depth. During the months of November through February, we offer a number of workshops related to sports activities and safety. Of course, you can book your adventure year round.

During the spring and fall seasons, temperatures can fluctuate quite a bit; and water temperatures are generally cool. Rain is sporadic. We supply wet suits, paddling pants, and jackets. We encourage you to add wool clothing such as sweaters, pants, hats, and socks for your comfort. Wool fabric insulates even when wet. Fleece and polypropylene synthetic material also provide insulating benefits.

During the summer season, you should wear a swimsuit, a T-shirt, tennis shoes, and a baseball hat. No matter what the season, you should bring one or two large towels and a change of clothes. Shower facilities are available at the termination points of many of our trips.

Invitation

What are you waiting for? Contact Star River Adventures today to arrange your exciting adventure. You can contact us at:

Address: Star River Adventures
                205 Riverview Drive
                Sutton, WV 26601-1311

Telephone: (304) 555-0110
Fax: (304) 555-0111
Email: StarRiver@trophe.com

Part 1

Marketing and Sales

In Part 1, you will complete projects for the Marketing and Sales Department of Star River Adventures. The jobs you will complete involve extensive use of word processing and integration with various other software applications such as spreadsheets, presentations, and databases. You will create a variety of documents. Your current job assignment is as an administrative assistant to Robert Jackson. However, you will also complete special projects for other departments and for Tommy Newland, the owner of Star River Adventures.

Preparing Marketing and Administrative Documents

Objectives

- ☐ Create and format letters, envelopes, and labels
- ☐ Produce documents from rough-draft copy
- ☐ Produce documents with hanging indents and automatic numbering
- ☐ Work with tables, including inserting formulas
- ☐ Use desktop publishing skills to design documents
- ☐ Input and format reports
- ☐ Insert a file into a document
- ☐ Print documents, envelopes, and labels

Summary of *Microsoft Office* Skills

- ✔ Correct spelling and grammar usage
- ✔ Enter and format date and time
- ✔ Apply character styles
- ✔ Modify paragraph formats
- ✔ Set and modify tabs
- ✔ Apply bullet, outline, and numbering format to paragraphs
- ✔ Apply paragraph styles
- ✔ Create and modify a document header and footer
- ✔ Modify document layout and Page Setup options
- ✔ Create and modify tables
- ✔ Preview and print documents, envelopes, and labels
- ✔ Manage files and folders for documents
- ✔ Save documents using different names and file formats
- ✔ Insert images and graphics
- ✔ Sort paragraphs in lists and tables
- ✔ Perform calculations in *Word* tables
- ✔ Control pagination

ST★R
River
Adventures

Job 1-1 Create Folders and Prepare Letters

Skills Applied

- Modifying page margins
- Using Spelling and Grammar checks
- Using Print Preview
- Printing documents and envelopes
- Using Save and Save As
- Creating folders for document storage

Before you begin creating documents, create folders in which to save and organize your documents. Follow your instructor's directions regarding where to save your files. You might save files on a local hard drive, a local area network, or some type of removable media. A floppy disk can be used to save many of the documents you create. However, some projects, such as related Web pages, may be too large to fit on a floppy disk.

Create a folder for each project that includes the project number and your name, your initials, or other identification as directed by your instructor. For example, for Project 1, the folder might be named *P1 Janna Arney,* where P1 stands for Project 1 and Janna Arney is your name.

As you create documents for each project, save those documents in the appropriate folder using the filenames given in the project.

Task 1 Answer Donation Request Letter

Success Tips

Unless instructed otherwise, assume that all letters you create will be printed on letterhead paper.

Robert Jackson has given you the edited hard copy of a letter explaining why Star River Adventures cannot grant a request for a free rafting trip. He asked you to prepare the final letter.

1. Review appropriate formatting for business letters in the Reference Guide on page 313.

2. Key the letter from the edited draft shown on page 12. Add any missing parts to the letter. If necessary, adjust the margins so the letter fits on one page.

3. Check the spelling and grammar. Proofread carefully and correct all errors. Save the file as **1-1 Request.** Preview the letter. Print the letter.

January 15, 20--

Ms. Marilyn McDowell
1572 Holly Drive
Cincinnati, OH 45202-1000

Dear Ms. McDowell

Thank you for your kind words concerning our company. We recently received your request for complimentary trips for your fund raising event, and we appreciate the importance of your request. Star River Adventures receives over 400 requests each year from organizations working to fund worthy causes. Requests come from our guests, *from* the local community, and from other states and countries. We are unable to honor all of the requests even though they are for worthy causes. ¶Although we are unable to honor your request for a free trip, you may purchase a gift certificate for any Star River Adventures one-day trip on the New River. The certificate is good for one year and for any day except Saturday. The cost of the gift certificate is $40 per person plus 6% sales tax. This amount helps to cover our ~~costs,~~ handling fees and some fixed costs *and* ~~While this amount~~ is well below our retail *price* ~~cost~~. Hopefully, you can auction the gift certificate for an amount that will allow you to make a fair return on your part. You may purchase a maximum of four gift certificates per year.

If you would like to order a gift certificate, please contact Upon receipt of your check or credit card information, you will receive a lovely portfolio that includes brochures and gift certificates.

Sincerely

Robert Jackson, Manager
Marketing and Sales
xx

Add the total amount in parentheses.

Joe Coward Administrative Assistant, at Star River Adventures.

We know that you understand our limitations in helping your cause due to the volume of similar requests we receive each year. We appreciate your business and look forward to rafting with you soon.

Task 2 Prepare Discount Request Letter

Mr. Jackson has also asked you to prepare a letter to a department store. In the past, this store has given Star River Adventures a discount on merchandise that it purchased and gave as gifts to less fortunate families.

1. Create a letter dated January 15 of the current year. Address the letter to:

```
Mr. J. Simon Hutcheson
Coins Department Store
790 Main Street
Sutton, WV 26601-7900
```

2. Use the following text as the body of the letter. Format the letter properly and add any missing parts using the letter example in the Reference Guide on page 313.

```
Thank you for helping us during the past five
years by giving us a discount on items that we
purchased for less fortunate families. Each
Christmas and Easter, we provide baskets for five
deserving families. We shop at your store using
money donations from our employees.

Without your assistance, it would be impossible to
provide such happy holidays for these people. We
hope that you will be willing, once again, to help
us with this philanthropic endeavor. At your
convenience, please call me at (304) 555-0110 to
discuss the details if you will be able to help us
help these families.
```

3. Save as **1-1 Baskets.** Print the letter.

Help Keywords

Envelope
   Create and print a
   single envelope

Challenge: Research Address Formats

Go to the World Wide Web site for the United States Post Office to find information on addressing envelopes. The URL is http://www.usps.gov. Choose the *Addressing and Packaging your Mail* link (or a similar link). Using the guidelines found at this site, prepare and print envelopes for the two letters you prepared in Job 1-1. Assume that you will be using envelopes with the return addresses already printed, so choose to omit the return address.

Job 1-2 Format Reading List

Skills Applied

- Modifying page margins
- Applying paragraph formats
- Applying character styles
- Using the Sort feature
- Creating a document footer
- Inserting date and time fields
- Printing documents*

Help Keywords

Hanging Indent
  Indent paragraphs
Sort
  Sorting

Tommy Newland, Robert Jackson, and Odessa Carr want the tour guides to realize that they are considered ambassadors for the company. One of the main reasons customers return to Star River Adventures for their outdoor adventures is that they are made to feel special by the guides. Tommy wants to give the river guides information that will help them build good customer service techniques. He has prepared a recommended reading list for the river guides.

1. Key the list shown on page 15 and format it in correct bibliographic format as illustrated in the Reference Guide on page 322.

   - For the heading, use a Times New Roman, bold, 14-point font and center alignment.
   - Use default margins and hanging indent format for the list.
   - Single-space (SS) each item and double-space (DS) between items.

2. Arrange the list alphabetically by author surname.

3. Add a footer to the document that contains your initials (in lowercase letters) and the date. Use a Times New Roman, 9-point font and the following format: xx: Month day, year.

4. Save the document as **1-2 List.** Print the document.

Challenge: Internet Research for Articles

Find three sites on the Internet that have information about the topic *customer service*. Add the reference notes for these sites to the Recommended Reading List document, using the format shown below. Save the updated list as **1-2 Challenge List.**

Author. "Article Title," *Source*. URL (date of online visit).
Example:
Ateineion, Bill. "Build Loyalty by Solving Problems," *Dartnell*. http://datrnellcorp.com/newssales.html (current date).

> Show underlined items as italic.

Recommended Reading List

Smith, Linda. "Difficult Customers and How to Help Them." *Salesmanship Quarterly*, Spring 2002, 4-8.

Howard, Kyle, and Beatrice Stone. "Having Fun in the Great Outdoors." *Outdoor Adventure Journal*, August 2003.

Harris, Paul, and Sara Riggs. "Five Steps to Effective Group Leadership." *Psychology In Action*, July 2001, 16-17.

Cleary, M. J., et al. "Tell Them Why." *America Tomorrow*, September 1999.

Charp, Mary, and Jim Doyle. "10 Steps To Assure Closing A Sale." *Salesmanship Quarterly*, Fall 2002, 8-9.

Tarrazo, Federick, and Samuel Ott. "Sell, Sell, Sell." *America Tomorrow*, December 2000.

Gilbert, Sue. "Pressure Points!" *Sales Monthly*, January 2001, 17-19.

Leifer, Seth. "TQM for Teams." *Sales Monthly*, May 2003, 9-10.

Amandam, Hal. "Personality Traits That Assure Sales." *Salesmanship Quarterly*, Spring 2001, 5-8.

Job 1-3 Create Petty Cash Table

Skills Applied

- Applying paragraph formats and character styles
- Creating and modifying tables
- Using formulas in tables
- Merging cells in tables
- Applying AutoFormat to tables

petty cash: funds kept on hand to pay small expenses

The Marketing and Sales Department begins each month with $100 in the petty cash fund. You will create a form and save it on your computer to track the payments made from petty cash. The same form can be used each month by changing the date and other data.

1. Create a table with 5 columns and 25 rows. Enter the data shown below. Use the example in Figure 1-1 for text placement.

Star River Adventures Marketing and Sales Petty Cash				
Date	Purpose	Cash Addition	Amount Dispersed	Total Available
January 1	Cash on hand	$100.00		$100.00
January 2	Stamps		$7.40	
(Rows omitted from example)				
	Totals			

Figure 1-1 Sample Petty Cash Table

2. Enter the following information from your handwritten notes in the petty cash table.

Star River Adventures_____

January 2, $7.40 for stamps
January 2, $2.50 tip for flower delivery
January 4, $12.48 for coffee supplies
January 10, 12.48 for coffee supplies
January 15, $7.40 for stamps
January 15, $40.00 cash addition
January 30, $12.48 for coffee supplies

3. Enter formulas to calculate the Total Available amounts. In the Totals row, insert formulas that total the Cash Additions and the Amount Dispersed columns.

4. In Column E of the Totals row, enter a formula to subtract the total amount dispersed from the total cash addition. The resulting figure should be the same as the total amount for January 30.

5. Apply the Table AutoFormat *Table Colorful 2*. Increase the table title to 14 point and make the title bold (as well as italic).

6. Save the document as **1-3 Petty Cash.** Print the document.

Thinking Critically

1. How do you calculate the Total Available amounts?

2. What formula can you use to total the Cash Addition column? the Amount Dispersed column?

Job 1-4 Use Desktop Publishing for Stickers and Thank-You Note

Skills Applied

- Applying paragraph formats and character styles
- Printing labels
- Adding images to documents
- Modifying and positioning graphics
- Modifying page margins and page orientation

When customers book their trips early in the season, scheduling employees and equipment is much easier for the Operations Department. For this reason, the company offers discounts for early-bird bookers.

Task 1 Format Labels for Stickers

Star River Adventures regularly sends out brochures advertising its services. You will create stickers to be placed on the covers of all brochures mailed in January and February.

1. Create a full page of Avery 3111 labels. Enter the text shown on the label below.

2. Format the first line of text for Garamond, 20-point, bold font. The remaining lines of text should be in Times New Roman, 14-point font. Use center alignment for all lines. Create the labels as a new document.

3. Your sticker should appear similar to Figure 1-2. Save the document as **1-4 Stickers.** Print the stickers.

Early-Bird Bookers!

Save 10% on all trips
booked before February 28.

Call (number) today.
Mention code F28Y04.

Figure 1-2 Sample Sticker

Task 2 Design Thank-You Note

You have been asked to design a thank-you note to be included with the confirmation of each early-bird booking. The note will be printed on 8 1/2″ × 5 1/2″ card stock in landscape orientation.

Help Keywords

Paper size
  Select a paper size
Page Setup
  Change the orientation
  of text

1. Create a thank-you note as requested. The text and format in Figure 1-3 show one possible layout. You are free to make other choices. If you do not have card stock, print on plain paper cut to 8 1/2″ × 5 1/2″.

2. Search the Internet to find an appropriate picture to include on the thank-you note. You may be able to find photos related to rafting on the Microsoft Design Gallery Live (http://dgl.microsoft.com). You can also use the photo file **WhitewaterNewRiver-def01** or graphic file **StarLogo1** found in your data files. Resize the image to an appropriate size, and position it attractively on the page.

3. Save the document as **1-4 Thank You.** Print the document.

Thank You

Thank you for the confidence you
have placed in Star River Adventures.
We are committed to providing you
with an outstanding outdoor adventure
that focuses on fun and safety. If you
have questions regarding your trip,
please call us at (304) 555-0110.

Figure 1-3 Sample Thank-You Note

Job 1-5 Prepare Section of Policy Manual

Skills Applied

- Applying paragraph formats and character styles
- Applying paragraph styles
- Modifying page margins
- Applying bullets
- Inserting page breaks and page numbers
- Managing orphans and widows

Mr. Newland is in the process of reworking the Employee Policy Manual. He has given you the first section marked with editing changes.

1. Key the section of the manual shown below and on pages 21–23 using the guidelines for reports provided in the Reference Guide on pages 319–321. Use the styles indicated so you can easily create a table of contents if one is needed later.

2. Insert a file as indicated on the draft at the end of the document to add another part of the Employee Policy Manual.

3. Save the document as **1-5 Manual.** Print the document.

POLICY MANUAL (Title Style)

Introduction *(Heading 1 Style)*

Purpose *(Heading 2 Style)*

The policies included in this policy manual were developed during the past ~~twenty~~ 20 plus years of Star River Adventures operation. All employees are expected to read, understand, and follow these policies as they pertain to their particular job assignments. Please review this manual on a regular basis to refresh your memory concerning its contents. THIS POLICY MANUAL IS NOT A CONTRACT. You are an employee "at will."

Keep in mind that this is a fluid document and will change. As changes are made, they will be posted on the company Web site and on the staff bulletin board. The manual is reviewed and reprinted in its entirety on an annual basis.

Revision Date (Heading 2)

Any part of the manual may be revised or deleted at any time. A current copy of the manual, including all revisions, will be available at the front desk.

Quality Policy (Heading 2)

The most important thing to know about Star River Adventures is that it is a service business. The safety and enjoyment of our customers is our up most main company concern. All aspects of our customer's experience, which are under our control, must meet with the customer's satisfaction.

Mission Statement (Heading 2)

Star River Adventures is focused on the customer. We plan professionally guided whitewater events that range from gentle, tranquil raft day trips down one of our scenic streams to wild and wet excursions that will challenge even the expert rafter. Whatever the adventure, safety is always our number one concern. Many amenities are available with our excursions, such as sleepovers at various sites, camping, bicycle tours, hiking, food services, and a variety of other special events.

Our mission at Star River Adventures is to:

Bulleted List

Offer the adventures that customers envision in a safe and exciting environment.

Provide the best value for the customer's dollar.

Make Have customers feel that as though they are a member of the Star River Adventures family.

Have customers return come back to Star River Adventures again and again because they have experienced excellent service at a fair price.

Facilities and Equipment *(Heading 2)*

Exceptional service includes providing clean, attractive, organized facilities and equipment to our guests (and each other). ~~Your responsibilities include:~~ *staff should:*

Bulleted List

Always park in designated areas. The areas with easiest access to facilities are reserved for our guests.

Clean up litter. Do not contribute to liter. Do not ignore a problem because "It is not my job."

Return all equipment to the appropriate locations. Report damaged equipment to the equipment manager.

Company Safety Philosophy *(Heading 2)*

Star River Adventures believes that the safety of both the guests and employees ~~if~~ *is* our first priority. Safe operating procedures result~~s~~ in the protection of both monetary and human value, with the human value being recognized by the employer and the community as having the greater value. Observe these principles concerning safety ~~concerns~~:

- Establishing and complying with safe work procedures will prevent all injuries and accidents from happening.

- The first consideration in all workplace actions is the prevention of bodily injury and the safeguarding of health. To prevent injury and maintain health, it is essential that employees be in good enough physical condition to do their assigned jobs.

- The written safety plan, provided in this manual, represents Star River Adventures' proactive safety position. It is the responsibility of all Star River Adventures employees to communicate and follow established safety practices.

- Failure to follow safety procedures will result in disciplinary action. Working safely is a condition of employment of Star River Adventures.

Star River Adventures complies with safety laws and regulations established by:

Occupational Safety and Health Association (OSHA). *&* *Administration*

(EPA).
(DOT).
(WVDNR). } *Spell out (Check the Internet for full spelling of acronyms.)*

All other applicable federal, state, and local safety and health regulations.

Employer Responsibilities *(Heading 3)*

Star River Adventures considers its responsibility to provide employees with a safe work environment to be a top priority. The following safety plans reflect Star's commitment to safety. It is the responsibility of Star River Adventures to provide:

Bulleted List {
Appropriate personal protective equipment and training.
A timely remedy for safety problems as managers become aware of them.
Facilities and equipment inspections in an effort to identify hazardous situations.
}

Safety Plan Administration *(Heading 3)*

lc Maria Inez, Operations Department, has overall responsibility for the Safety Plan. She will coordinate the plan and keep all safety records current.

The plan will be reviewed on a regular basis and changes made as needed. All employees are responsible for making Maria aware of any concerns they have with the safety plan.

Return-to-Work Policy *(Heading 2)*

(Insert file: Return to Work Policy B)

Job 1-6 Research River Classifications

Skills Applied

- Applying paragraph formats and character styles
- Applying paragraph styles
- Creating and modifying tables
- Setting and modifying tabs

Robert Jackson wants to prepare a page to include in the new advertising brochure that provides an explanation of each of the six classifications of whitewater. He also wants to include a chart listing the rivers where Star River Adventures operates and the classification of each river.

1. Work with another administrative assistant (a classmate). Use the Internet or the library to research the American Whitewater Affiliation's International Scale of River Difficulty. List the three classifications of moving water and the six classifications of white water. This information will be included in a brochure that will be distributed to customers. Note the source of each reference you use.

2. Create a table that presents the rivers where Star River Adventures operates and gives the classification of each river. The rivers include Big Sandy Creek, Bluestone River, Cheat River, Gauley River, Lower Meadow, Meadow River, New River, Potomac River, Tygart River, and Shenandoah River. A sample table showing the first two rivers is shown below.

River	Classification

Big Sandy Creek
    Upper Big Sandy
    Lower Big Sandy
	
	ClassIII/IV
	ClassIV/V

Bluestone River	Class I-III

3. Create a one-page final copy that includes:
   - The three classifications of moving water.
   - The six classifications of whitewater.
   - A table showing the rivers where Star River Adventures operates and the classification of each river.

4. Use an appropriate title for the page, and apply the Title style. Use *Moving Water, Whitewater*, and *Rivers* as subheads for the document. Format these subheads as style Heading 2. Use brief text to introduce the information presented. Format the page attractively.

5. Create a second page that lists the sources of your information. Format the list in correct bibliographic format as illustrated in the Reference Guide page on 322.

6. Save the document as **1-6 River Classifications.** Print the document.

Job 1-7 Prepare Injury Follow-up Form

Skills Applied

- Applying paragraph formats and character styles
- Applying paragraph styles
- Modifying page margins
- Setting and modifying tabs

Software Review

To make lines end at the same point at the right margin, set a tab where you want the lines to end. When you want to insert a line, turn on Underline before pressing the Tab key.

Mr. Newland has requested that an injury follow-up form be prepared. Impress the owner with the care you take in creating your documents by preparing an attractive form.

1. Prepare an injury follow-up form from the example shown in Figure 1-4. Make the top margin 2 inches and the side margins 1 inch. Apply the Title style to the title. Be sure that all lines that extend to the right margin end at the same point. Use your judgment regarding line spacing. The form should fit on one page.
2. Save the document as **1-7 Injury Follow-up.** Print the document.

prognosis: probable course of a disease and chance of recovery

INJURY FOLLOW-UP FORM

Name: ______________________________

Date of injury/accident: ______________________________

1. Did you see a doctor? Yes _____ No _____
2. What was the doctor's diagnosis? ______________________________

____

3. What was the doctor's prognosis? ______________________________

____

4. Did the doctor recommend treatment? Yes _____ No _____
5. If treatment was recommended, what type of treatment was suggested?

____

6. What type of treatment did you receive? ______________________________

____

7. How are you doing now? ______________________________
8. Is there any reason to believe that you will have future problems? Yes _____ No _____
9. Please elaborate. ______________________________

____

We hope that you are fully recovered and will be back on the river with us soon.

Figure 1-4 Sample Injury Follow-up Form

Project 2

Creating Personnel Documents

Objectives

- ☐ Create an organization chart
- ☐ Prepare documents using tabs, rotating text, inserting characters, sorting, and using outline numbered lists
- ☐ Prepare forms
- ☐ Work in a team to research topics related to rafting
- ☐ Write a report using research findings

Summary of *Microsoft Office* Skills

- ✔ Insert, modify, and move text and symbols
- ✔ Apply and modify text formats
- ✔ Correct spelling and grammar usage
- ✔ Modify paragraph formats
- ✔ Set and modify tabs
- ✔ Apply bullet, outline, and numbering format to paragraphs
- ✔ Apply paragraph styles
- ✔ Apply and modify column settings
- ✔ Modify document layout and Page Setup options
- ✔ Create and modify tables
- ✔ Preview and print documents
- ✔ Manage files and folders for documents
- ✔ Save documents using different names and file formats
- ✔ Insert images and graphics
- ✔ Create and modify diagrams and charts
- ✔ Create, modify, and position graphics
- ✔ Control pagination

STAR
River
Adventures

Job 2-1 Create Organization Chart

Skills Applied

- Modifying page margins and page orientation
- Creating and modifying charts
- Creating and inserting graphics in documents
- Applying and modifying character formats
- Applying paragraph formats

Organization charts help those inside and outside of an organization to understand the reporting structure within the company.

Help Keywords

Organization chart
Add an organization
chart

1. Create an organization chart that will eventually be distributed to all employees. Use the information provided on the organization chart presented in the Introduction to Star River Adventures on page 3. In the first box, enter only "Tommy Newland, Owner." Do not enter "Star River Adventures." Add a box with your name as an administrative assistant to Robert Jackson.

2. Use landscape orientation. Set left, right, top, and bottom margins to .5". Drag the boundary of the organization chart so it meets the margins. See Figure 2-1.

3. Increase the size of Tommy Newland's box so it measures .75" × 1.75". (**Hint:** Turn off AutoLayout.) For all other boxes, use the same size font, such as 10 point. Resize boxes, if needed, so all text in them displays.

4. Apply the Beveled Gradient diagram style to the organization chart.

5. Below the chart, create a text box centered horizontally on the page. In the box, enter "Star River Adventures" in a 36-point, bold font and "Organization Chart" in a 28-point, bold font.

6. Save the document as **2-1 Org Chart.** Print the chart.

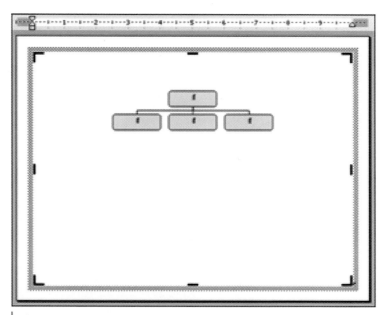

Figure 2-1 Organization Chart

Job 2-2 Prepare Job Descriptions

Skills Applied

- Applying character formats
- Applying paragraph formats
- Applying numbering
- Copying and pasting text
- Creating outlines

The company will be advertising open positions for several jobs for the coming season. Help prepare for this activity by creating updated job descriptions.

Task 1 Bus Driver Job Description

1. Key the job description for a bus driver shown on page 29. Use default margins and automatic numbering for duties and requirements. The numbers should be right-aligned.
2. Save the document as **2-2 Description Bus Driver.** Print the document.

Task 2 Administrative Assistant Job Description

1. Key a job description for an administrative assistant using the copy shown on page 30. Use the description for the bus driver as an example. Divide the list given into two sections, *Duties* and *Requirements*.
2. Use automatic numbering and copy the paragraph and signature lines from the bottom of the bus driver job description page.
3. Save the document as **2-2 Description Admin Assistant.** Print the document.

Help Keywords

Outline number
Modify bulleted or
numbered list formats
Customize numbered
list format

JOB DESCRIPTION
Bus Driver

Duties

1. Drive buses as assigned.
2. Transport guests and guides to drop-off and return to bus garage.
3. Perform CDL check on assigned vehicle each day.
4. Clean interior and exterior of assigned bus each morning.
5. Load designated number of life jackets.
6. Unload life jackets at drop-off.
7. Read and understand driving schedules.
8. Know access roads and CB calls.
9. Assume responsibility for general maintenance of bus, including fluids, tires, fuel, and so on.
10. Keep all Star River Adventures properties clean.
11. Follow all Star River Adventures policies.
12. Assist guests as needed.
13. Assist other employees as needed.
14. Work with management and employees.
15. Perform related duties as assigned.
16. Be familiar with all Star River Adventures trips and literature.

Requirements

1. CDL license (attach copy)
2. DOT card (attach copy)
3. Observance of all vehicular laws while operating a vehicle (county, state, and federal)
4. A preemployment drug test (federal law)
5. Random drug tests during period of employment (federal law)
6. An MVR (Department of Motor Vehicles Report) on all primary drivers (insurance requirement)

I have read and understand the duties and requirements as outlined on this sheet.

Name _____ Date _____

Administrative Assistant

- Assist owner and managers with projects and data input
- Assist river manager in contacting river guides and preparing DNR guide roster
- Prepare letters, documents, and files for owner and department managers
- Must be skilled in proper operation of Microsoft Office Suite components
- Must be able to use Dictaphone and transcriber
- Must be able to prepare letters from dictation on microcassettes
- Answer phones and screen calls for the owner and managers
- Maintain employee files, employee database mailing list, and payroll information
- Must be an authorized notary public in West Virginia
- Maintain owner's schedule and track days worked
- Maintain and distribute unemployment low earnings slips to employees during off-season
- Maintain office supplies and supplies for copy machine, printers, and fax machine
- Notarize documents
- Answer telephone reservation lines when needed
- Practice good diversity and teamwork skills

Task 3 Reservationist Job Description

Mr. Newland is considering using a different format for job descriptions. He has asked that one be prepared in outline format.

1. Key the job description shown below for a reservationist. Use default margins and automatic outlining as shown. Add an appropriate title.

2. Save the document as **2-2 Description Reservationist.** Print the document.

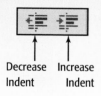
1) TAKE RESERVATIONS
   a) Answer Guest Questions According to Training
   b) Schedule Guests on Appropriate Raft Trips
   c) Sell Star River Adventures Trips and Packages
   d) Quote Prices and Take Payments

2) ANSWER PHONES
   a) Practice Good Customer Skills
   b) Transfer Calls Appropriately

3) EMPLOY KNOWLEDGE
   a) Be Familiar with All Star River Adventures Trips
   b) Be Familiar with All Star River Adventures Literature
   c) Be Familiar with All Star River Adventures Facilities
   d) Be Familiar with Local Attractions
   e) Be Familiar with All Star River Adventures Policies

4) OPERATE COMPUTERS
   a) Understand Reservation Programs
   b) Understand Data Entry Programs

5) COMPLETE CLERICAL WORK
   a) Enter Information from Mailing List Cards
   b) Complete Filing
   c) Help with Bulk Mailings

6) PERFORM OTHER DUTIES
   a) Interact with and Assist Guests as Needed
   b) Interact with and Assist Other Employees as Needed
   c) Perform Other Duties as Requested

Job 2-3 Create Name Cards

Skills Applied

- Creating and modifying tables
- Revising tables to modify cell formats
- Modifying table borders
- Applying character formats

Robert Jackson serves on the board of directors for the state Scouting organization. This year, the banquet for county directors will be held at a hotel ballroom in downtown Sutton. Although several members of the board are working to make the banquet a success, Mr. Jackson has accepted responsibility for many of the tasks. He has asked you to create the "tents" to be used as name cards for the head table.

1. Use an 8 1/2″ × 11″ sheet of paper for each tent. (Place one name on each tent). Create a table that has two columns and one row. Set the columns for a preferred width of 2.5″ each and the row for exactly 9″ in height. Center the table vertically and horizontally on the page.

2. Key Robert Jackson's name in the left and right cells. Use a Times New Roman, shadow, 72-point font. Rotate the text as illustrated. Set the cell alignment for the two cells at align center. Format the table for no border.

3. Save the document as **2-3 Tents.** Print the page. Fold the tent vertically in the center and vertically 1.5″ from the left and right edges. Staple or tape the sheet so it will maintain a triangular shape when it is placed on the table.

4. Repeat the process for the remaining four members of the board: David Bostic, Jessica Dials, Kelly Sprague, and John Thomas.

Help Keywords

Rotate text
  Change the position of
  text in a table
Table
  Resize all or part of a
  table

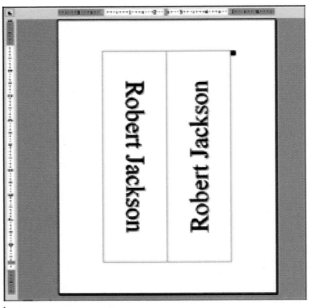

Figure 2-1 Name Card

Job 2-4 Prepare Information Sheet

Skills Applied

- Modifying page margins
- Applying character formats
- Applying paragraph formats
- Creating and modifying tables
- Revising tables to modify cell formats
- Modifying table borders
- Inserting page breaks
- Applying columns and modifying text alignment
- Revising column layout

The West Virginia Division of Natural Resources requires that guides "must have made a minimum of ten trips on a river or rivers of comparable or higher American Whitewater Affiliation class rating to the river portion to be guided . . . ." Prepare a form for guides to use in reporting their rafting experience as shown on the following page.

1. Set the left, right, top, and bottom margins for the page to .5".

2. Bold and center the title. Use a 12-point font for the first line of text and a 14-point font for the second line of text.

3. Insert a table with 3 columns and 20 rows. Set all rows to an exact height of .38". Set the border around the table, the border at the bottom of the first row, and the vertical lines in the table to a width of 1.5 points.

4. Bold and center the text in the first row vertically and horizontally.

5. Use a 10-point font for the text at the bottom of the page. Insert a Break, Continuous below the paragraph. Format two columns with 0.2" spacing between the columns to use for the signature lines.

6. Save the document as **2-4 Rafting Sheet.** Print the document.

Success Tips

To place text in columns in a document without changing the entire document, insert a Section Break, Continuous before and after the text.

WV DEPARTMENT OF NATURAL RESOURCES – LAW ENFORCEMENT DIVISION
WHITEWATER GUIDE – TRAINEE INFORMATION SHEET

Date	River and Section	Company
	use 20 rows in the table	

I hereby certify that I have successfully completed all of the listed whitewater trips as a guide trainee and have met or exceeded all requirements under state laws and regulations for a whitewater guide or trip leader within the state of West Virginia.

_____   State of _____, County of _____.
Guide–Trainee   *Date*   Taken, subscribed, and sworn to before me this _____
                                                         day of _____, 20 _____.
Address _____
                                                         My Commission expires_____.
_____
                                                         Notary Public _____

Job 2-5 Continue Work on Manual

Skills Applied

- Applying paragraph and character formats
- Applying paragraph styles
- Modifying page margins
- Applying bullets
- Inserting page breaks and page numbers
- Managing orphans and widows
- Applying columns and modifying text alignment
- Setting and modifying tabs
- Creating and modifying tables
- Inserting symbols

Help Keywords

Tabs
  Set tab stops
    To set tabs with
    leader characters

Success Tips

Use the Insert Symbols command to place happy face characters in a document.

Mr. Newland has requested that you add more information to the Employee Manual you worked on earlier.

1. Open the file **1-5 Manual,** which you created earlier.
2. Move to the end of the document and add the information from the hard copy provided below and on the following pages. Pay careful attention to the editing notations. Change all instances of *e-mail* to *email* (without a hyphen).
3. Save the document as **2-5 Manual.** Print the document.

Thinking Critically

1. What software feature can you use to create the diagonal border lines in the table cells of the report?

2. How do you access this feature?

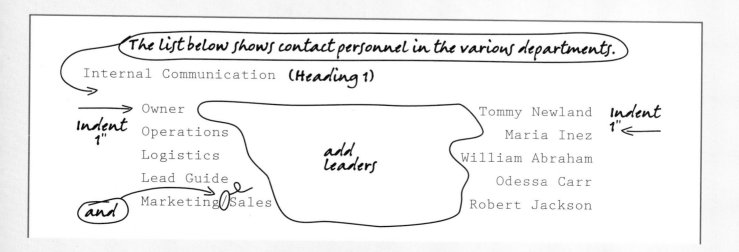

Indent 1"
Event Booking   Brenda Jenkins   Indent 1"
Administrative Assistant   Joe Coward
Payroll/Finance Accounting   Eric Collins   add leaders
and   Heather Taylor
Payroll   Joyce Forde
Administrative Assistant

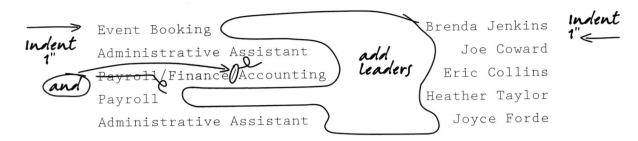

~~Communications~~

The following is a general listing of formal and informal means of communication regularly used at Star River Adventures.

Bulletin boards **are located** in the garage and office.

Department meetings **and**

~~The Spring Staff meeting held at the beginning of each rafting year.~~

Staff meetings **are** held as needed.

On busy weekends, ~~it is usual for~~ the owner, managers, or trip leaders **often** ~~to~~ request short meetings to discuss safety, policies, new information, problems, and suggestions.

After-trip meetings **are held** to debrief trip guides.

All employees will attend meetings scheduled to review policies, safety, and procedures as well as federal and state laws applicable to the operations of Star River Adventures.

Conflicts—Employees should speak directly to the individual with whom the conflict exists. Failing resolution, the employee may schedule a meeting with his **or** her manager or the owner.

The owner's and managers' doors are always open.

Information sheets are generally published to help organize busy days. These sheets are made available to guests and staff.

Memos may be inserted in payroll checks. See ~~Eric~~ **the Payroll Manager** if you want to include a memo to payroll.

Bulleted list

The Internet site for staff contains the following information.

Guide schedules

e-mail list

message board

river level

comments

staff meeting schedule

event calendar

Format in two columns.

Use Sentence case.

Employee Benefits *(Heading 1)*

Employee and Employee Guest Policy *(Heading 2)*

Full-paying guests have priority. Employees and employee guests ride the river on a "Standby Space Available Basis." Even with a reservation, employees or guests may be bumped from any trip.

Employees and their guests must make reservations 24 hours in advance of rafting trips. Each employee and employee's guest must read and sign a release form and follow the policies applicable to all other guests. The lead guide has the final say on whom may raft on any given day.

EMPLOYEE AND EMPLOYEE GUEST RAFTING DAYS

12.5% shading

	Mon	Tues	Wed	Thurs	Fri	Sat	Sun	Exceptions (No employee guest rafting allowed)
Apr	☺	☺	☺	☺	☺	☺	☺	
May	☺	☺	☺	☺	☺	☺	☺	Sunday, Memorial Day Weekend
June	☺	☺	☺	☺	☺	✕	☺	
July	☺	☺	☺	☺	☺	✕	☺	
Aug	☺	☺	☺	☺	☺	✕	☺	
Sept	☺	☺	☺	☺	☺	✕	☺	Sunday, Labor Day Weekend
Oct	☺	☺	☺	☺	☺	✕	☺	

Employee and Employee Guest Prices *(Heading 2)*

The following list shows the prices for employees and their guests: *stet*

- Employee—no charge
- Immediate Family—no charge for one-day trips
- Immediate Family—nominal multi-day charge as listed below

Multi-day charges for immediate family are as follows:

- One Day—$25 + 6% sales tax ( ) *Insert correct amounts*
- New River Two Day—$45 + 6% sales tax ( )
- Gauley River Two Day—$50 + 6% sales tax ( )

change hyphens to dashes

Company Rafting Equipment *(Heading 2)*

Rafting equipment, rental equipment, and/or two-day equipment may not be borrowed by anyone without the owner's approval.

Occasionally, raft*ing* equipment may be loaned to other companies. This is done only with ~~Maria's~~ *the Operations Manager's* approval. The equipment must be logged out and in.

Staff Rafting Equipment *(Heading 2)*

The staff owns two rafts, two kayaks, five life jackets, and *#* several paddles. Employees should sign the equipment in-and-out in the staff lounge. When employees finish using the equipment, they should return it to the boat garage. Employees are responsible for any damages which may occur as a result of usage (not normal wear and tear). Employees are not affiliated with Star River Adventures in any way while using staff rafting equipment. Employees are not covered by Star River Adventures' insurance policy while using staff rafting equipment. Taking a Star River Adventures guest on a private river trip for any type of compensation is reason for dismissal.

Guest Policy (Heading 1)

Cancellation and Refund Policy (Heading 2)

Guests are provided with Star River Adventures' cancellation policy through our printed literature, on our Web site, and on the back of each confirmation. Employees should familiarize themselves with this policy. If a guest asks for a refund, staff members can politely remind him where the information is located in our literature. Under no circumstances are staff members to inform guests that they are entitled to either a refund or a rain check. If guests have further questions concerning the matter, employees can politely refer them to the office staff.

In the event a rafting trip must be canceled due to weather or water conditions, the owner will take care of the problem. Even under these circumstances, employees are not authorized to mention anything about a refund or a rain check.

Release Forms and Photo Release (Heading 2)

Our insurance regulations require that every guest, employee guest, and off-duty employee must read and sign our release form. The bus must not leave before all release forms are signed and collected. Staff should allow sufficient time for guests to read and understand the form. Staff should also check each form as it is handed in to see that all areas are complete, that the handwriting is legible, and that it is signed.

Guests who are on multi-day trips must sign a release each day of the trip. Parents or legal guardians are responsible for signing the release forms for minors.

The only information on the release form that the guest may omit is the e-mail address. We use this address to send marketing information to guests five or six times a year.

Staff members should not pressure guests to provide this information if they do not volunteer it.

Late Guest Arrivals **(Heading 2)**

Our confirmation form notifies guests that they should allow at least 30 minutes prior to the trip to complete forms, change clothing, etc. Star River Adventures reserves the right to cancel trips for guests who arrive late.

Switching Sections of Rivers **(Heading 2)**

The opening manager makes the final decision concerning put-ins and take-outs. This decision is based on customer requests and efficient transportantion considerations.

sp   *requirements*

Job 2-6 Prepare Guide Information

Skills Applied

- Modifying page margins
- Applying character and paragraph formatting
- Setting and modifying tabs
- Applying bullets and numbering
- Inserting page numbers
- Creating outlines

Help Keywords

Sort
  Sorting

Mr. Newland has asked you to prepare a guide application form and a WVDNR list of regulations, both of which have signature lines. These forms must be ready for the new guides who will be hired soon.

Task 1 Guide Application

1. Key the Guide Application from the example on pages 42 and 43. Set the top margin at 1″ and the left, right, and bottom margins at .75″. Set the line spacing for the lists and lines at 1.5.

2. Alphabetize (sort) the list of whitewater skills. If necessary, make adjustments to margins or line spacing so the application fits on two pages.

3. Save the document as **2-6 Guide Application.** Print the document.

Task 2 Guide Regulations

1. Key the regulations from the text shown on pages 44 and 45. Use default margins and space as shown, using an outline numbered list. Place a page number in the upper right corner on page 2.

2. Save the document as **2-6 Regulations.** Print the document.

Star River Adventures
Guide Application
or
Application for Guide Training

Date: _____

Name: _____

Address: _____

Telephone: (H) _____ (W) _____

Are you 18 years of age or older? Yes No

Whitewater Experience

What year did you train and begin guiding commercial trips? _____

Did you start canoeing or kayaking before guiding? Yes No

If yes, when? _____

Local Experience

	Number of Trips	Dates
Big Sandy Creek		
Bluestone River		
Cheat River		
Upper Gauley		
Lower Gauley		
Upper New River (Meadow Creek to Prince)		
Middle New River (Prince to Thurmond)		
Lower New River		
Potomac River		
Tygart River		
Shenandoah River		

Initial Training

On the back of this page, describe your initial commercial rafting training. Include the name of the company doing the training, number of training trips, river rescue training, levels, and number of commercial trips. Include a list of what was covered during the training classes.

Whitewater Skills

Circle the number that best reflects your whitewater skills and experience (1 is lowest; 5 is highest).

a. Swimming ability	1	2	3	4	5
b. Teamwork ability	1	2	3	4	5
c. Interpretive speaking	1	2	3	4	5
d. Musical ability	1	2	3	4	5
e. Outdoor cooking ability (groups)	1	2	3	4	5
f. Camping ability	1	2	3	4	5
g. First aid skills	1	2	3	4	5
h. Whitewater ability	1	2	3	4	5

Physical Ability

Describe any physical challenges you have that might prevent you from guiding rafts or other guide-related duties. _____

First Aid/CPR

Submit with this application a recent photo of yourself and photocopies of valid CPR, First Aid, and EMT cards that you presently hold.

References

List the names of three people (not related to you) who have knowledge of your qualifications for the position.

Name	Address	Phone No.
_____	_____	_____
_____	_____	_____
_____	_____	_____

Present and Previous Employment

List your employers in the last two years, beginning with the most recent. If you need additional space, use the back of this page.

Name	Address	Phone No.
_____	_____	_____
_____	_____	_____
_____	_____	_____

May we contact these employers? Yes No

I hereby authorize the listed references and employers to disclose all requested information regarding my employment with said organization to Star River Adventures and agree to release said organization and its agents from all liability as a result of such disclosure.

_____   _____

Applicant's Signature   **Date**

WV DIVISION OF NATURAL RESOURCES REGULATIONS

SECTION 11.1–TRIP LEADERS AND TRIP GUIDES:

11.1 It shall be the responsibility of the licensee to instruct all Trip Leaders and Trip Guides in all applicable safety and emergency procedures.

11.2 Trip Leaders. Each commercial whitewater trip must include a Trip Leader. A Trip Leader must meet all trip guide qualifications specified in Section 11.3 of these regulations. In addition, a Trip Leader:

11.2.1 Must be at least 18 years old, unless approved in writing by the director.

11.2.2 Must have made a minimum of twenty trips on a river or rivers of comparable or higher American Whitewater Affiliation class rating to the river portion to be guided, of which six trips were on the river portion to be guided.

11.3 Trip Guides. A Trip Guide:

11.3.1 Must be at least 18 years old, unless approved in writing by the director.

11.3.2 Must have made a minimum of ten trips on a river or rivers of comparable or higher American Whitewater Affiliation class rating to the river portion to be guided, of which three trips were on the river portion to be guided.

11.3.3 Must be able to operate watercraft used in the licensee's commercial whitewater operation and assume responsibility for passenger safety.

11.3.4 Must have a VALID American Red Cross standard first aid card or the equivalent and CPR certification card or the equivalent.

11.3.5 Must have a thorough knowledge of the area traversed.

11.3.6 Must be familiar with floating in whitewater conditions in a personal floatation device.

11.4 For commercial whitewater operations on the Shenandoah River, a licensee may employ the services of trainee guides provided that all requirements concerning the number of trip guides set forth in Section 8.6 of these regulations are met. Trainee guides shall be at least 16 years old and otherwise meet the qualifications set forth in Section 11.3 of these regulations.

11.5 For commercial whitewater operations on the Gauley River, the director may require a trip guide to attest that he/she has made a minimum of three trips on the Gauley River when the river flow equaled or exceeded 1,000 cubic feet per second. The director may also require the licensee to submit a roster of trip guides who meet the qualifications set forth in this subsection and who are expected to be employed by the licensee throughout the designated peak season of the Gauley River. The director may also require the licensee to notify him/her of any changes in such roster made during the course of such season.

11.6 Variations from the qualifications of Trip Leader or Trip Guide as set forth in this section may be approved by the director. Requests for variation must be made in writing to the director, and such requests must substantiate that the variation does not reduce the intent of the qualifications set forth in these regulations.

11.7 Documents relating to the requirements of this section may be kept at the licensee's base camp for inspection by the director or his/her representative.

Date: _____

I, _____ , do hereby state that I have read the above-listed regulations and thereby know and understand the contents thereof.

_____
Signature

Job 2-7 Research Topics Related to Rafting

Skills Applied

- Modifying page margins
- Applying paragraph formatting
- Applying paragraph styles
- Inserting page numbers

To succeed in any job, an employee needs to learn as much as possible about the business in which he or she is working. There are several topics related to working in the whitewater rafting business in West Virginia that you want to research. Knowing more about these topics will make you a more valuable employee to Star River Adventures.

1. Work in a group with two other members (classmates) to complete this job. Use the Internet or the library to research the topics listed below. Each team member should research three topics (different from those chosen by other team members). Print or save copies of pictures, maps, and charts that are helpful to your understanding. Try to understand how these items relate to running a whitewater rafting business in West Virginia. Note the source information for the references you use.

   - Bridge Day
   - Department of Transportation (DOT)
   - Environmental Protection Agency (EPA)
   - Gauley Release Dates
   - Occupational Safety & Health Administration (OSHA)
   - River Classifications (difficulty class descriptions)
   - Tamarack
   - U.S. Army Corps of Engineers, Huntington Division
   - West Virginia Division of Natural Resources (WVDNR)
   - Summersville Dam

2. Write a summary paragraph or two (for each topic) containing the important facts you learned. Share your summaries with your teammates. Read the summaries prepared by your teammates and offer constructive feedback.

3. As a team, prepare an unbound report to include all of the information found by the team. Give the report an appropriate title and apply the Title style. Use the names of the topics for side headings in the report and use appropriate styles for the side headings. Include a References page to list the sources of information used for the report. Refer to pages 319–321 in the Reference Guide to review the unbound report format.

4. Save the report as **2-7 Rafting.** Print the report.

Preparing Administrative Documents

Objectives

- ☐ Produce documents for printed and online use
- ☐ Produce and complete *Word* forms
- ☐ Prepare agendas, minutes, and checklists
- ☐ Create documents using templates
- ☐ Save *Word* documents as Web files
- ☐ Create documents with graphics, tables, and footers
- ☐ Generate a directory, letters, and labels using mail merge
- ☐ Produce long documents from rough-draft copy

Summary of *Microsoft Office* Skills

- ✔ Insert, modify, and move text and symbols
- ✔ Apply and modify character format
- ✔ Correct spelling and grammar usage
- ✔ Apply font and text effects
- ✔ Enter and format date and time
- ✔ Modify paragraph formats
- ✔ Set and modify tabs
- ✔ Apply paragraph styles
- ✔ Create and modify a document header and footer
- ✔ Apply and modify column settings
- ✔ Modify document layout and Page Setup options
- ✔ Create and modify tables
- ✔ Preview and print documents, envelopes, and labels
- ✔ Manage files and folders for documents
- ✔ Create documents from a template
- ✔ Save documents using different names and file formats
- ✔ Insert images and graphics
- ✔ Insert, view, and edit comments

- ✔ Convert documents into Web pages
- ✔ Create and modify forms using various form controls
- ✔ Create forms and prepare forms for distribution
- ✔ Create, modify, and position graphics
- ✔ Merge letters with a *Word or Excel data* source
- ✔ Merge labels with a *Word or Excel data* source
- ✔ Track, accept, and reject changes to documents

ST★R River Adventures

Job 3-1 Create List of Food Service Options

Skills Applied

- Applying character and paragraph formats
- Setting and modifying tabs
- Adding images to a document
- Creating and modifying document footers
- Inserting date fields
- Creating custom forms using form controls
- Protecting forms

Star River Adventures contracts with a local restaurant that supplies meal packages. You will prepare a document showing the meal choices that are available for rafting tours. Guests will place the orders with Star River Adventures, which will arrange for the meals to be delivered to the appropriate location.

Create two versions of the document. One version will be a printed document to mail to prospective guests. The second version will be used by employees who complete the form in *Word*.

Task 1 Create Meal Packages Brochure

1. Use the information on page 49 to create a printed document showing the group meal packages. Use your creativity to format the page attractively. Add appropriate graphics.

2. Choose one font for the title and package headings. Choose a second font for all of the other text. (Do not use Times New Roman or Courier.) Make whatever font size and font style changes you choose.

Help Keywords

Date
  Insert the current date
  and time

3. Place one horizontal line between the different packages. Add lines at other locations and adjust the margins to make the page attractive and easy to read. Add a footer with Star River Adventures' name and phone number and the current date. Use the Insert Date feature so the date will be current whenever the document is printed. If anyone has two versions of a printout, they will know which is the most recent.

4. Save the document as **3-1 Meals.** Print the document.

Thinking Critically

Clients may call Star River Adventures to indicate their meal choices rather than mail a completed form. How can you use *Word's* form feature to create a form using the information in **3-1 Meals?** What text form fields, check boxes, and drop-down form fields can you use to allow company employees to quickly indicate the client's choices?

Group Meal Packages

Package 1: ($17.50/person plus tax)
Gourmet Buffet (All of the following are included:)
        Carved Roast Beef and Baked Ham
        Fresh Garden Vegetables
        Casseroles and Salad Bar
        Assorted Cheeses and Fruits
        Fresh Baked Breads
        Fresh Baked Cakes and Pies
        Coffee, Iced Tea, and Lemonade

Package 2: ($14.50/person plus tax)
Choose 1:   (A) Chicken Casserole
              (B) Roast Beef
              (C) Baked Ham
Choose 2:   (A) Salad
              (B) Corn on the Cob
              (C) Baked Potatoes
              (D) Green Beans
Includes all: Fresh Breads
              Desserts and Drinks (Coffee, Iced Tea, and Lemonade)

Package 3: ($9.50/person plus tax)
Choose 1:   (A) Hamburgers and Hot Dogs
              (B) Beef and Chicken Sandwich
Choose 1:   (A) Salad
              (B) Soup
Includes all: Desserts and Drinks (Coffee, Iced Tea, and Lemonade)

A minimum of 20 guests per group is required to reserve dinner packages. Advance reservations are required.

Breakfast Package: ($7.00/per person plus tax)
Includes all: Hot Breakfast Buffet
              Fresh Baked Breads
              Fresh Fruit
              Coffee, Tea, Milk, and Juice

A minimum of 8 guests per group is required to reserve the breakfast package. Advance reservations are required.

Task 2 Create Meal Packages Form

1. Open the file **3-1 Meals** that you created earlier. Use *Word's* form feature to create a form. Create text form fields, check boxes, and drop-down form fields that will allow employees to quickly indicate the group's choices. See Figure 3-1 for an example. Note that for Package 2, guests are allowed to make two vegetable choices. Decide how to accommodate this on your form. Figure 3-1 shows one possibility.

2. Use Times New Roman font for the entire document. This form is for internal use, so delete any graphics in the document. Leave the horizontal lines if you think they will improve readability.

3. Determine a logical place near the top of the page and add the following information.

   ```
   Group registration number: (insert text form field)

   Name of group contact: (insert text form field)
   ```

4. You may wish to protect the form before saving it. Use your first name as a password if you protect the form. (Using your password, unprotect the form later to make changes, if needed.) Save the document as **3-1 Meals Form.** Print the page.

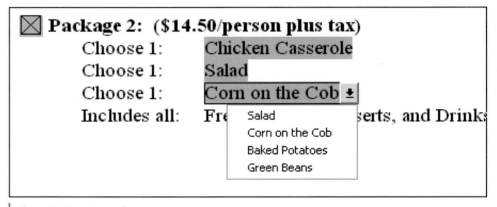

Figure 3-1 Form Example

Task 3 Complete Meals Form

1. Practice using the meals form you created. Open **3-1 Meals Form.** Complete the form using the following information.

   Group registration number: 1742

   Name of group contact: Howard Miller

   Meal package choice: Package 2

   Food choices: Roast Beef, Salad, Corn on the Cob

2. Save the completed document as **3-1 Meals for 1742.** Print the form.

Job 3-2 Prepare Agenda and Minutes

Skills Applied

- Applying character and paragraph formats
- Setting and modifying tabs
- Creating a document from a template
- Using Save As to save documents using different names
- Copying and pasting text
- Creating and modifying tables
- Inserting page numbers

agenda: a document that outlines the topics and order of the proceedings for a meeting

You will prepare agendas for upcoming meetings that Star River Adventures personnel will conduct. In addition to preparing the agendas, one of your responsibilities is to take minutes for the meetings.

Task 1 Key Agenda for Meeting

Success Tips

Remember to use leader tabs.

Tommy Newland conducts the general meetings for Star River Adventures. While Tommy is the sole owner of Star River Adventures and has the final say in all decisions, he likes to get input from key personnel.

1. Key the agenda shown below that will be passed out at the meeting. Format the agenda like the example on page 323 in the Reference Guide.

2. Save the document as **3-2 Meeting Agenda.** Print the document.

```
STAR RIVER ADVENTURES STAFF MEETING
February 14, 20--

Agenda

1. Call to order Tommy Newland
2. Approval of minutes from January 14 meeting
   Tommy Newland
3. Progress report on employee parking Joseph
   Coward
      Costs estimates Eric Collins
      Employee benefits Maria Inez
4. Decision on parking lot Tommy Newland
5. New business
      Buses Maria Inez
      Photocopier Robert Jackson
6. Adjournment
```

Task 2 Create Agenda for Mr. Newland

Help Keywords

Agenda
   Create an agenda

Mr. Newland needs an agenda with more detail to use while he conducts the meeting. You also need an agenda in a format that will be convenient for taking notes so that you can prepare the minutes efficiently following the meeting.

1. Use *Word's* Agenda Wizard to prepare the agendas for Mr. Newland and you. The first page will be for Mr. Newland to use and the following pages will be for your use.

2. Use this information as you follow the steps in the Agenda Wizard:
   - Choose the Standard style.
   - Add the correct date from the agenda you just created. The time is 1:30 p.m., and the Location is the Office Conference Room. Use SRA STAFF MEETING for the title.
   - Do not include any of the headings.
   - Omit the facilitator, time-keeper, and resource people.
   - Add the following agenda topic information:

       Progress report on employee parking, Joseph Coward, 15 minutes
       Cost estimates, Eric Collins, 5 minutes
       Employee benefits, Maria Inez, 5 minutes
       Decision on parking lot, Tommy Newland, 10 minutes
       Buses, Maria Inez, 10 minutes
       Photocopier, Robert Jackson, 5 minutes

   - Choose *Yes, you would like a form for recording the minutes.*

3. After completing the Wizard, add the following information to the first page:
   - Key the text *DRAFT FOR MR. NEWLAND* above the date so anyone reading the document will not think it is the final copy of the minutes.
   - The meeting will be called by Tommy Newland.
   - You will be the note taker.
   - The expected attendees are Tommy Newland, Maria Inez, Robert Jackson, Eric Collins, Joseph Coward, Joyce Forde, and you. (List the names in alphabetical order.)

4. Copy the first page of the document to a new file. Save the new document as **3-2 Agenda Newland.** Print the document.

5. Delete the first page from the original file. The other pages produced by the Wizard will be used for taking notes during the meeting. Add the text *DRAFT FOR MINUTES* above the date. Copy and paste the information for *Meeting called by, Note taker, and Attendees* from Mr. Newland's copy.

6. Insert an automatic page number at the horizontal center at the bottom of the page.

7. Save the pages as **3-2 Agenda for Notes.** Print the document.

Task 3 Create Minutes

minutes: a record of the discussions, proposals, and actions occurring in a meeting

As the meeting is held, you open the agenda file on your notebook computer. You edit and add information to the form to create minutes for the meeting. These informal minutes are kept on file in the company office.

1. Open **3-2 Agenda for Notes.** Delete, insert, and edit text as needed to make the form heading:

STAFF MEETING

STAR RIVER ADVENTURES
February 14, 20--
1:30–2:45 p.m.
Office Conference Room

2. Above the first item for discussion, change *Agenda* to *Minutes.*

3. The information below represents the issues and decisions you heard discussed during the meeting. Use this information to complete the form. Remove the number indicating minutes for all topics. Add a line at the bottom of the minutes where you will sign your name.

4. Save the document as **3-2 February Minutes.** Print the document.

Attendees: Eric Collins did not attend the meeting.

Progress report on employee parking:
Discussion: Joseph Coward distributed copies of the completed employee parking report. He reported that the option to purchase the property being considered for the lot will expire in 60 days.

Cost estimates:
Discussion: Joyce Forde reported in Eric's place. The parking lot can be constructed under budget only if gravel is used rather than asphalt. Gravel will be acceptable.

Employee benefits:
Discussion: The lot should alleviate tardiness caused by the difficulty employees have in finding appropriate parking close to the office. The proximity of the lot should make it safer for employees who leave after dark.

Decision on parking lot:
Conclusions: Tommy Newland decided that the company will proceed with purchasing land for the parking lot. Action items: Contact realtor. Person Responsible: Tommy Newland Deadline: February 20

Buses:
Discussion: Bus #3, which seats 16 passengers, has peeling paint. Conclusions: We will seek bids to have the bus painted. We need a firm commitment on when the bus will be available for use. Action items: Get three bids for painting the bus. Person responsible: Maria Inez Deadline: February 19

Photocopier:
Discussion: Robert Jackson distributed copies of bids for a new office copier. The lowest bid was from White's Office Machines. Conclusions: Tommy Newland decided that the company will purchase the copier from the lowest bidder. Action items: Place order for copier. Person Responsible: Eric Collins Deadline: February 19

Challenge: Create WV Scouts Meeting Agendas

Before the county director's banquet, Robert Jackson will chair a short meeting to review the water merit badges that are offered to WV Scouts.

1. Create a simple agenda to pass out to participants at the meeting. (Format the agenda like the example on page 323 in the Reference Guide.) Use the Agenda Wizard to create separate agendas for Robert to use while he conducts the meeting and for you to use to take notes during the meeting. Use the same general guidelines to set up the agendas that you used for the Star River Adventures staff meeting.

2. Meeting details include:

   - The meeting will be held at the Sutton Hotel on February 20 at 6 p.m. and is called by Robert Jackson.
   - There are no minutes from the previous meeting to approve, and there is no new business to discuss.
   - Robert will introduce the main topic for the meeting. This topic is the need for a third classification of water merit badge. (10 minutes)
   - While discussing the need for this badge, the group will review the current merit badges.
   - Jessica Dials will present the details of the canoe badge. (3 minutes)
   - Kelly Sprague will cover the whitewater badge. (3 minutes)
   - Robert will propose that an additional merit badge be added that will fall between the two existing badges. (2 minutes)
   - The expected attendees are John Thomas, David Bostic, Robert Jackson, Kelly Sprague, Jessica Dials, and you.

3. Save the documents as **3-2 Scouts Agenda, 3-2 Scouts Agenda Jackson,** and **3-2 Scouts Agenda for Notes.** Print the documents.

Job 3-3 Produce Rafting Checklists

Skills Applied

- Applying and modifying paragraph and character formats
- Adding images to documents and modifying graphics
- Inserting page numbers and date fields
- Creating a footer
- Saving *Word* documents as Web files
- Opening Web pages in *Word*
- Creating and modifying tables
- Modifying table borders and shading

Star River Adventures provides a variety of checklists for guests to use in preparing for river adventures. You need to prepare two of these checklists.

Task 1 Prepare Trip Checklist

1. Create a checklist for use by the person organizing the trip. Use the following information to create the list. Format the list attractively by making changes to fonts, cell borders, and placement that will improve the look and readability of the document.

> ORGANIZER'S CHECKLIST
> - Determine available dates and times for rafting trips
> - Check for availability of lodging needed for trip
> - Finalize number of participants
> - Make reservations for the rafting trip
> - Make reservations for lodging
> - Distribute trip information including dates and times of departure and return, release forms, payment dates and amounts, and cancellation policy
> - Collect deposit money
> - Collect release forms for minors (bring with you on the day of the trip)
> - Mail deposit payment
> - Collect balance of money
> - Mail balance payment
> - Distribute overnight checklist, maps, and directions for all members

2. Create lines or boxes for the organizer to check off when steps are complete. Provide an area for the organizer to make notes.

3. Add clip art or pictures to make the page more attractive.

4. Add the Star River Adventures name and phone number in a footer on the page. To easily identify the most recent copy of the form, add a date that will update automatically to the footer for the page.

Success Tips

Because you will later save the checklist as a Web page, you may want to create the list in a table. Using a table will help control the text width as it appears in a Web browser.

Help Keywords

Footer
  Insert footers

Help Keywords

Web page
  Create a Web page

5. Save the document as **3-3 Checklist.** Print the document.

6. The checklist you created will be mailed to individuals who request information. It will also be available on the Star River Adventures Web site. Open **3-3 Checklist.** Remove the footer. Include the Star River Adventures name and phone number on the page. Save the document as a Web page named **3-3 Checklist Online.**

7. Make any adjustments necessary so the page will appear attractively in a Web browser.

8. The users will print the page for their personal use. Open the file in a Web browser and print it. Use the printed checklist to help you decide whether to make adjustments to the page. Make changes, if needed.

9. Save the document again as a Web page using the same name.

Task 2 Create Sign-up Sheet

Organizers need a sign-up sheet to keep track of their group's registration information. Some of the information is general in nature and should be listed at the top of the page. Other information is specific and must be listed so the organizer can check it for each participant.

1. Using the information shown below, create a sign-up sheet (in table format) for mailing to organizers.

   SIGN-UP SHEET
   - Trip date
   - Deposit due date
   - Balance due date
   - Cost per person
   - Name, address, and phone number of participant
   - Deposit paid
   - Balance paid
   - Release forms signed and submitted
   - A place for notes

2. Follow the same guidelines that you used for the organizer's checklist (format attractively, provide space for checking off items, etc.).

3. Save the document as **3-3 Signup Sheet.**

4. Save **3-3 Signup Sheet** as a Web file named **3-3 Signup Sheet Online.** Make adjustments as needed so the document is attractive when displayed in the Web browser and easy to use when printed. Print the Web page.

Job 3-4 Generate Employee List and Directory

Skills Applied

- Applying and modifying paragraph and character formats
- Creating and modifying tables
- Modifying table borders and shading
- Applying AutoFormat to tables
- Creating a mail merge process for a directory
- Adding images to a document
- Modifying graphics
- Applying columns and modifying text alignment
- Inserting page numbers
- Modifying page margins and orientation

To make contacting employees easy, Star River Adventures periodically produces an employee directory that provides the names, addresses, and phone numbers of all employees. Additionally, each manager likes to have a one-page list of the employees with their telephone numbers.

Task 1 Create Employee Phone List

1. In *Word*, create a table with one row and three columns. Do not key any text in the table.

2. Start the Mail Merge Wizard. Choose to create a Directory.

3. Select the recipients from the *Excel* file **Roster** located in your data files. Select everyone on the Mail Merge Recipients list. Sort the list by last name.

4. In the first column of the table, insert the code for the last name, key a comma and a space, and then insert the code for the first name. In the second column, insert the code for the employee's phone number (home). In the third column, insert the code for the cell phone number.

«Empl_LName», «Empl_FName»	«Empl_Phone»	«Empl_Cell»

5. Save the document as **3-4 Employee List Setup**.

6. Complete the merge. Add a row at the top of the table that has the column headings NAME, HOME PHONE, and CELL PHONE. Apply the Table AutoFormat: Table Contemporary.

7. Add the following title above the table: EMPLOYEE PHONE LIST. Adjust column widths, fonts, and other settings for an attractive format.

8. Save the document as **3-4 Employee List Merged.** Print the document.

Task 2 Create Directory

1. Use the Mail Merge Wizard to create an employee directory. Use the *Excel* data file **Roster** as the data source. Sort the list by last name. In this directory include the following information:

   • Last Name, First Name
   • Street
   • City, State ZIP Code
   • Home Phone
   • Cell Phone
   • Extension

2. Add descriptive words to label the numbers for home phone, cell phone, and extension. Leave a blank line between entries to make the directory easy to read. (Place two hard returns after the Extension line in the merge setup document.) Format the document for two columns.

3. Save the document as **3-4 Employee Directory Setup.** Complete the merge to a new document. Save the document as **3-4 Employee Directory Merged.**

4. At the beginning of the document, insert a Section Break, Next Page. Create a cover page as the first page of the document. Use a one-column format for the cover page. Use your creativity to make the directory cover visually interesting. Change margins and fonts and add graphic elements to enhance the page.

5. On the second page of the document, apply a drop cap to the first name on the list. Choose *Dropped* for the position. For Lines to drop, enter *2*. Repeat for the rest of the employees.

6. Add page numbers to the directory at the bottom right of the page. Do not number the cover page. Begin the first page of names with page number 1.

7. The guides do not have phone extensions at the company. Delete the Extension line for employees who do not have an extension number. Format paragraphs so all information for an employee stays together on the same page and in the same column.

8. Save the document again using the same name. Print the document.

Challenge: Create Directory Booklet

Experiment with using a different format for the Employee Directory.

1. Open **3-4 Employee Directory Merged.** Format the document and print it as a folded booklet. Make changes as needed to enhance the new format. Add graphics or a place to record notes to blank pages if desired.

2. Save the document as **3-4 Employee Directory Booklet.** Print the document.

Job 3-5 Create Marketing Materials for WV Scouts

Skills Applied

- Modifying page orientation
- Creating and modifying tables
- Completing a mail merge process for form letters and mailing labels
- Viewing and editing comments
- Creating and modifying document headers
- Inserting date fields
- Inserting page numbers
- Finding and replacing text

WV Scouts have an opportunity to earn Whitewater Merit Badges. This is an excellent opportunity for Star River Adventures to market its services and to attract young guests to whitewater rafting. Robert Jackson knows that when individuals learn to raft at an early age, they are likely to become lifelong customers of Star River Adventures. You will prepare marketing items for WV Scouts groups.

Task 1 Create Data Source Table

Star River Adventures has received a list of WV Scouts troops interested in receiving information on whitewater rafting. You will create a table listing the contact information for the troops. Later you will merge this file with a cover letter.

1. Create a table with eight columns. Enter these column heads in the first row: Title, F_Name, L_Name, Address, City, State, ZIP, Troop.

2. Open and print the data file **Scouts.** Complete the table with the information given in the file. Change the page orientation to landscape. Save the document as **3-5 Scouts Troops.**

Task 2 Prepare Letter for Merge

Help Keywords

Comment
Delete a comment

1. Open the data file **Scouts Letter.** Read the comment in the letter from Robert Jackson and edit the letter according to his request. Delete the comment from the letter.

2. Prepare the letter to be merged with the table created in Task 1. Sort the list by last name. Assume that you are using letterhead paper. This letter will require two pages. Follow the guidelines for letters and second-page letter headings given in the Reference Manual on pages 313 and 315.

3. For the date line, insert a date/time code that will automatically insert the current date.

4. Insert appropriate text and codes for the letter address and the salutation as shown in Figure 3-2.

Help Keywords

Merge
  Create and print form letters

«Title» «F_Name» «L_Name»
WV Scouts Troop «Troop»
«Address»
«City», «State» «ZIP»

Dear «Title» «L_Name»

Figure 3-2 Sample Merge Codes

5. Create a header on the second page. Insert the proper codes to include the title, first name, and last name in the header. Insert the date to update automatically. See Figure 3-3.

«Title» «F_Name» «L_Name»
Page 2
October 6, 20--

Figure 3-3 Sample Merge Codes for Header

6. Save the document as **3-5 Scouts Letter Setup.** Merge **3-5 Scouts Troops** with **3-5 Scouts Letter Setup.** Save the document as **3-5 Scouts Letter Merged.** Print the document.

Task 3   Create Mailing Labels

1. Use *Word's* Mail Merge Wizard to create mailing labels for the five letters you created in Task 2. Use *Avery 5159 Address* for the label setup.

2. Use **3-5 Scouts Troops** as the data source. Sort the labels by last name. Use merge codes for the address as shown in Figure 3-2. Save the document as **3-5 Scouts Labels Setup.**

3. Complete the merge to a new document. Because only five records are in the data source file, the remaining labels on the page will show *WV Scouts Troop.* Delete this text from the otherwise blank labels.

4. Save the merged labels as **3-5 Scouts Labels Merged.** Print the document.

Job 3-6 Continue Work on Manual

Skills Applied

- Applying paragraph and character formats
- Applying paragraph styles
- Using AutoCorrect to insert frequently used text
- Setting and modifying tabs
- Inserting, copying, and pasting text and symbols
- Inserting, viewing, and editing comments
- Tracking changes
- Finding and replacing text

Mr. Newland has requested that you complete the last section of the manual that you worked on earlier.

1. Open the file **2-5 Manual,** which you created earlier. Review the procedures given earlier as you worked on the manual and refer to the Reference Guide for additional guidelines.

2. As you continue to key the manual, you will need to key the name of the company, "Star River Adventures," many times. To accomplish this more efficiently, create an AutoCorrect entry that will enter "Star River Adventures" every time you key "sra." If you find that this AutoCorrect entry causes problems with work you do later, simply delete it from the AutoCorrect dialog box.

3. Move to the end of the document. Add the text provided below and on the following pages. Pay careful attention to the editing notations.

4. Use Find and Replace to change all instances of *e-mail* to *email* (without a hyphen). Save the document as **3-6 Manual.**

5. Exchange files with a classmate. Proofread your classmate's document carefully. Use *Word's* track changes feature to mark corrections for errors in the document. Use Comments to insert questions about possible errors or formatting changes.

6. Review the comments and corrections your classmate made to your document. Accept or reject the changes as appropriate. Delete the comments. Save and print the document.

TEAMWORK

Employee Responsibilities   *(Heading 1)*

Courtesy *(Heading 2)*

We are all striving to provide quality service. Employees must keep in mind that guests are paying for a service/vacation. Employees should treat guests and coworkers as they themselves would like to be treated.

Confidentiality *(Heading 2)*

Employees are aware of confidential information such as payroll, ~~gross income~~ ~~user day numbers~~, mailing lists, etc. Staff should consider any information ~~confidential~~ that is not published in our literature or on our Web site confidential. Star River Adventures' mailing list is a valuable asset. Any unauthorized use or transfer of Star River Adventures' mailing list will result in the individual being criminally charged.

Clothing/Appearance *(Heading 2)*

General Appearance *(Heading 3)*

Clothes should be clean and neat and in good repair. Careful attention should be paid to personal hygiene (clean hair and body, use of deodorant, etc.).

Staff Shirts *(Heading 3)*

Staff must wear staff shirts and name tags while on duty. This applies to any marketing events that are attended by employees.

Staff clothing is provided for the use of employees only. Employees should not allow anyone else to use their staff shirts. Communication problems arise when guests cannot easily identify employees.

Jewelry *(Heading 3)*

Only earrings, finger rings, and necklaces may be worn by Star River Adventures employees while working. Facial/tongue jewelry is prohibited while working at any Star River Adventures job. Supervisors have the right to require that any item of jewelry be removed at any time ~~that they see fit~~.

Name Tags (Heading 3)

Star River Adventures employees are required to wear their name tags while at work. Name tags are supplied at no charge to each employee. Name tags are provided as a service to allow guests to identify employees easily.

Driving Star River Adventures' Vehicles (Heading 2)

Employees driving Star River Adventures' vehicles are required to have valid driver's license*s*. A commercial driver's license is required to drive a bus. The Administrative Assistant will run a *lc* Motor Vehicle Report on an employee before giving permission to drive a Star River Adventures vehicle.

If at any time a staff member finds something wrong with a Star River Adventures vehicle, he or she should fill out and submit a "Repair Sheet."

When removing a vehicle key from the key board in the garage, employees should replace it with a card indicating their name, the date, and the time they removed the key. When returning the key, employees should remove the card and delete their information.

The garage and all of the supplies and equipment in it are to be used for maintaining Star River Adventures' vehicles. You may use the garage for person*al* purposes only in the case of an emergency.

For the comfort of our guests, clean vehicles are a priority. Before returning a vehicle to the garage, an employee should thoroughly clean it and return all life jackets, helmets, etc. to the appropriate storage rooms.

Employees should check each vehicle for cleanliness before picking up guests.

Equipment, Building, and Property Maintenance *(Heading 1)*

Star River Adventures supplies all of the equipment needed to operate a rafting company. Employees are expected to respect the value of equipment, buildings, and property. The following individuals must be notified promptly when staff members notice any repairs that need to be made to equipment, buildings, or property.

~~Name~~ *Tommy Newland*   Buildings and property

~~Name~~ *Eric Collins*   Computer maintenance, security system, and phone

~~Name~~ *Maria Inez*   Rafting equipment

~~Name~~ *Maria Inez*   Vehicles and trailers

~~Name~~ *Eric Collins*   Office equipment

Office *(Heading 2)*

As the center of our business, the office is to be used for Star River Adventures business only. Office employees are involved in making reservations, doing accounting, scheduling, etc. Other employees should not disturb their work with general conversation.

Phone Calls *(Heading 2)*

Our phone lines are crucial to the operation of our business. While, at times, it may be necessary for employees to receive phone calls at work, calls should be kept to a minimum.

We have determined that it is not necessary for staff to carry personal cell phones at work. While ~~you are~~ working, employees are expected to concentrate on the needs of our guests, and we believe that having a cell phone that is turned on distracts from this purpose. There are, of course, special situations that might require an employee to carry a cell phone. If such a situation arises, staff members should discuss the issue with their supervisors.

Star River Adventures' toll free number is for business use only. The line is very expensive, and we appreciate the staff's help in keeping the cost down. If employees need to call the office or have someone call them at the office, they should remember to use the ^regular office number.

Move to end of section on Employee Responsibilities

Tardiness (Heading 2)

As soon as a staff member realizes that he or she will be late to work, the person should let his or her manager know. Our guests are excited about their adventures, and tardiness detracts from their enjoyment. In this ^ as in all matters, Star River Adventures wants its guests to enjoy a positive experience.

Smoking (Heading 2)

While we ~~never~~ ^do not discriminate against smokers, we ~~recognize~~ ^realize that smoking is a recognized social and health issue ~~in America~~. Star River Adventures allows smoking only outside of enclosed buildings and vehicles. Out of respect for our guests, we ask employees to abstain from smoking ~~at any time that~~ ^while they are "on the river".

Postage Meter (Heading 2)

Star River Adventures' postage meter is ~~never~~ ^not to be used for personal mail.

Copier (Heading 2)

Personal copies may be made on the office copier at 20¢ per copy.

Mail (Heading 2)

~~Luckily,~~ Star River Adventures receives a vast amount of mail. Staff should not use the company address for personal mail. We cannot be responsible for forwarding mail or for lost mail. If ~~you do~~ ^an employee does not want to rent a box at the local post office, ~~you may want to talk~~ ^we suggest talking to the postal clerk about "General Delivery" options.

Borrowing Vehicles (Heading 2)

Star River Adventures' insurance does not cover our vehicles for private use; therefore, we do not lend our company vehicles to anyone, including employees.

Move to end of section on Employee Responsibilities

Tips (Heading 2)

Staff members should not discuss tips in the presence of guests. It is unprofessional for our staff to ask for or imply in any way that they deserve tips. If employees receive tips, they must report them as income.

Theft (Heading 2)

Stealing will result in immediate dismissal. This includes all of Star River Adventures' property, food, names and addresses of guests, and guests' property.

Computer/E-mail (Heading 2)

Star River Adventures' computer system, including its e-mail system, is owned and maintained for the exclusive use of the business. It may be used for personal reasons only in the event of an emergency and with the office manager's or the supervisor's permission.

Employees of Star River Adventures need to use a password to operate the computer/e-mail system. Employees must disclose any password that used on the system to management. No employee is allowed to use unauthorized or undisclosed passwords.

When employees use Star River Adventures' computer/e-mail system, they are using a system that is not private. Employees are consenting to have all of their computer/e-mail work monitored. All online activity, including e-mail, can be traced to the author and may be used in court. The system must not be used in any way that is considered offensive to guests or to other Star River Adventures employees. This includes references to sexual orientation, race, national origin, disability, or any other area protected by state and federal law.

Move to end of Employee Responsibilities

Personnel File *(Heading 2)*

Employees may review their personnel files, by appointment, during regular office hours. Star River Adventures will have a manager present while an employee reviews his or her file. Employees may not mark on, destroy, or remove anything from a personnel file. They may request a copy of any document in the file. An employee may make a written rebuttal to anything in his or her file.

Discipline *(Heading 2)*

Star River Adventures exists to serve its guests. If an employee's job performance is not considered acceptable by management, that employee may be disciplined as management sees fit. Employees may be dismissed for first offenses if the owners or managers of Star River Adventures views the offense to be sufficiently serious.

Creating Materials to Promote the Company

Objectives

- ☐ Prepare a fax cover sheet, stationary, and notepads using mail merge
- ☐ Create document templates and create documents using templates
- ☐ Create bookmarks and insert text using bookmarked ranges
- ☐ Create printed forms, forms using *Word* form fields, and forms using form controls
- ☐ Save *Word* documents as Web pages
- ☐ Create a brochure with a three-column layout and custom graphics
- ☐ Update a long report to add footnotes, control pagination, and set page numbering options
- ☐ Create a report title page and table of contents

Summary of *Microsoft Office* Skills

- ✔ Insert, modify, and move text and symbols
- ✔ Correct spelling and grammar usage
- ✔ Enter and format date and time
- ✔ Modify paragraph formats
- ✔ Apply bullet, outline, and numbering format to paragraphs
- ✔ Apply paragraph styles
- ✔ Modify document layout and Page Setup options
- ✔ Create and modify tables
- ✔ Preview and print documents, envelopes, and labels
- ✔ Manage files and folders for documents
- ✔ Create documents from a template
- ✔ Save documents using different names and file formats
- ✔ Insert images and graphics
- ✔ Create, modify, and position graphics
- ✔ Create and edit Web documents in *Word*
- ✔ Create and modify forms using various form controls
- ✔ Create forms and prepare forms for distribution
- ✔ Merge letters with a *Word, Excel,* or *Access* data source
- ✔ Use *Excel* data in tables
- ✔ Control pagination
- ✔ Add and revise endnotes and footnotes
- ✔ Create and format document sections
- ✔ Create and update document table of contents
- ✔ Create presentations
- ✔ Import text from *Word* (to *PowerPoint*)
- ✔ Modify slide layouts
- ✔ Preview and print slides, outlines, and speaker notes

Job 4-1 Prepare Fax Cover Sheet, Stationary, and Notepads

Skills Applied

- Modifying table borders and shading
- Creating a document from a template
- Saving a document as a template
- Entering and formatting date and time
- Completing a mail merge process for letters
- Modifying page margins
- Applying paragraph formats
- Adding images to a document

As the company marketing manager, Robert Jackson emphasizes the importance of having Star River Adventures' name seen by the public as often as possible. He asks you to prepare a fax cover sheet, stationary, and notepads, all of which will help to advertise Star River Adventures.

Task 1 Create a Fax Cover Sheet Template

1. Use *Word's* Contemporary Fax template to create a fax cover sheet template to use with all outgoing faxes.

2. Add Star River Adventures' name, address, and phone number above *facsimile transmittal*. Move the text to the left so it does not fall on top of the vertical dots.

3. Add your name and *Administrative Assistant* in the From field. Change the Date field to Month day, year format that will update automatically. In the table near the bottom of the page, delete *CONFIDENTIAL* and the shading behind it.

4. Save the document as a document template named **4-1 Student Fax Cover Sheet.** (Use your full name for "Student"). Print the document.

5. Verify that the template is available for use by choosing *General Templates* from the Task Pane. The template **4-1 Student Fax Cover Sheet** should be available in the General folder.

Help Keywords

Template
   Create a document
   template

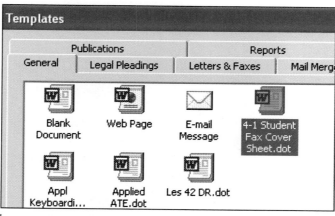

Figure 4-1 Templates Window

Task 2 Create a Letterhead Using Merge

You need to create one personalized letterhead design for each full-time employee. The file you create will be sent to an outside company that prints large quantities of letterheads on good quality paper.

1. Open the data file **Letterhead.** This document contains the company information in a header. You will enter merge codes to place the employee's name and phone number in the document.

2. Start the Mail Merge Wizard. Choose *Letters* for the type of document. Choose to use the current document to set up the letters. Under Choose an existing list, select *Browse*. Locate the *Access* file **P4 Employees** (found in your data files) as the data source file. Use the Employee Roster table. Select all of the full-time employees in the Mail Merge Recipients list.

3. Add the appropriate merge codes to the document. Include the Title, FirstName, LastName, and Extension fields as shown in Figure 4-2. Key *Extension:* before the Extension field code. Save the document as **4-1 Letterhead Setup.** Print the document.

ST★R River Adventures

205 Riverview Drive
Sutton, WV 26601-1311
Phone: (304) 555-0110

«Title» «FirstName» «LastName»
Extension: «Extension»

Figure 4-2 Merge Codes

4. Preview the letters; then complete the merge to a new document. Save the document as **4-1 Letterhead Merged.** Print the document.

Task 3 Design a Notepad Using a Watermark and Merge

All Star River Adventures employees have personalized company notepads. You will create a design for the notepads and use mail merge to enter the employee names. The printing company will use the sheets you design to create one gross of 5.5″ × 8.5″ pads for each employee.

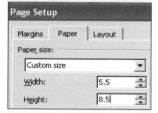

Software Review

To set a custom paper size:

• Select *Page Setup* from the File menu.

• Select the *Paper* tab.

• Select *Custom size* from the Paper size list.

• Enter the desired width and height.

• Click *OK*.

1. Create a document for the notepad for guides. You will modify this design for the full-time employees later. In Page Setup, set a custom paper size to 5.5″ by 8.5″. Set all margins to 0.5″.

2. Create a design for the notepad. Include the company name somewhere on the notepad. Include a place for the guide name followed by a comma and the position. Also include the company phone number. Use a graphic related to rafting as a watermark on the notepad.

3. Use the **P4 Employees** file for the data source. Use the Guide Roster table. Select all of the guides. Enter the appropriate merge codes in the document.

   ```
   «FirstName» «LastName», «Position»
   Phone: (304) 555-0110
   ```

4. Save the document as **4-1 Notepad Setup 1.** Print the document.

5. Preview your directory; then complete the merge to a new document. Save the document as **4-1 Notepad Merged 1.** Print the document, placing two pages per sheet. (Select this option in the Print dialog box.)

6. Open the file **4-1 Notepad Setup 1** that you created earlier. Save the file as **4-1 Notepad Setup 2.** Edit the design to create notepads for the full-time employees. Key *Extension:* below the phone number.

7. Use the **P4 Employees** file for the data source. Use the Employee Roster table. Select all of the employees. Add a merge code to insert the employee's phone extension as shown below. Save the file again using the same name. Print the document.

   ```
   «First_Name» «Last_Name», «Position»
   Phone: (304) 555-0110
   Extension: «Extension»
   ```

8. Preview your directory; then complete the merge to a new document. Save the document as **4-1 Notepad Merged 2.** Print the document, placing two pages per sheet.

Page Setup

| Margins | Paper | Layout |

Paper size:

| Custom size | ▼ |

Width: | 5.5 |
Height: | 8.5 |

Job 4-2 Create Printed, Onscreen, and Online Forms

Skills Applied

- Inserting text (using bookmarked ranges)
- Applying paragraph formats
- Applying paragraph styles
- Adding images to documents
- Creating custom forms using form controls
- Protecting forms
- Saving *Word* documents to the Web

A variety of information is available to people who are interested in Star River Adventures' services. Marketing materials that may be sent to these potential guests include brochures, videos, CDs, and e-newsletters. The information may be requested by mail, over the phone, or online.

Robert Jackson wants you to create a new form to use for these requests. He needs forms to:

- Insert in brochures and mailings to be returned via parcel post.
- Use onscreen when reservation assistants are taking calls.
- Allow users to submit information online.

Task 1 Create Bookmarks

Help Keywords

Bookmark
  Add a bookmark

Software Review

To bookmark text:

- Select the text.

- Select *Bookmark* from the Insert menu.

- Under Bookmark name, type or select a name, which must begin with a letter and cannot include spaces.

- Click *Add*.

As you create the forms, you will need to bring in information from other files. You will not insert the entire file, just part of the file. The first step in the process of bringing part of one file into another file is to place bookmarks in the original file. These bookmarks identify the selections or ranges of text you will import.

1. Create a separate folder in which to save your work for this job. Name this folder **Request Forms.** Open the data file **River Classifications.**

2. Select the text for the classifications of moving water. (Do not include the section heading or introductory sentence.) Create a bookmark for this text. Use the name *MovingWater* to bookmark the selection.

3. Select the text for the classifications of whitewater. (Do not include the section heading or introductory sentence.) Create a bookmark for this text. Use the name *Whitewater* to bookmark the selection.

4. Select the table listing the rivers. (Do not include the section heading or introductory sentence.) Create a bookmark for this text. Use the name *Rivers* to bookmark the selection.

5. Check that you have three properly named bookmarks in the document. Save the document in the Request Forms folder as **4-2 River Classifications.**

Task 2 Create Information Request

1. Open the data file **Printed Form.** Use the information provided in this document to design and create an information request form. This form will be provided in printed form to potential guests. As you design this form:

   - Include Star River Adventures' name, address, and phone number on the sheet.
   - Add section headings (similar to Customer Information) to make the form easier to use. Apply a paragraph style, such as Heading 1, to the headings.
   - Insert text from **4-2 River Classifications** as directed.
   - Include lines and/or checkboxes where the guest can write text or indicate choices.
   - Provide sufficient space for the information to be written on the form.
   - Plan the form so all of the information will fit on the front and back of one sheet of paper.
   - Format the form attractively. Use color and graphics to enhance the form.

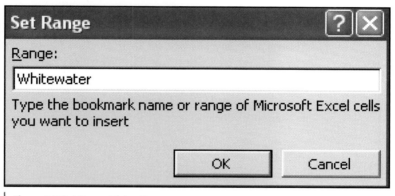
Figure 4-3 Set Range Dialog Box

2. Save the document as **4-2 Request Form Printed** in the Request Forms folder.

3. Ask a classmate to proofread your form and offer suggestions about improving the form design. Make changes as needed to correct errors or improve the form design. Print the document.

Task 3 Create a *Word* Form

1. Open the file **4-2 Request Form Printed** that you created earlier.

2. Edit this document to be completed using *Word*. Use *Word's* Form feature to add form fields to use in entering the information. Use these types of form fields:

   - Text form fields for varying information, such as name or address
   - Checkbox form fields for items where the prospective guests may choose more than one item
   - Drop-down form fields where prospective guests may choose only one item

3. Remove graphics and headers, footers, and other design elements that are not needed in this version of the form.

4. Protect the form. Save the document as **4-2 Request Form Onscreen** in the Request Forms folder. Print the form.

Sidebar

Success Tips

Search the Internet for information/brochure request forms for whitewater rafting businesses in West Virginia. Researching these forms will help you visualize how to construct your form.

Software Review

To insert bookmarked text from another file:
- Select *File* from the Insert menu.
- Find and select the file containing the bookmark.
- Click the *Range* button.
- Type the bookmark name in the Range text box.
- Click *OK*.
- Click *Insert*.

TEAMWORK

Challenge: Web Form

The form fields placed in a document using the *Word* Forms toolbar work when completing the form onscreen in *Word*. These fields no longer work when the file is saved as a Web page. You will replace the *Word* form fields with form controls as you create a version of the form that can be used as a Web page.

1. Open the **4-2 Request Form Printed** file that you created earlier. Save the document as a Web page (in HTML format) as **4-2 Request Form Challenge.**

2. Add textbox controls for name, phone, and email. Add text area controls for the address and estimated group size.

3. Add checkbox controls for preferred rafting adventure, types of information requested, and nonriver activities. Add drop-down box controls where clients can indicate how they found out about Star River Adventures and for the preferred method of contact.

4. Add a Reset button at the bottom of the page. Add a Submit button at the bottom of the page. Leave the Action property for the Submit button blank. The Action property allows you to indicate a file that will receive the information when a user clicks Submit. The Web developer will add this information when the form is placed on the company Web site.

5. Add a scrolling text control at the bottom of the page. Use Turquoise as the background color. Place this text in the box:

   ```
   Let Star River Adventures introduce you to the
   Big Sandy Creek - Bluestone River - Cheat River
   - Gauley River - Lower Meadow - Meadow River -
   New River - Potomac River - Tygart River -
   Shenandoah River!
   ```

6. Use Web Page Preview to view how the document will appear online. Make changes as needed for an attractive form. Save the document again in HTML format using the same name.

7. Open the form in your Web browser. Enter sample data to test the controls. Test the Reset button. It should clear data that has been entered into the form. Make corrections if needed. Print the form from your browser.

Help Keywords

Form controls
Form controls you can use on a Web page

Software Review

To insert a form control in a document:

- Select *Toolbars* from the View menu. Select *Web Tools.*

- Select the *Design Mode* button to switch to Design mode.

- Move to the location where you want the form control.

- Select a control button from the Web Tools toolbar.

Design Mode Button

Job 4-3 Create Fax and Presentation

Skills Applied

- Creating a document from a template
- Using object linking to display *Excel* worksheet data as a *Word* table or worksheet object
- Opening a *Word* outline as a presentation
- Changing the layout of individual slides
- Applying design templates to slides
- Printing handouts from slides

Today Tommy Newland is in Charleston, the state capital, preparing for tomorrow's meeting with the West Virginia Division of Natural Resources Law Enforcement Section. Mr. Newland sent Robert Jackson an urgent email with requests that you need to fulfill immediately.

Task 1 Create a Fax Using a Template

1. Open the data file **Email from Newland.** Read the email message.

2. Open the template **4-1 Student Fax Cover Sheet** that you created earlier. Fill in the following information.

   ```
   To: Tommy Newland
   Re: Classified Table
   Pages: Two including this one
   Paragraph Text: Tommy, the table you requested is
   on the next page. I am scheduled to leave the
   office today at 5:30. If you think that you will
   need additional information and would like me to
   stay later, just let me know. I'll be glad to
   help you prepare for tomorrow in any way that I
   can.
   ```

3. Delete the cc: row. Replace the boxes by *Urgent* and *Please Reply* with an *X*. Insert a hard page break after the paragraph.

4. Open the *Excel* data file **Classified.** Embed the data from the Accidents worksheet on the last page of the fax document. Save the fax as *Word* document **4-3 Fax.** Print the document.

Help Keywords

Embed
Insert information by creating a linked object or embedded object

Task 2 Create a Presentation from a *Word* Outline

1. Create the *PowerPoint* presentation from the data file **Special Use Request,** following Tommy's directions.

2. Save the presentation as **4-3 Special Use Request.** Print the presentation as handouts in black and white with six slides per page. Send the file as an email attachment to the address provided by your teacher, if so directed.

Help Keywords

Presentation
Create a *PowerPoint* presentation from a *Word* outline

Job 4-4 Create Three-Column Brochure

Skills Applied

- Creating a document from a template
- Applying paragraph styles
- Modifying paragraph formatting
- Applying bullets and numbering
- Creating and modifying graphics
- Copying and pasting text

Robert Jackson has prepared copy for you to use in creating a three-column brochure to use in marketing to the WV Scouts. The brochure will focus on the Whitewater Rafting Badge.

1. Create a new *Word* document using the Brochure template from the Publications templates. Use the existing styles that are saved with the template. Save the document as **4-4 Brochure.** Save often as you work on the document.

2. In the first column of the first page, key the following quotation to replace the text in the shaded box.

> *"Each of my three sons completed his Whitewater Merit Badge requirements at Star River Adventures. There were many companies to choose from, but Star River Adventures was our first choice because they are so safety conscious."*
> *(Louise Felder, Buckhannon, WV)*

3. Key the following text for the remainder of the first column. The text should not flow into the second column. (Do not use bold for the numbered list.)

STAR RIVER ADVENTURES' COMMITMENT TO SAFETY

Several basic guidelines are consistently followed, allowing Star River Adventures to maintain the best reputation for safety in the whitewater rafting industry.

1. The Upper New River is used for troops attempting the Whitewater Merit Badge because the rapids are less dangerous than the Lower New River.

2. A minimum of one certified river guide is provided for each group of eight scouts.

3. The "Rule of 100" is always enforced. No Scout troop is allowed to raft if the water temperature plus the air temperature is less than 100°F.

```
4. All appropriate licenses from the West
Virginia Division of Natural Resources Law
Enforcement Section are current and on file in
the company office.
```

Help Keywords

AutoShape
   Add a shape

4. For the second column, create a five-pointed star from Stars and Banners in AutoShapes. Apply a fill effect shaded from white in the center to blue at the outer edges. Replace the ampersand in the second column with the star you just created. Replace the name and address provided with Star River Adventures' name and address.

5. In the third column of the first page, replace the information at the top of the column with:

```
STAR RIVER ADVENTURES
WHITEWATER RAFTING FOR WV SCOUTS
```

6. Replace *Future Solutions Now* with:

```
Earn your Whitewater Merit Badge!
```

Software Review

To add text to an AutoShape:

• Right-click the AutoShape.

• Select *Add Text*.

• Key the text.

• Change the font, size, or alignment as desired.

7. Delete the graphic in the template. Create a new graphic similar to the one shown in Figure 4-4. Make three copies of the star AutoShape you created for the second column. Make the stars different sizes; then rotate and overlap them attractively.

8. The first star should contain the text *Star;* the second, *River;* and the third, *Adventures*. Rotate the images before you add text so the text remains level. Add text directly to the AutoShapes for the two smaller stars. To create text for the larger star, create a rectangle AutoShape with no fill and no line. Add the text *Adventures* to the rectangle shape. Place the rectangle shape over the largest star and group the shapes. Format the font, size, and alignment of the text for the stars to create an attractive graphic.

Help Keywords

AutoShape
   Rotate an AutoShape

Figure 4-4 AutoShapes with Text

9. Open the data file **Brochure Text.** In the first column on page 2 of the brochure, place the text sections shown under the heading *Page 2 Column 1* in the **Brochure Text** file.

10. In the second column on page 2, place the text from **Brochure Text** that is shown under the heading *Page 2 Column 2*.

11. Use the style *Block Quotation + Before: 0″ After: 0″* to create a new quotation at the bottom of the second column that will contain the following text.

> "Everything was 'just right.' I earned my merit badge, and as a reward, my parents are sending me back for the two-day trip." Sam Hobbs, Troop 422, Mineral Wells, West Virginia.

12. In the third column on page 2, place the text from **Brochure Text** shown under the heading *Page 2 Column 3*.

13. Change the phone number 555-0000 to Star River Adventures' phone number.

14. Proofread the document carefully. Check for consistent use of fonts and styles. Make corrections as needed. Print the brochure on the front and back of one sheet of paper.

Success Tips

If you do not have a duplex printer, select the Manual duplex option in the Print dialog box. This will allow you to print on both sides of a page.

☐ Print to file
☑ Manual duplex

Thinking Critically

1. When resizing an AutoShape, how can you make sure the shape maintains its original proportions?

2. When resizing an AutoShape, how can you make sure the center of the shape stays in its original location?

3. If text you key does not fit on an AutoShape without wrapping, what adjustments can you make so the text fits on one line?

Job 4-5 Complete Basic Work on Manual

Skills Applied

- Applying paragraph formats
- Inserting page numbers
- Managing orphans and widows
- Creating and formatting footnotes
- Finding and replacing text
- Inserting a table of contents
- Using header/footer and numbering options to format sections

You have completed a significant portion of the Employee Manual. Now you will add footnotes, control pagination, set page numbering options, and create a title page and table of contents.

1. Open the file **3-6 Manual** that you created earlier. Save the document as **4-5 Manual.** As you make the following changes, save the document periodically.

2. At the end of the first paragraph, insert a footnote. In the Footnote and Endnote box, key an asterisk (*) in the Custom mark box. For Numbering, select *Restart each page.* For Apply changes to, select *Whole document.* Key this text for the footnote:

```
An "at-will" employee may resign at any time and
may have his or her job terminated at any time.
```

Help Keywords

Footnote
  Insert a footnote or an
  endnote
    Custom footnotes or
    endnotes

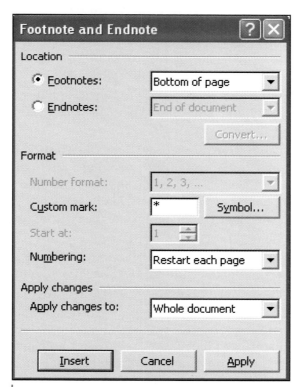

Figure 4-5 Footnote and Endnote Dialog Box

3. Find the side heading *Employee and Employee Guest Policy*. Insert a footnote after the word *Guest*. Follow the guidelines given for the first footnote.

   Footnote text:

   ```
   Employee guests must be immediate family members:
   mother, father, brother, sister, son, daughter,
   or spouse.
   ```

Help Keywords

Replace
   Find and replace text
   or other items

4. Search the entire document for the word *customer* and replace all occurrences with the word *guest*. Replace all occurrences of *multi-day* with *multiday*.

5. Run the Spelling and Grammar checker. Make all appropriate corrections.

Help Keywords

Pagination
   Control pagination

6. Verify that Widow/Orphan control is turned on. Check the top and bottom of each page and correct any text that does not flow to the appropriate page. Use the *Keep lines together* or *Keep with next* functions to make the adjustments. Avoid using hard returns or hard page breaks to push text to the next page. For numbered and bulleted items, at least two lines of the preceding paragraph should be on the same page as the first item. A single numbered or bulleted item may not appear at the top of a page. Include at least two lines of the preceding numbered or bulleted item on the page with the last item.

7. Move to the beginning of the document so you can insert a new blank page. Select *Break* from the Insert menu. Under Section break types, select *Next page*. This page will be used later for the title page. Move to the beginning of the document. Repeat this procedure to create a second blank page that will be used for the table of contents.

8. Move to the beginning of the document. Follow the example in the Reference Guide to create a title page for the document. The STAR RIVER ADVENTURES POLICY MANUAL was prepared for Star River Adventures employees by you on today's date. Use an Arial, 16-point, bold font for the title. (Do not apply the Title style. Doing so would cause the report title to be displayed twice in the table of contents.)

9. Notice whether the title page has a page number. If it does, view the header. Delete the page number and close the header. The title page should not display a page number.

10. Move to the second page, which is still blank. Follow the spacing guidelines from the Reference Guide for creating a report table of contents. Key the title (TABLE OF CONTENTS) for the page and press Enter twice. Use an Arial, 16-point, bold font for the title. (Do not apply the Title style.) You will insert a table of contents after you update the page numbering for the rest of the document.

Software Review

To disconnect a header or footer from those in a previous section:

• Select *Header and Footer* from the View menu.

• Click the *Same as Previous* button on the Header and Footer toolbar.

• *Same as Previous* will no longer display above the header or footer box.

Same as Previous Button

11. On the Table of Contents page, view the header and footer. For both the header and footer, click the *Same as Previous* button. This will cause *Word* to disconnect (not to repeat) the header and footer from the previous section.

12. On the Table of Contents page, insert page numbering. Position the number at the bottom of the page with center alignment. Format the number to show on the first page of the section and to use a Roman numeral number format (i, ii, iii). Start the page numbers for this section at ii. (The title page of the report is page i, but it should not display a page number.) See Figure 4-6.

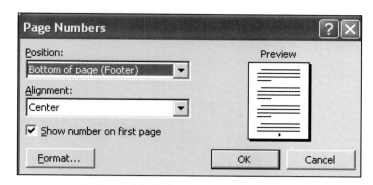

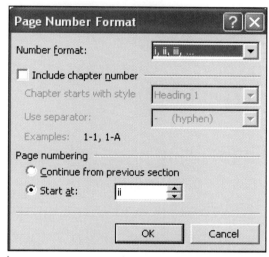

Figure 4-6 Page Number Options

13. Move to the first page of the body of the report. Add page numbers to the remaining sections of the report. Disconnect or connect header sections as needed to produce the desired numbering. The third page, which is the first page of the report body, should have no number. The fourth page, which is the second page of the report body, should have the Arabic numeral 2. The numbering for all of the following pages should flow logically (3, 4, 5, and so on).

14. Scroll through the document and visually check the page numbering. Recheck the first page, which is the title page; it should have no number. Recheck the second page, which is the table of contents. It should have the Roman numeral ii in the footer. If you have trouble with the numbering, check to see if the Different first page option is selected in the Page Setup box for a section. This will affect whether numbers appear on the first page of a section.

15. Because you applied styles to headings while creating the document, it will be simple to have *Word* generate the table of contents. On the Table of Contents page, insert a table of contents, accepting all default options.

16. Save the document as **4-5 Manual.** Print the document.

Help Keywords

Table of contents
  Create a table of contents

Project 5

Preparing Advertising Materials Using Desktop Publishing

Objectives

- ☐ Modify a template and develop certificates from templates
- ☐ Update and print *Excel* worksheets
- ☐ Prepare itineraries
- ☐ Use desktop publishing skills to prepare newsletters and brochures
- ☐ Create and apply styles in documents
- ☐ Create documents with WordArt and other graphics
- ☐ Save documents as Web pages and insert hyperlinks
- ☐ Copy and paste data from *Word* and *Access* files

Summary of *Microsoft Office* Skills

- ✔ Insert, modify, and move text and symbols
- ✔ Correct spelling and grammar usage
- ✔ Modify paragraph formats
- ✔ Set and modify tabs
- ✔ Create and apply paragraph styles
- ✔ Create and modify a document header and footer
- ✔ Modify document layout and Page Setup options
- ✔ Create and modify tables
- ✔ Preview and print documents, envelopes, and labels
- ✔ Manage files and folders for documents
- ✔ Create documents from a template
- ✔ Save documents using different names and file formats
- ✔ Insert images and graphics
- ✔ Create, modify, and position graphics
- ✔ Convert documents into Web pages
- ✔ Insert and modify hyperlinks to other documents and Web pages
- ✔ Use Mail Merge codes
- ✔ Enter and edit cell data including text and numbers

STAR River Adventures

Job 5-1 Design Gift Certificates

Skills Applied

- Entering, copying, and pasting text
- Modifying tables
- Applying paragraph formats
- Creating a document from a template
- Adding images to documents
- Inserting hyperlinks
- Entering and editing text in cells

Star River Adventures offers gift certificates that customers can purchase. Each certificate includes Star River Adventures' name, address, and phone number. Also printed on each certificate is the amount of the certificate and the date the certificate expires. For security purposes, each certificate is numbered and signed. You will create two sets of gift certificates—general certificates and certificates for WV Scouts. You will also record the sale and redemption of the certificates in an *Excel* worksheet.

Task 1 Create General Gift Certificates

1. Open the *Excel* file **Gift Certificates** from your data files. Update all dates on both sheets to reflect the current year. Save the file as **5-1 Certificate Record.** Close the file. You will use this file later.

2. Open the file **Certificate Template** from your data files. Save it as a *Word* template named **5-1 Certificate Template G** in the folder where you save your other solutions. You will update this file with information for Star River Adventures.

3. The certificate was created in a table. Make the width of the first column 1″. In the first column, insert an appropriate picture or clip art. Size the clip art so it is no more than .75″ in width.

4. Add Star River Adventures' name and address to the appropriate locations on the certificate.

5. Make the word *Number* a hyperlink to the *Excel* file **5-1 Certificate Record** that you saved earlier. Test the link to make sure it works properly. Format the hyperlink so it will display in black text, both before and after the link is used. (Modify the text color for the *Hyperlink* and *FollowedHyperlink* styles.)

6. Make two copies of the certificate table and place them on the same page (for three certificates on the page). Leave three blank lines between tables.

7. Save the template again using the same name. Print the template.

Task 2 Record Certificates Sales

Before you complete gift certificates for customers, you should review some general guidelines about preparing gift certificates. These guidelines have been placed on the company's local network for easy access.

1. Open the data file **Preparing Gift Certificates** in your browser. Read the guidelines. Close the file.

2. Open the template file **5-1 Certificate Template G** that you created earlier. Record the following information for the purchase and redemption of certificates. Use the current year in purchase and redemption dates.

   Phil Jones purchased an $85 certificate on March 12.
   Angie Maddox purchased three $50 certificates on March 15 (total $150).
   Certificate #502 was redeemed on March 17.
   Claude Raynes purchased a $250 certificate on March 23.
   Certificates #504 and #506 were redeemed on March 23.
   David Ellington purchased a $100 certificate on March 25.

3. Save the file as a *Word* document named **5-1 G Certificates Issued.** Print the document. Save the worksheet using the same name **5-1 Certificate Record.** Print the General worksheet.

Task 3   Create Certificates for WV Scouts

The company wants to recognize WV Scouts by offering a special gift just for this group. You will modify the gift certificate template to use for this purpose.

1. Open the file **5-1 Certificate Template G.** Save it as a template named **5-1 Certificate Template S** in the folder where you save your other solutions.

2. Keep all of the original certificate information, but change the design of the certificate to make it special for WV Scouts. Insert clip art or photos that are appropriate for scouting and/or whitewater rafting. Save the template again using the same name.

3. Complete gift certificates and record the following sales for WV Scouts.

   Joseph Musick purchased two $75 certificates on February 23.
   Angie Maddox purchased three $50 certificates on March 15 (total $150).
   Certificate #506 for $50 was redeemed on March 16.
   David Ellington purchased a $100 certificate on March 25.

4. Save the document as **5-1 S Certificates Issued.** Print the document. Save the worksheet as **5-1 Certificate Record.** Print the WV Scouts sheet.

Job 5-2 Prepare Itineraries

Skills Applied

- Inserting, copying, and pasting text
- Applying paragraph formats
- Creating and modifying tables
- Modifying table borders
- Modifying page margins

Tommy Newland and Robert Jackson will be traveling this month. You will create itineraries for their trips. Itinerary formats vary but should include who the itinerary is for, the purpose of the trip, and the days and times of the activities. The itinerary should also include any information that may be helpful to the person traveling. This includes contact information, such as names, addresses, and telephone numbers, as well as information about materials the traveler may need.

1. Tommy Newland will attend the National Whitewater Rafting Association Conference in Washington, D.C. Use the information shown in Figure 5-1 on page 86 to prepare an itinerary for his trip. Format the itinerary in a table approximately as shown. The itinerary should fit on one page.

2. Access the Internet and find a site that gives time and distances for travel by car. Find the travel time from Sutton, West Virginia, to Washington, D.C. Using this information, enter the appropriate times for leaving Sutton on April 7 and returning to Sutton on April 10.

3. Save the document as **5-2 NWRAC Itinerary.** Print the document.

4. Robert Jackson will attend the American Marketing Association's spring convention in Chicago, Illinois, from April 14–18.

5. Open the data file **Jackson Itinerary.** Use the information in this file to prepare an itinerary for Mr. Jackson. Use the same format as that for Mr. Newland's itinerary.

6. Save the document as **5-2 AMA Itinerary.** Print the document.

Thinking Critically

1. What Internet site can you use to find driving distances from one city to another?

2. What other resource can you use to find driving distances from one city to another?

ITINERARY FOR TOMMY NEWLAND
National Whitewater Rafting Association Conference
April 7–10, 20--

Date	Time	Activity
Wednesday April 7	12:30 p.m.	Leave Sutton, WV
	6 p.m.	Arrive, Washington, DC (check into hotel)
	7 p.m.	Dinner with Anderson Baker and Henry Watson Purpose: discussion of joint marketing proposal* Reservation for three at Chez Montgomery in Tommy Newland's name (1107 L Avenue, phone: 555-2087)
Thursday April 8	8 a.m.	Breakfast with Tory Daniels
	9–10:30 a.m.	Session on accounting practices
	11 a.m.–noon	Session on federal statutes relating to whitewater rafting
	noon–1:30 p.m.	Lunch with WV members of NWRA
	2–4 p.m.	Visit vendor booths
	7–9 p.m.	Banquet
Friday April 9	8 a.m.	Breakfast with Cheryl Fernandez, Sandy Fellows, and Jerry Sou
	9–10:30 a.m.	Session on safety practices
	11 a.m.–noon	Session on joint marketing opportunities
	noon–1:30 p.m.	Lunch with NWRA board of governors
	2–3:30 p.m.	Company president roundtable
	4–5 p.m.	Review of European whitewater rafting practices
	7–midnight	Dinner and closing party
Saturday April 10	9 a.m.	Breakfast and checkout
	10 a.m.–2 p.m.	Sightseeing
	2 p.m.	Depart Washington, DC
	7:30 p.m.	Arrive Sutton, WV

* All activities are at the hotel unless otherwise noted.
Three copies of joint marketing proposal are in the blue folder.

Enclosure: WV, VA, DC Map
               Hotel Confirmation
               Meeting Agenda

Figure 5-1 Travel Itinerary

Job 5-3 Create Newsletter for Print

Skills Applied

- Modifying page margins
- Applying paragraph formats
- Creating and modifying tables
- Revising tables by inserting rows and changing cell formats
- Modifying table borders and shading
- Creating and inserting graphics in documents
- Inserting Mail Merge codes
- Indenting paragraphs

You will prepare newsletters for February and April that will be mailed to customers. Guidelines for the February newsletter are given. Create the April newsletter so it follows the same basic format as the February newsletter.

Task 1 Prepare Newsletter Page 1

To reduce the cost of producing the newsletter, it will be printed on one sheet of paper (front and back). The newsletter is mailed to customers who prefer a hard copy or who do not have access to email. Refer to Figure 5-2 on page 89 as you create the first page of the newsletter.

1. Open a new blank *Word* document. Set all four margins to .5″.

2. Create a table that has two columns and one row. Set Column 1 (left column) to a preferred width of 1.5″ and Column 2 (right column) to a preferred width of 6″.

3. Shade Column 1 dark blue. Remove all border lines from Column 1. Remove the right border line from Column 2 (leaving the top and bottom border lines only).

4. Add a second row to the table. Right-align the text in Row 1 Column 2. This cell will contain the newsletter banner.

5. With the insertion point in Row 1 Column 2, insert WordArt. Select the WordArt style from the fifth column second row. Set the font size to 28 point. Key the text *Star River Adventures*. Change the fill color of the WordArt to dark blue.

6. Press Enter and insert a second WordArt below the first image. Use the same style, a 12-point font, and the text *Volume 12, Number 2*. Change the fill color to dark blue and the line weight to 1 point. Add one blank line above and below the WordArt in the cell.

7. In Row 2 Column 2, create WordArt for a side heading. Use the same style as for the other WordArt in the newsletter. Use dark blue fill and 1-point line weight. Use a 14-point font and key the following text:

        Skiing and Rafting, The Perfect Combination

banner: the information across the top of a publication with the name, volume number, etc.

Help Keywords

WordArt
  Add WordArt

8. Add one blank line above and below the WordArt in the cell. In Row 2 Column 2, enter the following body text using Times New Roman, 12-point for the font.

```
Let it snow, let it snow, let it snow. The heavy
snowfall this winter in the mountains of West
Virginia has created a bounty of opportunities
for outdoor activities. The ski areas in the
state have bountiful snow and will remain open
through March and April. In addition to
lengthening the skiing season, the abundant snow
provides the excitement of an early spring
whitewater season.

The serendipity of snow on the mountains and
water in the streams gives us a chance to offer
a special combination package available only in
March and April of this year. We have
arrangements with both Winterplace and Snowshoe
ski resorts that allow you to spend one day
skiing and the next day rafting.

This exceptional package is wild with activity
and wonderful with value. We are offering one
day of skiing, one night at the winter resort of
your choice, and one day of rafting for the
unbelievably low price of $220 per person. Lunch
is included on both days.
```

9. Add a new row below the last row. Enter the side heading *Spring Season Starts Early* as WordArt. Use the same guidelines as for the first side heading.

10. Open the data file **February Articles.** Under the side heading, enter the two paragraphs indicated for page 1.

11. Set the left indentation for all paragraphs in Column 2 to 0.15" and set the alignment to justify.

12. Add a new row below the last row. Split the new row into two columns. Remove the border between Columns 2 and 3.

13. In Column 2 of the new row, key this text using center alignment and a Times New Roman, 12-point, dark blue font:

```
For additional information, contact:
```

14. Under the text line, enter Star River Adventures' name, address, and phone number. Use center alignment and an Arial, 10-point, dark blue font for the text.

15. In Column 3 of the last row, insert an image. Use an appropriate clip art or picture that represents whitewater rafting or West Virginia. The right edge of the illustration should align with the right edge of the column.

16. In Row 1 Column 1, insert an AutoShape star. Use the colors white and dark blue for the star. Use a shading style that shades from white in the center to dark blue. Apply a white line to the star. Rotate the star to slightly off center.

Help Keywords

Graphic
Add shading, color, or
graphic fills

Help Keywords

Rotate
Rotate an object

17. Copy this star several times to display stars down Column 1, as shown in Figure 5-2. Rotate the stars in slightly different directions.

18. At the bottom of Column 1, key *February.* Use center alignment and a Times New Roman, 14-point, bold, white font. Save the document as **5-3 February Newsletter.** Your completed page should look similar to Figure 5-2.

Star River Adventures
Volume 12, Number 2

Skiing and Rafting, The Perfect Combination

Let it snow, let it snow, let it snow. The heavy snowfall this winter in the mountains of West Virginia has created a bounty of opportunities for outdoor activities. The ski areas in the state have bountiful snow and will remain open through March and April. In addition to lengthening the skiing season, the abundant snow provides the excitement of an early spring whitewater season.

The serendipity of snow on the mountains and water in the streams gives us a chance to offer a special combination package available only in March and April of this year. We have arrangements with both Winterplace and Snowshoe ski resorts that allow you to spend one day skiing and the next day rafting.

This exceptional package is wild with activity and wonderful with value. We are offering one day of skiing, one night at the winter resort of your choice, and one day of rafting for the unbelievably low price of $220 per person. Lunch is included on both days.

Spring Season Starts Early

The exceptional snow season promises a spectacular spring rafting season. The New River receives the flow from over three million acres of land. All rain and snow in the watershed contribute to the water rapids in the New River. The superb snow season that we experienced this winter, plus the expected heavy spring rains, promises fantastic spring whitewater. Summersville Dam is already full, so all excess water must be released. This means that in addition to the New River, we can begin rafting earlier on the Gauley River. Not every spring offers the promise of early rafting on the Gauley, so don't miss out on this spring's opportunity to raft early and raft often.

All packages and current prices are posted on our Web site. Remember that the earlier you book your trip, the bigger discount you can expect. Call our reservation line today and schedule the trip of a lifetime.

For additional information contact:

**Star River Adventures
205 Riverview Drive
Sutton, WV 26601-1311
Phone: (304) 555-0110**

Figure 5-2 February Newsletter Page 1

Task 2   Prepare Newsletter Page 2

Refer to Figure 5-3 on page 91 as you create page 2 of the newsletter.

1. Open the file **5-3 February Newsletter** that you created earlier. Go to the end of the document and insert a new row in the table. In Column 1 of the new row, insert a hard page break.

2. Open the data file **February Articles**. Locate the two articles indicated for page 2. Create WordArt for the heading of the first article for this page. Follow the same guidelines used for the previous side headings. Enter the text for the article. Repeat this process for the second article. Check to be sure the paragraphs in Column 2 on this page are indented like the ones on page 1.

3. Insert a new row after the last row. This row will contain the mailing information. Specify the row height to exactly 4.6″. Split Column 2 in this row into two columns and one row.

4. Move to Column 3 in the last row. Insert hard returns to position the cursor at about 8″. Use the Mail Merge Wizard to insert merge fields for a mailing address. Use the *Word* file **Newsletter List** found in your data files as the data source for the merge. (Do not complete the merge at this time; just enter the field codes.)

```
«Title» «First_Name» «Last_Name»
«Address»
```

Help Keywords

Merge
  Create and print form
  letters

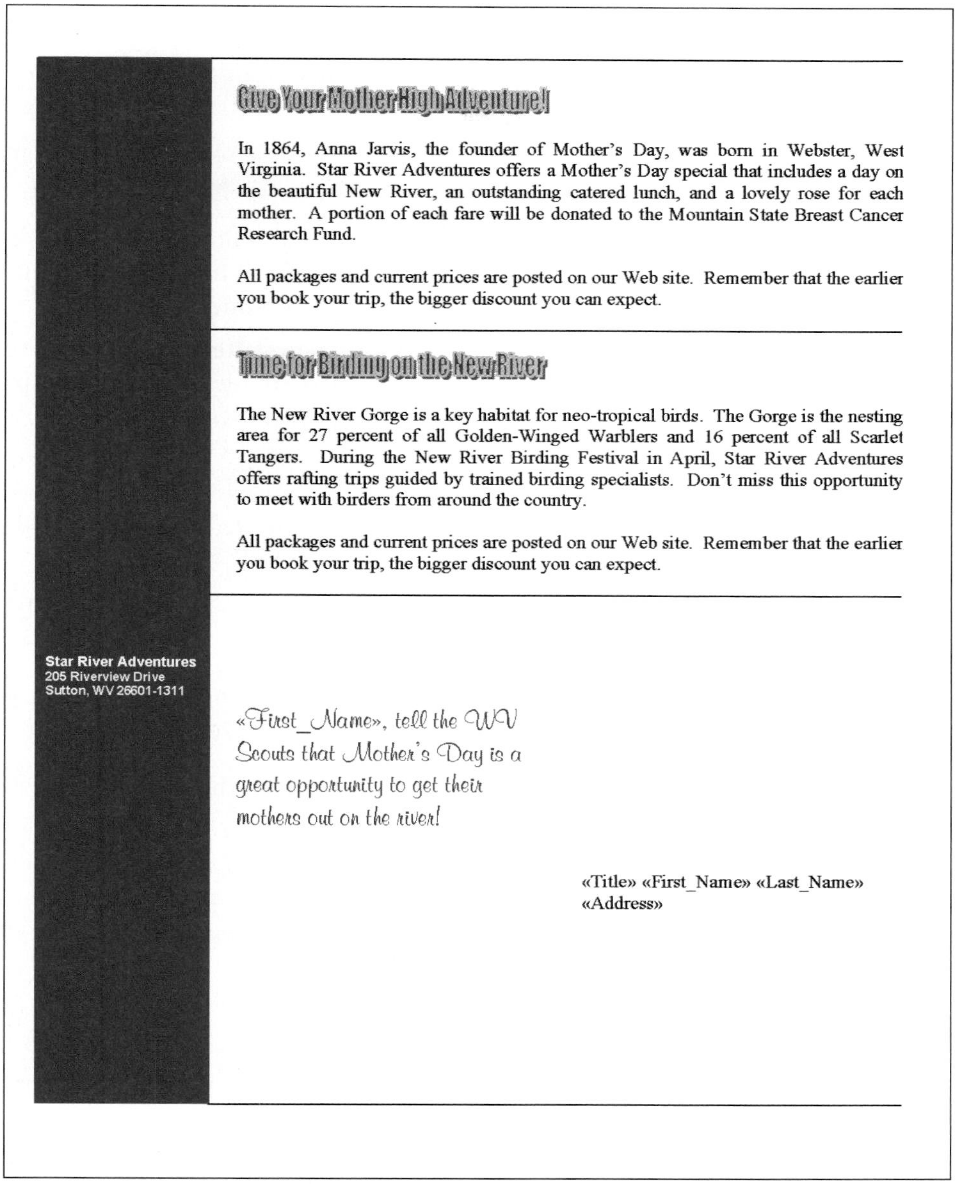

Give Your Mother High Adventure!

In 1864, Anna Jarvis, the founder of Mother's Day, was born in Webster, West Virginia. Star River Adventures offers a Mother's Day special that includes a day on the beautiful New River, an outstanding catered lunch, and a lovely rose for each mother. A portion of each fare will be donated to the Mountain State Breast Cancer Research Fund.

All packages and current prices are posted on our Web site. Remember that the earlier you book your trip, the bigger discount you can expect.

Time for Birding on the New River

The New River Gorge is a key habitat for neo-tropical birds. The Gorge is the nesting area for 27 percent of all Golden-Winged Warblers and 16 percent of all Scarlet Tangers. During the New River Birding Festival in April, Star River Adventures offers rafting trips guided by trained birding specialists. Don't miss this opportunity to meet with birders from around the country.

All packages and current prices are posted on our Web site. Remember that the earlier you book your trip, the bigger discount you can expect.

Star River Adventures
205 Riverview Drive
Sutton, WV 26601-1311

«First_Name», tell the WV Scouts that Mother's Day is a great opportunity to get their mothers out on the river!

«Title» «First_Name» «Last_Name»
«Address»

Figure 5-3 February Newsletter Page 2

5. In Column 2, enter hard returns to position the cursor at about 6.4″. Enter the following text to add a personalized note on the page. Insert the merge field to personalize the note. Use a dark blue font that simulates handwriting for the text.

    ```
    «First_Name», tell the WV Scouts that Mother's
    Day is a great opportunity to get their mothers
    out on the river!
    ```

6. In Column 1, enter hard returns to position the cursor at about 6″. Enter the Star River Adventures name and address. Use left alignment and an Arial, 9-point, bold, white font.

7. Save the file again using the same name. Print the newsletter on the front and back of one sheet.

Challenge: Prepare April Newsletter

The newsletter for April should follow the same basic guidelines as those used for the February newsletter. The April newsletter is Volume 12, Number 4. The newsletter will have two articles, one on each page.

1. Open the **5-3 February Newsletter** file that you created earlier. Save the file as **5-3 April Newsletter.** Edit the file to create the April newsletter. You may use the same illustration that you used in the February newsletter or insert a different illustration.

2. Open the data file **April Articles.** Use the text found in this file for the two articles. Edit the articles as needed so each fits within the space available on the page.

3. Delete the note about Mother's Day in the last row on page 2. Replace it with the following:

   ```
   «First_Name», let the parents know that we have
   an adventure for them, too!
   ```

4. Save the document again using the same name. Print the newsletter on the front and back of one page.

TEAMWORK

5. Exchange printed newsletters with a classmate. Read your classmate's newsletter and mark any errors you find or make suggestions for improvement. Update your newsletter as needed using comments from your classmate. Save and print a final newsletter.

Job 5-4 Produce Online Newsletter

Skills Applied

- Creating folders for document storage
- Saving documents as Web pages
- Creating and modifying tables
- Revising tables (inserting and deleting rows)
- Modifying table borders and shading
- Creating, modifying, and inserting graphics
- Finding and replacing text
- Inserting and modifying hyperlinks

In addition to a printed newsletter, the company posts a newsletter online. The online newsletter is enhanced by hyperlinks to additional information and other sites. Customers who access the online newsletter often choose to be dropped from the mailing list for printed newsletters. This helps reduce mailing and printing costs.

You will use the February newsletter to create a newsletter for the Web. All files must be saved as Web pages. You will need to preview the files as Web documents to see how they look. (Not all formatting from *Word* will be applied in the Web version of a document.) You should check each hyperlink you create to be sure that it works correctly.

1. Create a folder named *Newsletter.* Save all of the documents used for the online newsletter in this folder.

2. Open the file **5-3 February Newsletter.** Save the document as a Web page named **5-4 February Newsletter** in the Newsletter folder. Use *February Newsletter* for the page title.

3. Delete the last row with the return address, the personal note, and the mailing fields. Delete the page break and blank lines that were between pages 1 and 2.

4. Move the row that contains the company name, address, phone number, and graphic to the end of the document. Be sure that the row remains the same width as the other rows in the table. Delete *February* from Column 1.

5. Near the top of the document, add WordArt with the month (February) and the current year. Place the WordArt under the volume and issue number. Use the same WordArt setup used for the volume and issue information.

6. Use Find to locate and delete *All packages and current prices are posted on our Web site.* throughout the document.

7. At the end of each article except the last one, add this text:

   `Click here for additional information.`

8. You need to create each of the documents that the customer will access when he or she selects the link at the end of each article. For the first article, open the data file **Trip 800.** Note the formatting and layout used in the document. You will create similar documents later. Save the file as a Web page named **5-4 Trip 800** in your Newsletter folder. Use *Skiing and Rafting* as the page title.

9. Create a hyperlink from the newsletter text *Click here for additional information.* to the **Trip 800** file.

10. Create the document to link to the next article. Open the file **Spring Season** from your data files. This file contains handwritten notes for the article. Use this information to create a document with the same formatting and layout as that used for the **Trip 800** document. Add a table showing the current trip details (Trip 101 and 105). The information is available in the *Access* data file **Trip Packages.** Add an appropriate clip art or picture to the page.

11. Save the document as a Web page named **5-4 Spring Season** in your Newsletter folder. Add the appropriate link from the article in the February newsletter to the document **5-4 Spring Season.**

12. Create a Web page to link to the third article about Mother's Day. Open the file **Mothers Day** from your data files. This file contains handwritten notes for the article. Use this information to create a document with the same formatting and layout as that used for the **Trip 800** document. Add a table showing the current trip details (Trip 801). The information is available in the *Access* data file **Trip Packages.** Add an appropriate clip art to the page.

13. Save the document as a Web page named **5-4 Mothers Day** in your Newsletter folder. Add the appropriate link from the newsletter to the document **5-4 Mother's Day.**

14. A hyperlink is not used for the last article. At the end of the last article, add this text:

    `Call (304) 555-0110 for current information.`

15. Access the National Park Service Web site (http://www.nps.gov) and search for *Summersville Dam*. Review the search results and find an interesting article related to Summersville Dam. Note the URL for this article. Hyperlink the text *Summersville Dam* in the newsletter to the URL for the article.

16. Save the newsletter using the same name. Test all of the links in the article to make sure they work properly. Print the newsletter and the three related articles from your browser. Use landscape orientation for the articles.

Job 5-5 Prepare Marketing Brochure

Skills Applied

- Creating and applying paragraph styles
- Modifying page margins
- Inserting page breaks
- Creating and modifying tables
- Modifying table borders and shading
- Applying paragraph formats
- Creating, modifying, and inserting graphics in a document
- Creating and modifying document headers and footers
- Copying and pasting data (from *Word* documents and *Access* tables)
- Setting and modifying tabs

Throughout the year, Star River Adventures sends brochures to customers. You will begin work on this year's brochure. The brochure generally has 20 to 24 pages. You will create the first few pages of the brochure.

Task 1 Create Styles for Brochure

To establish consistency in the brochure, create styles to use for all of the paragraphs and headings.

1. Open the data file **Styles.doc.** This document shows the settings for styles that should be used for the brochure. Print and close the document.

2. Open a new blank *Word* document. Save the document as **5-5 Brochure.** Create styles to use for the paragraphs, the main headings, and the secondary headings. Use the settings shown on the printout when creating the styles.

3. Save the document again using the same name.

Task 2 Create Title Page

1. Open the file **5-5 Brochure** that you created earlier. Set all four margins to 0.5″. Create three pages by inserting a section break *Next page* between each of the pages.

2. On page 1, insert a two-column one-row table. Set the row height to exactly 10″. Set the width of Column 1 to 1.5″ and Column 2 to 6″. Remove the border lines from the table.

3. In Column 1, enter the company name using center alignment and a 72-point, Times New Roman font. Rotate the text for the company name as shown in Figure 5-4 on page 96.

4. Add pale blue shading to Column 1. Add dark blue shading to Column 2.

Help Keywords

WordArt
   Add WordArt

5. Create WordArt graphics for the text for Column 2 similar to that shown in Figure 5-4. Use a 36-point font for the first WordArt graphic and make the following three successively larger.

```
It's Wild!
It's Wonderful!
It's West Virginia
Whitewater!
```

6. Add an appropriate clip art at the bottom of Column 2. Save the brochure using the same name.

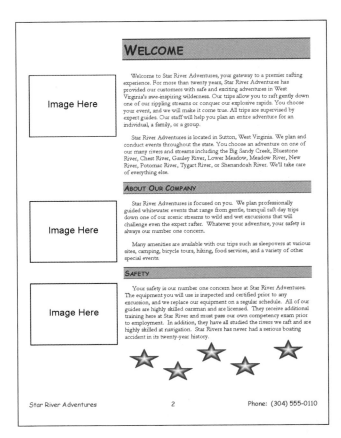

Figure 5-4 Brochure Pages 1 and 2

Task 3 Create Brochure Pages 2 and 3

1. Open the file **5-5 Brochure** that you created earlier. On page 2, create a footer to appear on page 2 and the following pages. Use 12-point, dark blue, Comic Sans or a similar font. In the footer, adjust the center tab so it is in the center of the page and the right tab so it is at the right margin. Place the company name at the left and the page number in the center. Place *Phone:* followed by the company phone number at the right.

2. On page 2, create a table with one row and two columns. Make the row height 9.5″. Set the first column width to 2.5″ and the second column width to 5″. Remove the table borders.

Help Keywords

Footer
   Insert footers

3. Insert three images in Column 1. Search the Internet and find appropriate photos or clip art related to rafting. Rafting images can be found on the Microsoft Design Gallery (http://dgl.microsoft.com). You may also use images from your data files: **Logaul01**, **Sittop01**, and **Logaul02**. Resize the images to 2.25″ wide.

4. In Column 2, enter the heading and text shown below. Apply Title 1 style to the heading and Paragraph style to the text.

   ```
   Welcome

   Welcome to Star River Adventures, your gateway to
   a premier rafting experience. For more than
   twenty years, Star River Adventures has provided
   our customers with safe and exciting adventures
   in West Virginia's awe-inspiring wilderness. Our
   trips allow you to raft gently down one of our
   rippling streams or to conquer our explosive
   rapids. You choose your event, and we will make
   it come true. All trips are supervised by expert
   guides. Our staff will help you plan an entire
   adventure for an individual, a family, or a
   group.

   Star River Adventures is located in Sutton, West
   Virginia. We plan and conduct events throughout
   the state. You choose an adventure on one of our
   many rivers and streams, including the Big Sandy
   Creek, Bluestone River, Cheat River, Gauley
   River, Lower Meadow, Meadow River, New River,
   Potomac River, Tygart River, or Shenandoah River.
   We take care of everything else.
   ```

5. Follow the *Welcome* section with the *About Our Company* and *Safety* sections. The text for these two sections is in the data file **Brochure page 2.** Copy and paste the text into the brochure file. Apply Title 2 style to the headings and Paragraph style to the paragraph text.

6. Insert AutoShape stars at the bottom of the cell. Format the stars to be shaded from white in the center to blue at the edge. Format the stars for blue line color.

7. Space the images in Column 1 so one is located beside each article. See Figure 5-4 on page 96 for an example of how page 2 should look.

8. On page 3, create a table with one row and two columns. Use the same row height as that used for page 2 (9.5″). On this page, place the larger column on the left. Set the first column width to 5″ and the second column width to 2.5″.

9. In Column 1, enter the main heading for the page *Special Packages* and apply the Title 1 style. Enter text for a side heading *Skiing and Rafting—The Perfect Combination.* Apply Title 2 style to the heading.

10. Open the file **5-4 February Newsletter** that you created earlier. Copy the text for the article from the February newsletter to the brochure. Apply the Paragraph style.

record selector: a small box or bar to the left of a record that can be clicked to select the entire record in Datasheet view

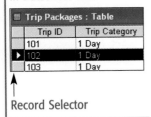

Record Selector

11. Open the *Access* file **Trip Packages** from your data files. Select and copy the record for Trip 800 from the Trip Packages table. Paste this data into your brochure after the last paragraph in the article.

12. This package is not available on weekends. Delete the cells referring to the weekend rate. (Be careful not to delete the first row of the table.) Delete the word *Trip* from the column headings. Change the shading in the first two rows to pale blue. Change the word *packages* from plural to singular. Resize the columns as needed so the table fits within Column 1. Apply All Borders border style to the table.

13. Below the table, enter a second side heading for this page: *Give Your Mother High Adventure.* Apply the Title 2 style. Copy the appropriate text from the February newsletter into the brochure. Apply the Paragraph style. Select and copy the record for Trip 801 from the **Trip Packages** database. Paste this data into your brochure after the last paragraph in the article.

14. Adjust the trip package table so the format is consistent with the other trip package table on the page.

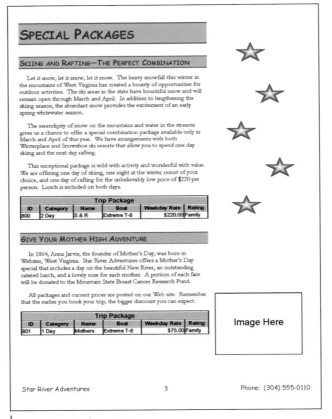

Figure 5-5 Brochure Page 3

15. Add AutoShape stars to Column 2 beside the first article. Format the stars as you did for page 2. Insert an image in Column 2 beside the Mother's Day article. Search the Internet and find appropriate photos or clip art. You may also use the image **Oaraft02** from your data files. Resize the image to 2.25″ wide.

16. See Figure 5-5 on page 98 for an example of how page 3 should look. Save the file using the same name. Print the brochure.

Challenge: Prepare Brochure Page 4

1. Open the file **5-5 Brochure** that you created earlier. At the end of the document, insert a section break *Next page* to create page 4. Create a table on page 4 with the same layout and format as the one on page 2.

2. In Column 2 (right column) on page 4, insert a graphic. Search the Internet or use clip art to find an image related to rafting, West Virginia, or mountain scenery. Adjust the height of the image to about 2″ and center it horizontally within the column. Readjust the size later, if needed, to fit the image and the following article on the page.

3. Below the image, enter the main heading *Raft in the Newest Duckies on the Oldest River in the World*. Apply the Title 1 style. Insert the appropriate text from the data file **April Articles.**

4. In Column 1, enter the main heading *Distances*. Apply the Title 1 style. Insert the paragraph and list of cities from the data file **Distances.** Apply the Paragraph style to the text. For the list of cities, change the paragraph spacing for *After* to 0 point.

5. Work with two or three classmates to find the driving distance in miles from Sutton to the cities listed. Use the Internet or other resources to find mileage numbers.

6. Enter the mileage numbers into the brochure. Use a right tab to align the numbers at the right edge of the column.

7. Near the bottom of Column 2, insert an appropriate image, such as a map of West Virginia.

8. Save the document as **5-5 Challenge Brochure.** Print the last page of the brochure.

Creating Training Presentations

Objectives

- ☐ Edit and format presentations
- ☐ Insert and modify graphics on slides
- ☐ Print slides, speaker's notes, handouts, and comments pages
- ☐ Create a presentation using a Wizard
- ☐ Modify title, slide, and notes masters
- ☐ Create and apply a design template
- ☐ Apply transitions and animation effects to slides
- ☐ Apply timing to a presentation
- ☐ Create hyperlinks and save presentations as Web pages
- ☐ Deliver presentations

Summary of *Microsoft Office* Skills

- ✔ Create presentations (manually and using automated tools)
- ✔ Add slides to and delete slides from presentations
- ✔ Modify headers and footers in the slide master
- ✔ Insert, format, and modify text
- ✔ Add tables, charts, clip art, and bitmap images to slides
- ✔ Customize slide backgrounds
- ✔ Add OfficeArt elements to slides
- ✔ Apply formats to presentations
- ✔ Apply animation schemes
- ✔ Apply slide transitions
- ✔ Customize slide formats
- ✔ Manage a slide master
- ✔ Rehearse timing
- ✔ Rearrange slides
- ✔ Modify slide layout

- ✔ Add links to a presentation
- ✔ Preview and print slides, outlines, handouts, and speaker's notes
- ✔ Deliver presentations
- ✔ Manage files and folders for presentations
- ✔ Publish presentations to the Web
- ✔ Review presentation comments

STAR River Adventures

Job 6-1 Update Existing Presentation

Skills Applied

- Creating folders for storing presentations
- Adding bitmap images to slides
- Changing the layout of individual slides
- Adding text to slides
- Adding slides to presentations
- Adding hyperlinks to slides
- Printing speaker's notes

The company provides training for all new employees. Several *PowerPoint* presentations will be needed for the training sessions. You will create new presentations and make changes to existing presentations.

Task 1 Create and Change Slides

Joseph Coward and you are charged with making a presentation to the office staff about how to create some of the documents produced at Star River Adventures. This presentation will be an introduction for new office staff and a refresher for others. Joseph has completed much of the work on the presentation. You will make additions and changes to his work.

1. Create a folder named **P6 Presentations.** Save your work for this project in this folder.

2. Open the *PowerPoint* presentation **Office Documents** found in your data files. Save the file as **6-1 Office Documents** in your P6 Presentations folder.

3. Carefully review the presentation, including the speaker's notes. Joseph set the vertical and horizontal guides so all graphics and illustrations can be placed consistently. Display the drawing guides onscreen so you can see the guides.

4. The second slide has too much information. Make a copy of Slide 2 by using the Insert Duplicate Slide command. Delete bulleted items on the slides so the first four items remain on Slide 2 and the last four items are on Slide 3.

5. In the notes pane on Slide 1, Joseph added the first definition/explanation and the spacing information for the first item (block format). Add explanations and spacing information for the next three bulleted items on the slide. (Use the Reference Guide on page 313 or a similar source for the definitions and spacing.)

6. Change the layout for Slide 3 to Title, Content and Text layout. Flip the clip art so it faces the center. Size the graphic so it fits within the guides.

7. Add the letter part *Sender's Name* in the appropriate bullet location on Slide 3.

8. Locate the file **Request** in your data files. Copy this file to your P6 Presentations folder.

9. On Slide 1, create a hyperlink for the letter graphic. Link the graphic to the file **Request** in your P6 Presentations folder. During the presentation, the letter can be accessed to demonstrate the centering process.

Success Tips

In the **Office Documents** file, the asterisks in the speaker's notes are to remind the presenter to demonstrate a *Word* function to the audience.

Help Keywords

Guides
   Show or hide guides

Help Keywords

Hyperlink
   Create a hyperlink
   Create a hyperlink to a file or Web page

10. In the notes pane on Slides 3 and 4, add explanations and spacing information for the terms on the slides. Save the file again using the same name.

Task 2 Create an Illustration

Slide 4 will be used to demonstrate how to create memos. You will prepare an illustration of a memo and add it to the content area of the slide.

1. In *Word*, open the file **Reading List Memo** from your data files. Save the file using the same name in your P6 Presentations folder.

2. Print preview the memo. Adjust the view/zoom so the entire memo is visible on the screen. Press the Print Screen key on the keyboard. This will place a copy of the screen on the clipboard. Close *Word*.

3. Open the file **6-1 Office Documents** that you created earlier. On Slide 4, change the layout to Title, Text and Content layout.

4. Paste the graphic of the memo into the content area. Crop the graphic so only the memo remains. Adjust the graphic size to fit in the content area at the right of the slide. Select the graphic and set the fill to No Fill. Set the line color to Automatic. This will create a border around the graphic.

5. Link the memo graphic to the file **Reading List Memo** in your P6 Presentations folder. The slide should look similar to Slide 1.

6. Save the presentation using the same name. View (play) the slide show and test the hyperlinks. Make adjustments if the links do not work correctly.

7. Print notes pages in pure black and white.

Help Keywords

Crop
    Crop a picture

Success Tips

When you access a *Word* document from a link in a presentation, click the *Back* button on the Web toolbar to return to the slide show. If the Web toolbar is not displayed, choose *View, Toolbars, Web*.

Job 6-2 Prepare to Present Slide Show

Skills Applied

- Running slide shows
- Customizing slides
- Copying and altering clip art on slides
- Adding slides to a presentation
- Adding, editing, and formatting text
- Changing the layout of individual slides
- Printing speaker's notes
- Creating OfficeArt elements and adding them to slides
- Rehearsing presentations
- Changing the order of slides in a presentation

Task 1 Practice Presenting

You will help with the presentation to the staff. Practice presenting **6-1 Office Documents.** While in the slideshow view, experiment with using the pen to mark on the slides.

1. Open the file **6-1 Office Documents** that you saved earlier. View the show. Set the pointer options to Pen. On Slide 1, circle the first bullet in black and draw a vertical line along the left margin of the letter to emphasize that it is straight.

2. Change the pen color to red and circle the second bullet. Indicate with red circles that there is no punctuation at the end of the salutation and complimentary close.

3. Change the pen color to green. Circle the third bullet and indicate the side margins on the letter.

4. Use the Print Screen key to capture a copy of Slide 1 showing the marks made by the pen. Paste this screen capture into a *Word* document. Save the document as **6-2 Slide Capture.** Print the *Word* document.

Task 2 Enhance a Presentation

A presentation can be more attractive and interesting with a colorful background. Changing the color of clip art can also add variety to the presentation. In this task, you will work with color changes and add a final slide to summarize the presentation. You will also add a title slide at the beginning of the presentation.

1. Open the file **6-1 Office Documents** that you saved earlier. Format the background so it shades from medium blue at the top of the slides to light blue at the bottom. Apply the background to all of the slides.

2. On Slide 2, change the color of the woman's hair from brown to blond.

3. Select all of the slides in the presentation and generate a summary slide. Move the summary slide to the end of the presentation. Change the title of the slide to *Questions?*. Delete the bullet item *Business Letter Parts*.

4. Add a new slide to the beginning of the presentation using the Title Slide layout. Add an appropriate title and graphic to the slide. Add *Presented by* and your name as the subtitle. Resize the graphic as needed.

Success Tips

Hold down the Shift key while drawing on a slide with the pen to create a straight line.

Help Keywords

Recolor clip art
  Recolor a picture from the Clip Organizer

Help Keywords

Summary Slide
  Create a slide containing titles of other slides

Software Review

To record timings while you rehearse:

- Select *Rehearse Timings* on the Slide Show menu.
- Click the *Advance* button to move to each slide.
- Allow time for discussion before moving to another slide.
- Click *Yes* to accept the timings after the last slide.

Help Keywords

Timing
   Set timings for a slide show

5. Add a new slide at the end of the presentation using the Title Only layout. Enter the title *Make Your Documents Stars*.

6. Copy the clip art from Slide 3 to the new slide. Select the clip art and ungroup the image. Delete the computer from the clip art.

7. Create an AutoShape star with yellow or gold fill color. Send the star image backward. Place the star so it appears to be in the woman's hands.

8. Group the images and adjust the size and placement on the slide, if necessary. The woman should be facing right, as shown in Figure 6-1.

9. Save the presentation as **6-2 Office Documents.** Print notes pages to use as you rehearse presenting the slides.

10. Start the slide show in rehearsal mode. While rehearse timing is activated, practice giving the entire presentation, including using the pen. Allow time for following the links to other files. Accept the timings for the show.

Figure 6-1 Slide with Clip Art

11. Save the presentation as **6-2 Office Documents Timed.** Use the Screen Print button to capture the slide sorter view, which shows the time set for each slide. Paste the image into a new *Word* document. Save the document as **6-2 Sorter Capture** and print.

12. Practice presenting both **6-2 Office Documents** and **6-2 Office Documents Timed**. Decide which one you prefer presenting.

Task 3 Create Handouts

Software Review

To send slides to a *Word* document:

- Select *Send To* from the File menu.
- Select *Microsoft Word*.
- Select a page layout option.
- Select a paste option.
- Click *OK*.

Help Keywords

Callout
   Add a callout (shape)

Staff members who participate in the office training will want to take notes during the presentation. Having copies of the slides, the letter, and the memo to use for taking notes would be helpful.

1. Send the file **6-2 Office Documents** to *Microsoft Word*. Choose *Blank lines next to slides*. The *Word* document will be used for handout pages.

2. At the end of the *Word* file on a new page, insert the letter file **Request.** Then insert the memo file **Reading List Memo** on a new page. Create a document footer to contain *Office Documents Presentation* at the left, the page number in the center, and your name at the right.

3. On the letter and memo, add callouts from AutoShapes for each document part. An example is shown in Figure 6-2. Key the name of the document part in each callout shape. Change the line color and text color of the callouts to red. Center the text in the callouts.

4. Save the document as **6-2 Handouts** and print it.

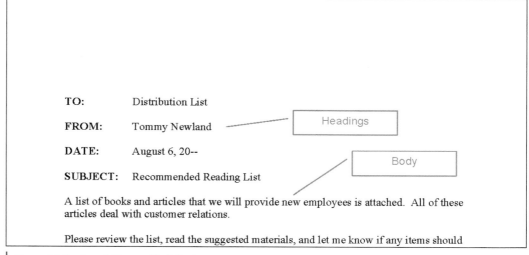

TO: Distribution List

FROM: Tommy Newland   Headings

DATE: August 6, 20--

SUBJECT: Recommended Reading List   Body

A list of books and articles that we will provide new employees is attached. All of these articles deal with customer relations.

Please review the list, read the suggested materials, and let me know if any items should

Figure 6-2 Portion of Memo with Callouts

Job 6-3 Create Design Template

Skills Applied

- Adding bitmap graphics to slides or backgrounds
- Creating and managing slide masters
- Creating and customizing design templates

Rather than using one of the standard templates provided in *PowerPoint*, you will create an original design to use for some of the office training presentations.

1. Open a blank *PowerPoint* presentation. In the slide master view, add a title master. (Right-click on the slide in the Outline panel; select *New Title Master*).

2. On the title master, insert an image. Use clip art or photos of interesting scenery, such as mountains or rivers. You may wish to search the Web for images. You can also use the picture file **New River** found in your data files as shown in Figure 6-3.

3. Adjust the picture by moving, cropping, and resizing so the desired portion of the image fills the slide. Send the image to the back.

4. Your image may have dark colors that will interfere with reading title text placed over the image. If that is the case, select the text box for the title and apply a light fill color to the box. An example is shown in Figure 6-3. Repeat for the subtitle text box. You may wish to resize the text boxes so they do not cover too much of the image.

Figure 6-3 Title Master

5. Save the file as a design template named **6-3 Template** in your P6 Presentations folder.

6. Switch to the slide master. Format the background using custom colors. Choose a color that coordinates with the image you used for the title slide. Apply the background to all slides.

7. Reduce the size of the Title Area for AutoLayouts to 1.25″ by 7″. Reduce the size of the Object Area for AutoLayouts to 4.95″ × 7″.

8. Delete the text box for the Number Area in the lower right corner of the master slide. Move the text box for the Footer Area to the right so it aligns with the right edge of the Object Area for Auto Layouts. Move the text box for the Date Area so it aligns at the left with the Object Area for Auto Layouts as shown in Figure 6-4.

9. Insert the image file that you used on the title master. Crop or resize the image to 7.5″ tall by 2.25″ wide. Move the picture to the left edge of the slide master.

10. Save the design template again using the same name, **6-3 Template.** You will apply this design template in a later job.

Figure 6-4 Slide Master

Thinking Critically

1. What is the advantage of making formatting or other changes to a slide master rather than to each slide in a show?

2. If you wish to display text over a dark image on a slide, what alternative can you use to applying a light fill to the text box?

Job 6-4 Edit and Format Presentation

Skills Applied

- Creating presentations using design templates
- Editing and formatting text on slides
- Adding slides to a presentation
- Changing the order of slides in presentations
- Creating footers for slides
- Printing comments pages, handouts, and speaker's notes
- Reviewing and deleting comments in a presentation

Tommy Newland has worked on a presentation of the Employee Manual. He wants you to "clean up" the presentation before he continues his work. You will use several *PowerPoint* functions to help you manage the presentation.

Task 1 Check Style and Spelling

1. Open the presentation **Manual** found in your data files. Save the file as **6-4 Manual** in your P6 Presentations folder. Read the presentation carefully to become familiar with the content.

2. Apply the design template **6-3 Template** that you created earlier to the presentation. You may need to select the Browse option at the bottom of the Slide Design pane and navigate to your P6 Presentations folder to find the template.

3. On Slide 1 in the subtitle text box, insert the current date. Use the *Month day, year* format and set the date to update automatically. Adjust the size of the text box to make it smaller and to show more of the background image, if desired.

4. Activate *PowerPoint's* Check Style function. Set the Slide title style to *Title Case,* the body text style to *Sentence case,* and the End punctuation/body punctuation to *Paragraphs do not have punctuation.* Make the appropriate changes indicated by the style checker so there is consistency in the presentation.

Help Keywords

Style
　Turn style checks on
　or off
　Change options for
　style checks

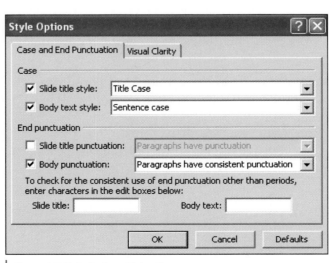

Figure 6-5 Style Options Dialog Box

5. Check for spelling errors and make corrections.

6. Manually check the font sizes and make corrections as needed. All titles on the slides should be Arial 44 normal. (This does not include the title slide.) All text for first-level bullet items on the slides should be Arial 32 normal. The second-level bullets should be Arial 28.

7. Throughout the presentation, replace *SRA* with *Star River Adventures*. Turn off the check style option because *PowerPoint* will interpret Star River Adventures as being incorrect. It does not follow the guideline to use sentence case.

8. Save the presentation again as **6-4 Manual.**

Task 2 Edit and Add Slides

Some of the text and slides are in the wrong order. You will move them so they are in the same order as the information in the Employee Manual. You will also add slides with new information.

1. Open the file **6-4 Manual** that you edited earlier. Move the Revisions slide so it follows the Purpose slide. Move the Quality Policy slide so it follows the Revisions slide.

2. Find the comment that Robert Jackson left in the presentation. Print the slide using the current slide selection and the *Include comment page* choice. Complete the work that Robert requested and delete the comment. (See the file **4-5 Manual** that you created in Project 4.)

3. Insert a new slide that uses the Title and Content layout. Enter the title *Organization Chart*. Use the Insert Object function to insert the organization chart from the file **2-1 Org Chart** that you created in Project 2.

4. Double-click the chart object to select it for editing. Delete the words *Organization Chart* in the text box below the chart. After deleting the text, resize the text box to make it smaller. Click outside the chart object to deselect it.

5. Click the chart image once to select the image. Use the Crop tool to remove blank space around the edge of the image. Increase the size of the chart image, but do not allow it to extend into the picture area at the left of the slide.

6. Add a footer to appear on all slides except the title slide. In the footer, include the current date in *Month day, year* format to update automatically. Also include the company name in the footer.

Task 3 Edit Notes Master and Print

Mr. Newland has asked you to make adjustments to the notes pages. He prefers that the area for notes be larger and that the text of the notes be in a larger size font so they are easy to read.

1. Open the file **6-4 Manual** that you edited earlier. View the notes master. Adjust the notes master so the size of the slide representation is approximately 2″ in height.

2. Increase the size of the Notes Body Area to about 6″. If necessary, move the Notes Body Area up so it does not overlap the Footer Area and Number Area. Align the left edges of the slide representation and the Notes Body Area.

Help Keywords

Comments
  Print reviewer
  comments

Software Review

To insert an object created from a file:

• Select *Object* from the Insert menu.

• Select *Create* from file.

• Browse to locate the file.

• Enter the filename.

• Click *OK*.

Help Keywords

Master
  Format, position, and
  resize placeholders

3. Set the Notes Body Area to a font size of 16 point. Save the presentation again as **6-4 Manual.** Print notes pages for Slides 7, 9, and 11. Print handouts for all slides with six slides per page. Print using grayscale or pure black and white.

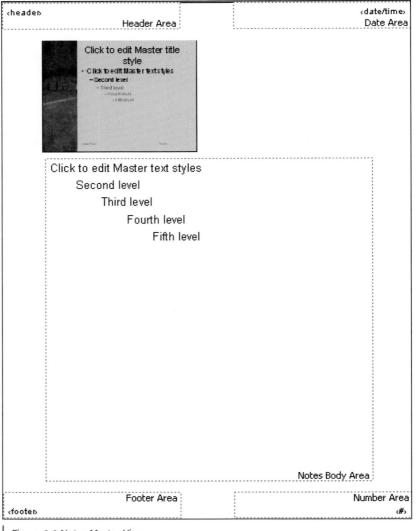

Figure 6-6 Notes Master View

TEAMWORK

Challenge: Create Team Presentation

1. Work with a classmate to create a presentation about formatting documents. Include topics such as second-page headers for letters and memos, envelopes, email, agendas, itineraries, cover pages, bibliographies, or reports. Save the presentation as **6-4 Formatting.**

2. Add notes, as well as appropriate illustrations and links. Print handouts for the presentation.

3. Present the slides to your class as though you were teaching staff members how to format these documents.

Job 6-5 Create Presentation Using a Wizard

Skills Applied

- Creating presentations using the AutoContent Wizard
- Adding text to slides
- Customizing slides
- Applying custom animation to slides
- Changing the layout of individual slides
- Saving presentations as HTML pages
- Applying transition effects to slides
- Printing slides

Task 1 Create Training Presentation

1. Create a new presentation using the AutoContent Wizard. Choose *Training* for the type of presentation. The output will be an onscreen presentation. The presentation title is *Athlete's Foot,* and the footer is *Star River Adventures.*

2. Save the presentation as **6-5 Athlete's Foot** in your P6 Presentations folder. On Slide 1, change or add text in the subtitle box to display *Odessa Carr.* Omit the footer from this slide only.

3. Open and print the *Word* data file **Training.** This file contains handwritten text to use for the slides. Replace the text in the presentation with this text.

4. To keep the bulleted text from overlapping the puzzle pieces on the Slide 4 (Overview), apply the Title, Text and Content layout.

5. On Slide 4, add words that represent problems associated with athlete's foot to replace *Text* on the puzzle pieces. Change the size of the font so the words do not wrap. Select all of the puzzle pieces and group them together. Move the grouped image on the slide so it is opposite the bulleted text.

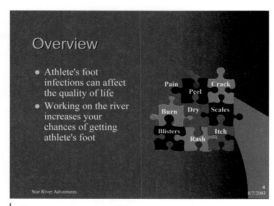

Figure 6-7 Overview Slide

6. View the title master. Select the pale blue graphic. Apply the Spin custom animation from the Emphasis group to this graphic. Set the animation to start With Previous. Set the amount to Two Spins.

7. Change the slide design color scheme. Choose the second choice on the top row (pale background with blue graphic).

8. Save the presentation again as **6-5 Athlete's Foot.** Print the presentation as a handout with nine slides per page in pure black and white.

Task 2 Save Presentation as Web Page

Odessa Carr wants to make the athlete's foot presentation available on the company Web site. You will convert the presentation file to a Web page.

1. Open the file **6-5 Athlete's Foot** that you created earlier.

2. On Slide 1, remove the name *Odessa Carr*. Remove the custom animation effect for both text boxes on this slide.

3. On the title master, remove the custom animation effect for the blue graphic (that you added earlier).

4. Change the transition effect for all slides to Box In.

5. Save the presentation as a Web page named **6-5 Athlete's Foot Online.** Use *Athlete's Foot* as the page title. View the presentation in a browser. Check that all links work and play the show. Make corrections if needed.

6. Print the first slide of the presentation from *PowerPoint*.

Challenge: Create Hyperlinks to Web Sites

1. Access the Internet and find two Web sites that provide information about athlete's foot. Note the Web site name and the URL for each site. Note the name of the article about athlete's foot.

2. Open the **6-5 Athlete's Foot Online** file in *PowerPoint*. On the last slide under *Internet articles*, add the name of each Web site followed by the article name found on that site. Example: *American Podiatric Medical Association, Athlete's Foot: Information From The APMA*

3. Create a link to the Web page for each article. Save the file as a Web page using the name **6-5 Challenge.** Test the page in your browser.

Part 2

In Part 2, you will complete projects for the Finance and Accounting Department of Star River Adventures. The jobs will involve extensive use of spreadsheet applications. They will also require integration with various other software applications such as word processing, presentations, and databases. The jobs in this part are related to payroll, budgets, travel expenses, data analysis, what-if scenarios, financial documents, Internet activities, and research.

Finance and Accounting

Project 7

Managing Payroll Records

Objectives

- ☐ Understand basic payroll terminology
- ☐ Create payroll worksheets
- ☐ Use formulas and functions in a worksheet
- ☐ Add columns and rows to a worksheet
- ☐ Sort data in a worksheet
- ☐ Name and manage multiple sheets in a workbook
- ☐ Lock cells and protect sheets in a workbook
- ☐ Link data in a workbook
- ☐ Paste a worksheet into a memo

Summary of *Microsoft Office* Skills

- ✔ Insert, delete, and move cells
- ✔ Enter and edit cell data including text, numbers, and formulas
- ✔ Check spelling
- ✔ Find and replace cell and data formats
- ✔ Manage workbook files and folders
- ✔ Save workbooks using different names and file formats
- ✔ Apply and modify cell formats
- ✔ Modify row and column settings
- ✔ Modify row and column formats
- ✔ Use automated tools to format worksheets
- ✔ Modify Page Setup options for worksheets
- ✔ Preview and print worksheets and workbooks
- ✔ Insert and delete worksheets
- ✔ Modify worksheet names and positions
- ✔ Use 3-D references
- ✔ Create and revise formulas

- ✔ Use statistical, date and time, financial, and logical functions in formulas
- ✔ Work with ranges
- ✔ Modify passwords, protections, and properties
- ✔ Import data to *Excel*
- ✔ Export data from *Excel*

STAR
River
Adventures

Job 7-1 Create Payroll Worksheet for Salaried Employees

Skills Applied

- Locating and opening existing workbooks
- Creating folders for saving workbooks
- Inserting worksheets into a workbook
- Formatting worksheet tabs
- Entering and editing text and numbers in cells
- Formatting cells
- Modifying alignment
- Applying cell formats
- Creating and editing formulas using the Formula Bar
- Using VLOOKUP
- Creating formulas using functions
- Entering a range within a formula by dragging
- Using references (absolute and relative)
- Using Save As to store workbooks to different locations/unique filenames
- Freezing and unfreezing rows and columns
- Adding cell protection and protecting individual worksheets
- Modifying worksheet orientation
- Setting a print area and printing a print area

Understanding Payroll

Success Tips

If you have not already done so, create folders in which to save the workbook files for this part. See Job 1-1 on page 11 for more details.

Eric Collins is the manager of the Finance and Accounting Department, and Heather Taylor is the payroll manager in this department. Employees' salaries or wages are identified in the contract they sign when employed by Star River Adventures. Star River Adventures' fiscal year is the same as the calendar year. New contracts are effective January 1 of each new year.

The owner, managers, administrative assistants, and the lead guide are full-time employees of Star River Adventures and are paid a yearly salary. They are paid monthly on the last working day of the month. All other employees are paid an hourly rate. This rate varies based on their experience and the number of years they have worked for the company.

All guides are given one-year contracts and must apply for employment each year. Guides for the season are usually hired during the months of January to March each year, but they usually begin work on April 1. They must complete training during January or February and pass a required examination to be considered for employment. Guides must be licensed prior to completing additional required Star River Adventures training. Guides are paid biweekly on Friday of the week following the last working day of the payroll period.

Employee's Withholding Allowance Certification

Each employee is required to complete an Employee's Withholding Allowance Certification, Form W-4. Each allowance is equal to $3,000 (in 2003). The information the employee provides on this form determines the amount of federal income tax withheld from the employee's paycheck. Generally, four factors determine the amount of tax withheld:

- Marital status
- Number of withholding allowances claimed
- Any additional amount the employee wants withheld
- Any exemptions from withholding the employee claims

Cut here and give Form W-4 to your employer. Keep the top part for your records.

Form **W-4** — Department of the Treasury, Internal Revenue Service

Employee's Withholding Allowance Certificate

▶ For Privacy Act and Paperwork Reduction Act Notice, see page 2.

OMB No. 1545-0010 — **2003**

1 Type or print your first name and middle initial | Last name | 2 Your social security number

Home address (number and street or rural route) | 3 ☐ Single ☐ Married ☐ Married, but withhold at higher Single rate.
Note: *If married, but legally separated, or spouse is a nonresident alien, check the "Single" box.*

City or town, state, and ZIP code | 4 **If your last name differs from that shown on your social security card, check here. You must call 1-800-772-1213 for a new card.** ▶ ☐

5 Total number of allowances you are claiming (from line **H** above **or** from the applicable worksheet on page 2) 5

6 Additional amount, if any, you want withheld from each paycheck . . . . . . 6 $

7 I claim exemption from withholding for 2003, and I certify that I meet **both** of the following conditions for exemption:
- Last year I had a right to a refund of **all** Federal income tax withheld because I had **no** tax liability **and**
- This year I expect a refund of **all** Federal income tax withheld because I expect to have **no** tax liability.

If you meet both conditions, write "Exempt" here . . . . . . ▶ 7

Under penalties of perjury, I certify that I am entitled to the number of withholding allowances claimed on this certificate, or I am entitled to claim exempt status.
Employee's signature
(Form is not valid unless you sign it.) ▶ **Date** ▶

8 Employer's name and address (Employer: Complete lines 8 and 10 only if sending to the IRS.) | 9 Office code (optional) | 10 Employer identification number

Cat. No. 10220Q

Source: Form W-4 (2003) U.S. Department of the Treasury, Internal Revenue Service

Figure 7-1 Form W-4 Employee's Withholding Allowance Certificate

Tax Rates

The progressive tax rates used to calculate the amount of income taxes employees pay are determined by the legislature and occasionally change based on the economy and the needs of government. The following table shows an example of the percentage of income that must be paid as income tax.

Income $	Rate
0–27,050	10%
27,051–65,550	27.50%
65,551–136,750	30.50%
136,751–297,350	35.50%
297,351–Up	39.10%

The actual rate will vary based on marital status and the number of allowances an employee claims on Form W-4. The Internal Revenue Service (IRS) provides tables so businesses and individuals can look up the taxes on income earned based on marital status and allowances. A portion of a table showing taxes due from married employees who are paid monthly is shown in Figure 7-2 on page 117. According to this table, a married employee with two withholding allowances who earned between $1,240 and $1,280 must pay $21 in federal withholding tax.

MARRIED Persons—MONTHLY Payroll Period

(For Wages Paid in 2003)

If the wages are—		And the number of withholding allowances claimed is—							
At least	But less than	0	1	2	3	4	5	6	7
		The amount of income tax to be withheld is—							
$0	$540	$0	$0	$0	$0	$0	$0	$0	$0
540	560	1	0	0	0	0	0	0	0
560	580	3	0	0	0	0	0	0	0
580	600	5	0	0	0	0	0	0	0
600	640	8	0	0	0	0	0	0	0
640	680	12	0	0	0	0	0	0	0
680	720	16	0	0	0	0	0	0	0
720	760	20	0	0	0	0	0	0	0
760	800	24	0	0	0	0	0	0	0
800	840	28	3	0	0	0	0	0	0
840	880	32	7	0	0	0	0	0	0
880	920	36	11	0	0	0	0	0	0
920	960	40	15	0	0	0	0	0	0
960	1,000	44	19	0	0	0	0	0	0
1,000	1,040	48	23	0	0	0	0	0	0
1,040	1,080	52	27	1	0	0	0	0	0
1,080	1,120	56	31	5	0	0	0	0	0
1,120	1,160	60	35	9	0	0	0	0	0
1,160	1,200	64	39	13	0	0	0	0	0
1,200	1,240	68	43	17	0	0	0	0	0
1,240	1,280	72	47	21	0	0	0	0	0
1,280	1,320	76	51	25	0	0	0	0	0
1,320	1,360	80	55	29	4	0	0	0	0
1,360	1,400	84	59	33	8	0	0	0	0
1,400	1,440	88	63	37	12	0	0	0	0
1,440	1,480	92	67	41	16	0	0	0	0

Source: Publication 15, Circular E, Employer's Tax Guide, U.S. Department of the Treasury, Internal Revenue Service

Figure 7-2 Sample Tax Table

Other Taxes and Deductions

gross income: income before deductions

In addition to income tax, employers are also required to deduct payroll taxes from each employee's gross income. The two basic payroll taxes are Social Security, also called FICA (Federal Insurance Contribution Act) tax, and Medicare tax.

Social Security tax: provides retirement benefits to employees and their dependents

The current Social Security tax (in 2003) is 6.20 percent of gross income earned up to an income of $87,000. Gross income over that amount is not taxed for Social Security. Currently all employees at Star River Adventures earn less than $87,000 per year. The current Medicare tax rate is 1.45 percent. There is no limit on the amount of wages subject to Medicare tax.

Medicare tax: provides medical benefits to individuals when they reach the age of 65

In addition to income taxes and payroll taxes, employees can request that their employer take additional deductions for retirement accounts or other benefits available, such as dental or eye care insurance. At this time, no employee of the company has requested additional deductions.

Most states require employers to deduct state income taxes. The state tax rate for West Virginia is currently (in 2003) 6.5 percent of gross earnings. The yearly salaries for the current fiscal year for the full-time employees of Star River Adventures are shown in Figure 7-3 on page 118.

SALARIED EMPLOYEES				
Employee	**Marital Status**	**Allowances**	**Position**	**Salary**
Abraham, William	Married	2	Manager, Logistics	$48,500
Carr, Odessa	Single	1	Lead Guide	$31,000
Collins, Eric	Married	3	Manager, Finance and Accounting Dept.	$43,000
Coward, Joseph	Single	0	Administrative Assistant	$24,800
Forde, Joyce	Married	0	Administrative Assistant	$23,400
Inez, Maria	Married	1	Manager, Operations Dept.	$45,300
Jackson, Robert	Single	1	Manager, Marketing and Sales Dept.	$49,300
Jenkins, Brenda	Single	0	Manager, Event Booking	$42,800
Newland, Tommy	Married	4	Owner	$65,000
Taylor, Heather	Married	0	Manager, Payroll	$41,900

Figure 7-3 Salaried Employees

Creating a Payroll Worksheet

The company has decided to automate its payroll. You have been asked by Heather Taylor, Payroll Manager, to design a worksheet for calculating the monthly payroll for salaried employees. Ms. Taylor suggests a layout similar to the worksheet shown in Figure 7-4 on page 119.

1. Open the *Excel* data file **Monthly Payroll.** Insert a new worksheet. Name the sheet *April.*

2. Enter the worksheet titles in Rows 1–3 as shown in Figure 7-4. Use bold for the titles. Use a larger font for the company name. Use the current year in the date. Center the titles over the worksheet.

3. Enter the column headings as shown in Figure 7-4. Bold and center the column headings. Apply pattern to Rows 6 and 17 as shown.

4. Refer to Figure 7-3 above. Enter the names, salary, marital status, and number of withholding allowances for each employee.

STAR RIVER ADVENTURES
Payroll for Salaried Employees
Payroll Period: April 1–30, 20--

Personnel	Marital Status	Annual Salary	Allowance from W4	Monthly Salary	Income Tax	Social Security (FICA)	Medicare	State Tax	Other	Net Pay
Abraham, William	Married	48,500	2	4,041.67	402.00	250.58	58.60	262.71		3,067.77
Carr, Odessa	Single	31,000	1	2,583.33	291.00	160.17	37.46	167.92		1,926.79
Collins, Eric										
Coward, Joseph										
Forde, Joyce										
Inez, Maria										
Jackson, Robert										
Jenkins, Brenda										
Newland, Tommy										
Taylor, Heather										
Totals				6,625.00	693.00	410.75	96.06	430.63		4,994.56

Figure 7-4 Salaried Payroll Worksheet

5. Create the appropriate formulas for the first employee and copy them to other cells as needed. Enter formulas to calculate the following:

   - Monthly Salary = Annual Salary / 12
   - Social Security Tax = Monthly Salary * 6.2%
   - Medicare Tax = Monthly Salary * 1.45%
   - State Tax = Monthly Salary * 6.5%

6. For Income Tax amounts, look up the tax amount (based on the monthly salary, marital status, and number of allowances) using the tables provided in the workbook.

   Example: William Abraham is married, claims two allowances, and earns $4,041.67 per month. To determine his tax amount, go to the Married Monthly Payroll Tax sheet. In the Wages column, locate an amount that is closest to but not more than 4,041.67. That amount is 4040. Read across to the Allowances, 2 column. The tax amount is 402. Enter 402 for the tax amount on the April sheet for this employee.

   Alternative method: As an alternative to manually looking up the tax amounts, you can use the VLOOKUP function to determine the income tax. If you want to use this method, see the Challenge option at the end of this job for more instructions. Then continue with the rest of this job.

7. Enter a formula to find Net Income:

   Net Income = Monthly Salary − All Deductions

8. Enter the label **Totals** in A18. Total Columns E through I and K. Format all cells that contain dollar amounts as currency, but with no dollar sign. Use no decimal places in Column C. Use two decimal places in Columns E through I.

9. Check spelling in the worksheet. Freeze the panes so all row headings and employee names remain displayed on the screen.

10. You want to protect the worksheet data and formulas for use in future months. However, an employee's marital status or the number of allowances claimed may change during the year. Unlock the cells for Marital Status (B7:B16) and for Allowance from W4 (D7:D16). Protect the worksheet.

11. Save the workbook as **7-1 Payroll.** Print the April worksheet using landscape orientation. Your completed worksheet should look similar to Figure 7-4, showing data for all of the employees. The total for Net Pay should be 25,679.26.

Help Keywords

Freeze pane
  View two parts of a worksheet . . .
Unlock Cells
  About worksheet and workbook protection

Challenge: Use VLOOKUP Formula

Follow these steps to use the VLOOKUP function to determine the Income Tax amounts for the April payroll worksheet.

1. In Cell F7, enter a formula that will find the proper tax amount and place it in the cell. Use an absolute cell reference for the data range on the tax table. A sample formula is shown below.

   =VLOOKUP(E7,'Married Monthly Payroll Tax'!$A$3:$G$137,4)

Software Review

In a VLOOKUP formula, the column to look in is referenced by a number. Column A is 1, Column B is 2, and so on.

Help Keywords

VLOOKUP worksheet
function
References
  About cell and range
  references

2. Copy the formula to Cell F8. Change the name of the tax table sheet if the employee is single. Change the last number in the formula to reference the column that has the proper number of allowances. Repeat this process for all employees.

Challenge: Learn about Income and Payroll Taxes Online

1. Access the Internal Revenue Service, Department of Treasury Web site at http://www.irs.gov. On that site, you have access to tax-related forms, instructions, and a variety of activities that will enable you to learn more about the U.S. tax system.

2. Search the IRS site for *Understanding Taxes*. Look for the link to *Student Lessons*. Complete modules to learn about income and payroll taxes and related forms.

Thinking Critically

Employees are able to adjust the amount of their net income each pay period by adjusting the number of allowances they claim on their Form W-4. An employee does not have to claim any allowances. Discuss the advantages and disadvantages of claiming zero allowances.

Success Tips

The payroll worksheet for salaried employees will not change much from month to month. The worksheet might change when:

- An employee is paid additional salary for extra services.
- A change in allowances is made.
- An employee is added or deleted from payroll.
- A tax rate change occurs.
- An employee is given unpaid leave from work.
- An employee's salary changes.

Help Keywords

Worksheet
  Move or copy sheets
Insert
  Insert blank cells, rows, or columns

Job 7-2 Update Payroll Workbook

Skills Applied

- Locating and opening existing workbooks
- Inserting worksheets into a workbook
- Formatting worksheet tabs
- Going to a specific cell
- Inserting columns
- Entering and editing text and numbers in cells
- Creating and editing formulas using the Formula Bar
- Formatting cells
- Adding cell protection and protecting individual worksheets
- Modifying worksheet orientation

Ms. Taylor has asked you to prepare a payroll worksheet for May for salaried employees.

1. Open the payroll workbook **7-1 Payroll** that you created earlier.

2. Create a copy of the April worksheet and rename it May. Go to cell A3. Change the date in the title.

3. Ms. Taylor has indicated that one employee, Robert Jackson, was given a $500 bonus by the owner for his outstanding performance during April. You need to modify the worksheet so such adjustments are possible. Insert a column to the right of the Allowance from W4 column. Key a column heading, *Other Earnings*, for the new column. (You must unprotect your worksheet before you can make this change.)

4. Key the bonus amount for Robert Jackson in the Other Earnings column.

5. Change the formula for Monthly Salary for all employees. The formula should allow for the possibility of an employee earning additional income:

   Monthly Salary = Annual Salary / 12 + Other Earnings

6. If you did not use a VLOOKUP formula for the income tax amounts, find the new tax amount for Robert Jackson.

7. Check your worksheet for accuracy. The Total amount for Net Pay should be 25,967.83.

8. Unlock the cells for Other Earnings (E7:E16). Protect the worksheet.

9. Save the workbook as **7-2 Payroll.** Print the May sheet in landscape orientation to fit on a single page.

Job 7-3 Create Payroll Worksheet for Hourly Employees

Skills Applied

- Locating and opening existing workbooks
- Inserting worksheets into a workbook
- Formatting worksheet tabs
- Entering and editing text and numbers in cells
- Formatting cells
- Modifying alignment
- Bringing information into *Excel* from external sources
- Creating and editing formulas using the Formula Bar
- Creating formulas using functions
- Applying cell formats
- Using references (absolute and relative)
- Using VLOOKUP
- Freezing and unfreezing rows and columns
- Adding cell protection and protecting individual worksheets
- Modifying worksheet orientation

Success Tips

Employees who work in a service industry, such as the guides at Star River Adventures, often receive tips from customers in addition to their hourly wages. Tips are often as much or more than hourly wages. These employees are responsible for paying federal income tax on tips they receive.

Ms. Taylor just received a list of the guides hired for the coming season. These guides completed the additional training required. They were recommended by Willie Abraham and Odessa Carr. Mr. Newland hired these individuals and determined their hourly salary based on their education, experience, and qualifications.

Ms. Taylor asked you to create a payroll worksheet to calculate payroll for these hourly employees. You must allow for overtime for any individual who works over 80 hours during a payroll period. The overtime rate is 1.5 times the hourly rate. The guides and their hourly salary, marital status, and federal withholding allowances are recorded in the Star River Adventures database in the Guide Roster table as shown in Figure 7-5.

Guide Roster				
Guide FName	**Guide LName**	**Guide Marital Status**	**Guide Allowances**	**Guide Hourly Rate**
Robin	Nichols	Single	1	6.10
Carson	Forde	Married	1	7.20
Tamara	Gibson	Single	0	7.00
Heather	Goldman	Single	1	7.00
Laura	Robinson	Single	0	7.00
Tinukwa	Okojie	Single	0	6.50
Alan	Jackson	Married	0	7.10
Sidney	Miller	Single	0	6.90
Nicholas	Goetze	Married	1	7.80

Figure 7-5 Portion of the Guide Roster Table

Biweekly tax tables for single and married employees (similar to the monthly table shown in Figure 7-2 on page 117) are used to determine federal income withholding tax for hourly employees.

Ms. Taylor recommends that you use a layout for your hourly payroll worksheet similar to the worksheet shown in Figure 7-6 on page 125.

1. Open the data file **Biweekly Payroll.** This workbook contains the tax tables you need for the hourly payroll. Insert a new worksheet.

2. Enter the worksheet titles in Rows 1–3 as shown in Figure 7-6. For the payroll period date range, identify the first two full weeks in April of the current year. Use the date for Sunday in the first week as the beginning date. Use the date for Saturday in the second week for the ending date. Use bold for the titles. Use a larger font for the company name. Center the titles over the worksheet.

3. Rename the worksheet with the payroll period dates; for example, *April 1–14.*

4. Enter the column headings as shown in Figure 7-6. Bold and center the column headings.

Software Review

When copying data from an *Access* table, select and copy an entire column, including the column head. Then delete or edit the column head in the new document or worksheet.

5. Open the *Access* data file **Star River Adventures P7.** Open the Guide Roster table. Copy and paste data from the Guide Roster table into the appropriate columns in your April 15 worksheet for the guides' last names, first names, hourly rates, allowances, and marital status. Enter the hours worked for each employee as shown below.

Nichols, Robin	80 hours	Okojie, Tinukwa	65 hours
Forde, Carson	80 hours	Goldman, Heather	72 hours
Gibson, Tamara	82 hours	Miller, Sidney	80 hours
Jackson, Alan	92 hours	Goetze, Nicholas	80 hours
Robinson, Laura	80 hours		

STAR RIVER ADVENTURES
Payroll for Hourly Employees
Payroll Period: April X–XX, 20--

Last Name	First Name	Marital Status	Allowance from W4	Hourly Rate	Hours Worked	Wages Earned	Income Tax	Social Security (FICA)	Medicare	State Tax	Other	Net Pay
Nichols	Robin	Single	1	6.10	80.00	488.00	29.00	30.26	7.08	31.72		389.95
Forde	Carson	Married	1	7.20	80.00	576.00	20.00	35.71	8.35	37.44		474.50
Totals						1,064.00	49.00	65.97	15.43	69.16		864.44

Figure 7-6 Hourly Payroll Worksheet

6. Create the appropriate formulas for the first employee and copy them to other cells as needed. If an employee worked 80 or fewer hours during a payroll period: Wages Earned = Hours Worked * Hourly Rate.

If an employee worked more than 80 hours during a payroll period: Wages Earned = (80 * Hourly Rate) + (Hours over 80 * 1.5).

You need to enter a formula that takes into account whether individuals work more or less than 80 hours during a payroll period. Create a nested formula that uses the IF function. A sample formula is shown below.

=IF(F7>80,(80*E7)+((F7−80)*1.5*E7),F7*E7)

Help Keywords

IF worksheet function

7. The other columns use the same formulas you used to calculate deductions for salaried employees: Income Tax, Social Security Tax, Medicare Tax, State Tax, and Net Pay. Refer to Job 7-1 if you need to review these formulas.

8. Apply pattern to Rows 6 and 16 as shown. Enter the label *Totals* in A17. Total Columns G through K and M. Format all cells that contain dollar amounts as currency with two decimal places, but with no dollar sign.

9. Check spelling in the worksheet. Freeze the panes so all row headings and employee names remain displayed on the screen. Unlock the cells for Marital Status (C7:C15), Allowance from W4 (D7:D15), and Hours Worked (F7:F15). Protect the worksheet.

10. Save the workbook as **7-3 Payroll.** Print the April 15 worksheet using landscape orientation to fit on one page. Your completed worksheet should look similar to Figure 7-6, showing data for all of the employees. The total for Net Pay should be 3,915.33.

Job 7-4 Change Data in Locked Cells

Skills Applied

- Opening a workbook from a folder created for workbook storage
- Inserting (copying) worksheets in a workbook
- Formatting worksheet tabs
- Entering and editing text and numbers in cells
- Clearing cell content
- Modifying worksheet orientation
- Protecting individual worksheets

Ms. Taylor wants you to calculate the payroll for June for the salaried employees. In this pay period, Odessa Carr earned $1,500 of Other Earnings.

1. Open the file **7-2 Payroll** that you created earlier. Unprotect the sheet.

2. Copy the May worksheet. Rename the new worksheet *June.* Change the date in Row 3 on the June sheet.

3. On the June sheet, enter 1,500 in the Other Earnings column for Odessa Carr. Clear the cell (500) in the Other Earnings column for Robert Jackson.

4. Check the accuracy of your worksheet. The total Net Pay amount should be 26,578.04. Protect the sheet again.

5. Save the workbook as **7-4 Payroll.** Print the June sheet in landscape orientation to fit on one page.

Job 7-5 Add Records and Sort Lists

Skills Applied

- Opening a workbook from a folder created for workbook storage
- Inserting (copying) worksheets in a workbook
- Formatting worksheet tabs
- Entering and editing text and numbers in cells
- Inserting rows
- Creating and editing formulas using the Formula Bar
- Using references (absolute and relative)
- Modifying worksheet orientation
- Protecting individual worksheets

Ms. Taylor asked that you complete the next April payroll for hourly employees. In addition, you must add the two new employees who have been hired.

Guide	Hourly Wages	Marital Status	Allowances
Farley, Josh	6.10	Single	1
Du, Chien	6.50	Single	0

1. Open the file **7-3 Payroll** that you created earlier. Make a copy of the first April sheet. Rename the new sheet with the date range; for example, *April 15-28.* Change the date in the title.

2. Unprotect the new sheet. Insert two new rows below the last employee name. For the two new employees, enter employee names, hourly wages, marital status, and allowances as shown above. Sort the payroll records so they are in alphabetic order by employee last name.

3. Key the hours worked for this payroll as shown below. Copy the formulas, as needed, for the new employees. Be sure to use absolute cell references where necessary.

Du, Chien	60 hours	Jackson, Alan	40 hours
Farley, Josh	80 hours	Miller, Sidney	80 hours
Forde, Carson	80 hours	Nichols, Robin	80 hours
Goetze, Nicholas	80 hours	Okojie, Tinukwa	85 hours
Gibson, Tamara	80 hours	Robinson, Laura	80 hours
Goldman, Heather	80 hours		

4. Check the accuracy of your worksheet. The total Net Pay amount should be 4,436.17. The records should be in the order shown above.

5. Unlock the cells for Marital Status, Allowance from W4, and Hours Worked for the two new employees. Protect the worksheet.

6. Save the workbook as **7-5 Payroll.** Print the sheet in landscape orientation to fit on one page.

Help Keywords

Insert
  Insert blank cells, rows, or columns
Sort
  Sort a list

Job 7-6 Create Quarterly Summary Report

Skills Applied

- Opening a workbook from a folder created for workbook storage
- Inserting (copying) worksheets in a workbook
- Formatting worksheet tabs
- Entering and editing text and numbers in cells
- Formatting cells
- Modifying alignment
- Merging cells
- Creating and editing formulas using the Formula Bar
- Using references (absolute and relative)
- Creating formulas using functions
- Sharing data among worksheets using 3-D cell references in formulas
- Modifying worksheet orientation
- Applying AutoFormats to worksheets
- Deleting rows
- Exporting structured data from *Excel*
- Pasting data into *Word*

Ms. Taylor wants you to prepare a Quarterly Summary Report for Mr. Newland, showing total wages earned for the quarter for salaried employees.

1. Open the file **7-4 Payroll** that you created earlier. Insert a new sheet and rename the sheet *Quarterly Report*.

2. Enter titles for the report. Leave a blank row after the titles. Use the current year in the date.

   STAR RIVER ADVENTURES
   2nd Quarter Salaried Payroll
   June 30, 20--

3. In Row 5, enter these column headings: Personnel, Salary, Income Tax, Social Security (FICA), Medicare, State Tax, Other, Net Pay.

4. Format the titles and column headings similar to those on the June sheet. Add pattern to Row 6 as on the June sheet. Copy the names for employees from the June sheet and paste them to the Quarterly Report sheet.

5. An easy way to summarize data from multiple worksheets is to link the worksheets. Create formulas on the Quarterly Report worksheet to sum the amounts for each employee for the three-month period April through June. (There will be no amounts in Column G because no Other deductions have been made this quarter.)

   Example: To find the Salary amount for the Quarterly Report sheet, add the Monthly Salary amounts for April, May, and June. The following formula is used to find the Salary amount for William Abraham on the Quarterly Report sheet: =April!E7+May!F7+June!F7.

6. Add pattern to Row 17 as on the June sheet. Enter the label *Totals* in A18. In Row 18, find the sum of each column for Columns B through F and H.

7. Check the accuracy of your worksheet. The total amount for Net Pay is 78,225.13. Save the workbook as **7-6 Payroll.** Print the Quarterly Report sheet in portrait orientation to fit on one page.

Challenge: Create Memo with Worksheet

Ms. Taylor has asked you to prepare a memo to Mr. Newland that includes the Quarterly Report worksheet.

1. Open the file **7-6 Payroll** that you created earlier. Save the file as **7-6 Payroll Challenge.**

2. On the Quarterly Report worksheet, select Rows 5 through 18. Apply an AutoFormat to your worksheet. Choose a simple format (such as Accounting 2) that will look attractive when the data is copied into a memo. If desired, delete blank rows in the worksheet where pattern was applied in the original format. Save the file again using the same name.

3. Review memo format on page 314 in the Reference Guide. Prepare a memo to Tommy Newland from you. Use July 1 of the current year as the date. Use *Quarterly Payroll Report* as the subject. Key the paragraph shown below.

   The payroll report you requested is shown below. This table summarizes the total salary, taxes, and net pay for salaried employees for the months of April, May, and June. If you have any questions about the data, please let me know.

4. Leave a blank line after the paragraph. Paste a copy of the data from the Quarterly Report worksheet into the memo as a worksheet object. Center the table horizontally on the page. Make adjustments to column widths, headings, and formatting as needed for an attractive table.

5. Save the memo as **7-6 Challenge Memo.** Print the memo. Close the worksheet without printing.

Thinking Critically

In the Job 7-6 Challenge, you pasted a copy of a worksheet into a word processing document. You could have used one of the Paste Special options to link it as a worksheet object. What would be an advantage of this approach?

Managing Budgets

Objectives

- ☐ Create a workbook with multiple linked sheets
- ☐ Work with complex formulas
- ☐ Add sheets, name sheets, and move sheets in a workbook
- ☐ Format cells for number, font, alignment, and pattern
- ☐ Key data from source documents
- ☐ Create a chart
- ☐ Copy and paste workbook data into a *Word* document

Summary of *Microsoft Office* Skills

- ✔ Insert, delete, and move cells
- ✔ Enter and edit cell data, including text, numbers, and formulas
- ✔ Check spelling
- ✔ Manage workbook files and folders
- ✔ Save workbooks using different names and file formats
- ✔ Apply and modify cell formats
- ✔ Apply styles
- ✔ Modify Page Setup options for worksheets
- ✔ Preview and print worksheets and workbooks
- ✔ Insert and delete worksheets
- ✔ Modify worksheet names and positions
- ✔ Use 3-D references
- ✔ Create and revise formulas
- ✔ Use statistical, date and time, financial, and logical functions in formulas
- ✔ Create, modify, position, and print charts
- ✔ Export data from *Excel*
- ✔ Apply and modify text formats
- ✔ Modify paragraph formats
- ✔ Create and format document sections
- ✔ Insert images and graphics
- ✔ Insert and modify text and symbols

STAR River Adventures

Job 8-1 Create Budget Worksheet

Skills Applied

- Entering and editing text and numbers in cells
- Formatting cells
- Modifying alignment
- Merging cells
- Creating and editing formulas using the Formula Bar
- Creating formulas using functions
- Applying styles
- Freezing and unfreezing rows and columns
- Modifying worksheet orientation

budget: a plan for how a company's resources (money, goods, equipment) will be used

The owner and the manager of each department at Star River Adventures have separate budgets. The company divides its expenses into categories that reflect its business operations. Most of the expenses and income occur at the department level. Therefore, the department budgets are much larger than the budget for Tommy Newland, the owner of the company. All of these separate budgets combined show what the entire company expects to spend. The general budget categories include the following:

- **Salary:** amounts paid to salaried employees
- **Wages:** amounts paid to hourly employees
- **Fringes:** benefits paid by the company for things such as retirement and health insurance
- **Travel:** amounts paid for travel by company employees for reasons such as public relations, conventions, and adventure trips
- **Recurring Expenses:** amounts paid each month, such as rentals (copy machines and/or other equipment), long-term purchases, and utilities
- **Supplies:** amounts paid for miscellaneous supplies such as paper, toner, and office supplies
- **Equipment:** amounts paid for equipment such as boats, computers, and furniture
- **Miscellaneous:** amounts paid for items not covered in one of the other expense categories

fiscal year: the 12-month period used for accounting purposes

According to company policy, amounts that the company budgets for salary, wages, and fringes cannot be used for any other purpose. Department managers are free to transfer funds among other budget categories as needed. They can also transfer additional funds into the salary, wages, and fringes categories. The company budget for the current fiscal year is shown in Figure 8-1 on page 133.

Items	Owner	Operations	Marketing and Sales	Finance and Accounting	Totals
	STAR RIVER ADVENTURES				
	Budget for 2003				
Salaries	$ 65,000.00	$ 96,900.00	$116,900.00	$108,300.00	$387,100.00
Wages	$ 16,000.00	$ 96,000.00	$ 16,000.00	$ 16,000.00	$144,000.00
Fringes	$ 20,250.00	$ 48,225.00	$ 33,225.00	$ 31,075.00	$132,775.00
Travel	$ 5,000.00	$ 6,000.00	$ 6,000.00	$ 2,000.00	$ 19,000.00
Recurring Expenses	$ 20,000.00	$ 40,000.00	$ 10,000.00	$ 10,000.00	$ 80,000.00
Supplies	$ 25,000.00	$ 40,000.00	$ 8,000.00	$ 8,000.00	$ 81,000.00
Equipment	$ 10,000.00	$ 50,000.00	$ 5,000.00	$ 3,000.00	$ 68,000.00
Miscellaneous	$ 5,000.00	$ 1,000.00	$ 1,000.00	$ 1,000.00	$ 8,000.00
Total	$166,250.00	$378,125.00	$196,125.00	$179,375.00	$919,875.00

Figure 8-1 Star River Adventures' Budget

Ms. Taylor has asked you to prepare a workbook containing the four main budgets for Star River Adventures: Owner, Operations, Marketing and Sales, and Finance and Accounting. Each department will provide monthly reports with figures for each budget category. You should create the worksheets similar to the one shown in Figure 8-2 on page 134. In this job, you will create a worksheet for the Owner budget. You will create worksheets for other budgets in later jobs.

1. Open a new blank workbook. Name the first sheet tab *Owner*. This worksheet will contain the budget of Tommy Newland, owner of Star River Adventures.

2. Key the titles and column heads as shown in Figure 8-2 on page 134. Use wrap text and center alignment for the column headings. Center the worksheet title lines (company name and address) across all columns. Use bold as shown. Use a 12-point font for the company name.

Fiscal Year Budget—Owner

STAR RIVER ADVENTURES
205 Riverview Drive
Sutton, WV 26601-1311

Date	Salary	Wages	Fringes	Travel	Recurring Expenses	Supplies	Equipment	Misc.	Monthly Total	Annual Budget	Year-to-Date Expenditures	Percent of Budget Remaining
1/31/20-	5,416.67	1,333.33	1,687.50	556.67	1,766.67	1,851.18	925.48	316.67	13,854.17	166,250.00	13,854.17	91.67%
2/28/20-									0.00		13,854.17	91.67%
3/31/20-									0.00		13,854.17	91.67%
4/30/20-									0.00		13,854.17	91.67%
5/31/20-									0.00		13,854.17	91.67%
6/30/20-									0.00		13,854.17	91.67%
7/31/20-									0.00		13,854.17	91.67%
8/31/20-									0.00		13,854.17	91.67%
9/30/20-									0.00		13,854.17	91.67%
10/31/20-									0.00		13,854.17	91.67%
11/30/20-									0.00		13,854.17	91.67%
12/31/20-									0.00		13,854.17	91.67%
Total Expenditures	5,416.67	1,333.33	1,687.50	556.67	1,766.67	1,851.18	925.48	316.67	13,854.17			
Annual Budget	65,000.00	16,000.00	20,250.00	5,000.00	20,000.00	25,000.00	10,000.00	5,000.00	166,250.00			
Balance	59,583.33	14,666.67	18,562.50	4,443.33	18,233.33	23,148.82	9,074.52	4,683.33	152,395.83			
Percent Remaining	91.67%	91.67%	91.67%	88.87%	91.17%	92.60%	90.75%	93.67%	91.67%			

Figure 8-2 Owner's Budget

3. Enter the dates in Column A. Key the amounts spent for January. Enter formulas to sum the amounts spent in the Monthly Total column.

4. Enter the Annual Budget amount as shown. This amount was taken from the company budget (shown in Figure 8-1).

5. Enter formulas for all of the months (even though you have data now for only January) in the following columns:

   • Year to Date Expenditures = Monthly totals to date
   • Percent of Budget Remaining = (Annual Budget − Year to Date Expenditures) / Annual Budget

6. Key the labels below the dates as shown in Column A. Enter formulas to sum the columns in the Total Expenditures row. Enter the Annual Budget amounts as shown. These amounts were taken from the company budget (shown in Figure 8-1). Sum the Annual Budget row in the Monthly Total column as a check figure. It should be the same as the amount shown in the Annual Budget cell.

7. Enter formulas for:

   • Balance = Annual Budget − Total Expenditures
   • Percent Remaining = (Annual Budget − Total Expenditures) / Annual Budget

8. Format all columns with dollar amounts as currency, but with no dollar signs. Format the appropriate columns for percent style with two decimal places. Add pattern to the row above the column headings and below the last date to divide your worksheet into sections.

9. Freeze panes so the column and row headings remain displayed on the page when you navigate through the document.

10. Check the spelling of the worksheet. Use landscape orientation and fit the worksheet on one sheet when printed. Save your workbook as **8-1 Budget.** Print the worksheet. Your completed worksheet should look similar to Figure 8-2 on page 134.

Job 8-2 Update Owner Budget

Skills Applied

- Locating and opening existing workbooks
- Opening a workbook from a folder created for workbook storage
- Entering and editing text and numbers in cells
- Adding footers to worksheets
- Using Save As to save a workbook to a different name

1. Open the data file **Expenditures.** This file shows the expenditures reported by the four budget divisions of Star River Adventures for the months of January, February, and March.

   In the future, you will receive reports on the first working day of each month from Mr. Newland and each department manager listing their expenditures for the previous month. It will be your job to keep the budget worksheets up to date.

2. Open the file **8-1 Budget** that you created earlier. Enter the figures for the Owner budget for the months of February and March. You will work with the other departments later.

3. Save the updated worksheet as **8-2 Budget.** Print the worksheet.

Challenge: Custom Footer

confidential: private or secret in nature

Company financial documents and information such as budgets are usually considered confidential. Financial worksheets often carry a reminder of this fact by using the word *Confidential* in a header or footer.

1. Create a custom footer for the **8-2 Budget** worksheet. In the footer, include the company name, the current date, and the word *Confidential*.

2. Save the workbook as **8-2 Challenge Budget.** Print the Owner worksheet.

Help Keywords

Footer
   Add headers and
   footers for printing

Job 8-3 Copy and Update Budget Sheets

Skills Applied

- Locating and opening existing workbooks
- Opening a workbook from a folder created for workbook storage
- Entering and editing text and numbers in cells
- Inserting (copying) worksheets in a workbook
- Formatting worksheet tabs
- Deleting cells
- Repositioning worksheets in a workbook

Help Keywords

Copy
Copy sheets

Ms. Taylor likes the budget worksheet you prepared for Mr. Newland. She now wants you to create worksheets for the other three departments.

1. Open the file **8-2 Budget** that you created earlier. Make a copy of the Owner worksheet. Rename the sheet *Operations*.

2. Edit the new sheet to change the department name: *Fiscal Year Budget-- Operations*. Delete the data for Owner expenditures. Enter the data for January, February, and March for the Operations Department as shown on the **Expenditures** worksheet.

3. Refer to the annual budget shown in Figure 8-1 on page 133. Edit the Annual Budget figure in Column K to show the annual budget figure for this department. Edit the Annual Budget row to show figures for this department from the company budget.

4. Repeat this process to create budget sheets for the Marketing and Sales Department and the Finance and Accounting Department.

5. Move the sheets, if needed, to arrange the sheets in alphabetic order.

6. Check your worksheets for accuracy. The Percent Remaining figures for the four worksheets are shown below.

7. Save the workbook as **8-3 Budget.** Print the worksheets for Operations, Finance and Accounting, and Marketing and Sales.

Check Figures for **8-3 Budget**

	Salary	Wages	Fringes	Travel	Recurring Expenses	Supplies	Equipment	Misc.	Monthly Total
Finance and Accounting									
Percent Remaining	75.00%	75.00%	75.00%	58.33%	75.83%	98.21%	83.33%	75.03%	76.04%
Marketing and Sales									
Percent Remaining	75.00%	84.79%	75.00%	32.11%	76.37%	89.02%	85.23%	77.96%	75.40%
Operations									
Percent Remaining	75.00%	100.00%	75.00%	82.55%	75.08%	88.46%	91.67%	67.62%	85.08%
Owner									
Percent Remaining	75.00%	80.41%	76.04%	84.36%	75.10%	82.19%	90.75%	90.57%	78.44%

Job 8-4 Link Worksheets and Prepare Report (Challenge Job)

Skills Applied

- Locating and opening existing workbooks
- Opening a workbook from a folder created for workbook storage
- Entering and editing text and numbers in cells
- Inserting (copying) worksheets in a workbook
- Formatting worksheet tabs
- Deleting cells
- Creating and editing formulas using the Formula Bar
- Creating formulas using functions
- Using references (absolute and relative)
- Sharing data among worksheets using 3-D cell references in formulas

In this job, you will link multiple worksheets to prepare a summary report of the budget records. The report will include figures for the first quarter for the four budget divisions of the company: Finance and Accounting, Marketing and Sales, Operations, and Owner. Your work can be greatly reduced by using linking, copy, and fill functions.

1. Open the file **8-3 Budget** that you created earlier. Create a copy of the Owner worksheet. Rename the new sheet *First-Quarter Report*.

2. Edit the new sheet to change the sheet title in Row 5: *Fiscal Year Budget--First-Quarter Report*. Delete the data for Owner expenditures in Rows 9, 10, and 11.

3. Refer to the annual budget shown in Figure 8-1 on page 133. Edit the Annual Budget figure in Column K to show the annual budget figure for the entire company. Edit the Annual Budget row to show figures for the entire company.

4. For the expenditures in Columns B through I for January through March, use formulas to calculate the totals for the expenditures for the four departments. For example, to calculate the total salary for January for the four divisions you need to add:

January 31 salary for:

Finance and Accounting + Marketing and Sales + Operations + Owner

Sample formula:

='Finance and Accounting'!B9+'Marketing and Sales'!B9+Operations!B9+Owner!B9

5. After you have created the formula for Salary for January, use the copy and fill functions to enter formulas for the other expenditures.

6. Check your worksheet for accuracy. The last four rows of worksheet are shown on the following page. Save the workbook as **8-4 Budget.** Print the First-Quarter Report worksheet.

Help Keywords

Fill Cell
  Fill data within a row
  or column

Check Figures for **Budget 8-4**

	Salary	Wages	Fringes	Travel	Recurring Expenses	Supplies	Equipment	Misc.	Monthly Total
Total Expenditures	96,775.02	9,567.65	32,983.74	6,735.43	19,728.34	10,087.95	6,330.85	1,265.54	183,474.52
Annual Budget	387,100.00	144,000.00	132,775.00	19,000.00	80,000.00	81,000.00	68,000.00	8,000.00	919,875.00
Balance	290,324.98	134,432.35	99,791.26	12,264.57	60,271.66	70,912.05	61,669.15	6,734.46	736,400.48
Percent Remaining	75.00%	93.36%	75.16%	64.55%	75.34%	87.55%	90.69%	84.18%	80.05%

Thinking Critically

1. In Project 8, you created a budget workbook with multiple budget sheets. Explain the relationship between the workbook and worksheets.

2. In what other instances would you want to place several sheets in a workbook? How does placing related sheets in a workbook increase work productivity?

Job 8-5 Create Chart

Skills Applied

- Locating and opening existing workbooks
- Creating column charts
- Formatting and positioning charts
- Printing charts

Ms. Taylor asks you to prepare an expenditures chart. The chart should compare the expenditures for each budget area for the months of January, February, and March.

1. If you completed Job 8-4, open the file **8-4 Budget.** If you did not complete Job 8-4, open the data file **Budget Summary.** Go to the First-Quarter Report worksheet.

2. Use the data in the rows showing expenditures for January, February, and March to create a column chart. Use rows for the data series. Use a legend to identify the dates. Title the chart *FIRST-QUARTER EXPENDITURES*. Place the chart on a chart sheet.

3. Format the chart title for a 20-point font. Format the Value axis for currency with no decimal places and a 12-point font. Format the Category axis for bold and an 11-point font. Resize or reposition chart elements, if needed, for attractive placement. Change colors for the plot area or the columns, if desired, to create an attractive chart. Your chart should look similar to the one shown in Figure 8-3.

4. Save the workbook as **8-5 Budget.** Print the chart.

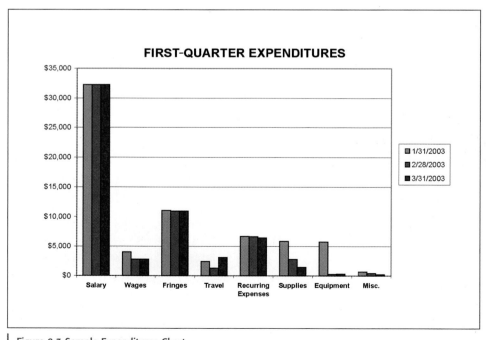

Figure 8-3 Sample Expenditures Chart

Job 8-6 Prepare Report

Skills Applied

- Applying paragraph formats and character styles
- Applying paragraph styles
- Modifying page margins
- Inserting page breaks and page numbers
- Managing orphans and widows
- Using Page Setup options to format sections
- Adding images to a document
- Using Paste Special

Ms. Taylor asks you to prepare a short report for Mr. Newland that will briefly summarize the budget records for the first quarter. She also wants you to include the worksheet showing the expenditures in each budget category and the chart you prepared. She has drafted a report and asks you to insert material where indicated.

1. Key the following text as an unbound report. Refer to page 319 in the Reference Guide to review unbound report format. Insert information where requested. Insert a Next Page section break before page 2. Remember to number page 2.

2. Check the spelling and proofread carefully. Save the report as **8-6 Report.** Print the report.

STAR RIVER ADVENTURES
First-Quarter Fiscal Report

The percent of the budget remaining, approximately 80 percent, is above the level expected at the end of the first quarter. Details are provided in the table on the following page. We have this favorable balance primarily because the guides for the season were not yet employed during the first quarter, causing the Wages category to be low.

Note that all of the budget categories except Travel have remaining balances above those expected at the end of the first quarter. The Travel budget category has approximately 64.55 percent of the funds remaining. This amount is slightly below that expected at the end of the first quarter.

The following chart compares budget expenditures for each month in the first quarter. Supporting details for the chart are shown in the table on the following page.

(Insert First-Quarter Expenditures chart here.)

(Create a second page for the report. Format the page for landscape orientation. Place the First-Quarter Report budget worksheet on the page.)

Managing Business Travel Documents

Objectives

- ☐ Understand terminology related to travel
- ☐ Build travel request and travel expense report templates
- ☐ Use advanced formatting of cells
- ☐ Build complex formulas
- ☐ Prepare an electronic presentation with drawings, clip art, and hyperlinks to the Internet and other documents
- ☐ Paste a portion of a worksheet into a memo

Summary of *Microsoft Office* Skills

- ✔ Insert, delete, and move cells
- ✔ Enter and edit cell data including text, numbers, and formulas
- ✔ Check spelling
- ✔ Manage workbook files and folders
- ✔ Create workbooks using templates
- ✔ Save workbooks using different names and file formats
- ✔ Apply and modify cell formats
- ✔ Modify row and column formats
- ✔ Modify Page Setup options for worksheets
- ✔ Preview and print worksheets and workbooks
- ✔ Create and revise formulas
- ✔ Use statistical, date and time, financial, and logical functions in formulas
- ✔ Create hyperlinks
- ✔ Create, edit, and apply templates
- ✔ Apply and modify text format
- ✔ Modify paragraph formats
- ✔ Set and modify tabs
- ✔ Create and modify tables
- ✔ Insert images and graphics

- ✔ Create presentations (manually and using automated tools)
- ✔ Add slides to and delete slides from presentations
- ✔ Insert, format, and modify text
- ✔ Modify headers and footers in the Slide Master
- ✔ Add tables, charts, clip art, and bitmap images to slides
- ✔ Add OfficeArt elements to slides
- ✔ Apply slide transitions
- ✔ Modify slide layout
- ✔ Add links to a presentation

STAR River Adventures

Job 9-1 Create Request for Travel Template

Skills Applied

- Entering and editing text and numbers in cells
- Modifying alignment
- Merging cells
- Applying cell formats
- Creating and editing formulas using the Formula Bar
- Entering a range within a formula by dragging
- Modifying worksheet orientation
- Creating a workbook template

Employee Travel

per diem: a daily allowance

Star River Adventures employees must sometimes travel on company business. All travel arrangements are made through the Finance and Accounting Department. Individuals are reimbursed for business travel expenses. However, the trip must be approved by a manager prior to requesting travel arrangements. The employee must submit a Request for Travel form for the manager's approval prior to departure. No *per diem* advance requests are processed without a Request for Travel form approved by a manager.

The Request for Travel Form

template: a model or guide

Mr. Collins, manager of the Finance and Accounting Department, wants to increase employee efficiency by converting as many paper forms as possible to electronic templates. He asks you to prepare a worksheet template for the Request for Travel form shown in Figure 9-1 on page 145.

Most of the first two sections of the form will already be completed when the Finance and Accounting Department receives the form. Once you have prepared the template, employees will use the template to prepare electronic copies for travel requests. A manager will email the partially completed form to you and request that you process the form.

A member of the support staff will make the air transportation arrangements, hotel reservations, and auto rental reservations and will provide that information to you. You will enter the cost of air transportation, hotel, auto rental, registration, total estimated miles if personal auto is used, and any other expenses approved. For example, other expenses might include entertainment costs for business associates.

From the information provided on the form, you will enter the information in the last section of the form. Automate the form as much as possible by using appropriate formulas. This section requires the following entries:

- **Date processed.** The date processed is the date the Request for Travel form is received and processed. This cell should be formatted for text input.

- **Number of nights.** The number of nights is equal to the number of nights a hotel room is required. If an employee is staying with family or friends, no charges for lodging can be submitted.

	A	B	C	D	E	F	G	H	I
1		**STAR RIVER ADVENTURES**							
2		**205 Riverview Drive**							
3		**Sutton, WV 26601-1311**							
4									
5		**Request for Travel**							
6	**Section 1**								
7	Date:	_____							
8	Department name:	_____							
9	Traveler's name:	_____							
10	Manager's signature:	_____							
11	Traveler's signature:	_____							
12									
13	**Section 2**								
14	Travel destination:	_____							
15	Purpose of travel:	_____							
16	*Description of travel:	_____							
17	Departure date and approximate time:	_____							
18	Return date and approximate time:	_____							
19	Total hours:	_____							
20	Air transportation request, if needed:	_____							
21	Hotel request and desired accommodation type:	_____			Rate: _____		Days: _____		
22	Auto rental request, if needed:	_____			Rate: _____		Days: _____		
23	Registration request, if not already made:	_____					_____		
24	Personal auto:	Enter estimated miles in the space provided.					Miles: _____		
25	Other requests: _____	Explain: _____							
26									
27	**Section 3**								
28	*Completed by Finance and Accounting Dept.*								
29	Date processed:	_____							
30	Number of nights:	_____							
31	Number of per diem days:	0.00							
32	Estimated total costs:	$0.00							
33	Amount available for advance:	$0.00							
34	Summary of arrangements made:								
35									
36	*Attach a copy of flyer and/or registration form for event, if any. Registration for events should be								
37	completed prior to deadlines and are claimed on the Travel Expense Report.								

Figure 9-1 Request for Travel Form

- **Number of per diem days.** The number of per diem days is equal to the total number of hours of travel divided by 24. The per diem allowance is $42 per day. Individuals are not reimbursed for meals and do not need to keep receipts. Their daily expenditures for food are included in the per diem allowance.

- **Estimated total costs.** The total estimated costs include airfare, hotel, auto rental, registration, mileage allowance for personal auto, per diem allowance, and other approved expenses. The mileage allowance is 39 cents per mile.

- **Amount available for advance.** The amount available for advance is equal to total estimated costs less airfare times 80 percent.

- **Summary of arrangements made.** This section is for your use to indicate any special notes to the traveler, such as required receipts, required notification for any changes or cancellations, and so on. This range of cells should be formatted for text.

The company guarantees the first-night hotel stay and auto rental through charges to the company credit card. Registration fees, too, are paid by the company in advance if the traveler submits travel requests before any deadline. Travelers can draw a travel advance equal to 80 percent of the total estimated costs, less the cost of airline travel, which is paid by the company in advance.

Creating the Form Template

1. Open a new blank worksheet in *Excel*. Create a Request for Travel form as shown in Figure 9-1 on page 145.

2. Enter the three lines for the worksheet titles (company name and address) in bold as shown. Enter the name of the form, Request for Travel, in bold. Center the titles and the form name across all columns. Apply a heavy border to the cells in Row 5, as shown.

3. Format the range of cells used in Section 1 on the form for text. Enter the labels in Column A as shown. Format the cells in Columns B through H for a single underline, as shown.

4. Format the cells in Section 2 (A13:H26) for text. Enter the labels as shown. Format the cells in Columns B through H that will hold the information for a single underline, as shown. Apply a heavy border to the cells in Row 12, as shown.

5. Format the cell for the total hours value for number with two decimals. Use the comma separator for thousands.

6. Format the cells that will hold values for air transportation, hotel rate, auto rental rate, registration, and other requests for currency with two decimals and a dollar sign.

7. Format the cell for the estimated personal auto miles value for a number with no decimal places. Use this same format for the days values for hotel and auto rental.

8. In Section 3, format cells A27:H34 for text. Enter the labels and format cells for a single underline, as shown. Apply a heavy border to the cells in Row 26 and Row 35, as shown.

9. Format the cell for the Number of nights value for a number with no decimals.

10. Format the cell for the Number of per diem days for a number with two decimals. Enter an appropriate formula to calculate the number of per diem days:

Number of per diem days = Total hours/24

11. Format the cell for the Estimated total costs value for currency with two decimals and a dollar sign. Enter a formula to determine the value:

    Estimated total costs = Air transportation + (Hotel rate * Days) + (Auto rate * Days) + Registration + (Personal auto miles * .39) + Other requests + (Number of per diem days * 42)

12. Format the cell for the Amount available for advance value for currency with two decimals and a dollar sign. Enter a formula to determine the value:

    Amount available for advance = (Estimated total costs − Air transportation) * .80

13. Enter the note below Section 3. Format the sheet for landscape orientation. Center the worksheet horizontally on the page.

14. Spell-check and proofread the worksheet carefully. Save your completed worksheet as a template. Name the file **9-1 Request for Travel Template.** Save the template file in the same folder as your other solutions.

Help Keywords

Template
  Create a template

Job 9-2 Process Travel Requests

Skills Applied

- Creating a workbook from a template
- Entering and editing text and numbers in cells
- Locating and opening existing workbooks

Task 1 Travel Request for Carr

The department received a Request for Travel form from Maria Inez, the manager of the Operations Department. (She has not yet received a copy of your electronic form.) The request is for Odessa Carr, who will be traveling to Seattle, Washington, to view the operations of another rafting company. Our staff has already made the airline, hotel, and auto reservations as shown on the form.

1. Open the **9-1 Request for Travel Template** file you created earlier. Enter the necessary information to process this request. Use the partial form below that shows Sections 1 and 2 of the form. You must determine the number of hours of travel.

2. Enter April 15, 20-- for the date processed. All calculations for Section 3 of the form should be completed automatically using the formulas you entered into the template.

	A	B	C	D	E	F	G	H	I
1				STAR RIVER ADVENTURES					
2				205 Riverview Drive					
3				Sutton, WV 26601-1311					
4									
5				Request for Travel					
6	Section 1								
7	Date:	April 14, 20--							
8	Department name:	Operations							
9	Traveler's name:	Odessa Carr							
10	Manager's signature:								
11	Traveler's signature:								
12									
13	Section 2								
14	Travel destination:	Seattle, Washington							
15	Purpose of travel:	Visit Carter Rafting, Inc.							
16	*Description of travel:	View operations of company							
17	Departure date and approximate time:	April 22, 1:00 p.m.							
18	Return date and approximate time:	April 26, 9:00 p.m.							
19	Total hours:								
20	Air transportation request, if needed:	$619.00							
21	Hotel request and desired accommodation type:	Clairmont Hotel				Rate:	$85.00	Days:	5
22	Auto rental request, if needed:	Custom Auto Rental				Rate:	$26.00	Days:	6
23	Registration request, if not already made:								
24	Personal auto:	Enter estimated miles in the space provided.					Miles:	0	
25	Other requests:		Explain:						
26									

3. Check your work. The Estimated total costs amount should be $1,271.00. The Amount available for advance should be $521.60.

4. Save the completed form as **9-2 Carr Travel Request.** Remember to select *Microsoft Excel Worksheet (*.xls)* as the file type. Print the form for the manager's signature.

Task 2   Travel Requests for Jackson and Inez

Our staff has forwarded two additional Request for Travel forms to you for processing. The reservation information has already been entered.

1. Open the data file **Jackson Travel Request.** This file contains a partially completed Request for Travel form that was prepared using your template file.

2. Complete the form. Determine the total hours and enter the number. Use April 15, 20--, as the date processed. Enter the number of nights. The per diem days, the estimated costs, and the available advance will be calculated using the formulas you entered in the template.

3. Check your work. The Estimated total costs amount should be $495.25. Save the form as **9-2 Jackson Travel Request.** Print the form.

4. Open the data file **Inez Travel Request.** This file contains a partially completed Request for Travel form that was prepared using your template file. Follow the instructions in Step 2 to complete the form.

5. Check your work. The Estimated total costs amount should be $1,158.20. Save the form as **9-2 Inez Travel Request.** Print the form.

Challenge: Research Travel Options

1. Mr. Collins has asked you to check possible airline reservations for a trip he must take to Seattle, Washington. He will leave from Sutton, West Virginia, on the morning of May 11 and return the morning of May 16. There is no major airport in Sutton. He must use an airport in a neighboring city.

   Search the Internet for flight information for Mr. Collins. Provide three options, including itineraries and sample fares. You might want to use one of the following two Web sites as a resource:

   • Travelocity.com (http://www.travelocity.com)
   • Priceline.com (http://www.priceline.com)

2. Mr. Collins will need to drive to Huntington, West Virginia, next week. Search the Internet to locate a map and driving directions for him. Include an estimate of the mileage. You might want to use MapQuest (http://www.mapquest.com) to complete this assignment.

Job 9-3 Create Rafting Competition Presentation

Skills Applied

- Applying character and paragraph formats
- Setting and modifying tabs
- Applying border and shading
- Creating and modifying tables
- Creating and inserting graphics in documents
- Creating presentations from a blank presentation
- Adding slides to presentations
- Adding text to slides
- Adding clip art and bitmap images to slides and backgrounds
- Adding hyperlinks to slides and *Word* documents
- Adding information to the Footer area, Date/Time area, or Number Area of the Slide Master
- Applying transition effects to slides
- Creating OfficeArt elements and adding them to slides
- Changing the layout of individual slides
- Saving *Word* documents in HTML format

Mr. Collins knows you have had experience developing electronic presentations. He asks you to prepare a short electronic presentation that he can show on an upcoming trip. The presentation will advertise the Gauley River Rapids Challenge event to be held on May 2–3. You will also prepare an application form for this event.

Mr. Collins has provided you with sample slides. You must find pictures and clip art to use in the presentation. You also may need to do some drawing. You might want to locate media from the Microsoft Design Gallery Live Web site (http://dgl.microsoft.com). You will need a map of West Virginia and various media to develop an effective presentation. Use the Internet and clip art or pictures available to you.

Task 1 Event Application

1. Open a new word processing document. Prepare an application for the Gauley River Rapids Challenge similar to the one shown in Figure 9-2 on page 151.

2. In the application document, include WordArt for the title of the event. Include clip art near the top of the form, as shown by the placeholder in Figure 9-2. In Task 2, you will create a presentation about this event. After creating that file, you will make the clip art image in the application a hyperlink to the presentation file.

3. Save the document as **9-3 Application.** Print the document.

Help Keywords

WordArt
  Add WordArt
Clip art
  About finding clips

Click picture for more
information.

**Star River Adventures
205 Riverview Drive
Sutton, WV 26601-1311**

Gauley River Rapids Challenge
May 2–3

Preregistration is April 15–25. Final registration is on site on May 1. No participants
will be accepted after that date. Teams include four or five individuals. All participants
must be 18 or older. The registration fee is $250. The fee must be included with your
registration form. (See the payment options below.)

To register, provide the following information:

Name	Address	Phone Number
Team Leader		
Team Members		

If paying by check or money order, make the check payable to Star River Adventures and
attach it to this application. If paying by credit card, provide the following information:

Type of card: ____American Express ____MasterCard ____Visa
Name on card: _____
Card number: _____
Expiration date (month and year): _____

Mail your registration form to the address above!

Figure 9-2 Sample Application

Task 2   Event Presentation

1. Open a new blank presentation in *PowerPoint*.

2. Access the slide master and insert a picture or motion clip representing river rafting. Format the picture or motion clip so it appears as the background image for all slides. You might use a small image and place it in a top or bottom corner of the slide. You might use a large image that covers most of the slide. If you use a large image, apply the washout effect to the image so it does not overpower the contents of the slide.

3. Enter a footer that displays the name of the event, *Gauley River Rapids Challenge,* and the slide number.

4. Create Slide 1 using the information shown in Figure 9-3. Insert an outline of the state of West Virginia. (If you cannot find an outline graphic, you might want to paste a picture of a West Virginia map and use the line drawing tool to trace the outline of the map; then delete the map.) You can usually locate maps of all states in clip art.

5. Use the appropriate layout and add a title and subtitle as shown. Add text to show the location of Sutton, West Virginia. Add clip art to mark the location. Note that the motion clip or image that should appear as the background for all slides is not shown on the sample slides. Sample slides show black text. You should choose an attractive color scheme for your slides.

Figure 9-3 Sample Slide 1

Success Tips

To create effective slides:
• Limit the amount of text on each slide.
• Use bulleted lists rather than long sentences.
• Do not use punctuation at the end of text lines.
• Be consistent in the use of fonts and colors.

6. Prepare Slides 2–5 using the following information. Format the slides for bulleted text. Choose attractive bullets and a font that is easy to read.

Slide 2

Registration

• Preregistration: April 15–25
  ▪ Contact Star River Adventures at 304-555-0110 to register
  ▪ Teams of four or five people and guide provided by Star River Adventures
  ▪ Registration fee for two-day event: $250 per team
  ▪ Total prize money awarded: $2,500
  ▪ Entry fee includes:
    • Equipment
    • Meals
    • One-night accommodations, two or three people per room

Slide 3

Description of Event

• May 2
  ▪ 7:00–8:00 a.m. Continental breakfast at Summerville Lake, launch site of event
  ▪ 8:30–9:30 a.m. Pick up equipment, meet assigned guide, and make plans for the event
  ▪ 10:00 Gauley River Rapids Challenge begins
  ▪ 12:00–1:00 p.m. Completion of Segment 1; time recorded
  ▪ 1:30 p.m. Barbecue lunch

Slide 4

Description of Event

• May 2 continued
  ▪ 3:00 p.m. Begin Segment 2 of Challenge
  ▪ 5:00–6:00 p.m. Completion of Segment 2; time recorded
  ▪ 7:00 p.m. Dinner at lodge; daily prizes awarded
• May 3
  ▪ 7:00–8:00 a.m. Continental breakfast at lodge
  ▪ 8:30 a.m. Begin Segment 3 of Challenge
  ▪ 10:30–11:30 a.m. Completion of Segment 3; time recorded

Slide 5

Description of Event

• May 3 continued
  ▪ 12:00 p.m. Box lunch
  ▪ 1:30 p.m. Begin Segment 4 (last segment) of Challenge
  ▪ 3:30–4:30 p.m. Completion of Segment 4
  ▪ 5:00 p.m. Barbecue and awards ceremony
  ▪ 6:30 p.m. End of Challenge, ground transportation back to launch site

7. Create Slide 6 using Figure 9-4 as a guide. This slide shows a drawing of the Gauley River. You can find maps of the Gauley on the Internet. Look on Web sites such as the National Park Service (http://www.nps.gov) or American Whitewater (http://www.americanwhitewater.org) and search for *Gauley River*. You can also use the **Gauley.bmp** image file located in your data files. Add text, lines, arrows, and symbols similar to those shown to indicate the route of the event.

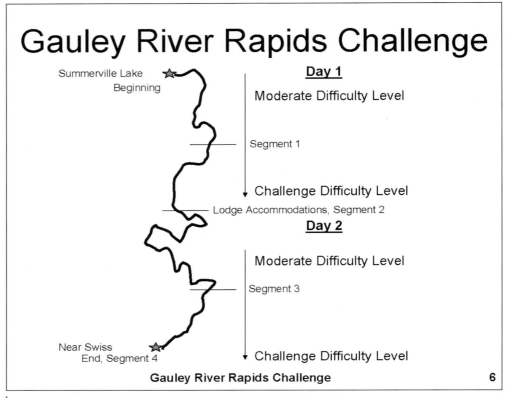

Figure 9-4 Sample Slide 6

8. Create Slide 7 using the title and text shown below. Include an appropriate image, such as a map of West Virginia or an "Information" icon. Make the image a hyperlink to an Internet location such as http://www.mapquest.com, at which you can obtain maps, driving directions, and mileage. Test the hyperlink to be sure it works properly.

Slide 7

Driving Directions

- Click on the image below to access:
  - Driving directions from your location to Sutton, WV
  - Maps
  - Mileage estimates

(Place the image here.)

9. Create Slide 8 using the title and text shown. Include an appropriate image to represent the event application. Make the image a hyperlink to the application you prepared in *Word* (**9-3 Application**). Test the hyperlink to be sure it works properly.

Slide 8

Application Form

- Click on the image below to access an application form
- Complete and print the form
- Mail the form to Star River Adventures

(Place the image here.)

Help Keywords

Transition
Add transitions
between slides

TEAMWORK

10. Check spelling and proofread the slides carefully. Make necessary adjustments to the font color, style, fill color, and so on to make the format consistent on all slides and to improve the appearance of your presentation. Add appropriate slide transitions.

11. Save the file as **9-3 Presentation.** Ask a classmate to review your presentation as you review his or her presentation. Discuss any errors you find and share ideas for how to make the presentation better. Make changes as needed and save again using the same name.

12. Ask your teacher whether you should print the slides or submit your work electronically.

13. Open **9-3 Application** in *Word*. Make the clip art image in the application a hyperlink to the **9-3 Presentation** file. Save the file using the same name. Test the hyperlink to be sure it works properly.

Challenge: Create Application Web Page

Help Keywords

HTML
About creating a Web
page

1. Open the **9-3 Application** file you created for this job.

2. Save the file in HTML format so it can be displayed on a Web site. Name the file **9-3 Challenge Application.** Make the page title *Gauley River Rapids Challenge.*

3. Open the **9-3 Challenge Application** file in your Web browser and view the page. Test the link to the presentation to be sure it works properly.

4. Make changes to the file in *Word,* if needed, for an attractive Web page. For example, you might want to place the document in a table to control the width of the text display or add a background color to the page.

5. Print the **9-3 Challenge Application** Web page from your browser.

Job 9-4 Create Expense Report Template

Skills Applied

- Entering and editing text and numbers in cells
- Formatting cells
- Modifying alignment
- Merging cells
- Applying cell formats
- Creating and editing formulas using the Formula Bar
- Creating formulas using functions
- Entering a range within a formula by dragging
- Creating a workbook template

Once an employee returns from company-sponsored travel, that employee must submit required receipts (for airfare, hotel, registration, auto rental, taxi, and miscellaneous). Mr. Collins wants you to prepare a worksheet template to automate this form. The worksheet should be similar to the one shown in Figure 9-5 on page 157.

1. Open a new blank worksheet in *Excel*. Enter the three lines for the worksheet titles (company name and address) in bold as shown. Enter the name of the form, *Travel Expense Report*, in bold. Center the titles and the form name across all columns.

2. Enter the labels in Columns A and F as shown. Format cells that will hold the payee name and address, the date submitted, the department, and the reason for travel for text. Enter the column heads in Columns B through I. Apply bold and center the heads.

3. Format the range of cells used for the calendar dates for mm/dd/yy format.

4. Format the range of cells used for miles driven for a number with no decimals. Format the range of cells used for per diem hours for a number with two decimals. Format other cells in the Total Cost column, cells in the Totals row, and cells in the Summary section for currency with two decimal places and a dollar sign, as shown.

5. Format the cells that hold daily amounts and daily totals (B18:H39) for a number with two decimal places and the comma separator.

6. Enter a formula to find the reimbursement amount for mileage.

   Reimbursement = Miles Driven * .39.

7. For airfare, the employee will enter one amount on the flight out date. For auto rental, the employee will enter one amount on the date the auto is returned to the rental agency. Enter formulas to sum the daily totals for Transportation.

	A	B	C	D	E	F	G	H	I	J
1				STAR RIVER ADVENTURES						
2				205 Riverview Drive						
3				Sutton, WV 26601-1311						
4										
5				Travel Expense Report						
6										
7	Payee Name and Address:					Date Submitted:				
8						Department:				
9										
10										
11	Event or Reason for Travel:									
12										
13		Day 1	Day 2	Day 3	Day 4	Day 5	Day 6	Day 7	Total Cost	
14	Calendar Date									
15										
16	**Transportation**									
17	Miles Driven (personal auto)	0							0	
18	Reimbursement	0.00	0.00	0.00	0.00	0.00	0.00	0.00	$0.00	
19	Airfare	0.00							$0.00	
20	Auto Rental							0.00	$0.00	
21	Taxi	0.00							$0.00	
22	Other	0.00							$0.00	
23	Total Transportation	0.00	0.00	0.00	0.00	0.00	0.00	0.00	$0.00	
24										
25	**Lodging and Meals**									
26	Per Diem Hours	0.00	0.00	0.00	0.00	0.00	0.00	0.00	0.00	
27	Reimbursement	0.00	0.00	0.00	0.00	0.00	0.00	0.00	$0.00	
28	Hotel							0.00	$0.00	
29	Other	0.00							$0.00	
30	Total Lodging and Meals	0.00	0.00	0.00	0.00	0.00	0.00	0.00	$0.00	
31										
32	**Miscellaneous Expenses**									
33	Entertainment	0.00							$0.00	
34	Rentals	0.00							$0.00	
35	Phone or Fax	0.00							$0.00	
36	Copying and Printing	0.00							$0.00	
37	Registration	0.00							$0.00	
38	Other	0.00							$0.00	
39	Total Miscellaneous Expenses	0.00	0.00	0.00	0.00	0.00	0.00	0.00	$0.00	
40										
41	**Totals**	$0.00	$0.00	$0.00	$0.00	$0.00	$0.00	$0.00	$0.00	
42										
43	**Summary**									
44	Total Expenses		$0.00							
45	Advance Received	$0.00								
46	Airfare Paid in Advance	$0.00								
47	Other Expense Paid in Advance	$0.00								
48	Total Advance		$0.00							
49										
50	**Amount Due Employee**		$0.00							
51										
52										
53	Employee Signature					Date				
54										
55	Manager's Approval					Date				
56										

Figure 9-5 Travel Expense Form

8. Enter a formula to calculate the reimbursement amount for per diem hours. Reimbursement = (Per diem hours/24) * 42. For hotel, the employee will enter one amount on the day of checkout. Enter formulas to sum the daily totals for Personal Lodging and Meals.

9. Enter formulas to sum the daily totals for Miscellaneous Expenses.

10. Enter formulas to calculate the total expenses for each day in Row 41.

11. Enter formulas in appropriate cells in Column I to total each item and each category. Enter a formula in Cell I41 to sum the three expense categories.

12. In the Summary section, to find the Total Expenses amount, enter a formula to sum the totals for each day's expenses (B41:H41). This Total Expenses number should be equal to the total shown in Cell I41.

13. The advance amounts will come from the Request for Travel form. Enter a formula to sum the advance amounts to find the Total Advance. Enter a formula to subtract the Total Advance from the Total Expenses to find the Amount Due Employee.

14. Format cells above totals for a single underline, as shown in Figure 9-5. Format Cell C50 for a double underline. Enter the labels and underline cells as shown in Rows 53 and 55 for the signatures and dates.

15. Format the worksheet to print in portrait orientation, to be centered horizontally, and to fit on one page. Proofread the sheet carefully.

16. Save the worksheet as a template named **9-4 Expense Report Template.** Print the worksheet.

Thinking Critically

Sometimes the expenses for a trip are less than the amount planned. For example, an employee might be able to complete a trip in two days instead of three days, as planned. When this happens, the employee may owe the company money because the travel advance was issued for three days of travel.

1. How would you modify the travel expense report to show an amount an employee owes the company?

2. What formula would you use to compute the amount the employee owes?

Job 9-5 Process Travel Expense Report

Skills Applied

* Creating a workbook from a template
* Entering and editing text and numbers in cells

Employees can use the new travel expense template to prepare their expense reports. Sometimes, however, managers who are busy with other tasks may ask you to complete forms for them. You have received an email from Mr. Jackson, shown below. He asks that you prepare a travel expense form for him.

1. Open the **9-4 Travel Expense Template** you created earlier. Complete the form using the information Mr. Jackson provides in the email. Use April 30 as the date submitted. Use the current year in all dates. The payee name and address are:

   Mr. Robert Jackson
   440 Bluejay Drive
   Sutton, WV 26601-0440

2. Save the completed report as **9-5 Jackson Expense Report.** Print the report.

Email: Travel Expense Report	
From:	Robert Jackson
To:	Administrative Assistant
Date:	April 30
Subject:	Travel Expense Report

Please prepare a travel expense report for me. Details of my trip that you will need are given below. I received a travel advance of $396.20 before my trip.

* Event/reason for travel: Visit to an excursion company in Deep Creek, PA.
* My travel dates were April 24, 25, and 26.
* My mileage for April 24 was 325 miles; April 25, 21 miles; and April 26, 310 miles.
* My total hotel bill at checkout on April 26 was $128.55.
* My per diem hours for April 24 were 15 hours; April 25, 24 hours; and April 26, 14 hours.
* For entertainment, I spent $18.50 on April 24 and $80.75 on April 25.
* On April 24, I spent $7.00 on copying.

Please send me a printed copy of the form. I will attach the receipts and get the appropriate signatures. Let me know if you have any questions. Thanks for your help.

Robert

Job 9-6 Correct Expense Report and Prepare Memo

Skills Applied

- Locating and opening existing workbooks
- Entering and editing text and numbers in cells
- Applying character and paragraph formats
- Setting and modifying tabs
- Exporting structured data from *Excel*

Mr. Collins has asked you to check an expense report submitted by Maria Inez. In looking over the form and comparing it to her Request for Travel form, you discover a discrepancy in the amounts for the registration fee that was paid in advance. Also, the registration fee amount is not listed in the Summary section of the report. You need to correct the form and write a memo to Ms. Inez about the error.

1. Open the data file **Inez Expense Report.** Refer to the file **9-2 Inez Travel Request** that you created earlier to find the amount paid for registration. Enter this amount in the appropriate cells on Ms. Inez's expense report. (Update the year portion of the calendar dates to the current year if needed.)

2. Save the updated worksheet as **9-6 Inez Updated Report.** Print the updated report.

3. Create a memo to Maria Inez from you dated May 3 of the current year. Use an appropriate subject line. See page 314 in the Reference Guide to review memo format.

4. Key the paragraphs below as the body of the memo.

> Ms. Inez, I found a discrepancy between your travel expense report dated May 2 and our records. Our records show an advance for (insert amount) was paid for the convention registration. Taking the advance into account changes the amount that is due to you to (insert amount), as shown below in the Summary portion of your updated travel expense report.
>
> I will route the updated report to Mr. Newland for his signature. Please send me the receipt for the convention registration to attach to your report.

5. Copy the Summary and Amount Due Employee data from the updated travel expense report into the memo. Save the memo as **9-6 Inez Memo.** Print the memo.

Help Keywords

Copy
  Copy *Excel* data and
  charts to *Word* or
  PowerPoint

Determining Prices for Trip Packages

Objectives

- ☐ Apply advanced formatting
- ☐ Work with multiple workbook sheets
- ☐ Insert clip art
- ☐ Use Goal Seek
- ☐ Work with the Scenario feature
- ☐ Display only the result of a formula in a cell
- ☐ Filter lists
- ☐ Paste special a worksheet object in a word processing document
- ☐ Download and link to videos

Summary of *Microsoft Office* Skills

- ✔ Insert, delete, and move cells
- ✔ Enter and edit cell data, including text, numbers, and formulas
- ✔ Check spelling
- ✔ Work with a subset of data by filtering lists
- ✔ Manage workbook files and folders
- ✔ Save workbooks using different names and file formats
- ✔ Apply and modify cell formats
- ✔ Modify row and column settings
- ✔ Apply styles
- ✔ Modify Page Setup options for worksheets
- ✔ Preview and print worksheets and workbooks
- ✔ Insert and delete worksheets
- ✔ Modify worksheet names and positions
- ✔ Create and revise formulas
- ✔ Create, modify, and position graphics
- ✔ Create and display scenarios
- ✔ Export data from *Excel*
- ✔ Insert, modify, and move text and symbols
- ✔ Insert, view, and edit comments
- ✔ Apply bullet format to paragraphs
- ✔ Modify document layout and Page Setup options
- ✔ Create presentations
- ✔ Insert, format, and modify text
- ✔ Add tables, charts, and clip art to slides
- ✔ Apply animation schemes
- ✔ Apply slide transitions
- ✔ Add links to a presentation
- ✔ Preview and print slide handouts
- ✔ Import *Excel* charts to slides
- ✔ Deliver presentations
- ✔ Manage files and folders for presentations

Job 10-1 Create Trip Package Cost Worksheet

Skills Applied

- Entering and editing text and numbers in cells
- Merging cells
- Formatting cells
- Applying cell formats and styles
- Creating and editing formulas using the Formula Bar
- Adding functions to formulas
- Using references (absolute and relative)
- Creating, modifying, and positioning graphics

management cost: overhead; indirect costs associated with a product or service

direct cost: expenses that can be associated with a trip, such as equipment and food

Help Keywords

Clip art
  About drawing objects and pictures

Mr. Collins has given you information about a new excursion Star River Adventures plans to offer. He has estimated some of the costs. He asks you to prepare a worksheet to automate most of the process of determining prices for the trip package.

Guides are included in the number of participants when determining the costs for equipment, meals, and transportation for a trip. Each raft has one guide. A certain amount of work is required of the office staff and for expenses such as advertising for each trip. This cost is figured into the total cost of the trip and is called management cost. Management cost is estimated to be 38 percent of direct costs of the trip.

1. Open a new blank workbook. Enter the labels as shown in Figure 10-1 on page 163. Apply bold as shown. Insert clip art that represents rafting. Insert row shading as shown.

2. Enter the values shown in Columns C and D.

3. Format the cells to hold values or formulas as follows:
   - Format Number of rafts, Individuals per raft, and Participants as number, no decimals.
   - Format cost amounts in Column D for equipment, meals, transportation, and guides as number, two decimals.
   - Format all cells in the Total column (F) except Profit margin percent as number, two decimals.
   - For the Profit margin percent, apply percent style.

4. Enter formulas in cells:
   - Participants (all categories except for Guides) = Number of rafts * Individuals per raft
   - Participants for Guides category = Number of rafts
   - Total amounts for equipment, meals, transportation, and guides = Participants * Cost amount
   - Subtotal = SUM of above amounts in the Total column
   - Management cost = Subtotal * Management cost percent (38%)
   - Total cost = Subtotal + Management costs
   - Cost per person = Total costs / Number of participants (not including guides)

5. You will add formulas for Total income, Profit margin percent, and Profit margin amount in a later job.

6. Save your completed worksheet as **10-1 Pricing.**

	A	B	C	D	E	F
1		STAR RIVER ADVENTURES				
2		205 Riverview Drive				
3		Sutton, WV 26601-1311				
4					Place Rafting Image Here	
5	**Excursion:**	New River Discovery				
6	**Difficulty level:**	Level I–III rapids, small but exciting				
7	**Location:**	Scenic New River Gorge				
8	**Restrictions:**	Ages 6 to adult, children under the age of 12 must be accompanied by an adult				
9	**Length of trip:**	Approximately 6 hours				
10	**Trip includes:**					
11		Equipment (life jacket, helmet, paddle)				
12		Transportation to and from river				
13		Breakfast rolls and drinks (juice, coffee, tea, milk)				
14		Raft guide				
15		Riverside barbecue lunch				
16		Refreshments at end of excursion				
17						
18	**Projected costs:**					
19		Number of rafts (4–10)		6		
20		Individuals per raft (4–9 including guide)		8		
21			**Cost Amount**	**Participants**		**Total**
22		Life jacket	1.50	48		72.00
23		Helmet	1.50	48		72.00
24		Paddle	1.00	48		48.00
25		Breakfast	2.50	48		120.00
26		Lunch	7.00	48		336.00
27		Refreshments	2.50	48		120.00
28		Transportation	8.50	48		408.00
29		Guides (each per day)	52.00	6		312.00
30		**Subtotal**				1,488.00
31		Management cost	38%			565.44
32		**Total cost**				2,053.44
33		**Cost per person**				48.89
34		**Total income**				
35		**Profit margin percent**				
36		**Profit margin amount**				
37						
38						

Figure 10-1 Trip Cost Worksheet

Job 10-2 Price Trips Using Goal Seek

Skills Applied

- Locating and opening an existing workbook
- Entering and editing text and numbers in cells
- Creating and editing formulas using the Formula Bar
- Inserting worksheets in a workbook
- Formatting worksheet tabs
- Adding footers to worksheets

Goal Seek: a form of *what-if* analysis in which you know the desired result of a formula, but not the input value

Earlier you determined the cost per person for the trip package. The way Star River Adventures makes a profit is by charging its customers an amount larger than the cost of an excursion (cost per person). Your job will be to determine how much we must charge each customer to make a certain amount of profit. You could do this by trying different amounts in the cost per person cell until you discover an amount that generates the desired profit, but that would be a long process. The easiest way is to use the Goal Seek function.

1. Open **10-1 Pricing** that you created earlier. Name the sheet with your cost figures *Cost*.

2. Enter formulas for total income, profit margin percent, and profit margin amount.

   - Total income = Cost per person * Number of participants (not including guides)
   - Profit margin percent = Total income − Total costs / Total income
   - Profit margin amount = Total income − Total cost

3. Insert a footer on the Cost sheet that contains the sheet name, *Confidential*, and the page number.

4. Make copies of the Cost sheet. Rename the new sheets *5% Profit, 10% Profit, 15% Profit, 20% Profit,* and *25% Profit.*

5. On the 5% Profit sheet, change the cell containing the Cost per person formula from a formula to its value (the result of the formula).

6. Use the Goal Seek feature to determine the price per person that must be charged to make a 5% profit. See Figure 10-2.

   - Click in the Profit margin percent cell (F35).
   - Choose *Goal Seek* from the Tools menu.
   - Enter *5%* in the To value box.
   - Enter *F33* (Cost per person) in the By changing cell box.
   - Click *OK*.

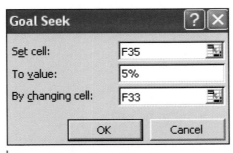

Figure 10-2 Goal Seek Dialog Box

7. The value in Cell F33 now represents the price the company must charge to make a 5% profit. Change the label in Cell B33 to Price per person.

8. Repeat Steps 4 through 6 for the sheets named 10% Profit, 15% Profit, 20% Profit, and 25% Profit.

9. Save your completed workbook as **10-2 Pricing.**

10. Compare your worksheet results with those of a classmate. Did you find the same amounts for Price per person and Profit margin amount? If not, examine your formulas to determine how they differ. Make changes to your worksheets if needed.

11. Print a copy of each worksheet. Each sheet should be formatted to fit on one page.

Job 10-3 Create Profit Margin Report

Skills Applied

- Locating and opening an existing workbook
- Exporting data from *Excel*
- Using copy and paste special
- Applying paragraph styles
- Modifying page margins
- Inserting page numbers
- Applying bullets
- Viewing and editing comments

Success Tips

Select *Markup* from the View menu to see the changes and comments Mr. Collins has made in the document if they are not already visible.

Help Keywords

Select
   Select sheets

Now that you have completed the analysis requested by Mr. Collins, you need to prepare a report for him that he can share with other personnel. The report will describe the excursion, summarize costs, and present various options for price per customer for the trip.

1. Open the data file **Pricing Report.** This file contains Mr. Collins's draft of the report. Review unbound format in the Reference Guide on pages 319–321. Prepare a two-page unbound report using the information in the **Pricing Report** file.

2. Apply Title style to the report title. Apply Heading 1 style to the side headings. Accept the changes Mr. Collins has made to the draft. Read and follow the directions in his comments. Delete the comments after reading them.

3. Open the **10-2 Pricing** workbook. Save the workbook as **10-3 Pricing.** Change the setup of the worksheets to make more attractive tables for the report. Hold down the CTRL key and click the sheet tabs for 5% Profit, 10% Profit, 15% Profit, 20% Profit, and 25% Profit to select all of these sheets.

4. Select Cells B33:36. Move these labels to Cells D33:36. With the same five sheets still selected, change the text font and size of Cells D33:F36 to match the font and size used in the report. Change the format of Cells F33, F34, and F36 to currency, two decimals, dollar sign. Verify that changes were made to all five sheets. Save the worksheet.

5. Use the Copy and Paste Special features to place sections of the workbook **10-3 Pricing** in the report as Mr. Collins directs in the report draft. Align the objects you paste at the center. Leave one blank line between the objects.

6. Insert a page number on page 2. Insert a hard page break, if needed, to break the pages at an appropriate location. Edit each worksheet section in the report to remove bold from the labels.

7. Save the report as **10-3 Pricing Report.** Print the report.

Job 10-4 Work with Scenarios

Skills Applied

- Locating and opening existing workbooks
- Creating scenarios
- Repositioning worksheets in a workbook
- Deleting worksheets from a workbook

Scenario: the *Excel* command that performs a type of *what-if* analysis similar to Goal Seek

Help Keywords

Scenario
   Create a scenario

Software Review

To create a scenario:

- Select *Scenarios* from the Tools menu. Click *Add*.

- Enter a name for the scenario.

- In the Changing cells box, enter the references for the cells you want to change.

- Under Protection, select the options you want.

- Click *OK*.

- In the Scenario Values dialog box, type the value you want for the changing cell.

- Click *OK*.

Mr. Collins was very pleased with the pricing report you prepared. After reading the report, he decides that he needs more information. He wants to know the amount of profit Star River Adventures would make from the New River Discovery excursion if the number of rafts included in a trip were varied. Eight people per raft, including the guide, will be required. You will find this information by using *Excel's* Scenario feature.

1. Open the **10-3 Pricing** file that you created earlier. Go to the 5% Profit worksheet.

2. Create the first scenario.

   - Click on the cell that shows the number of rafts.
   - Select the *Scenario* command and add a new scenario named *Four Rafts*.
   - Enter the cell reference for the number of rafts (D19) if not already shown.
   - Do not select any options under Protection. Click *OK*.

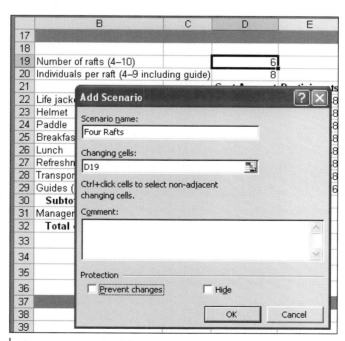

Figure 10-3 Scenario Dialog Box

3. In the Scenario Values dialog box, enter *4*. Click *OK*.

4. In the Scenario Manager dialog box, select *Show*. Your worksheet should be updated to show the profit based on four rafts as shown in Figure 10-4. Save your workbook as **10-4 Pricing.**

Number of rafts (4–10)		4	
Individuals per raft (4–9 including guide)		8	
		Price per person	$51.46
		Total income	$1,440.89
		Profit margin percent	5%
		Profit margin amount	$71.93

Figure 10-4 Four Rafts Scenario

Software Review

To create a scenario summary:

- Select *Scenarios* from the Tools menu.
- Select *Summary*.
- Select *Scenario Summary*.
- Enter or confirm the cells in the Result cells box.
- Click *OK*.

TEAMWORK

5. Create scenarios based on five, six, seven, eight, nine, and ten rafts. Save the worksheet using the same name.

6. Create a scenario summary. Your sheet should look similar to Figure 10-5. Move the Scenario Summary sheet to place it after the 25% Profit sheet.

7. Go to the 25% Profit sheet. Complete scenarios to determine the amount of profit based on the number of rafts launched, 4 to 10. Give each scenario a different name than those already used, such as *4 Rafts.*

8. Create a scenario summary for the 25% Profit sheet. The new sheet will be named *Scenario Summary 2*. Move this sheet to the end of the sheets you have created. Delete any blank sheets from the workbook. Save your workbook again using the same name. Print the two scenario summary sheets in landscape to fit on one page each.

9. Compare your two scenario summary sheets to those of a classmate. If your results differ, determine which is correct. Make adjustments to your worksheet if needed.

Scenario Summary								
	Current Values:	Four Rafts	Five Rafts	Six Rafts	Seven Rafts	Eight Rafts	Nine Rafts	Ten Rafts
Changing Cells:								
$D$19	4	4	5	6	7	8	9	10
Result Cells:								
$F$35	5%	5%	5%	5%	5%	5%	5%	5%
$F$36	$71.93	$71.93	$89.92	$107.90	$125.88	$143.86	$161.85	$179.83

Notes: Current Values column represents values of changing cells at time Scenario Summary Report was created. Changing cells for each scenario are highlighted in gray.

Figure 10-5 Scenario Summary Sheet

Job 10-5 Prepare Multimedia Presentation

Skills Applied

- Creating presentations from a blank presentation
- Adding text to slides
- Creating tables on slides
- Adding clip art images to slides
- Applying an animation scheme
- Applying transition effects
- Adding hyperlinks to slides
- Inserting *Excel* worksheets on slides
- Running slide shows
- Printing handouts

Mr. Collins has asked you to prepare a presentation about the New River Discovery excursion. This presentation will be used to introduce the new trip to company personnel. It can be modified later to show to travel agencies that may be able to assist in recruiting potential customers.

1. In *Word*, open the data file **New River Trip.** Print this file, which contains content and notes for the slides.

2. Open a new blank presentation in *PowerPoint*. Enter the text for each slide as shown on New River Trip document. Create a table for Slide 7 as shown.

3. Format Slide 1 as a title slide for the presentation. Format Slides 2 through 5 for title and text (bulleted list). Format Slides 6 and 7 for title only.

4. On Slide 1, use an entrance effect to have the lines of text appear on the screen. Select a suitable slide transition and transition to the next slide automatically after five seconds. Apply the same transition to the other slides, but do not transition automatically.

5. Use an appropriate background for all of the slides or apply a template design to all of the slides. Choose an appropriate color scheme.

6. Select appropriate clip art or motion clips or use the drawing tools or WordArt to create art that reflects the theme of the show. Place graphics on Slides 1 and 2 and on other slides, as desired, for an attractive and interesting presentation.

7. On Slide 6, paste the worksheet section from **10-4 Pricing** as directed.

8. Go to Slide 2. Create a menu using the bulleted items to hyperlink to the appropriate slides and to exit the slide show. (Use Action Settings to create a hyperlink that will exit the slide show.)

9. Once the hyperlinks are created, you may wish to change the color of the text used for the hyperlinks to a color that displays clearly. You can accomplish this by editing the color schemes for accents and hyperlinks.

10. Add action buttons to Slides 3 through 7. On Slides 3 through 6, place an action button that takes the user to the next slide. On Slides 3 through 7, place an action button that takes the user to the menu (Slide 2).

Help Keywords

Transitions
  Add transitions
  between slides

Software Review

To insert an action button on a slide:

- Select the slide you want to place a button on.

- Select *Action Buttons* from the Slide Show menu.

- Select the button you want.

- Click the slide.

- Select *Hyperlink to*.

- Select *OK* to accept the proposed hyperlink or click the arrow and select the link you want.

Help Keywords

Hyperlink
    Insert an action button

11. Save the show as **10-5 New River Discovery Show.** Run the slide show to test the links and to determine whether adjustments are needed. Make changes to fonts, colors, graphics, and so on, as needed, for an attractive presentation.

12. Print handouts four per page using grayscale.

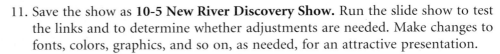

Challenge: Add Link to a Rafting Video

1. Open the **10-5 New River Discovery Show** that you created earlier.

2. On Slide 2, add a menu option: Rafting Video.

3. Do one of the following:

   • Create a menu link to a rafting video stored on your local hard drive or network.
   • Create a menu link to a Web site that has rafting videos available for viewing. (You may need to search the Internet to find sites about rafting.)

4. Save your presentation as **10-5 Challenge Show.**

Job 10-6 Alphabetize and Filter Lists

Skills Applied

- Locating and opening existing workbooks
- Filtering lists using AutoFilter
- Setting Page Setup Options for printing
- Inserting worksheets into a workbook

The response to the Gauley River Rapids Challenge has been very good. Nearly one hundred individuals have entered the competition, many more than expected. Mr. Collins has asked that you assist in getting some of the paperwork ready for the competition. All participants have provided their names and telephone numbers. Only the team leader's address was recorded. The team leader was responsible for paying the $250 entry fee.

Task 1 Sort the List

Help Keywords

Sort
  Sort a list

1. Open the data file **Gauley List.** This worksheet contains data for the participants.

2. Sort the records in alphabetic order based on participants' names. Be sure to keep the entire record for each individual together. Indicate that you have a header row so the headings will not be sorted with the data.

3. Name the sheet tab *By Name*. Make a copy of the sheet. Rename the sheet *By Team*.

4. On the By Team sheet, sort the list first by Team Number and then by Name. Insert blank rows between teams. Apply a pattern in the blank rows that separate teams.

5. Adjust Page Setup options so the By Team sheet will print on two pages in portrait orientation. Print the By Team worksheet. Save your workbook as **10-6 Gauley List.**

Task 2 Filter the List

Mr. Collins has requested a list that shows just the team leaders and their information. He also wants a list of any teams that have not paid the full registration fee.

1. Open the **10-6 Gauley List** worksheet that you created earlier. Make a copy of the By Name sheet. Name the new sheet *Leaders*.

2. Filter the Leaders sheet to display only records for team leaders. Save the workbook using the same name.

3. Make a copy of the Leaders sheet. Name the new sheet *Fee*.

Filter: the feature used to display a subset of data based on criteria

4. Go to the Fee sheet. Create a custom filter that will show records where the Registration Fee does not equal 250. See Figure 10-6.

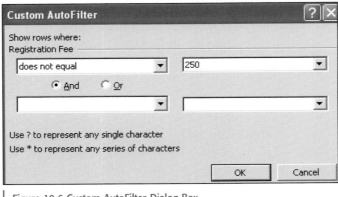

Figure 10-6 Custom AutoFilter Dialog Box

5. Save the workbook using the same name. Print the Leaders and the Fee sheets formatted to fit on one page each.

Challenge: Filter Using Wild Cards

Mr. Collins asks that you print a list showing records for teams from outside West Virginia.

1. Open the **10-6 Gauley List** file that you created earlier.

2. Make a copy of the Leader sheet. Name the new sheet *Outside WV*.

3. Create a custom filter that will find records that do not contain WV in the Address field. You will need to use wildcards in your filter criteria.

4. Save the workbook as **10-6 Gauley List Challenge.** Print the Outside WV sheet.

Performing Statistical Analyses

Objectives

- ☐ Format cells—borders, font, alignment, conditional formatting
- ☐ Use Page Setup options
- ☐ Work with named ranges
- ☐ Create formulas with functions
- ☐ Create charts
- ☐ Create memos and reports with title pages and table of contents
- ☐ Create and format tables
- ☐ Import data from *Excel* into *Word*

Summary of *Microsoft Office* Skills

- ✔ Insert, delete, and move cells
- ✔ Enter and edit cell data, including text, numbers, and formulas
- ✔ Check spelling
- ✔ Manage workbook files and folders
- ✔ Save workbooks using different names and file formats
- ✔ Apply and modify cell formats
- ✔ Modify row and column settings
- ✔ Modify row and column formats
- ✔ Modify Page Setup options for worksheets
- ✔ Preview and print worksheets and workbooks
- ✔ Insert and delete worksheets
- ✔ Modify worksheet names and positions
- ✔ Use statistical, date and time, financial, and logical functions in formulas
- ✔ Create, modify, position, and print charts
- ✔ Use named ranges in formulas

- ✔ Export data from *Excel*
- ✔ Modify paragraph formats
- ✔ Create and modify tables
- ✔ Apply bullet, outline, and number formats to paragraphs
- ✔ Control pagination
- ✔ Create document table of contents
- ✔ Modify document layout and Page Setup options
- ✔ Insert, modify, and move text and symbols

ST★R
River
Adventures

Job 11-1 Design Customer Evaluation Form

Skills Applied

- Applying paragraph formats
- Creating and modifying tables
- Modifying table borders and shading
- Modifying cell formats

The staff at Star River Adventures believes that customers are the company's most important asset. To keep the excellent reputation the company has earned throughout the years, the company seeks feedback from its customers and modifies operations when necessary.

At the end of each excursion, participants are asked to complete a short evaluation form. These forms are then given to the owner, Tommy Newland. He reviews them and takes whatever action he thinks is necessary.

Mr. Newland thinks that his brief review of these forms does not give him the full potential of this important source of customer feedback. He wants a more in-depth analysis that will aid him in making important management decisions.

Mr. Collins, the manager of the Finance and Accounting Department, has been asked to redesign this form to make it more user-friendly. In the future, Mr. Collins will receive these forms after each excursion. He will analyze them and provide a report to Mr. Newland. Mr. Collins has made some changes to the form to make it easier for the participants to complete and for him to analyze the data. He has asked you to update the document incorporating these changes.

1. In *Word*, open and print the data file **Evaluation Form.** This file contains the evaluation form currently used.

2. Edit the directions to read:

   > **Directions:** Circle the number that best reflects your impression of our staff and the service you received from Star River Adventures.

3. Leave the Raft Number and Excursion line as is. Delete the numbered list. Enter the following table that contains revised questions and rating numbers. Align question numbers at the right. Enter the additional instructions above the numbers, as shown. Center the text over the numbers.

Help Keywords

Table
   Create a table

		Circle One Number 1 = poorest rating and 5 = best rating				
1.	Was the process of booking your excursion easy and convenient?	1	2	3	4	5
2.	Was your excursion guide friendly and competent?	1	2	3	4	5
3.	Was the cost of your excursion a good value?	1	2	3	4	5
4.	Was the appropriate equipment provided, and was the equipment in good condition?	1	2	3	4	5
5.	Was the food provided as ordered and of good quality?	1	2	3	4	5
6.	How would you rate the overall services provided by the staff of SRA?	1	2	3	4	5
7.	How would you rate your overall excursion experience?	1	2	3	4	5
8.	How would you rate the overall safety of the excursion?	1	2	3	4	5
9.	Was the ground transportation comfortable and convenient?	1	2	3	4	5
10.	Did your excursion progress according to the planned time schedule?	1	2	3	4	5

Help Keywords

Cell
  Change the position of
  text in a table

4. The table shows cell borders to help you set up the table. Do not display cell borders in your document. Align the text and numbers as shown in the sample table. Leave the Comments section at the bottom of the document.

5. Save the document as **11-1 Evaluation Form.** Print the document.

Job 11-2 Create Data Entry Worksheet

Skills Applied

- Entering and editing text and numbers in cells
- Formatting cells
- Merging cells
- Freezing and unfreezing rows and columns
- Modifying row height and column width
- Checking spelling on worksheets
- Modifying worksheet orientation and printing options

The evaluation form you designed in Job 11-1 will be completed by each participant at the end of each excursion. The data on these forms will be entered so that analyses can be performed. Mr. Collins asks you to prepare a worksheet that can be used to enter the data.

1. Print **11-1 Evaluation Form** if you have not already done so. Beginning in A1 of a new *Excel* worksheet, enter the three-line main heading as shown on the evaluation form. Center this heading across columns after you have completed the rest of the worksheet. Bold the company name.

2. Enter the label *Excursion:* in A5 in bold. Enter the heading *Questions* in A6 in bold. You will center this heading across columns later.

3. Enter column headings in cells C7 through L7 that are abbreviated forms of the questions on the evaluation form. See Figure 11-1 on page 177 for examples. For the headings, use initial caps for all important words, change the font size to 9 point, wrap text within the cells, change cell widths, align text with a 90 degree orientation, and center text within the column.

4. Enter the labels in Row 8 in bold. Enter *Participant* in A8, *Raft Number* in B8, and *Comments* in M8. Increase the width of the Comments column to allow for the entry of short comments. Format the cells in the column to have the text wrap.

5. Enter the numbers 1 through 10 in cells C8:L8. Center each number within the cell and bold the numbers. Place a single line border at the bottom of cells A8 through M8. Center the *Questions* label across the columns used to designate questions 1 through 10.

6. Freeze panes so labels remain on the screen as you scroll through entries. Check the spelling.

7. Use Page Setup to format this worksheet for printing 1 page wide by 2 pages tall in landscape orientation. Print the worksheet. Save the worksheet as **11-2 Evaluation Analysis.**

	A	B	C	D	E	F	G	H	I	J	K	L	M
1							STAR RIVER ADVENTURES						
2							205 Riverview Drive						
3							Sutton, WV 26601-1311						
4													
5	Excursion:												
6							Questions						
7			1 Process of Booking Excursion	2 Your Excursion Guide	3 Cost of Your Excursion	4 Equipment Provided	5 Food Provided	6 Services Provided by the Staff of SRA	7 Excursion Experience	8 Safety of Excursion	9 Ground Transportation	10 Time Schedule	
8	Participant	Raft Number											Comments
9													

Figure 11-1 Evaluation Worksheet

Job 11-3 Analyze Feedback Data

Skills Applied

- Locating and opening existing workbooks
- Entering and editing text and numbers in cells
- Formatting cells
- Merging cells
- Freezing and unfreezing rows and columns
- Formatting worksheet tabs
- Naming ranges and using named ranges in formulas
- Inserting columns
- Creating formulas using functions

In Job 11-2, you prepared the data entry sheet for analyzing feedback from excursions. In this job, you will enter that data into your worksheet and analyze the data. Ms. Forde has entered the raw data into a worksheet named **New River Excursion Data.**

1. Open the file **11-2 Evaluation Analysis** that you created earlier.

2. Open the **New River Excursion Data** data file. Copy the data from this worksheet into your **11-2 Evaluation Analysis** worksheet. Copy only the range of data you need. Be sure to enter the name of the excursion and the date in the appropriate cell. Close the **New River Excursion Data** file.

3. Rename the sheet *New River*. Save your workbook as **11-3 New River Data.**

4. Name the range that represents the responses to each question 1 through 10. For example, Question 1 is represented by the range C9:C50. Name this range *Question1*. The dialog box in Figure 11-2 shows examples of the named ranges.

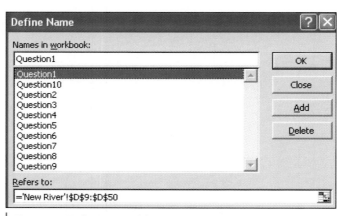

Figure 11-2 Define Name Dialog Box

5. Insert a new column to the right of Column A. Move the title of the excursion back to Column B.

6. Leave one blank row after the data and enter the label *Basic Analyses* in Column A.

7. Unfreeze the panes. Freeze the panes again below the column labels and after Column B.

8. Enter these labels in bold in Columns A and B below your data:

Basic Analyses	Count
	Average
	Max
	Min
	Mode

mode: the most frequently occurring, or repetitive, value in a range of data

9. Calculate the Count, Average, Max, Min, and Mode for each question. Use the named ranges you created in your formulas. Use one decimal place for the average. Figure 11-3 shows the use of the MAX function for Question 1.

10. Save your workbook again using the same name. Print the worksheet.

11. Compare your results with those of a classmate. If your results differ, examine your formulas and data. Make corrections if needed. The results for the first question are Count, 42; Average, 4.5; Max, 5; Min, 3; and Mode, 5.

TEAMWORK

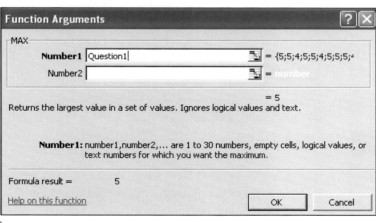

Figure 11-3 Function Arguments Dialog Box

Job 11-4 Refine and Expand Data Analyses

Skills Applied

- Locating and opening existing workbooks
- Inserting worksheets in a workbook
- Formatting worksheet tabs
- Repositioning worksheets in a workbook
- Freezing and unfreezing rows and columns
- Deleting selected cells
- Modifying worksheet orientation

Mr. Newland was very pleased with the worksheet you prepared and the initial analyses you performed. When scanning the raw data, he noticed low evaluations of one or two of the guides and only an average rating of the food services. He wants to know how:

- Guides are evaluated by the customers on the raft assigned to each guide.
- Evaluations of guides compare to one another.
- The individuals on each raft rate the services.

He hopes to use this information to identify some trends.

The guides for the New River Excursion were as follows:

Raft Number	Guide
1	Carson Forde
2	Josh Farley
3	Nicholas Goetze
4	Robin Nichols
5	Heather Goldman
6	Sidney Miller
7	Laura Robinson

Software Review

To sort data in a worksheet:

- Select the data to be sorted.
- Select *Sort* from the Data menu.
- Select an option under Sort by.
- Indicate whether the selection includes a header row.
- Click *OK*.

1. Open the file **11-3 New River Data** that you created earlier. Create a copy of the New River sheet. Rename the sheet *Carson Forde*, the name of the guide on Raft 1. Unfreeze the panes.

2. Sort the data in Rows 9 through 50 by Column C, Raft Number.

3. Make a copy of the Carson Forde worksheet. Rename the sheet *Josh Farley*. Repeat this procedure to create a sheet for each guide.

4. On the Carson Forde sheet, delete the rows that hold data for the other guides (Rows 15 through 50, Rafts 2 through 7). Do not delete the Basic Analyses data rows. The range for each question will be updated to reflect the reduced number of rows. The Basic Analyses results will also be updated.

5. Repeat Step 4 for each guide. Arrange the sheets representing guides in alphabetic order.

6. Use Page Setup to format the sheet for each guide to fit on one page in landscape orientation. A sample worksheet for a guide is shown in Figure 11-4.

7. Save the workbook as **11-4 New River Data.** Print the worksheet for each guide.

8. Compare your worksheets for the guides with those of a classmate. If the sheets differ, examine the data and formulas to determine why they differ. Make corrections to your workbook if needed.

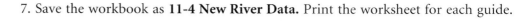

TEAMWORK

	A	B	C	D	E	F	G	H	I	J	K	L	M	N
1							STAR RIVER ADVENTURES							
2							205 Riverview Drive							
3							Sutton, WV 26601-1311							
4														
5	Excursion:	New River, June 9												
6							Questions							
7	Participant		Raft Number	Process of Booking Excursion 1	Your Excursion Guide 2	Cost of Your Excursion 3	Equipment Provided 4	Food Provided 5	Services Provided by the Staff of SRA 6	Excursion Experience 7	Safety of Excursion 8	Ground Transportation 9	Time Schedule 10	Comments
9	1		7	5	2	4	4	4	4	2	5	4	5	Guide was not friendly.
10	10		7	4	3	5	5	4	5	3	5	4	5	The guide didn't seem to like children.
11	17		7	5	3	4	4	4	4	3	5	4	4	The guide wasn't very friendly.
12	28		7	5	3	5	5	4	5	4	5	4	5	
13	35		7	4	2	4	4	3	4	2	4	3	4	The guide was terrible.
14	36		7	4	3	5	4	4	5	3	5	4	4	
15														
16	Basic Analyses	Count		6	6	6	6	6	6	6	6	6	6	
17		Average		4.5	2.7	4.5	4.3	3.8	4.5	2.8	4.8	3.8	4.5	
18		Max		5	3	5	5	4	5	4	5	4	5	
19		Min		4	2	4	4	3	4	2	4	3	4	
20		Mode		5	3	4	4	4	4	3	5	4	5	
21														

Figure 11-4 Guide Worksheet

Job 11-5 Add Conditional Formatting and Create Charts

Skills Applied

- Locating and opening existing workbooks
- Entering and editing text and numbers in cells
- Formatting cells
- Inserting worksheets and formatting worksheet tabs
- Creating and printing charts
- Hiding rows and columns in a worksheet

Task 1 Create Guide Evaluation Sheets

Mr. Newland was very pleased with the worksheets you prepared for the guides. He would like you to make a few additional changes.

1. Open the **11-4 New River Data** workbook that you created earlier.
2. Go to the Josh Farley worksheet. In A4, key *Guide:* in bold. In B4, key *Josh Farley*. Repeat this process, using the appropriate guide name, on all guide sheets.
3. Go to the Josh Farley worksheet. Add conditional formatting to the cells containing the averages for each question. Show any value less than 3 in italic and in red. Show any value greater than 4.5 in italic and in blue. Figure 11-5 shows a sample entry for conditional formatting. Repeat this process for each guide sheet.
4. Save the file as **11-5 New River Data.**

Help Keywords

Condition
  Add, change, or
  remove conditional
  formats

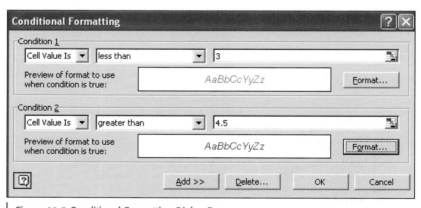

Figure 11-5 Conditional Formatting Dialog Box

Task 2 Create Guide Evaluation Chart

1. Open the **11-5 New River Data** workbook that you created earlier. Add a new sheet and name the sheet *Guide Evaluation*.
2. Enter the data shown on page 183. Use conditional formatting for the average evaluations using the same criteria as in Task 1, Step 3.

NEW RIVER EXCURSION	
Guide Evaluation	
Guide Name	**Average Evaluation**
Josh Farley	3.8
Carson Forde	*4.8*
Nicholas Goetze	4.2
Heather Goldman	4.0
Sidney Miller	*5.0*
Robin Nichols	*2.8*
Laura Robinson	*2.7*

Help Keywords

Chart
  Create a chart

3. Use the information in this worksheet as the basis for creating a 3-D column chart similar to the one shown in Figure 11-6. Format the worksheet attractively to fit on one printed page in portrait orientation. Print the worksheet containing the chart.

4. Save the workbook using the same name.

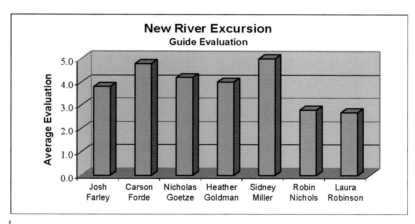

Figure 11-6 Guide Evaluation Chart

Task 3 Create Average Responses Chart

1. Make a copy of the New River worksheet and rename the sheet *Average Responses*.

2. Hide Columns C and N. Hide Rows 9 through 52. The average for each question should now appear below the question number.

3. Create a 3-D column chart. Chart the question numbers and the average scores for questions. Answer the Thinking Critically questions on page 184 to help you plan the chart design.

4. Use *New River Excursion* for the chart title. Add a subtitle for the chart, *June 9.* For the Category axis title, use *Question.* For the Value axis title, use *Average Responses.* Your chart should look similar to Figure 11-7 on page 184.

5. Format the worksheet attractively to fit on one page in portrait orientation. Print the worksheet, including the chart. Save the workbook as **11-5 New River Data.**

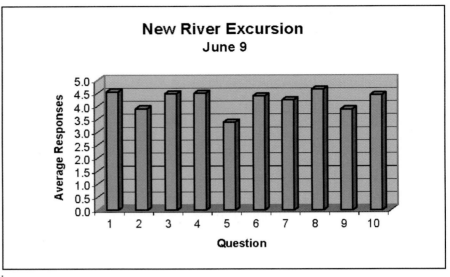

Figure 11-7 Average Responses Chart

Thinking Critically

1. Describe how to align text in the Value axis title for vertical alignment (as shown in Figure 11-7).

2. What range of cells do you need to select to create the chart for Job 11-5, Task 3 (shown in Figure 11-7)?

Job 11-6 Create Integrated Report

Skills Applied

- Applying paragraph formats
- Applying bullets and numbering
- Creating and modifying tables
- Setting line and page breaks
- Inserting a table of contents
- Exporting structured data from *Excel*
- Copying and pasting text
- Inserting page numbers
- Creating formulas using functions
- Entering and editing text and numbers in cells

Mr. Newland wants you to prepare a report that highlights the overall performance of Star River Adventures as evaluated by customers on the New River Excursion. He has given you general guidelines for the report.

1. Open the data file **Evaluation Report.** Read Mr. Newland's instructions regarding what to include in the report under each report heading. Delete his instructions and key your text for the report.

2. Format the report in unbound style. Refer to the Reference Guide pages 319–321 to review unbound report format.

3. Prepare a title page and table of contents for your report.

4. Save your report as **11-6 Evaluation Report.** Print the report.

Help Keywords

Pearson worksheet function
   Pearson worksheet function

correlation: a relationship or connection

Success Tips

For the Pearson correlation, Question 2 is the dependent variable and the other questions are the independent variables.

Challenge: Create Correlations Memo

Mr. Newland would like to know whether the client's evaluation of the guide influenced his or her evaluation on the other questions. You can use a worksheet function, Pearson product moment correlation, to find this information. This function gives you a correlation. A correlation above .60 shows that a client's evaluation on another question was strongly influenced by his or her opinion of the guide.

1. Open the file **11-3 New River Data.** Enter the Pearson product moment correlation calculations below the other data in the worksheet.

TEAMWORK

2. In Column B, enter a label to describe the questions being compared. For example, for the first correlation, you might compare Question 2 (guide evaluation) to Question 1 (process of booking excursion). In Column F, enter the formula for the calculation. Sample formula: =PEARSON(E9:E50,D9:D50)

	B	C	D	E	F	G
58	Pearson: Question 2:Question 1				0.28	
59	Pearson: Question 2:Question 3				0.63	Strong Association

3. Enter labels and formula to compare each remaining question to Question 2.

4. Use the IF function in the cell to the right of each correlation to display the words *Strong Association* if the correlation is greater than or equal to .60. Sample formula: =IF(F59>=0.6,"Strong Association"," ")

5. Save the workbook as **11-6 Challenge.** Print the worksheet.

6. Compare your worksheet to a classmate's. Do the correlation results match? If not, examine your formulas to determine why they differ. Make corrections as needed.

7. Refer to the Reference Guide page 314 to review memo format. Write a memo to Mr. Newland from you. Use the current date and appropriate subject line. In the body of the memo, give a summary of your findings about which response ratings seem to be influenced by the client's opinion of his or her guide. Include a table in the memo showing the relationship of the other nine evaluation questions to Question 2. (Copy the Pearson calculations and related labels from **11-6 Challenge.**) Indicate that Mr. Newland should refer to an attached evaluation form to see the text of the questions.

8. Save the memo as **11-6 Challenge Memo.** Print the memo.

Preparing Financial Documents

Objectives

- ☐ Build financial document worksheets
- ☐ Create templates
- ☐ Create and run macros
- ☐ Create and edit graphics
- ☐ Track precedents and dependents
- ☐ Work with print areas
- ☐ Save a worksheet as a Web page
- ☐ Create and format charts

Summary of *Microsoft Office* Skills

- ✔ Insert, delete, and move cells
- ✔ Enter and edit cell data, including text, numbers, and formulas
- ✔ Check spelling
- ✔ Manage workbook files and folders
- ✔ Save workbooks using different names and file formats
- ✔ Apply and modify cell formats
- ✔ Modify Page Setup options for worksheets
- ✔ Preview and print worksheets and workbooks
- ✔ Insert and delete worksheets
- ✔ Modify worksheet names and positions
- ✔ Create and revise formulas
- ✔ Use statistical, date and time, financial, and logical functions in formulas
- ✔ Create, modify, position, and print charts
- ✔ Create, modify, and position graphics
- ✔ Convert worksheets into Web pages
- ✔ Create hyperlinks
- ✔ View and edit comments
- ✔ Create, edit, and apply templates
- ✔ Create, edit, and run macros
- ✔ Compose and send messages to workgroup and Internet addresses

ST★R River Adventures

Job 12-1 Create Balance Sheet Worksheet

Skills Applied

- Entering and editing text and numbers in cells
- Formatting worksheet tabs
- Formatting cells
- Merging cells
- Creating and editing formulas using the Formula Bar
- Creating formulas using functions
- Setting Page Setup options for printing
- Creating a workbook template

Mr. Collins, the manager of the Finance and Accounting Department, is continuing to automate financial processes. With the assistance of other department personnel, he has converted payroll, budget, travel documents, cost projections, and customer feedback records to electronic format.

He now wants to begin converting basic financial documents to electronic format. The first document he wants to convert is the balance sheet. The balance sheet shows the financial condition of the company on a specific date. The Finance and Accounting Department prepares a balance sheet for Mr. Newland that shows the financial condition of the company on the last working day of each month. The four main sections of a balance sheet are described below.

- *Heading:* The heading includes the company name and address, the name of the document, and the date.

- *Assets:* Assets are things of value owned by the company. *Current assets* include cash and other things of value that can be converted to cash quickly. *Fixed assets* include items such as equipment and real estate that cannot be converted to cash quickly. The *other* category is used for miscellaneous things of value, such as such as patents and trademarks.

- *Liabilities:* Liabilities are debts or obligations the company must pay. Obligations that must be paid in a relatively short period of time are *current liabilities*. Those obligations that are paid over a long period of time are referred to as *long-term liabilities*.

- *Owner's Equity:* Owner's equity is equal to assets minus liabilities. The basic accounting equation is stated as follows: Assets = Liabilities + Owner's Equity. The balance sheet is said to be in balance when the total assets are equal to the total liabilities plus the owner's equity.

Mr. Collins has provided a sample balance sheet format. He wants you to prepare an electronic template. Using this template, only the balances will have to be entered each month. All calculations will be completed automatically.

1. Create a new folder on your disk or hard drive. Name the folder **Balance Sheets**. Save the balance sheet documents you complete in Project 12 in this folder.

2. Open a new workbook. Rename the first sheet *Balance Sheet Template*. Create a template that Star River Adventures can use to prepare its balance sheet each month. Use the sample balance sheet shown in Figure 12-1 on page 190 as your guide in creating the template.

Help Keywords

Increase indent
  Position data in a cell

3. Enter the labels as shown in Column B. Use the indent command to make the necessary indentions. Center the headings (company name, address, document name, and date) across columns after you have completed the worksheet. Use the current year for the date. Use bold as shown. Fill cells with pattern as shown.

4. Format the first cell in each section in which a value is to be entered and all totals for currency with a dollar sign and two decimals. Format other cells in which values will be entered for currency with no dollar sign.

5. Format cells that indicate the last value to be entered in a series for single accounting underline style.

6. Format cells that hold the values for Total Assets, Total Liabilities, Owners Equity, and Total Liabilities and Owner's Equity for double accounting underline style.

7. Enter a formula with the SUM function in the cell to hold the sum of Total Current Assets. Repeat for Total Fixed Assets and for Total Other Assets. Enter the necessary formula to calculate Total Assets.

8. Enter formulas with the SUM functions in necessary cells to sum Total Current Liabilities and Long-term Liabilities. Enter the necessary formula to calculate Total Liabilities.

9. Enter the necessary formula to determine Owner's Equity (Assets − Liabilities). Enter the necessary formula to determine Total Liabilities and Owner's Equity.

10. Place a border around the data in your template. Select A1:E44 as the range for the border. Center the worksheet horizontally on the page.

11. Save the workbook as a template named *12-1 Balance Sheet Template* in your Balance Sheet Documents folder. (Be sure to choose *Template (*.xlt)* in the Save as type list.)

12. Verify that all functions and formulas are accurate by using Formula Auditing and tracing your precedents and dependents. Remove all arrows after you have verified that all functions and formulas are accurate.

13. Once you are sure your worksheet is accurate, save it again using the same name. Print the worksheet.

	A	B	C	D	E
1					
2		**STAR RIVER ADVENTURES**			
3		**205 Riverview Drive**			
4		**Sutton, WV 26601-1311**			
5					
6		**Balance Sheet**			
7		**May 31, 20– –**			
8					
9		**Assets**			
10		**Current Assets**			
11		Cash		$0.00	
12		Inventory		0.00	
13		Prepaid Expenses		0.00	
14		Other		0.00	
15		**Total Current Assets**		$0.00	
16		**Fixed Assets**			
17		Real Estate/Buildings		$0.00	
18		Furniture and Fixtures		0.00	
19		Equipment		0.00	
20		Other		0.00	
21		**Total Fixed Assets**		$0.00	
22		**Other Assets**			
23		Miscellaneous		0.00	
24		**Total Other Assets**		$0.00	
25		**Total Assets**		$0.00	
26					
27		**Liabilities and Owner's Equity**			
28		**Current Liabilities**			
29		Accounts Payable		$0.00	
30		Taxes Payable		0.00	
31		Notes Payable (within 12 months)		0.00	
32		Other		0.00	
33		**Total Current Liabilities**		$0.00	
34		**Long-term Liabilities**			
35		Notes Payable (greater than 12 months)		$0.00	
36		Other		0.00	
37		**Total Long-term Liabilities**		$0.00	
38		**Total Liabilities**		$0.00	
39					
40		**Owner's Equity**		$0.00	
41					
42		**Total Liabilities and Owner's Equity**		$0.00	
43					
44					

Figure 12-1 Sample Balance Sheet Format

Job 12-2 Add Graphic and Macro to Template

Skills Applied

- Creating a workbook from a user-defined template
- Entering and editing text and numbers in cells
- Formatting worksheet tabs
- Editing a workbook template
- Creating, modifying, and positioning graphics
- Creating and running macros

Task 1 Create May Balance Sheet

1. Open and print the data file **May Balance Sheet.** This file contains handwritten data needed for the May balance sheet. Close the document. Open the template file **12-1 Balance Sheet Template** that you completed earlier.

2. Enter data from the printout to prepare the May 31, 20-- balance sheet. Use the current year for the date. If your worksheet is accurate, the Total Assets amount and the Total Liabilities and Owner's Equity amount should be $1,046,002.28.

3. Rename the sheet tab *May, 20-- Balance Sheet*. Use the current year for the date. Save the workbook in your Balance Sheets folder as **12-2 May Balance Sheet.** Print the worksheet and close the workbook.

Task 2 Edit a Template

Mr. Newland is very pleased with the balance sheet worksheet you prepared. He asks that you add a macro to the template.

1. Open the template file **12-1 Balance Sheet Template** that you created earlier. You will create a macro button to appear outside the print range.

2. Near the top of Column G, draw a rectangle. Apply 3-D format to the rectangle and a light fill color. Add the text *Clear Entries* to the rectangle.

Clear Entries

3. Create a macro that will clear the values you enter in the worksheet. Clear only the contents. Do not clear functions, formulas, and formatting. Name the macro *ClearEntries*. Assign the macro ClearEntries to the object you created in Step 2. Key sample data in the cells. Run the macro to make sure it clears all entries.

4. Save the template in your Balance Sheets folder as **12-2 Balance Sheet Template.**

Job 12-3 Access Financial Documents from Web Pages

Skills Applied

- Creating a workbook from a template
- Entering and editing text and numbers in cells
- Formatting worksheet tabs
- Using Web Page Preview
- Saving worksheets as Web pages
- Creating, sending, and printing email messages
- Inserting hyperlinks in documents

Task 1 Create June Balance Sheet

1. Open the data file **June Balance Sheet** and print the file. Close the file.

2. Open the **12-2 Balance Sheet Template** file that you created earlier. Complete the June 30, 20-- balance sheet using the data provided. Rename the sheet tab *June 20-- Balance Sheet*. Use the current year for the date.

3. Save the file in your Balance Sheets folder as **12-3 June Balance Sheet**. Set an appropriate print area (that does not include the macro button) and print the sheet. Close the workbook.

Task 2 Create Web Page and Email with Link

Mr. Newland has asked you to prepare an email to Star River Adventures employees telling them about the plans for placing financial documents on the company Web site. You need to save the June balance sheet as a Web page to link to the memo.

1. Open the **12-3 June Balance Sheet** file that you created earlier. Preview the document as a Web page. Notice whether the macro button appears in the Web page. Close the preview.

2. Right-click the macro button and choose *Assign Macro*. Delete the macro name *ClearEntries* assigned to this button. Delete the macro button from the sheet.

3. Save the worksheet as a Web page using the filename **12-3 June Balance Sheet Online** in your Balance Sheets folder. Make the sheet title *June Balance Sheet*. Open the file from a Web browser to make sure the file displays properly. Close the file.

4. Create an email message to the group address *Employees.StarRiver@trophe.com* (or an address specified by your instructor). The email is from you on the current date. Use *Electronic Financial Management System* as the subject.

5. Write the body of the email. Explain the following points:
   - Star River Adventures is creating a new electronic financial management system. Nearly all company records will be available on the Web site.
   - Employees will have access to the company's public information. Each employee will also have access to confidential information required for his or her job.

Success Tips

If you do not have access to email software, create a "simulated" email message in a *Word* file. You should be able to complete all of the instructions except sending the message.

- Employees will access the Web site in the normal manner and enter authorized areas by using an ID number and password.
- In the near future, we will add a Financial Documents button and menu option to the Web page so documents such as balance sheets and income statements are accessible to the public.
- Employees can see how the June balance sheet will look on the Web by clicking a link in this message.

6. At the end of the message, key this text to be used as a hyperlink:

```
Click to View Balance Sheet
```

Help Keywords

Hyperlink
Hyperlinks, inserting

path: the URL or drive, folder names, and filename that tell the exact location of stored data

7. Create a hyperlink from the text to the **12-3 June Balance Sheet Online** file. (For this exercise, you will link to a file on your hard drive or local network where your Web page is stored in your Balance Sheets folder. You need to know the complete path to where the **12-3 June Balance Sheet Online** file is stored. If you were really working at Star River Adventures, you would store the Web page file on the company's local network or Web site and link to that location.)

8. Choose the option in your email software to keep a copy of the message when it is sent. Send the message. If you used the Employees.StarRiver@trophe.com address, you will receive a return message telling you that the message cannot be delivered (because this is not a real address). However, you will still have a copy of the message in your Sent folder.

9. Access your copy of the sent email message. Test the link in your sent message. Print the email message.

Challenge: Research Financial Documents on the Web

Mr. Newland has asked you to research how other companies present financial documents on their Web sites. Access the Internet. Use a search engine to find the URLs for three large companies (for example: Wal-Mart, Microsoft, and General Motors). Record the company name and Web site URL for each company. Access each company's Web site. For each company, answer the questions below.

1. What types of financial documents are available on the site?

2. What links from the financial documents to other pages or sites are provided?

3. Does the site home page have a link directly to financial documents? If not, what path or method did you use to find the financial documents?

4. What suggestions can you provide for the Star River Adventures Web site after viewing other company sites?

Job 12-4 Create Income Statement Worksheet

Skills Applied

- Entering and editing text and numbers in cells
- Formatting cells and merging cells
- Creating and editing formulas using the Formula Bar
- Creating formulas using functions
- Setting Page Setup options for printing
- Formatting worksheet tabs
- Adding footers to spreadsheets
- Adding and editing comments attached to worksheet cells
- Creating a template
- Creating, modifying, and positioning graphics
- Creating and running macros
- Setting print areas and printing print areas
- Previewing and printing nonadjacent selections

net income: the income remaining after expenses are deducted

An income statement is a financial document that shows the income and expenses over a period of time. A variety of formats can be used for income statements. Star River Adventures' income statement shows the income, expenses, and net income.

Task 1 Create Second-Quarter Income Statement

1. Create a new folder named **Income Statements** on your disk or hard drive. Save the income statement documents you complete in Project 12 in this folder.

2. Open a new workbook. Rename the first sheet *2nd Quarter 20--*. Use the current year in the date. Use the sample income statement shown in Figure 12-2 on page 195 as your guide in creating the worksheet.

3. Enter the labels as shown in Column B. Use the indent command to make the necessary indentions. Center the headings (company name, address, document name, and date) across columns after you have completed the worksheet. Use the current year for the date. Use bold as shown. Fill cells with pattern as shown.

4. In Column C, enter the values for the income and expense amounts as shown. Format the first cell to hold values in each category (Income and Expenses) for currency, dollar sign, and two decimals.

5. Format the cells to display values for Total Income, Total Expenses, and Net Income for currency, dollar sign, and two decimals and for double accounting underline style.

6. Format the cells to hold values as currency, no dollar sign, and two decimals. Format the cells that display values for the last cell in each category (Special Fees and Miscellaneous) for single accounting underline style.

7. Enter formulas using the SUM function to calculate the amounts for Total Income and Total Expenses. Enter a formula to calculate Net Income (Total Income − Total Expenses). If your income statement is accurate, the Net Income should be $106,044.59.

	A	B	C	D
1				
2		**STAR RIVER ADVENTURES**		
3		205 Riverview Drive		
4		Sutton, WV 26601-1311		
5				
6		**Income Statement**		
7		April 1 - June 30, 20 - -		
8				
9		**Income**		
10		Excursions	$312,502.50	
11		Gifts and Novelties	9,893.22	
12		Food Services	7,500.10	
13		Special Events	12,376.09	
14		Miscellaneous Equipment Rentals	3,285.17	
15		Special Fees	3,030.06	
16		**Total Income**	$348,587.14	
17				
18		**Expenses**		
19		Salaries	$95,260.59	
20		Wages	35,280.00	
21		Fringes	31,210.22	
22		Travel	4,781.93	
23		Recurring Expenses	19,003.20	
24		Supplies	10,607.30	
25		Equipment	15,350.80	
26		Outside Services	8,250.00	
27		Legal	325.00	
28		Taxes (Real Estate)	3,909.50	
29		Depreciation	4,880.38	
30		Advertising	482.33	
31		Memberships	150.00	
32		Gift and Novelties for Resale	11,250.80	
33		Miscellaneous	1,800.50	
34		**Total Expenses**	$242,542.55	
35				
36		**Net Income**	$106,044.59	
37				
38				
39				

Figure 12-2 Sample Income Statement

8. Place a border around the data in your worksheet. Center the worksheet horizontally on the page. Add a custom footer to contain *Unaudited* and the current date.

9. Enter a comment in the cell that indicates the period of time covered by the income statement:

    Do not enter a specific date; enter a period of time.

10. Save the file as **12-4 2nd Quarter Income Statement.** Print the worksheet.

11. Save the sheet as a Web page named **12-4 2nd Quarter Income Statement Online** in your Income Statements folder. Use an appropriate title for the page. Access the Web page from your browser to make sure it displays properly. Close the file.

Task 2   Print Ranges and Create a Template

1. Open the file **12-4 2nd Quarter Income Statement** that you created earlier.

2. Set the print area to include only the Income section of the worksheet. Print this section.

3. Select the worksheet headings, the Total Income label and value, the Total Expenses label and value, and the Net Income label and value. Print these nonadjacent selections. Reset your original print range to include the entire document.

4. Edit the comment for the date range cell. Add this additional information:

   For example: April 1 - June 30, 20--

5. Save the worksheet as a template file named **12-4 Income Statement Template** in the Income Statements folder.

6. Near the top of Column E (outside the print area), draw a rectangle. Apply 3-D format to the rectangle and a light fill color. Add the text *Clear Entries* to the rectangle. This button should look similar to the one you used in the balance sheet template.

7. Create a macro named *ClearEntries* that will clear the contents of only those cells in which you entered values (individual income items and expense items). Assign the macro ClearEntries to the object you created in Step 6. Run the macro to make sure it clears all entries. (Key sample data in the cells first if needed.)

8. Save the template again using the same name and location.

Job 12-5 Complete First-Quarter Income Statement

Skills Applied

- Creating a workbook from a template
- Entering and editing text and numbers in cells
- Formatting worksheet tabs
- Using Web Page Preview
- Saving worksheets as Web pages
- Editing comments attached to worksheet cells

Mr. Newland wants you to convert the first-quarter statement to electronic format to match the one you prepared for the second quarter.

1. Open the file **12-4 Income Statement Template** that you created earlier. Complete the first-quarter income statement using the data below. Remember to change the date range in the heading.

2. Rename the sheet tab *1st Quarter 20--*. Use the current year in the date. Save the workbook as **12-5 1st Quarter Income Statement** in your Income Statements folder.

TEAMWORK

3. Format the sheet to print on one page in portrait orientation. Print the worksheet. Compare your worksheet with a classmate's worksheet. Do the Net Income amounts agree? If not, check the data and make changes as needed.

4. Preview the worksheet as a Web page. Make changes to the worksheet as needed so the macro button does not appear on the Web page. Delete the comment attached to the date range cell.

5. Save the sheet as a Web page named **12-5 1st Quarter Income Statement Online** in your Income Statements folder. Use an appropriate page title. View the page from a Web browser to make sure it displays properly.

Income		Expenses	
Excursions	$225,005.50	Recurring Expenses	15,050.01
Gifts and Novelties	4,213.73	Supplies	11,078.25
Food Services	2,350.05	Equipment	4,040.06
Special Events	8,005.32	Outside Services	750.00
Miscellaneous Equipment Rentals	1,765.32	Legal	100.00
Special Fees	1,050.23	Taxes (Real Estate)	3,909.50
		Depreciation	4,280.00
Expenses		Advertising	75.00
Salaries	$94,287.23	Memberships	0.00
Wages	4,280.00	Gifts and Novelties for Resale	3,389.10
Fringes	24,641.81	Miscellaneous	250.25
Travel	1,090.00		

Job 12-6 Create and Format Charts

Skills Applied

- Opening a workbook from a folder created for workbook storage
- Creating charts using at least two chart types
- Formatting charts
- Printing charts
- Inserting worksheets into a workbook
- Entering text into cells
- Inserting selected cells
- Creating, modifying, and positioning graphics

Mr. Newland is considering expanding Star River Adventures. In the near future, he wants to begin publishing the balance sheets and income statements as he seeks potential investors. You will create charts using the two balance sheets and the two income statements that can be published with the statements.

Task 1 Create Balance Sheet Charts

1. Open the file **12-2 May Balance Sheet** that you created earlier.

2. Create a pie chart on a new sheet. Chart the Total Assets, Total Liabilities, and Owner's Equity values.

3. Enter the company name, document name, and date from the worksheet as the chart title. Show values for the data labels. Change font sizes and alignment of chart elements as needed for an attractive chart similar to Figure 12-3 on page 199. Save the file as **12-6 May Chart.** Print the chart.

4. Open the file **12-3 June Balance Sheet** that you created earlier.

5. Create a clustered column chart with 3-D effect on a new sheet. Chart the Total Assets, Total Liabilities, and Owner's Equity values. Enter the company name, document name, and date from the worksheet as the chart title. Enter the title *Amount* for the Z axis. Display a legend. Show a data table with the chart. Change font sizes, move chart elements, and adjust the chart depth, if desired, for an attractive chart similar to that shown in Figure 12-3 on page 199.

6. Save the file as **12-6 June Chart.** Print the chart.

Help Keywords

Chart
Create a chart

---

data series: related data points that are plotted in a chart

Software Review

To adjust the depth on a 3-D chart with axes:

- Click a data series in the 3-D chart you want to change.

- Choose *Selected Data Series* on the Format menu.

- Select the *Options* tab.

- Change the settings for Gap depth, Gap width, or Chart depth.

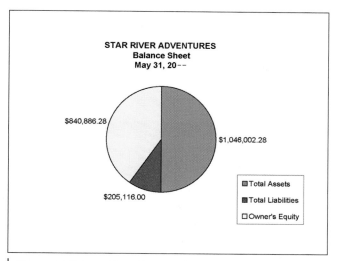

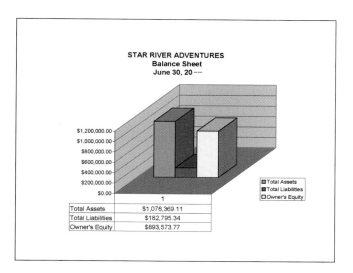

Figure 12-3 Balance Sheet Charts

Task 2 Create Income Statement Charts

1. Open the file **12-4 2nd Quarter Income Statement** that you created earlier.

2. Create a 3-D bar chart on a new sheet. Chart the Total Income, Total Expenses, and Net Income values.

3. Enter the company name, document name, and date range from the worksheet as the chart title. Use *Amount* for the title of the Z axis. Show values for the data labels. Display a legend.

4. Format the data labels using a 16-point, bold format to display zero decimal places. Move the data labels onto the bars. Format the values on the Z axis for zero decimal places and increase the font size. Change the color of each bar and add a fill effect. Make other formatting changes as desired for an attractive chart. A sample chart is shown in Figure 12-4 on page 200.

5. Save the file as **12-6 2nd Quarter Chart.** Print the chart.

6. Open the file **12-5 1st Quarter Income Statement** that you created earlier. The **12-4 2nd Quarter Income Statement** file should also be open.

7. Copy the 2nd Qtr 20-- sheet to the **12-5 1st Quarter Income Statement** file. Close the **12-4 2nd Quarter Income Statement** file. Save the workbook that contains sheets for both quarters as **12-6 Comparison Chart.**

8. Copy the income, expense, and net income figures (Column C) from the 1st Qtr sheet and paste them into the same rows on the 2nd Qtr sheet in Column D. Enter column headings in Row 9 to identify each quarter.

9. Create a 3-D column chart on a new sheet. Chart the Total Income, Total Expenses, and Net Income values for both quarters.

10. Enter *Income Statement Comparison* as the chart title. Use *Amount* as the title for the Value axis. Display a legend.

11. Change the series names to *Quarter 2, 20--* and *Quarter 1, 20--*. Format the numbers on the Value axis for zero decimal places and increase the font size. Use WordArt to create the company name and display it above the title.

12. Make other formatting changes as desired for an attractive chart. A sample chart is shown in Figure 12-4. Save the file as **12-6 Comparison Chart.** Print the chart.

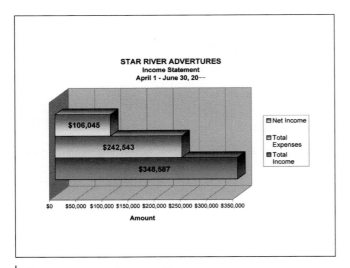

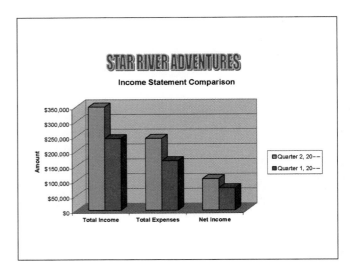

Figure 12-4 Income Statement Charts

Thinking Critically

1. You created different types of charts in Project 12. What chart types are appropriate for summarizing balance sheet data? Why?

2. What chart types are appropriate for summarizing income statement data? Why?

3. A pie chart shows the relationship of parts to a whole. What do each of these chart types show: column, bar, line, area?

Creating Presentations for July 4th Extravaganza

Objectives

- ☐ Create electronic presentations
- ☐ Insert sounds, images, tables, files, and motion clips
- ☐ Apply design templates, layouts, custom animations, and transitions
- ☐ Create hyperlinks and save a presentation as a Web file
- ☐ Work with action buttons and menus for navigation
- ☐ Insert slides to combine presentations
- ☐ Link slides to *Word* and *Excel* documents
- ☐ Package a presentation

Summary of *Microsoft Office* Skills

- ✔ Create presentations (manually and using automated tools)
- ✔ Add slides to and delete slides from presentations
- ✔ Insert, format, and modify text
- ✔ Add tables, charts, clip art, and bitmap images to slides
- ✔ Add OfficeArt elements to slides
- ✔ Apply custom formats to tables
- ✔ Apply animation schemes
- ✔ Apply slide transitions
- ✔ Rearrange slides
- ✔ Modify slide layout
- ✔ Add links to a presentation
- ✔ Preview and print slides, outlines, handouts, and speaker notes

- ✔ Add sound and video to slides
- ✔ Deliver presentations
- ✔ Manage files and folders for presentations
- ✔ Publish presentations to the Web
- ✔ Use Pack and Go
- ✔ Create, edit, and apply templates (worksheets)
- ✔ Find and replace cell data and formats
- ✔ Enter and edit cell data
- ✔ Create, modify, and position graphics
- ✔ Apply and modify cell formats
- ✔ Create and revise formulas
- ✔ Modify paragraph formats
- ✔ Create and modify tables

Job 13-1 Create July 4th Extravaganza Presentation

Skills Applied

- Creating folders for storing presentations
- Creating presentations from a blank presentation
- Adding slides to presentations
- Adding text to slides
- Editing and formatting text on slides
- Creating tables on slides
- Applying user-defined formats to tables
- Creating OfficeArt elements on slides
- Applying animation to slides
- Adding transition effects to slides
- Changing the layout of slides
- Printing handouts
- Adding sound effects to slides

The July 4th holiday is an important event for Star River Adventures. The special events scheduled on this day usually draw large crowds, and significant profits are generated. This year the company is planning its largest extravaganza ever. To make this event even more successful, the staff plans to prepare a comprehensive advertising campaign.

An important advertising item will be slide shows. These shows will be sent to travel agents and posted on the company Web site. All departments will be asked to help with various parts of the campaign. Because of your experience in developing electronic presentations, you have been asked to assist in that area.

1. Search the Internet for a variety of clip art, photos, sound files, and motion clips related to the July 4th holiday. Look for media that represent West Virginia (map), basketball, bicycling, fireworks, cooking, barbecue, rivers, the sun, sunglasses, swimming, horseback riding, picnics, rafting, fishing, softball, and children's games. These files will be helpful in developing your presentations. A good source of media is the Microsoft Design Gallery Live (http://dgl.microsoft.com).

2. Create a folder named **P13 Presentations.** Save all documents and media related to this project in that folder.

3. Open a new blank presentation file in *PowerPoint*. Save the file as **13-1 July 4** in your P13 Presentations folder. Insert a title slide with the following title and subtitle. See Figure 13-1 for an example title slide.

   ```
   Star River Adventures

   July 4th Extravaganza
   ```

4. Add an animation entrance effect to the title and the subtitle text boxes, such as *Fly In* with the direction *From Left*. Have the effect start *With Previous*.

5. Select and apply a design template that is appropriate for the presentation, such as *Fireworks*.

Figure 13-1 July 4th Show Title Slide and Table Slide

6. Insert a sound on the title slide. You can use the sound file **July 4 Sound** found in your data files, a sound from the Clip Organizer, or a sound file you found on the Internet. Have the sound play automatically and loop to continue playing until a new slide is displayed. Drag the sound icon off the slide so it does not display when the slide show is played.

7. Open and print the *Word* data file **July 4 Text.** Use the information on this printout to create the slides. Use a Bulleted List layout for Slides 2 through 4. Add an entrance effect for the bullet list.

8. Select *Title Only* layout for Slide 5. Key the title *Location.* Insert clip art for a map of West Virginia. Indicate the location of the event, Fayetteville, West Virginia, by drawing a star AutoShape on the map. Add an entrance effect to the star. Add the city name, Fayetteville, if it is not already shown on the map.

9. For Slide 6, select *Title and Table* layout. Create a table with two columns and ten rows as shown in Figure 13-1. Key the slide title and the driving times from various cities as shown on the printout. Reduce the font size of the text in the table so it fits on the slide. Add shading to the headings row to match the border color and change the font to white.

10. For Slide 7, select *Bullet List* layout and add the title and text. Add the same entrance effect for the bullet list as used for other slides.

11. Add an appropriate transition effect to all slides. Check the spelling and proofread carefully. Save the file again using the same name. Print handouts of all slides, nine per page in black and white.

Job 13-2 Create Registration Presentation

Skills Applied

- Editing and formatting text on slides
- Deleting slides
- Adding clip art and sounds to slides
- Adding hyperlinks to slides
- Printing slides
- Entering and editing text and numbers in cells
- Using Find and Replace to change cell contents
- Creating a workbook template
- Creating, modifying, and positioning graphics in worksheets
- Formatting cells
- Creating and editing formulas

Task 1 Create Slides

The next slide show you will develop provides registration information for the July 4th Extravaganza. Because this presentation and others will be linked to the first slide show you prepared, you should use the same design and color scheme for all of the shows.

1. Open the presentation file **13-1 July 4** that you created earlier. Save the file as **13-2 Register** in your P13 Presentations folder.

2. Open the *Word* data file **Register Text** that contains handwritten notes for the slides. Edit slides from the **13-1 July 4** show to contain the text for this show. Delete unneeded slides.

3. Delete the sound file from the title slide. Insert clip art and sounds on the slides as desired.

4. Use Spell Check and proofread the slides carefully. Save again using the same name. Close the file and *PowerPoint*.

Task 2 Complete Registration Form

You will complete a registration form in *Excel* that was begun by a coworker. This form will be used by travel agents who receive the promotional slide shows. When the slide shows are placed on the company Web site, the Web developer will create a Web form using your form as an example. Customers can complete the form and submit it online or print a form and mail or fax it in.

1. Open the data file **Registration Form** in *Excel*. Save the file as a template named **13-2 Registration Form** in your P13 Presentations folder.

2. Enhance the form by adding an appropriate clip art image near the top left of the form. Add pattern to the column heading cells in a color that coordinates with the slide show.

3. Use Find and Replace to change all instances of *AM* to *a.m.* Change all instances of *PM* to *p.m.*

4. Format all amounts in the Price and Total columns for currency, dollar sign with two decimals. Format the cells where the number of persons will appear for number with no decimal places.

5. Enter formulas in the Total column to multiply the number of persons times the price per person for each event that has a price. Enter a formula to sum the Total column.

6. Save the template again using the same name. Print the worksheet.

7. Open the presentation file **13-2 Register** that you created earlier. On Slide 3, add a hyperlink to the words *registration form*. Link to the *Excel* file **13-2 Registration Form** in your P13 Presentations folder. Play the show and test the link. (In *Excel*, click the *Back* button on the Web toolbar to return to the presentation.)

Task 3 Record Registration Information

You have created a registration form that can be completed and sent to Star River Adventures. Now you will record information for a customer who wants to register by phone.

1. Open the *Excel* template file **13-2 Registration Form** that you created earlier. Save the file as **13-2 Dorazio**.

2. Use the information below to complete a registration form for this customer. The customer will mail a check for the registration fee. Save the file again using the same name and print the worksheet.

```
Mr. Don Dorazio
107 Main Street
Sutton, WV 22601-2232
Email: ddorazio@trophe.com

Two adults are to be registered for each of these
events:
Continental Breakfast (Adult)
Buffet Lunch (Adult)
5-Mile River Raft Race
Kayak Race
Early Evening Barbecue (Adult)
```

Job 13-3 Create Events Presentation

Skills Applied

- Editing and formatting text on slides
- Deleting slides
- Adding images and sounds to slides
- Printing handouts
- Creating tables on slides
- Adding sound effects to slides

You need to develop a slide show that includes the events schedule for the July 4th Extravaganza. If you have not already located the media (clip art, photos, sounds, or motion clips) suggested at the beginning of Project 13, you should do so before completing this job.

1. Open the presentation file **13-1 July 4** that you created earlier. Save the file as **13-3 Events** in your P13 Presentations folder.

2. Open the *Word* data file **Events Text** that contains handwritten notes for the slides. Edit slides from the **13-1 July 4** show to contain the text for this show. Delete unneeded slides.

3. Delete the sound file from the title slide. Insert clip art and sounds on the slides as directed in the notes. Figure 13-2 shows an example of Slide 3.

4. Use Spell Check and proofread the slides carefully. Save again using the same name. Print the file as handouts, four per page in black and white.

Figure 13-2 Events Slide with Table

Job 13-4 Create Clothing Presentation

Skills Applied

- Editing and formatting text on slides
- Deleting slides
- Adding images and sounds to slides
- Printing handouts
- Adding sound effects to slides
- Adding hyperlinks to slides

You need to develop a slide show that describes the proper clothing needed for river excursions at various times of the year.

1. Open the presentation file **13-1 July 4** that you created earlier. Save the file as **13-3 Clothing** in your P13 Presentations folder.

2. Open the *Word* data file **Clothing Text** that contains handwritten notes for the slides. Edit slides from the **13-1 July 4** show to contain the text for this show.

3. Delete the sound file from the title slide.

4. On Slide 2, insert a text box and add the text shown in the notes. Format the text box with a fill color that complements the slide color scheme. Add an entrance effect to the text box. Add a motion clip or photo of a river. Using WordArt, create an image of the word *Summer* as shown in Figure 13-3. Create another WordArt image of the words *Spring or Fall.*

5. Create the remaining bullet list slides. Insert text boxes, images, and sounds on the slides as directed in the notes.

6. Add a hyperlink from the WordArt image *Summer* to Slide 3. Add a hyperlink from the WordArt image *Spring or Fall* to Slide 5. Play the show and test the hyperlinks. Save the file again using the same name. Print the file as handouts, four per page in black and white.

Help Keywords

Text box
  Add text to a slide

Figure 13-3 Slide with Custom Text Box

Job 13-5 Create Forms Presentation and Document

Skills Applied

- Editing and formatting text on slides
- Deleting slides
- Adding images and sounds to slides
- Printing handouts
- Adding hyperlinks to slides
- Applying paragraph formats
- Creating and modifying tables
- Modifying table borders and shading

You need to develop a slide show that describes the forms customers must complete before embarking on a river excursion.

1. Open the presentation file **13-1 July 4** that you created earlier. Save the file as **13-5 Forms** in your P13 Presentations folder.

2. Open the *Word* data file **Forms Text** that contains handwritten notes for the slides. Edit slides from the **13-1 July 4** show to contain the text for this show.

3. On Slide 4, insert a text box and add the text shown in the notes. Format the text box with a fill color that complements the slide color scheme. Later you will add a hyperlink to the text box.

4. Delete the sound file from the title slide. Save the file again using the same name. Close the file and *PowerPoint*.

5. In *Word*, create an information form as shown on page 209. Format the form approximately as shown. Create a two-column table for the customer information. Remove all border lines except the ones shown.

6. Save the form as **13-5 Information Form** in your P13 Presentations folder. Print and close the form.

7. Open the **13-5 Forms** presentation file that you created earlier. Add a hyperlink from the text box on Slide 4 to the file **13-5 Information Form** that you created.

8. Play the show and test the hyperlink. Print the file as handouts, four per page in black and white.

Star River Adventures
205 Riverview Drive
Sutton, WV 26601-1311

CUSTOMER INFORMATION FORM

Star River Adventures is required by state law to obtain customer information. Please complete this form and print legibly.

Last Name _____

First Name _____

Address _____

City _____

State _____

ZIP Code _____

Day Phone _____

Night Phone _____

Email _____

Birth Date _____

Legal Guardian _____
(Complete for minors.)

Signature _____
(To be signed by customer or legal guardian of minor.)

Thank You!

Job 13-6 Combine Presentations and Create Web File

Skills Applied

- Adding text to slides
- Adding slides to presentations
- Editing and formatting text on slides
- Changing the order of slides in a presentation
- Running slide shows
- Saving a presentation in HTML format
- Preparing a presentation for delivery using Pack and Go

Task 1 Insert Slides and Add Navigation Buttons

At times, company personnel may wish to use the shows you created separately. However, the shows should be combined before being sent to travel agents.

1. Open the presentation file **13-1 July 4** that you created earlier. Save the file as **13-6 July 4.** Move to the last slide. Insert all of the slides from the file **13-2 Register.**

2. Move to the last slide. Insert all of the slides from the file **13-3 Events.**

3. Move to the last slide. Insert all of the slides from the file **13-4 Clothing.**

4. Move to the last slide. Insert all of the slides from the file **13-5 Forms.**

5. Move to the Menu slide. Add a bulleted item at the beginning of the list to read *Event highlights*. Move the Menu slide so it becomes Slide 2.

6. Insert a new slide with the Title layout as Slide 3. Enter the following title and subtitle.

       July 4th Extravaganza

       Event Highlights

7. Move to the Dress for Success slide. Play the show and test the links on this slide. If the links do not go to the proper slides, edit the links.

8. Move to the Menu slide. Create a hyperlink from each bulleted item in the menu to the appropriate title slide in the presentation.

9. Develop a navigation scheme for the slides. Beginning on the Menu slide, insert two action buttons. One button should move to the previous slide. The other button should move to the next slide in the presentation. See Figure 13-4 on page 211 for an example. Beginning on the slide after the Menu slide, insert a button that moves to the Menu slide. Place only the Forward button on Slide 1.

10. Use colors and a font for the navigation buttons that complement the presentation color scheme. Place the buttons in the same location on each slide, near the bottom of the slide. Use grids and guides to help you place the buttons evenly. After you create the first set of buttons, use the Copy and Paste commands to copy them to the other appropriate slides.

11. Play the show and test your navigation menus to make sure everything works properly. Save the file again using the same name.

Software Review

To insert slides from another file:

- Move to the location where you wish to insert slides.
- Select *Slides from Files* from the Insert Slides menu.
- Browse to find the file that contains the files to insert.
- Select *Insert All* to insert all slides in the file or select individual slides and click *Insert*.

Help Keywords

Hyperlink
    Create hyperlink

Success Tips

Use the *Format AutoShape, Size* options to help you make buttons the same width and height.

TEAMWORK

12. Ask a classmate to review your presentation at your computer while you review his or her presentation. Look for errors or inconsistencies in the slides. Check to be sure that the slide transitions are consistent throughout the slide show and that all slide designs complement one another. Give feedback to one another regarding the slides. Make changes as needed and save the file again using the same name.

Figure 13-4 Slides with Navigation Buttons

Task 2 Create Web File

The July 4th Extravaganza combined slide show is almost ready to convert to an HTML file that can be posted on the company Web site. You will remove links to forms from the presentation. Using your forms as examples, the Web developer will create forms that can be completed and submitted online. These forms will be linked to the appropriate slides.

1. Open the presentation file **13-6 July 4** that you created earlier. Move to the By Fax slide. Delete the link to the registration form.

2. Move to the last slide, Information Form. Delete the link from the text box to the form.

Help Keywords

Web page
   Save a presentation as
   a Web page

3. Preview your presentation as a Web page. Make any necessary changes as a result of your preview. Save your presentation as a Web page named **13-6 July 4 Online.** Use *July 4th Extravaganza* as the page title.

4. View your presentation using your Web browser. Play the presentation and check all of the links. If corrections are needed, open the presentation in *PowerPoint* and make the corrections. Then save the file again using the same name and format.

Thinking Critically

While viewing your presentation as a Web page, you probably noticed a few differences between viewing it as a presentation and as a Web page. What recommendations or suggestions would you make to others who might want to prepare presentations and then convert them to Web pages?

Challenge: Use Pack and Go

Help Keywords

Pack and Go
  Package a presentation
  to run on another
  computer

This presentation may be sent to travel agents or potential customers, but you do not know if they have appropriate software on their computers to run the presentation. To overcome this problem, you can package your presentation to run on another computer. You can even include a viewer so it is not necessary for the other computer to have *PowerPoint* to play the show.

Note: You need two or three floppy disks to complete this task.

1. Open the presentation file **13-6 July 4** that you created earlier. Use Pack and Go to package the presentation. Save your packaged presentation on floppy disks. Choose to include linked files and the *Viewer for Microsoft Windows*.

2. Unpack the presentation and view it on another computer.

Part 3

Operations

In the projects for Part 3, you report to Maria Inez, manager of the Operations Department. As part of your job duties, you are responsible for designing and maintaining databases. Although the jobs involve extensive database applications, they also require integration with various other software applications, such as word processing, presentations, and spreadsheets. You will create and modify database tables, queries, forms, and reports related to the guides and the equipment used at Star River Adventures. You will also create multimedia presentations and Web pages to present information effectively to coworkers and clients.

Project 14

Managing Guides and Their Certifications

Objectives

- ☐ Create a table
- ☐ Define data relationships
- ☐ Define new data fields
- ☐ Edit data field definitions
- ☐ Design and run simple reports and queries
- ☐ Create forms
- ☐ Print tables and reports
- ☐ Use *Access* and *Word* files to create merged documents

Summary of *Microsoft Office* Skills

- ✔ Open database objects in multiple views
- ✔ Move among records
- ✔ Format datasheets
- ✔ Create and modify tables
- ✔ Add a predefined input mask to a field
- ✔ Modify field properties
- ✔ Create and modify Select queries
- ✔ Create and display forms
- ✔ Modify form properties
- ✔ Enter, edit, and delete records
- ✔ Create queries
- ✔ Sort records
- ✔ Create one-to-one relationships
- ✔ Enforce referential integrity
- ✔ Create and format reports
- ✔ Preview and print reports
- ✔ Export data from *Access*
- ✔ Sort and group data in reports
- ✔ Merge letters with *Access* data source

STAR River Adventures

Job 14-1 Edit the Guide Roster Table

Skills Applied

- Opening *Access* objects in the appropriate views
- Formatting a table or query datasheet for display
- Using navigation controls to move among records
- Editing records from a table using a datasheet or form
- Entering records into a datasheet (table or query)
- Changing the field properties of one or more fields to display an input mask
- Modifying field properties for one or more tables in Table Design View
- Using the Input Mask Wizard
- Sorting records in a datasheet

Task 1   Edit Data and Add Fields

Each guide has been asked to provide changes to his or her personal information. These changes are shown in the table in Figure 14-1 on page 216. You need to edit data in the Guide Roster table and add a new field to hold other data.

1. Open the *Access* data file **Star River Adventures P14.** If directed to do so by your instructor, rename the Guide Roster database table as described in the Success Tips at the left.

2. Open the Guide Roster table. Adjust the column widths to accommodate the longest entry. Save your layout changes.

3. Review the information for each guide and become familiar with the guide names. You will be hearing more about the guides in later jobs.

4. In the Guide Roster table, edit the addresses for Laura and Heather to include the new information shown in Figure 14-1.

5. In Design View, add a phone number input mask for the Guide Phone field and for the Guide Cell field. Choose to store the data without keying the symbols in the mask. Save the table.

6. In Datasheet View, enter the phone numbers from Figure 14-1. Notice that the phone number input masks reduce the chance of making errors in the data entry. Change the column widths, if necessary, to display all of the data. Verify your edits carefully. Errors can affect future jobs.

Success Tips

Your instructor may want you to rename database tables, queries, and reports by adding your name to the existing name. For example, the table named *Guide Roster* would be renamed *Guide Roster your name.* This naming scheme can be helpful in identifying each student's work when several students print tables or reports.

Help Keywords

Resize
   Resize a column or row

Software Review

To create an input mask:

- In Design View, select a field.
- Select *Input Mask* from the Field Properties list.
- Select the *Build* button.
- Use the Input Mask Wizard to define an input mask.

PERSONAL DATA UPDATES						
Guide Name	**Guide Address**	**City**	**State**	**ZIP**	**Guide Phone**	**Guide Cell**
Robin Nichols					3045550156	3045550031
Carson Forde					3045550143	3045550078
Tamara Gibson					3045550167	3045550020
Josh Farley					3045550158	3045550060
Laura Robinson	89222 River Way			26601-4473	3045550149	3045550044
Tinukwa Okojie					3045550162	3045550055
Heather Goldman	735 Ridgeline Boulevard			26601-1812	3045550128	3045550089
Sidney Miller					3045550142	3045550039
Nicholas Geotze					3045550113	3045550047
Alan Jackson					3045550127	3045550037
Chien Du					3045550141	3045550026

Figure 14-1 Personal Data Updates

7. In Design View, insert a row below the Guide ZIP Code field. Name the new field *Guide DOB*. Assign a data type of Date/Time and a description of Guide Date of Birth. Use the Input Mask Wizard to define a short date input mask. Save the table.

8. In Datasheet View, enter the following dates of birth. Notice how the date input mask controls the data entry. Verify your dates carefully. Errors can affect future jobs. Print the table in landscape orientation. Close the database.

Robin	06/12/1984	Heather	10/30/1981
Carson	01/31/1985	Sidney	07/27/1984
Tamara	05/22/1976	Nicholas	08/04/1985
Josh	02/08/1979	Alan	01/20/1983
Laura	04/16/1982	Chien	10/03/1979
Tinukwa	12/09/1984		

Task 2 Assign a Primary Key

When the Guide Roster table was created, no primary key was assigned. In this task, you assign a primary key and sort the records in the Guide Roster table.

1. Open the **Star River Adventures P14** database file that you edited earlier. Open the Guide Roster table.

2. In Datasheet View, enter a Guide ID for each guide. The ID will be the first and last initials of the guide plus 001. For instance, the Guide ID for Robin Nichols should be RN001.

3. In Design View, make the Guide ID field the primary key for the records in the Guides Roster table. Switch to Datasheet View. Notice that the records have been automatically sorted in order by the Guide ID field.

4. Print the table in landscape orientation.

Task 3 Sort Records

Help Keywords

Sort
  Sort records

In Task 2, the Guide Roster table was sorted automatically by Guide ID. Occasionally you must sort the table in a different order. Ms. Inez requests two printed lists of the guides—one sorted by Guide LName and one sorted by Guide City.

1. Open the **Star River Adventures P14** database file that you edited earlier. Open the Guide Roster table.

2. While in Datasheet View, position your cursor anywhere in the Guide LName column. Select the *Sort Ascending* button. Notice the record order now. Chien Du should be your first record. Print the table in landscape orientation.

3. Position your cursor anywhere in the Guide City column. Select the *Sort Descending* button. Sutton should be the Guide City value in your first record. Print the table in landscape orientation.

4. Close the table without saving changes. Close the database.

Thinking Critically

In Task 2, you used the first and last initials of the guide plus 001 for the Guide ID. What might you use for a primary key value for two people with the same initials?

Job 14-2 Automate Certifications Tracking

Skills Applied

- Opening *Access* objects in the appropriate views
- Creating tables
- Using the Input Mask Wizard
- Creating forms using the Form Wizard
- Modifying the properties of a form
- Entering records using a form
- Creating a one-to-one relationship using the Relationships window
- Enforcing referential integrity in a one-to-one relationship

As you learned in Project 7, guides are given one-year contracts. They must reapply for employment each year. To be eligible to work for Star River Adventures, a guide must have current First Aid and CPR certifications. Guides must also complete 300 miles of river time over a period of two months.

Up to this point, Maria Inez, Operations Manager, has manually kept track of the required certifications. Because certifications are so important to the company's reputation, Ms. Inez has decided to automate this process. You will create a certifications table to keep track of each guide's certifications and the expiration dates. Because it is the end of the season, you will create a table in preparation for next season. Initially the certification fields will be set to No for each guide and the expiration dates will be set to the last day of the current year. The certification information will be updated later for each guide.

Task 1 Create a Guide Certifications Table

1. Open the **Star River Adventures P14** database file that you edited earlier.

2. In Design View, create a new table named *Guide Certifications*. (Add your name as part of the table title if your instructor has asked you to name tables in this way.)

3. Create the fields shown in the table on page 219. Use the Input Mask Wizard to define a short date input mask for the Cert CPR Exp, Cert First Aid Exp, and Cert River Miles Exp fields. Set the Guide ID field as the primary key.

4. Close the table, saving your changes.

Field Name	Field Type	Field Size	Description
Guide ID (Primary Key)	Text	5	Guide Identification Number
Cert CPR	Yes/No		Red Cross CPR Certification?
Cert CPR Exp	Date/Time	Short date	Red Cross CPR Certification Expiration Date
Cert First Aid	Yes/No		Red Cross First Aid Certification?
Cert First Aid Exp	Date/Time	Short date	Red Cross First Aid Certification Expiration Date
Cert River Miles	Yes/No		300-Mile River Requirement?
Cert River Miles Exp	Date/Time	Short date	300-Mile Certification Expiration Date
Cert Training	Yes/No		Star River In-House Training Workshop
Cert Exam	Number		Star River In-House Exam Score

Task 2 Create a Form and Enter Data

1. Open the **Star River Adventures P14** database file that you edited earlier. Create a simple form using the Form Wizard. The form should be based on the Guide Certifications table and should include all of the fields.

2. Select a columnar layout and the *Ricepaper* style. Make the title of the form *Guide Certifications Form*.

3. In Design View, modify the form's design by adding the title *Certifications Data Entry Form* in the Form Header. Use the Label icon from the Toolbox to add the title. Change the title font to 14 point. Add or change any formatting you wish to make the form easy to use. Your form should look similar to Figure 14-2 on page 220 after you enter data in the next step.

4. Use the form to enter data for all of the guides. To find the Guide ID data, open the Guide Roster table. Copy and paste the Guide ID data or key the data into the form.

5. Enter the last day of the current year in the Cert CPR Exp, Cert First Aid Exp, Cert River Miles Exp fields.

6. To indicate No in the Yes/No fields, do not check the boxes for the Cert CPR, Cert First Aid, Cert River Miles, and Cert Training fields. Enter 0 in the Cert Exam field.

7. Save the changes and close the form.

Guide Certifications Form

Certifications Data Entry Form

Guide ID	AJ001
Cert CPR	☐
Cert CPR Exp	12/31/2003
Cert First Aid	☐
Cert First Aid Exp	12/31/2003
Cert River Miles	☐
Cert River Miles Exp	12/31/2003
Cert Training	☐
Cert Exam	0

Record: ◀ ◀ 1 ▶ ▶▶ ▶✱ of 11

Figure 14-2 Certifications Data Entry Form

Help Keywords

Relational
  Define relationships
  between tables

Thinking Critically

1. Open the Relationships window in the **Star River Adventures P14** database file. What relationship currently exists? What type of relationship is it, one-to-one or one-to-many?

2. What is the primary key of each table shown?

Task 3 Define Relationships

1. Open the **Star River Adventures P14** database file that you edited earlier.

2. Close any open tables. Open the Relationships window.

3. Define a one-to-one relationship between the Guide Roster table and the Guide Certifications table. Relate the Guide ID field in the Guide Roster table to the Guide ID field in the Guide Certifications table. Select the *Enforce Referential Integrity* option in the Edit Relationships dialog box. Then create the relationship.

4. The Relationships window should look similar to Figure 14-3. Select *Print Relationships* from the File menu to print the Relationships window. Close the Relationships window.

5. Check your work. Open the Guide Certifications table. Click the plus sign by the Guide ID field for the first record. Data for that guide from the Guide Roster table should appear. Click the minus sign to hide the data. Close the database.

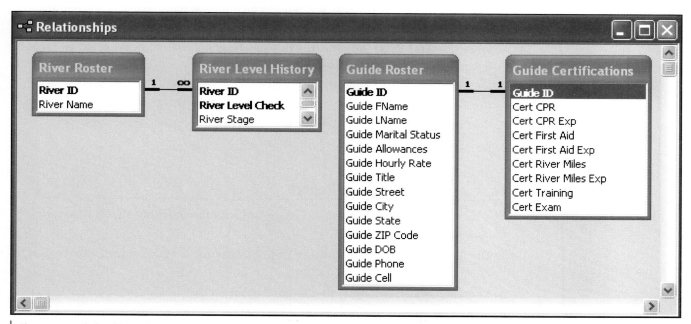

Figure 14-3 Relationships Window

Job 14-3 Run Queries and Print Reports

Skills Applied

- Opening *Access* objects in the appropriate views
- Running queries
- Previewing and printing a report
- Editing and deleting records from a table using a datasheet or form

Maria Inez has asked for your help in finding some data from the Star River Adventures database. You will help Ms. Inez by running queries and a report that have already been created. You will also update some fields in the Guide Certifications table.

Task 1 Run and Print Queries

Ms. Inez needs to know which guides live nearby in Sutton and, therefore, may be available to come to work on short notice if an unexpected need arises. The City Guide Query will provide this information.

Mr. Newland is considering raising the hourly rate that guides are paid so all guides make at least $7 per hour. Ms. Inez asks you to run a query that lists all guides who make less than $7 per hour. The Guide Rate query will provide this information.

1. Open the **Star River Adventures P14** database file that you edited earlier. Select *Queries* from the Objects column.
2. Rename the Guide City Query and the Guide Rate Query to add your name to the titles if your instructor has asked you to follow this procedure.
3. Run the Guide City Query. Print the results of the query.
4. Run the Guide Rate Query. Print the results of the query.

Task 2 Run and Print a Report

Ms. Inez has requested a report to use for quick reference that shows the guide names and their ID numbers.

1. Open the **Star River Adventures P14** database file that you edited earlier. Select *Reports* from the Objects column.
2. Rename Guide ID Report to add your name to the title if your instructor has asked you to follow this procedure.
3. Use Print Preview to determine whether the report should be printed in landscape or portrait orientation. Select the appropriate orientation. Print the report.

Task 3 Update Certifications Table

1. Open the **Star River Adventures P14** database file that you edited earlier. Open the Guide Certifications Form.

2. Make these updates to the Cert CPR and Cert CPR Exp fields. Use next year as the year in the expiration date.

Guide ID	Cert CPR	Cert CPR Exp
AJ001	Yes	1/31
CD001	Yes	3/31
CF001	Yes	4/31
JF001	Yes	2/28
NG001	Yes	1/31
RN001	Yes	5/31
TG001	Yes	3/31

3. Make these updates to the Cert First Aid and Cert First Aid Exp fields. Use next year as the year in the expiration date.

Guide ID	Cert First Aid	Cert First Aid Exp
AJ001	Yes	1/31
CD001	Yes	4/31
CF001	Yes	2/28
LR001	Yes	1/31
RN001	Yes	5/31
TG001	Yes	3/31

4. Close the Star River Adventures database.

Help Keywords

Query
   About Designing a
   Query

Thinking Critically

1. Open the **Star River Adventures P14** database file that you edited earlier. Open Query 1 in Design View. What is the name of the table used in this query? Which data fields have been included in this query? What does the * symbol mean? What is the advantage of using this symbol?

2. Open the Guide City Query in Design View. Which data fields have been included in this query? What criteria are used to limit the records retrieved? Which field is used to sort the records? What is the sort order?

3. Open the River Level Report in Design View. Which tables were used to create this report?

Job 14-4 Create Queries and Reports

Skills Applied

- Opening *Access* objects in the appropriate views
- Creating queries using Wizards and in Design View
- Creating reports using the Report Wizard
- Setting sorting options for reports
- Formatting reports in Design View

Software Review

To create mailing labels:

- Select *Reports* on the Objects bar.
- Select *New*.
- Choose *Label Wizard* from the list.
- Select options and enter data to complete the wizard.

One of Maria Inez's projects is to send a notification to this year's guides reminding them to apply for employment next year. You will create queries and reports based on the Guide Roster table and the Guide Certifications table to help Ms. Inez complete this task.

1. Open the **Star River Adventures P14** database file that you edited earlier.

2. Create a query based on the Guide Roster table. Include the following fields: Guide Title, Guide FName, Guide LName, Guide Street, Guide City, Guide State, and Guide ZIP Code. Save the query as *Guide Address Query*. Run the query. Examine the query results table to see that the correct information is included.

3. Create mailing labels using the Label Wizard based on the Guide Address Query. Select the *Avery 5160* label. Adjust the font and color if desired. Construct your label as shown below. Sort on the Guide LName field. Name the report *Guide Address Labels*. Print the report.

Prototype label:

{Guide Title} {Guide FName} {Guide LName}
{Guide Street}
{Guide City}, {Guide State} {Guide ZIP Code}

4. Create a query in Design View based on the Guide Roster table and the Guide Certifications table. From the Guide Roster table, include the Guide FName and Guide LName fields. From the Guide Certifications table, include the Cert CPR, Cert CPR Exp, Cert First Aid, and Cert First Aid Exp fields. Run the query. Examine the query results table to see that the correct information is included. Save the query as *Guide Cert Query*.

5. Create a report using the Report Wizard based on Guide Cert Query. Include all of the fields. Sort the data by Guide LName. Select the *Corporate* layout and accept all other defaults. Name the report *Guide Cert Report*.

6. Preview the report and notice the headings. To make this report more readable, rename the column headings. For example, change *Guide LName* to *Last Name*. Change *Cert CPR* to *CPR*. Use your judgment regarding the other column heads. Make adjustments to the spacing or alignment of headings and data, as needed, for an attractive report. Change the main title of the report to *CPR and First Aid Certifications*.

7. Preview and print the report.

Job 14-5 Merge Data with *Word* Document

Skills Applied

- Modifying page margins
- Using Spelling and Grammar checks
- Exporting data from *Access* tables or queries
- Completing a mail merge process for form letters

Maria Inez has asked for your help in preparing a letter to the guides, reminding them of next year's hiring and certification requirements.

1. Review letter format on page 313 in the Reference Guide. Open a new blank document in *Word*. Compose a letter to the guides. Date the letter October 20 of the current year. Leave the address and salutation information blank for now. Include these points in the letter body:

    - Congratulate the guides for completing a record season and wish everyone a great winter break.
    - Ask the guides to contact you no later than January 15 to reapply for the new season.
    - Remind the guides that to be considered for employment they need to provide proof of current Red Cross CPR certifications and Red Cross First Aid certifications.
    - Remind the guides that they need to complete the 300-Mile River Requirement, the Star River Adventures Training, and an exam during January through March of next year.
    - Refer to an enclosed report (CPR and First Aid Certifications prepared in the previous job) that lists the certification status for CPR and First Aid.
    - Ask the guides to let you know if they have more current certification information.

2. Use an appropriate complimentary close. Use Ms. Inez's name and title in the signature block. Use your reference initials and an enclosure notation.

Help Keywords

Merge
   Create and print form
   letters

3. To personalize the memo, use the *Word* Mail Merge Wizard. Merge the letter created in the previous steps with the *Access* Guide Roster table. Choose to sort the letters by the Guide LName field.

4. Insert Merge Fields for the letter address as shown below. Save the file as **14-4 Letter.** Print the source document showing the merge fields.

    «Guide_Title» «Guide_FName» «Guide_LName»
    «Guide_Street»
    «Guide_City», «Guide_State» «Guide_ZIP_Code»

    Dear «Guide_FName»:

5. Complete the merge, opening a new document that contains all of the merged letters. Save the merged file as **14-4 Merged Letters.**

6. Ask your instructor whether you should print just the first letter or all of the letters in the merged file. Print as directed.

Challenge: Research American Red Cross

1. Access the Internet and find a chapter of the American Red Cross near Star River Adventures. Hint: Enter a WV ZIP Code on the American Red Cross site to find local chapters. Use the company ZIP Code or a ZIP Code from one of the guides' addresses.

2. Open **14-4 Letter** that you created earlier. Add sentences to the letter from Ms. Inez to give the name and phone number of the local chapter. Suggest that guides contact this chapter for information about CPR and First Aid certification programs being offered. Save the file as **14-4 Challenge Letter.**

3. Merge the letters with the database table again. Name the revised letters **14-4 Challenge Merged.** Print the first letter from the merged file.

Thinking Critically

1. In an *Access* table, how do you move quickly to the last record? to the first record in the table? from field to field within the same record?

2. Assume an *Access* table contains the list of names shown below.
   - If sorting by last name in ascending order, what is the full name of the first record?
   - If sorting by last name in descending order, what is the full name of the first record?
   - If sorting in ascending order by last name then by first name, which of the Smiths will appear first?

First Name	Last Name
John	Smith
Dave	Salley
Connie	Ngim
Jim	Berry
Mike	Parra
Barbara	Row
Jill	Eiken
Beth	Lopez
Suzie	Parra
Diana	Smith

3. List three reasons why proofreading your data entry work is important. Think of this in terms of what might result if data is inputted incorrectly into the Guide Roster table.

Managing Equipment

Objectives

- ☐ Create a table
- ☐ Create validation rules
- ☐ Create data relationships
- ☐ Define and edit data fields
- ☐ Create forms
- ☐ Design and run queries
- ☐ Create memos and email

Summary of *Microsoft Office* Skills

- ✔ Open database objects in multiple views
- ✔ Move among records
- ✔ Create and modify tables
- ✔ Add a predefined input mask to a field
- ✔ Create Lookup fields
- ✔ Modify field properties
- ✔ Create and modify Select queries
- ✔ Add calculated fields to Select queries
- ✔ Create and display forms
- ✔ Modify form properties
- ✔ Enter, edit, and delete records
- ✔ Create queries
- ✔ Sort records
- ✔ Create one-to-many relationships
- ✔ Enforce referential integrity
- ✔ Use data validation
- ✔ Specify multiple query criteria
- ✔ Using aggregate functions in a query
- ✔ Apply and modify text formats
- ✔ Apply bullet, outline, or numbering formats

STAR River Adventures

Job 15-1 Create Equipment Table

Skills Applied

- Opening *Access* objects in the appropriate views
- Creating one or more tables using the Table Design Wizard
- Modifying field properties for one or more tables in Table Design View

Task 1 Design Equipment Table

Star River Adventures' goal is to be the leader in the rafting industry in terms of quality of trips and equipment. To help the company reach this goal, you will create a database table to keep track of equipment and the required service for the equipment.

1. Review the following sample record. Design a new table to accommodate the equipment data records.

2. For each field, list a field name, field length, description, and data type you will use for the field. (Do not create the table yet; just plan the design.) Complete the Thinking Critically questions below to help you design the table.

SAMPLE RECORD	
Equipment ID	RFT346
Equipment Name	Avon Professional T-8
Equipment Category	Raft
Equipment Cost	$2,099
Equipment Quantity	1
Equipment Purchase Date	02/03/1993
Equipment Serviced?	Y or N (FYI: The data for this field is entered upon inspection.)
Equipment Last Service Date	10/01/--
Equipment Inspection Frequency	2 (FYI: The data for this field is expressed in years.)

Thinking Critically

1. How should field names be defined? Why should you not name fields as field1, field2, field3, and so on?

2. Which field should be designated as the primary key field in the Equipment table? Why would you select this field?

3. How will you determine the length for each field?

Task 2 Create Equipment Table

Help Keywords

Table
Create a table

1. Open the *Access* data file **Star River Adventures P15.** Compare your design for the Equipment table to the design shown below.

2. In Design View, create a new table named *Equipment*. (Add your name as part of the table name if your instructor has asked you to name tables in this way.)

3. Create the fields listed below. Set the Equip ID field as the primary key. Close the table, saving your changes. Close the database.

Field Name	Field Type	Field Size	Description
Equip ID (Primary Key)	Text	6	Equipment Identification Number
Equip Name	Text	25	Equipment Name
Equip Category	Text	8	Equipment Category
Equip Cost	Currency		Initial Cost of Equipment
Equip Qty	Number	Long Integer	Quantity of Equipment on Hand
Equip Purchase Date	Date/Time	Short date	Equipment Purchase Date
Equip Serviced?	Yes/No		Has equipment been serviced?
Equip Last Service Date	Date/Time	Short date	Date of Last Service
Equip Inspection Frequency	Number	Long Integer	Inspection Frequency

Challenge: Find Clip Art on the Internet

1. Access the Internet. Search for graphics related to rafting. The graphic (clip art or photo) should not be copyrighted or should give you permission to use the file for personal use. Consult with your instructor if you are unsure about the acceptable use of graphics that you find.

2. Select an image and save it with an appropriate name. You will use this image on a data entry form in the next job.

Job 15-2 Create Validity Checks

Skills Applied

- Opening *Access* objects in the appropriate views
- Using the Input Mask Wizard
- Adding a Lookup field to a table using the Lookup Wizard
- Specifying data validation criteria and text for fields

validation rules: criteria used to ensure that data is entered correctly

Although Maria Inez and her staff do their best to enter data into the database correctly, errors still occur. For instance, the cost of a wet suit might be entered as $2,999.98 instead of $299.98. An error such as this would overstate the cost of equipment, causing errors in the financial reports.

To help prevent errors, you can set up validity checks based on validation rules. Validity checks can be used to establish a range of acceptable values, specific acceptable values, required fields, default values, input formats, and referential integrity.

1. Open the **Star River Adventures P15** database file that you edited earlier. Open the Equipment table in Design View.

2. Create a validity check indicating that all of the fields are required fields. These fields may not be left blank when entering new equipment. Test the rule by attempting to leave the required fields blank.

3. Create a Lookup field for Equip Category. Click in the Data Type for the field. Click the down arrow and select *Lookup Wizard*. Select the option allowing you to type in the values you want. Enter *1* for the number of columns. Finish the Wizard. On the Lookup tab under Field Properties, enter three categories for the Row Source: Raft, Clothing, Sleeping.

4. Create a validation rule for the Equip Inspection Frequency field. Require that the number be greater than 0 but less than 7 (>0 And <7). Create an appropriate validation text message, such as "Enter an inspection frequency between 0 and 7 years."

5. Use the Input Mask Wizard to define a short date input mask for the Equip Purchase Date and Equip Last Service Date fields.

6. Close the table, saving your changes. Close the database.

Software Review

To make a field a required field:

- Open the table.
- In Design View, select the *General* tab under Field Properties.
- Set the Required property to *Yes*.

Help Keywords

Lookup Wizard
   Create a field that looks up or lists values in tables
Validation
   Validate or restrict data entry in tables

Job 15-3 Create Equipment Data Entry Form

Skills Applied

- Opening *Access* objects in the appropriate views
- Creating forms using the Form Wizard
- Modifying the properties of a form
- Entering records using a form
- Using navigation controls to move among records

Up to this point, Maria Inez has kept a journal describing the equipment and the service requirements. Because the equipment is so important to Star River Adventures' success, you will create a data entry form to enter the current inventory of equipment and any future equipment acquisitions.

Task 1 Create a Form

1. Open the **Star River Adventures P15** database file that you edited earlier.

2. Create a simple form using the Form Wizard. The form should be based on the Equipment table and should include all of the fields. Select a columnar layout and the *Ricepaper* style. Make the title of the form *Equipment Form*.

Help Keywords

Form
   Create a form

3. In Design View, modify the form's design by eliminating *Equip* from all of the labels. In the Form Header, use the Label tool from the Toolbox to add the main title *Star River Adventures*. Use a bold, 22-point font for the title.

4. Below the main title, add the subtitle *Equipment Data Entry Form*. Use a bold, 16-point font for the subtitle. Center the titles over the equipment fields.

5. Insert the rafting image you saved in Job 15-1, Task 3, or select an appropriate image from the Microsoft Clip Art collection or from the Microsoft Design Gallery Live. Your form should look similar to Figure 15-1 on page 232.

TEAMWORK

6. Work with a classmate to compare form designs. Using your classmate's suggestions, add or change formatting or text to correct errors or to make the form easy to use. Widen the form as needed and move the titles, if necessary, to keep them centered.

7. Save and close the form. Close the database.

Figure 15-1 Equipment Form

Task 2 Enter Data

1. Open and print the *Word* data file **Equipment.** Close *Word*. This file contains notes about the equipment.

2. Open the **Star River Adventures P15** database file that you edited earlier. Open the Equipment form.

3. Enter the sample of equipment data shown in the *Word* file that you printed using the Equipment form. Replace the *xxxx* in the date fields with the current year.

4. Go to Record 6 and print this record only.

5. Close the form and the database.

Job 15-4 Create Supplier Roster Table

Skills Applied

- Opening *Access* objects in the appropriate views
- Creating tables using the Table Design Wizard
- Modifying field properties in Design View
- Using the Input Mask Wizard

Maria Inez would like to keep track of equipment suppliers as well as equipment. Suppliers are often contacted about new purchases, billing questions, and equipment service questions. You will create a table to keep track of equipment suppliers.

1. Open the **Star River Adventures P15** database file that you edited earlier.

2. Design a new table using the Table Wizard to store information about suppliers. Start the Wizard and select *Suppliers* under Sample Tables.

3. Select these sample fields: *SupplierID, SupplierName, ContactName, Address, City, StateorProvince, PostalCode, PhoneNumber,* and *FaxNumber.*

4. Rename the following fields:

   - SupplierID to Supplier ID
   - SupplierName to Supplier Name
   - ContactName to Supplier Contact
   - Address to Supplier Address
   - City to Supplier City
   - StateorProvince to Supplier State
   - PostalCode to Supplier ZIP
   - PhoneNumber to Supplier Phone
   - FaxNumber to Supplier Fax

5. Name your table *Supplier Roster.* (Add your name as part of the table name if your instructor has asked you to name tables in this way.) Allow the Wizard to set a primary key for you.

6. Do not relate this table to any other table in your database at this time. You will establish relationships later.

7. Choose to modify the table design. Review the properties for each of the fields.

8. Select the Supplier ID data type. Press F1 for a definition of the AutoNumber data type. Close Help. Change the AutoNumber data type to Text with a field size of 3.

9. Select the Supplier ZIP field. Under Field Properties, click in the Input Mask field. Select the *Build* button. From the list of input masks, select *ZIP Code.* Accept the defaults for the input mask and store the data without the symbols in the mask. This saves storage space by allowing you to *view* the data formatted but not to *store* the formatting symbols.

Help Keywords

Input Mask
  Validate or restrict
  data in a form

10. Follow similar procedures to create an input mask for the Supplier Phone and Supplier Fax fields. Use the Phone Number input masks for both fields.

11. Select the Supplier State field. Under Field Properties, enter the greater than sign (>) in the Format field. Change the field size to 2. Save the table.

12. In Datasheet View, enter a sample record to test the format property for the Supplier State field and the input masks for the Supplier Phone and Supplier Fax fields. Exit the table without saving the sample record.

Thinking Critically

1. How does the format property affect the data entered into the Supplier State field?

2. How does the input mask affect the data entered into the Supplier Phone and Supplier Fax fields?

Job 15-5 Create Supplier Roster Data Entry Form

Skills Applied

- Opening *Access* objects in the appropriate views
- Creating forms using the Form Wizard
- Modifying the properties of a form
- Entering records using a form
- Using navigation controls to move among records
- Creating one-to-many relationships
- Enforcing referential integrity in one-to-many relationships

Task 1 Create a Data Entry Form

1. Open the **Star River Adventures P15** database file that you edited earlier.

2. Create a simple form using the Form Wizard. The form should be based on the Supplier Roster table and should include all of the fields. Select a columnar layout and the *Ricepaper* style. Make the title of the form *Supplier Roster Form.*

3. In Design View, modify the form's design by removing *Supplier* from all labels. In the Form Header, use the Label tool from the Toolbox to add the main title *Star River Adventures.* Use a bold, 22-point font. Below the main title, add the subtitle *Equipment Data Entry Form.* Use a bold, 16-point font. Center the titles over the fields.

4. Work with a classmate to compare form designs. Using your classmate's suggestions, add or change formatting or text to correct errors or to make the form easy to use. Widen the form as needed and move the titles, if necessary, to keep them centered. Save the form. Your form should look similar to Figure 15-2.

Figure 15-2 Supplier Roster Form

5. Enter the supplier data shown below using the Supplier Roster Form. Go to Record 2 and print this record only.

ID	Name	Contact	Address	City	State	ZIP	Phone	Fax
450	WWR Suppliers	Roberts, Jane	253 Northfield Drive	Pocatello	ID	83201-2620	208-555-0103	208-555-0104
550	USA Rafting	Davidson, Gina	7343 Montgomery Road	Chillicothe	IL	61523-1085	309-555-0197	309-555-0198
650	AVON Rafts	Washington, Gamal	271 Winter Lane	Portland	ME	04101-2518	207-555-0111	207-555-0112
750	Sports Unlimited	O'Malley, Steve	70 Middlebury Drive	Rochester	NH	03867-5664	603-555-0190	603-555-0191
850	Camping USA	Patel, Makkari	229 Bretton Way	Morgantown	WV	26505-2290	304-555-0123	304-555-0120
950	Outfitters	Perez, Juan	6326 Cannon Drive	Morgantown	WV	26505-6611	304-555-0103	304-555-0104

Success Tips

Common fields are used to link tables together. The Supplier ID in the Supplier Roster table is considered to be the parent (primary) because each Supplier ID occurs only once. The Supplier ID in the Equipment table is considered to be the child (foreign) since any one Supplier ID could occur multiple times. This relationship between tables is called a *one-to-many relationship*. This relationship ensures that a Supplier ID is not listed on the Equipment table if the supplier does not first exist on the Supplier table. The validity check that ensures that the value of a foreign key matches the value of a primary key is called *referential integrity*.

Task 2 Create a Validation Rule with Referential Integrity

An employee should not be able to enter data into the equipment table for a supplier that does not first exist in the Supplier Roster table. Therefore, you need to establish a relationship between these tables to prevent this from happening.

1. Open the Equipment table in Design View. Below the last field, insert the new field named *Supplier ID*. For the new field, use a data type of Text, a field size of 3, and a description of *Supplier Identification Number*. Save the table.

2. In Datasheet View, add the following Supplier IDs to the Equipment table. Save the changes and close the table.

Equip ID	Supplier ID	Equip ID	Supplier ID
CTH101	450	RFT603	650
CTH201	450	RFT801	550
CTH301	750	RFT802	550
CTH401	950	RFT803	550
RFT401	550	SLP101	850
RFT402	550	SLP102	850
RFT601	650	SLP201	950
RFT602	650		

3. Additional suppliers and equipment may be added to the database at a later time. To ensure that a Supplier ID entered in the Equipment table exists first in the Supplier table, establish a relationship between the Equipment table and the Supplier Roster table. Close any open tables.

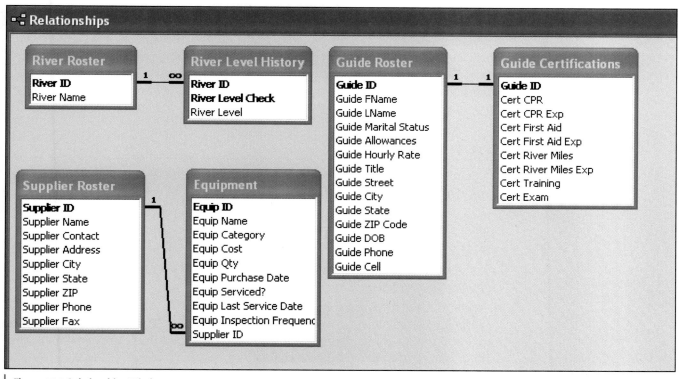

Help Keywords

Relational
   Define relationships
   between tables

4. Open the Relationships window. Define a one-to-many relationship between the Equipment table and the Supplier Roster table. Relate the Supplier ID field in the Supplier Roster table to the Supplier ID field in the Equipment table.

5. Select the *Enforce Referential Integrity* option in the Edit Relationships dialog box. Then create the relationship.

6. The Relationships window should look similar to Figure 15-3. Select *Print Relationships* from the File menu to print the Relationships window. Close the Relationships window.

7. Check your work. Open the Supplier Roster table. Click the plus sign by the Supplier ID field for the first record. Data for that supplier from the Equipment table should appear. Click the minus sign to hide the data. Close the database.

Figure 15-3 Relationships Window

Thinking Critically

In the relationship between the Supplier Roster and Equipment tables, which table contains the primary key? Which table contains the foreign key?

Job 15-6 Query Equipment and Supplier Tables

Skills Applied

- Opening *Access* objects in the appropriate views
- Creating queries using Wizards and in Design View
- Sorting records in a query
- Creating and running queries with AND or OR conditions
- Specifying and applying advanced filters in a query
- Using the AVG, SUM, or COUNT functions in a query
- Applying character and paragraph formats
- Setting and modifying tabs
- Applying bullets and numbering

Now that you have automated the equipment inventory, company personnel will be able to get quick responses to common inquiries. Maria Inez and her staff often have questions about the current state of the equipment and when it was serviced. You will prepare queries to answer these questions. The printed query results can be used as an informal report to be forwarded to the person who requests the information. You will use your word processing skills to write transmittal memos for some of the information.

Task 1 Query All Records

1. Open the **Star River Adventures P15** database file that you edited earlier.

2. Ms. Inez has requested a list of all of the records in the Equipment table. Create a query to include all fields. Sort the results by Equipment Cost in ascending order. Name the query *Equipment Cost Sort.*

3. Print the query results table. Prepare an email to MariaInez.StarRiver@trophe.com to let her know that you have placed the information in her mailbox. Print the email.

4. William Abraham, manager of Logistics, needs a list of all suppliers in the Supplier Roster table. Create a query named *Suppliers List.* Include the following fields: Supplier Name, Supplier Contact, Supplier City, and Supplier Phone. Sort the results by Supplier Name in descending order. Print the results.

Task 2 Query with Criteria/Conditions

1. Joseph Coward has asked for several printouts for a report. Using the Equipment table, create queries to find the information. Print the results. If requested by your instructor, write the criteria that were used for each of the queries on your printout.

   - A list of all of the rafts in inventory. Include the Equip Name, Supplier ID, and Equip Category fields. Save the query as *Rafts.*

   - All of the equipment with a cost greater than $3,000. Include the Equip Name, Supplier ID, and Equip Cost fields. Save the query as *Cost Over $3,000.*

   - All of the equipment purchased in this calendar year. Include the Equip Name and Equip Purchase Date fields. Save the query as *This Year's Purchases.*

- Equip Name and Equip Cost fields for all equipment with a category of clothing. Save the query as *Clothing*.

2. Once you have the four printouts, create a cover memo to Joseph Coward from you. Refer to Reference Guide pages 314–315 to review memo format. Use the current date. Include a bulleted list of the printouts that are attached. Express your willingness to provide further information, if necessary, and your hope that the printouts will assist in the preparation of his report.

3. Save the document as **15-6 Memo1.** Print the memo.

Thinking Critically

1. How can a field (such as Category in the Clothing query) be part of the query without being shown in the query results?

2. What option can be used to select all of the fields from a table when creating a query?

Task 3 Queries with Criteria, AND, and OR

Maria Inez is working with Robert Jackson, manager of Marketing and Sales, who is interested in negotiating price breaks with suppliers. He needs contact information for suppliers in West Virginia.

1. Create a query named *Supplier Contacts*. Include the following information: Supplier ID, Supplier Name, and Supplier Phone for all suppliers in West Virginia (WV). Print the results.

2. William Abraham needs printouts to answer the following requests from Maria. Include only the Equip Name and Equip Cost fields in the results. Print the results.

   - All of the clothing that costs less than $100. Save the query as *Clothing Less Than $100.*

   - All of the sleeping equipment available that costs more than $100 but less than $200. Save the query as *Sleeping $100 to $200.*

   - All of the rafts with an equipment inspection frequency of less than two years. Save the query as *Rafts Insp Freq Less Than 2 Yrs.*

   - All of the rafts with an equipment inspection frequency of greater than four years. Save the query as *Rafts Insp Freq Over 4 Yrs.*

   - All of the equipment with a category of clothing or sleeping. Save the query as *Clothing and Sleeping.*

3. Close the database.

4. Create a cover memo to William Abraham from you. Use the current date. Mention the printouts that are attached. Express your willingness to provide further information, if necessary.

5. Save the document as **15-6 Memo2.** Print the document.

Help Keywords

Total
  About calculations in a query

Software Review

To assign a format to a field in a query:

- In Design View, right-click the field.

- Choose *Properties* from the pop-up menu.

- On the General tab, click in the Format field.

- Click the down arrow and select a format.

See Figure 15-4.

Challenge: Create Queries with Calculated Fields

1. Open the **Star River Adventures P15** database that you edited earlier.

2. Create a query named *Total Cost* using the Equipment table. The query results should include the Equip Name, Equip Cost, and Equip Qty fields and a calculated field named Total Cost (Equip Qty * Equip Cost). Assign a format of standard to the calculated field. Print the query results.

3. Create a query using the Equipment table. In the query results, show the Equip Category and the average of Equip Cost for all of the rafts. Name the query *Average Cost of Rafts*. Print the query results.

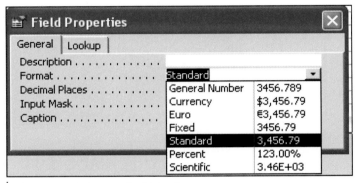

Figure 15-4 Field Properties Dialog Box

Managing an Off-Season Speaking Schedule

Objectives

- ☐ Create a database using the Database Wizard
- ☐ Modify a Switchboard form
- ☐ Review data relationships
- ☐ Enter data in Datasheet View
- ☐ Create an AutoForm and enter data
- ☐ Import and export data and link tables
- ☐ Create, modify, and delete reports
- ☐ Save reports in HTML format
- ☐ Create a multimedia presentation

Summary of *Microsoft Office* Skills

- ✔ Create *Access* databases
- ✔ Open database objects in multiple views
- ✔ Move among records
- ✔ Format datasheets
- ✔ Create Lookup fields
- ✔ Modify field properties
- ✔ Create and display forms
- ✔ Modify form properties
- ✔ Enter, edit, and delete records
- ✔ Create and format reports
- ✔ Preview and print reports
- ✔ Import data to *Access*
- ✔ Export data from *Access*
- ✔ Link tables
- ✔ Group and sort data in reports

- ✔ Create presentations (manually and using automated tools)
- ✔ Add slides to and delete slides from presentations
- ✔ Modify headers and footers in the slide master
- ✔ Insert, format, and modify text
- ✔ Add tables, charts, clip art, and bitmap images to slides
- ✔ Apply animation schemes
- ✔ Apply slide transitions
- ✔ Modify slide layout
- ✔ Preview and print slides, outlines, handouts, and speaker notes

Job 16-1 Create Database Using the Database Wizard

Skills Applied

- Creating databases using the Database Wizard
- Modifying the properties of a form or specific form controls
- Opening *Access* objects in the appropriate views

In the off-season, Maria Inez, Operations Manager, and her salaried staff are active in promoting whitewater rafting to the community. The goal of Star River Adventures is to be a leader in the rafting industry by promoting the sport of rafting and by promoting rafting safety. Because this is a separate component of the business, you will create a new database to keep track of speaking contacts and scheduled events for the off-season.

Software Review

To create a database from a template:

- Select *New* from the File menu.
- Select *General Templates* in the Task Pane.
- Select a database from the available templates.
- Indicate a folder in which to store the file in the Save in box.
- Enter a name for the database.
- Click *Create*.

See Figure 16-1.

Task 1   Create a New Database

1. Create a new database using an *Access* Database Wizard. Select *Event Management* from the available database templates. Name the database **SRA Event Management P16.**

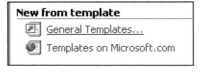

Figure 16-1 Choosing a Database Template

2. In the Database Wizard, review the list of tables that the Event Management database will store. Click *Next* to continue.

3. For the Event Information table, review the list of preselected fields. Select (add) *Notes* to the fields in the table. Review the list of preselected fields for the following tables to become familiar with the tables:

   - Event Attendee Information
   - Event Registration Information
   - Event Type Information
   - Information About Employees

4. For the Information About Employees table, select (add) the Email Name field. Click *Next* to continue.

5. Select the *Ricepaper* style for your screen displays. Select the *Bold* style for the printed reports.

6. The title of the database should be *SRA Event Management P16*. Select *Yes, I'd like to include a picture*. Select the *Picture* button. Select the picture you saved in

Job 15-3. You may also select an appropriate image from the Microsoft Clip Art collection or from Microsoft Design Gallery Live. This graphic will appear on some reports generated by the database so it should be a small graphic. Click *Next* to continue.

7. Select *Yes* to start the database. Click *Finish*.

8. Once the database has been built, click *OK* to indicate that you will complete the company information.

9. Complete the company information form as shown in Figure 16-2. Company information can also be found in the Introduction on page 7. Use 6% for the sales tax. Leave the Payment Terms and Invoice Descr fields blank. Close the My Company Information dialog box.

10. Close the database.

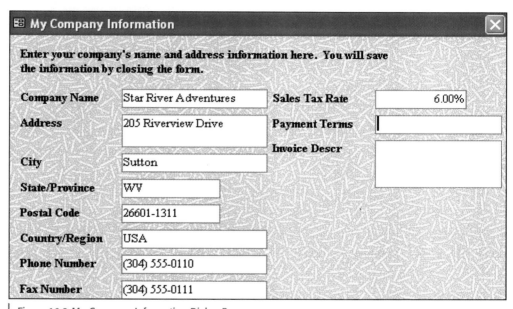

Figure 16-2 My Company Information Dialog Box

Task 2 Modify the Switchboard Form

The Database Wizard created a standard Switchboard form that appears when the database is opened. By default, the Switchboard form has a picture of balloons. You will replace the balloon image with a more appropriate image for the company.

1. Access the Internet and use a search engine to search for sites related to whitewater rafting or for sites that offer free clip art. Select an appropriate image to include on the Switchboard form.

2. Save the image using an appropriate name. You can also save an image from the Microsoft Design Gallery Live (http://dgl.microsoft.com). Be sure that any image you save is not copyrighted or that the site gives permission for personal use of the image.

3. Open the **SRA Event Management P16** database file that you created earlier.

Success Tips

When you use the Database Wizard to create a database, *Access* automatically creates a Switchboard form that helps you navigate the database. This Switchboard has buttons that you can click to enter data, open forms and reports, quit *Access*, or customize the Switchboard. The Switchboard form can also be modified in Design View.

4. With the Switchboard form onscreen, change to Design View. Delete the balloon image. Insert the image you saved in the previous step or as directed by your instructor.

5. Delete the two boxes that hold the title labels. Add a new label and enter the main title *Star River Adventures*. Format the title in bold with an 18-point font. Add another label and enter the subtitle *Event Management*. Format the subtitle in italics with a 16-point font. Center the subtitle beneath the main title.

6. Using your own preferences, change the foreground, background, and/or font colors.

7. View the Form Header/Footer. Add a label in the Form Footer to contain your full name. Place your name near the left edge of the form and use a 14-point font.

8. A sample form is shown in Figure 16-3. Save the changes to the form. Preview and print the Switchboard form. Close the database.

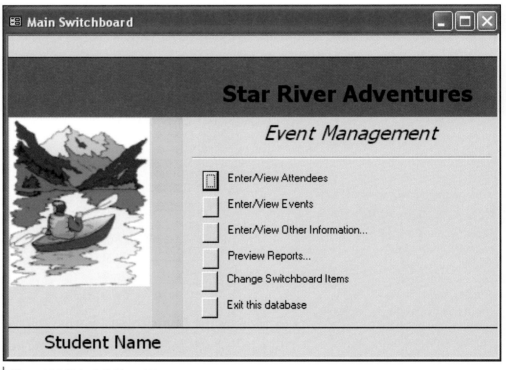

Figure 16-3 Main Switchboard Form

Job 16-2 Customize Database

Skills Applied

- Opening *Access* objects in the appropriate views
- Deleting reports in a database
- Modifying the properties of a form or specific form controls

In this job, you will review the database relationships to help you better understand how to use the database tables. You will also customize the database to fit your specific needs.

Task 1 Review the Database Relationships

Help Keywords

Relational
   Print the design of a
   database object
   Edit an existing
   relationship

1. Open the **SRA Event Management P16** database file that you created earlier. Minimize or close the Switchboard form and maximize the database window.

2. Open the Relationships window. Rearrange (click and drag) the tables and relationships so they appear approximately as shown in Figure 16-4. Select *Print Relationships* from the File menu to print the Relationships window.

3. Right-click each relationship line and select *Edit Relationships* to familiarize yourself with the tables included in the relationship. On your Relationships printout, record the following for each relationship: the relationship type, whether referential integrity has been enforced, and whether the options for Cascade Update Related Fields and Cascade Delete Related Records is selected.

4. Close the Relationships window.

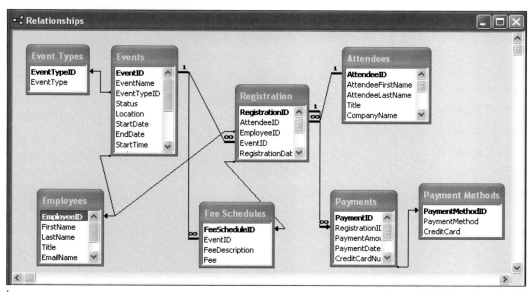

Figure 16-4 Relationships Window

Help Keywords

Referential integrity
  About relationships in
  an *Access* database
  Cascading updates
  and deletes

Thinking Critically

Open the **SRA Event Management P16** database file that you created earlier. Open the Relationships window.

1. What is the relationship between the Attendees and Registration tables? Has referential integrity been enforced?

2. What is the relationship between the Event Types and Events tables? Has referential integrity been enforced?

3. Which table represents the core of the database by having the most relationships tied to it? How many tables are related to this table?

4. Use *Access* Help to learn more about the Cascade Update Related Fields and Cascade Delete Related Records. Write a brief explanation of each option.

Task 2 Delete Reports and Update the Switchboard

Using the Database Wizard is very helpful in setting up an initial database. However, you need to customize it to fit your specific needs. For instance, at Star River Adventures, speaking events are free. Therefore, the Sales by Employee and Sales by Event Type reports are not needed. Occasionally participants do pay a fee for meals or supplies that accompany a meeting, so you will keep the tables related to payments.

1. Open the **SRA Event Management P16** database file that you edited earlier. Minimize or close the Switchboard and maximize the database window.

2. Delete the Sales by Employee and Sales by Event Type reports.

3. Restore the Switchboard. On the Main Switchboard window, select *Preview Reports*. Note that two reports listed relate to the tables that have been deleted. Return to the Main Switchboard window.

4. Update the Switchboard to reflect this change in available reports. On the Main Switchboard window, select *Change Switchboard Items*. On the Switchboard Manager window, select *Reports Switchboard* and click *Edit*.

5. Select *Preview the Sales by Event Type Report*. Click *Delete* and then *Yes*. Repeat for the Preview the Sales by Employee Report. Select *Close, Close*.

6. On the Main Switchboard window, select *Preview Reports*. Note that only one report is now listed. Exit the database.

Job 16-3 Populate Events Management Tables

Skills Applied

- Opening *Access* objects in the appropriate views
- Using navigation controls to move among records
- Formatting a table datasheet for display
- Entering records using a form and using a datasheet
- Exporting data from tables or queries
- Linking tables between *Access* databases
- Adding a lookup field to a table
- Importing structured data into *Access* tables
- Creating AutoForms
- Printing a report
- Modifying field properties

Now that you are familiar with the database structure, you are ready to enter the data to keep track of the off-season speaking schedule. In this job, you will use several methods to populate the Events Management database tables.

Task 1 Enter Data Using a Switchboard Form

The speaking engagements are one of three types: Demonstration, Panel Discussion, or Presentation. You will enter this data in the Event Types table using the Switchboard. One employee is assigned to be in charge of each event. You will also enter data for the Employees table. Only full-time employees handle speaking engagements. Guides are not included in this table.

1. Open the **SRA Event Management P16** database file that you edited earlier.

2. On the Main Switchboard window, select *Enter/View Other Information*. Select *Enter/View Event Types*. In the first record, enter *Demonstration* in the Event Type field. Note that the Event ID is numbered automatically.

3. Click the right arrow in the navigation bar to move to the next record. Enter *Panel Discussion* in the Event Type field.

4. Move to the next record. Enter *Presentation* in the Event Type field. Close the form window.

5. On the Switchboard, select *Enter/View Employees*. Enter the employee data shown in the table on page 248. Note that the Employee ID is an AutoNumber field that will be filled automatically. You should have ten records. After entering the last record, close the form window.

First_Name	Last_Name	Title	Work Phone	Extension	Email_Name
William	Abraham	Manager, Logistics	(304) 555-0110	485	WilliamAbraham.StarRiver@trophe.com
Odessa	Carr	Lead Guide	(304) 555-0110	310	OdessaCarr.StarRiver@trophe.com
Eric	Collins	Manager, Finance and Accounting	(304) 555-0110	430	EricCollins.StarRiver@trophe.com
Joseph	Coward	Administrative Assistant	(304) 555-0110	248	JosephCoward.StarRiver@trophe.com
Joyce	Forde	Administrative Assistant	(304) 555-0110	234	JoyceForde.StarRiver@trophe.com
Maria	Inez	Manager, Operations	(304) 555-0110	453	MariaInez.StarRiver@trophe.com
Robert	Jackson	Manager, Marketing and Sales	(304) 555-0110	493	RobertJackson.StarRiver@trophe.com
Brenda	Jenkins	Manager, Event Booking	(304) 555-0110	428	BrendaJenkins.StarRiver@trophe.com
Tommy	Newland	Owner	(304) 555-0110	650	TommyNewland.StarRiver@trophe.com
Heather	Taylor	Manager, Payroll	(304) 555-0110	419	HeatherTaylor.StarRiver@trophe.com

Help Keywords

Export
  Export data or
  database objects

Software Review

To export a table to
another *Access*
database:

• In the Database
  window, click the
  name of the table you
  want to export.

• Select *Export* from the
  File menu.

• Select the database
  you want to export to.

• In the Export dialog
  box, indicate a name
  for the table or accept
  the name shown.

• Select whether you
  want to export the
  table's definition and
  data or just the table's
  definition.

6. Minimize the Switchboard. Maximize the Database window and select *Tables*. Open the Employees table. Widen the columns to accommodate the longest entry. Print the table. Close the database.

Task 2   Export Data and Link Tables

The employee data would also be useful stored as part of the Star River Adventures database. Rather than entering the data again into that database, you will export the Employees table to the **Star River Adventures P16** database file, keeping the same name for the table.

1. Open the **SRA Event Management P16** database file that you edited earlier. Export the Employees table definition and data to the **Star River Adventures P16** file found in your data files.

2. Close the **SRA Event Management P16** database. Open the **Star River Adventures P16** database found in your data files. Verify that the Employees table is there and that all of the data was exported.

3. To ensure that the two tables always reflect the same information for the employees, you can link the two tables together. Open the **Star River Adventures P16** database if it is not already open.

4. From the File menu, select *Get External Data, Link Tables*. Select the **SRA Event Management P16** database from the file list. Select *Link*. In the Link Tables dialog box, select *Employees*. Click *OK*.

5. To test the link, open the new linked table named *Employees1*. Change the extension for William Abraham from 485 to 685. Close the table. Close the database.

6. Open the **SRA Event Management P16** database. Open the Employees table and verify that the extension has been updated for William Abraham. Close the table and close the database.

Task 3 Enter Data in Datasheet View

Some of the tables in the database have fields that you will not use or that would be more useful if their properties were changed. You will change the properties for the Events table and enter data using Datasheet View.

1. Open the **SRA Event Management P16** database that you created earlier.

2. Because you will be working with Datasheet View for the next few tasks, close the Switchboard.

3. Open the Events table in Design View. Delete the Status, EndDate, EndTime, Event Description, and Notes fields.

4. Because speaking engagements are held at the Star River Adventures site or at the customer's site, create a lookup field for the Location field. Select *Combo Box* for Display Control. Select *Value List* for Row Source Type. For Row Source, enter two locations: *On-site, Off-site*. Change the field size to 20. Save and close the table.

5. Select the Events table and open it in Datasheet View. Enter the four events currently scheduled into the Events table. More events will be added as other organizations request speakers. Note that the EventID is an AutoNumber field that will be filled automatically. Replace the year shown in the StartDate field with the current year. All events are confirmed. Widen the columns to accommodate the longest entries. Save and close the table.

Help Keywords

Link
  Import or link data
  and objects

Software Review

To disable the Switchboard form:

• Select *Startup* from the Tools menu.

• In the Startup dialog box, change the Display/Form page from *Switchboard* to *None*.

• Select *OK*.

Event Name	EventTypeID	Location	Start Date	Start Time	Required Staffing	Available Spaces	EmployeeID
Chamber of Commerce Meeting	Panel Discussion	Off-site	11/1/2003	9:00 AM	1	18	Newland, Tommy
Sutton Junior Boaters	Presentation	Off-site	12/15/2003	9:00 AM	2	25	Carr, Odessa
WV Scouts	Demonstration	On-site	11/9/2003	2:30 PM	3	10	Jackson, Robert
Kenton Science Club	Presentation	Off-site	11/18/2003	1:45 PM	1	25	Inez, Maria

Task 4 Import Data from *Excel*

The leader of the WV Scouts group has sent you a list of the members who will attend Odessa Carr's demonstration. The list is in an *Excel* file. You will import this table into your SRA Events Management database.

1. Open the **SRA Events Management P16** file that you created earlier.

2. Import the *Excel* file **WV Scouts Attendees** (from your data files) into the database. Locate the file *WV Scouts Attendees* in your data files. (Choose *Microsoft Excel* for Files of Type.) You want to import Sheet 1. Indicate that the first row does contain column headings. You want to store your data in an existing table. Select *Attendees* from the list.

3. Select *Tables* in the Database window. Open the Attendees table and view the data. Resize the other columns to display all of the data. Print the table in landscape orientation.

Task 5 Populate the Registration Table

1. Open the **SRA Event Management P16** database file that you edited earlier.

2. Open the Switchboard form. Select *Enter/View Attendees*. All of the people currently in the Attendees table should be registered as part of the WV Scouts event. On the first record, select the *Register* button near the bottom of the screen. A form for registration information will appear for this record.

3. The Registration ID (AutoNumber), Registration Date (current date), and the Attendee will appear automatically. Click the down arrow for the Event field and select *WV Scouts Meeting*. Click the down arrow for the Salesperson field and select *Jackson, Robert*. Click the *Close* button to close the Registration form.

4. Move to Record 2 in the Attendees form. Click the *Register* button. Select *WV Scouts Meeting* for the Event field and *Jackson, Robert* for the Salesperson. Close the Registration form.

5. Repeat this process for the remaining seven records. Close the Attendees form.

6. In the Database window, select *Tables*. Open the Registration table. Note that the data you entered using the form is displayed in the table. Close the table.

7. On the Main Switchboard window, select *Preview Reports*. Select *Preview the Attendee Listing Report*. Note that the report shows all attendees, the organization, and the number of events for which each person is registered. Also note that the report contains the image you selected when creating the database with the Database Wizard. Close the report.

Challenge: Modify Report Design

1. Open the **SRA Event Management P16** database file that you edited earlier.

2. Open the Attendees Listing Report in Design View. Modify the design to remove the Fax Number field. Adjust the placement of the remaining elements for an attractive appearance. Move or resize the image, if needed. Save the form design.

3. Preview and print the form. Close the database.

Task 6 Add Records Using an AutoForm

AutoForm: a form created automatically by *Access* that displays all fields and records in the underlying table or query

Help Keywords

Form
  Create a form

1. Open and print the data file **Sutton Junior Boaters.** This letter contains a list of people who will attend the Sutton Junior Boaters meeting. Note that a phone number is provided only for the adult leader of the group.

2. Open the **SRA Event Management P16** database file that you edited earlier.

3. In the Database window, select the Attendees table (but do not open it.) Select *AutoForm* from the Insert menu. A form appears in which you can enter data. Move to a new blank record. Enter the title, name, and address data for the attendees. Enter *Sutton Jr. Boaters, Advisor* in the Company Name field for Gary Volz. Enter just the organization name for all other records. Do not enter registration information at this time. Close the form without saving.

4. Open the Switchboard form. Select *Enter/View Attendees*. Move to the record showing the first name that you entered in Step 3. Register this person for the Sutton Junior Boaters Meeting. Select *Carr, Odessa* for the Salesperson. Repeat for the remaining records.

5. Preview the Attendees Listing report. This report should contain attendees for both events. Print the report. Close the database.

Job 16-4 Create Events Management Reports

Skills Applied

- Opening *Access* objects in the appropriate views
- Creating and modifying reports
- Previewing and printing reports
- Setting sorting and grouping options for reports

Ms. Inez is interested in knowing the status of the events schedule. You will create two reports to answer her questions about the scheduled events.

Task 1 Create a Report and Save in HTML Format

1. Open the **SRA Event Management P16** database file that you edited earlier.
2. Use the Report Wizard to create a report based on the Events table. Include all of the fields. Do not use grouping. Sort based on the EventTypeID field. Select a tabular layout and a landscape orientation. Select the *Corporate* style. The title of the report should be *Events by Event Type.*
3. In Design View, delete the EventID and EmployeeID fields. Evenly distribute the label controls and text box controls across the page. Widen column heading labels to accommodate the headings.
4. In the Page Footer, use the Label tool from the Toolbox to add the company name centered. Save the report design. Preview the report and print it. Your report should look similar to Figure 16-5 on page 253.
5. Export the Events by Event Type report to a static HTML file. Name the file **16-4 Events by Event Type Report.** View the report in your default Web browser. Preview and then print the Web page in landscape orientation. Close the browser. Close the database.

Task 2 Create a Report with Grouping

1. Open the **SRA Event Management P16** database file that you edited earlier.
2. Use the Report Wizard to create a report. From the Employees table, include the LastName field. From the Events table, include the EventName and StartDate fields. From the Attendees table, include the AttendeeLastName and AttendeeFirstName fields.
3. Group the data first by EventName and then by LastName. Sort the data by AttendeeLastName and then by AttendeeFirstName in ascending order.
4. Select a stepped layout and a portrait orientation. Select the *Corporate* style. The title of the report should be *Registration by Event.*
5. In Design View, change the LastName column head to *Employee.* Add a space between words in the column heads; for example, change *EventName* to *Event Name.* Evenly distribute the label controls and text box controls across the page. Widen column heading labels to accommodate the headings. In the Page Footer, use the Label tool from the Toolbox to add the company name centered. Your report should look similar to Figure 16-5 on page 254.
6. Save the report. Preview the report and print it.

Software Review

To save an *Access* report as an HTML file:

- In the Database window, select the report name.
- Select *Export* from the File menu.
- In the Save As Type box, click *HTML Documents (*.html; *.htm).*
- Select the drive or folder to export to and enter the file name.
- Check the Autostart box so the file opens in your browser after saving.
- Click *Export.*
- Choose the Default encoding option.
- Click *OK.*

Help Keywords

Group
  About grouping
  records

Events by Event Type

Event Type ID	Event Name	Location	Start Date	Start Time	Required Staffing	Confirmed	Available Spaces
Demonstration	Chamber of Commer	Off-site	11/1/2003	9:00 AM	1	Yes	18
Panel Discussion	WV Scouts Meeting	On-site	11/9/2003	2:30 PM	3	Yes	10
Presentation	Kenton Science Club	Off-site	11/18/2003	1:45 PM	1	Yes	25
Presentation	Sutton Junior Boaters	Off-site	12/15/2003	9:00 AM	2	Yes	25

Monday, July 21, 2003   *Star River Adventures*   *Page 1 of 1*

Figure 16-5 Event and Registration Reports

Registration by Event

Event Name	Employee	Last Name	First Name	Start Date
Sutton Junior Boaters				
	Carr			
		Black	Irene	2/15/2003
		Chang	Lilly	2/15/2003
		Park	Kim	2/15/2003
		Patel	Joe	2/15/2003
		Perez	Rosa	2/15/2003
		Rodriguez	Al	2/15/2003
		Van Cleve	Roger	2/15/2003
		Volz	Gary	2/15/2003
		York	Diane	2/15/2003
WV Scouts Meeting				
	Jackson			
		Adams	Clara	11/9/2003
		Castillo	Hilda	11/9/2003
		Chen	Rudy	11/9/2003
		Ho	Ben	11/9/2003
		Jones	Irma	11/9/2003
		Price	Sam	11/9/2003
		Ramos	Jake	11/9/2003
		Rodriguez	Sally	11/9/2003
		White	Joe	11/9/2003

Monday, July 21, 2003   *Star River Adventures*   *Page 1 of 1*

Figure 16-5 Event and Registration Reports (continued)

Job 16-5 Create Multimedia Presentation

Skills Applied

- Creating presentations using design templates
- Adding slides to presentations
- Adding information to the footer area of the slide master
- Adding text to slides and formatting text on slides
- Adding clip art images or bitmaps to slides
- Applying an animation scheme to slides
- Applying transition effects to slides
- Changing the layout of individual slides
- Printing handouts

One event sponsored by Star River Adventures is the presentation on West Virginia's Whitewater Responsibility Act. Maria Inez is responsible for organizing these presentations. She presents to local school districts and to customers planning a whitewater trip with Star River Adventures. The presentation contains the main points of the Responsibility Act, but the narrative and details presented vary as appropriate for the audience.

Task 1 Create a Presentation

1. The West Virginia Whitewater Responsibility Act is posted on the West Virginia state Web site. For your convenience, the part of the document you need to create the presentation has been downloaded to a *Word* file.

2. Open the data file **WV Act.** Read the document to become familiar with the laws governing commercial whitewater rafting companies.

3. In *PowerPoint*, create a presentation to include information from the **WV Act** file. Create the new presentation using a design template. Select a design template appropriate for a business presentation and apply it to all of the slides.

Help Keywords

Layout
   Apply a slide layout

4. For Slide 1, select the title slide layout. Enter the following information:

        WV Whitewater Responsibility Act
        Presented by
        Maria Inez
        Star River Adventures

5. Use a bulleted list layout for the remaining slides. For Slide 2, enter the heading *Purpose of Act.* Create bullet items summarizing the purpose of the Act. (Hint: The purpose can be found in the last sentence in the section entitled *Legislative purposes.*)

6. For all bulleted lists, make your bullets brief and concise. Do not use complete sentences. Use brief action phrases instead. Place enough words on the slide to introduce the thought—not to show everything the speaker will say. More detailed information for the presenter can be placed in the Notes for each slide, if desired. Do not place punctuation at the end of bulleted items (except for Slide 7). Follow this style for all bulleted lists.

7. For Slide 3, enter the heading *Duties of Outfitters and Guides*. Create bullets that summarize the section entitled *Duties of Commercial Whitewater Outfitters and Commercial Whitewater Guides*.

8. For Slides 4 and 5, enter the heading *Duties of Participants*. Create brief, concise bullets that summarize the duties of participants. Use two slides for this topic to prevent one slide from being overcrowded.

9. For Slide 6, enter the heading *Liability of Outfitters and Guides*. Key concise bullets that summarize the most important points from this section of the document.

10. For Slide 7, enter the heading *Conclusion*. Enter these bullets:
    - Act responsibly
    - Have fun!
    - Questions

11. Save the presentation as **16-5 WV Whitewater Act.**

12. Ask a classmate to review your presentation as you review his or her presentation. Discuss both presentations. Make corrections or changes to your presentation using the feedback from your classmate. Close the presentation.

TEAMWORK

Task 2 Modify a Presentation

1. Open the **16-5 WV Whitewater Act** presentation that you created earlier.

2. On the slide master, replace the footer placeholder with a copyright symbol and the company name: *©Star River Adventures*. Increase the font size of the footer to 18 points. Using the Header and Footer dialog box, apply the footer to all slides except the title slide.

3. Change the slide layout of Slide 7 to text and clip art. Add an appropriate image from the clip art or from another source.

4. Apply a preset animation or custom animation of your choice to all of the slides. Apply a transition with sound to all slides. Test the animation and transitions by viewing the slide show. Save the presentation using the same name.

5. Preview and then print handouts, four per page. Close the presentation.

Help Keywords

Footer
  Add headers and
  footers

Help Keywords

Animation
  Animate text and
  objects

Managing Information Requests

Objectives

- ☐ Create and modify tables, forms, queries, and reports
- ☐ Use the Find and Replace feature
- ☐ Use Filter by Form and Filter by Selection
- ☐ Create a data access page
- ☐ Create Select and Update queries
- ☐ Create reports with calculated controls
- ☐ Create a subform
- ☐ Create a new database and import tables

Summary of *Microsoft Office* Skills

- ✔ Create *Access* databases
- ✔ Open database objects in multiple views
- ✔ Move among records
- ✔ Format datasheets
- ✔ Create and modify tables
- ✔ Add a predefined input mask to a field
- ✔ Create lookup fields
- ✔ Modify field properties
- ✔ Create and modify Select queries
- ✔ Create and display forms
- ✔ Modify form properties
- ✔ Enter, edit, and delete records
- ✔ Create queries
- ✔ Sort records
- ✔ Filter records

- ✔ Create one-to-many relationships
- ✔ Enforce referential integrity
- ✔ Create and format reports
- ✔ Add calculated controls to reports
- ✔ Preview and print reports
- ✔ Import data to *Access*
- ✔ Create a simple data access page
- ✔ Add subform controls to *Access* forms
- ✔ Use aggregate functions in queries

ST★R River Adventures

Job 17-1 Manage Prospective Client Data

Skills Applied

- Opening *Access* objects in the appropriate views
- Creating tables in Design View
- Using the Input Mask Wizard
- Modifying field properties in Table Design View
- Creating forms using the Forms Wizard
- Modifying the properties of a form
- Entering records using a form
- Sorting records in a datasheet
- Filtering datasheets by selection and by form
- Formatting a datasheet for display

The Star River Adventures Web site has been an excellent tool for promoting the company. However, Robert Jackson thinks more can be done to capture information about people who visit the site or call the company. Currently, when a prospective client phones Star River Adventures, a staff member records the information and sends a brochure through the mail. However, the company does not keep a permanent record of the client information.

To improve this process, Mr. Jackson has asked his administrative assistant, Joseph Coward, and you to create a database table and form so the company can keep prospective client information. The goal is to use this form to collect client information from phone calls. Mr. Jackson also plans to post the form on the company Web site so clients can provide information online.

Task 1   Create Prospective Client Table

1. Open the **Star River Adventures P17** data file.

2. In Design View, create a new table named *Prospective Clients*. (Add your name as part of the table if your instructor has asked you to name tables in this way.) Create the fields listed below. Set the PClient ID field as the primary key. Save the table.

Field Name	Field Type	Field Size	Description
PClient ID (Primary Key)	Text	5	Prospective Client Identification Number
PClient Title	Text	5	Prospective Client Title
PClient FName	Text	35	Prospective Client First Name
PClient LName	Text	50	Prospective Client Last Name
PClient Address	Text	75	Prospective Client Address
PClient City	Text	25	Prospective Client City
PClient State	Text	2	Prospective Client State
PClient ZIP	Text	10	Prospective Client ZIP
PClient Brochure	Yes/No		Prospective Client Brochure Request?

To create a lookup field that lists values:

- Open the table in Design View.

- Insert the field if it is not already in the table.

- In the Data Type column, click the arrow and select *Lookup Wizard*.

- In the first Lookup Wizard dialog box, click the option that indicates you will type in the values that you want.

- Click *Next* and follow the directions in the remaining Lookup Wizard dialog boxes.

3. In Design View, create an input mask for the PClient ZIP field. Select the *Build* button. From the list of input masks, select *ZIP Code*. Accept the defaults for the input mask. Store the data with the symbols in the mask. Save the table.

4. Select the Format Property for the PClient State field. Enter the greater than sign (>). Save the table.

5. Create a lookup field for the PClient Title field using the Lookup Wizard. Select the option allowing you to type in the values that you want. Enter the following titles in one column (in five cells): *Mr., Ms., Mrs., Miss,* and *Dr.*

6. Save and then close the table.

Task 2 Create Client Data Entry Form

1. Open the **Star River Adventures P17** database file that you edited earlier. Create a simple form using the Form Wizard. Base the form on the Prospective Clients table and include all of the fields.

2. Select a columnar layout and the Ricepaper style. Make the title of the form *Prospective Clients Form*.

3. In Design View, modify the form's design by eliminating *PClient* from all of the labels. Change two of the name labels. Change *FName* to *First Name* and *LName* to *Last Name*.

4. In the Form Header, use the Label icon from the Toolbox to add the main title of *Star River Adventures*. Make the font weight bold and the font size 22 point. Below the main title, add the subtitle *Prospective Client Data Entry Form*. Make the font weight bold and the font size 16 point. Center the titles over the client fields.

5. In the Detail section, add a label above the PClient fields identifying this section as *PERSONAL INFORMATION*. Assign light gray for the back color, red for the fore color, and 14 point for the font size. Center the label over the client fields.

6. In the Detail section, add a second label above the PClient Brochure field identifying this section as *BROCHURE REQUEST*. Assign light gray for the back color, red for the fore color, and 14 point for the font size. Center the label over the client fields.

7. Replace the Brochure label with *Please send me a brochure.*

8. In the Footer section, add the current date. To enter the current date in the form footer, add a text box. Enter the expression *=Date()* in the control. Change the text box label to *Current Date*.

9. Add any additional formatting you wish to make the form easy to use. Widen the form as needed and move the titles, if necessary, to keep them centered. Your form should look similar to Figure 17-1 on page 260. Save and close the form.

Figure 17-1 Prospective Clients Form

Help Keywords

Sort
  Sort records

10. Open and print the *Word* data file **New Clients.** Close the file. Open the *Access* form Prospective Clients. Enter the client data from the printout.

11. Place your cursor in the PClient State field. Sort the records in ascending order.

12. Go to Record 14 and print this record only. Close the form.

Task 3   Find, Replace, and Edit Client Data

1. Open the **Star River Adventures P17** database file that you edited earlier.

2. Open the Prospective Clients table in Datasheet View. Widen the columns to accommodate the longest entries. Save the table.

3. Place the cursor in the PClient LName column in the table. Use the Find feature to find the client whose last name begins with *To.* Select the *Match: Start of Field* option. When you find the name, change the spelling of the name from *Tomshow* to *Tomshowe.*

4. To be consistent with the other tables in the database, change the abbreviations in the street addresses to complete words. Select the PClient Address column. Use the Find and Replace feature and the Match: Any Part of Field option. Replace all abbreviations in the addresses. Review each replacement by using the Find Next and/or Replace buttons. Replace the following: *Dr.* with *Drive, Rd.* with *Road, Ave.* with *Avenue,* and *Blvd.* with *Boulevard.*

5. Widen the address column to accommodate the longest entry. Verify that all addresses have been updated. Save the table.

Software Review

To find a value in a field:

• In Form or Datasheet View, select *Find* from the Edit menu.

• In the Find What box, type the value you want to find.

• Set any other options you want to use in the Find and Replace dialog box.

• Click *Find Next.*

Help Keywords

Filter
    Create a filter
    Remove a filter

6. Joseph would like a list of prospective clients from West Virginia. Rather than using a query, use the Filter by Selection option. Select any West Virginia entry in the PClient State field. Select the *Filter by Selection* button on the toolbar. Select the *PClient LName* field and sort alphabetically.

7. Print the table showing a list of the prospective clients who live in West Virginia. Select the *Remove Filter* button to remove the filter.

8. Joseph would like a list of prospective clients from the midwestern states Ohio and Michigan. Select the *Filter By Form* button on the toolbar. On the Filter form, select *OH* from the drop-down list in the PClient State field. Select the *OR* tab near the bottom of the window. Select *MI* from the drop-down list in the PClient State field. Select the *Apply Filter* button on the toolbar. Select the *PClient LName* field and sort in descending order.

9. Print the table showing a list of the prospective clients who live in Ohio or Michigan. Select the *Remove Filter* button to remove the filter.

10. Sort the table in ascending order by the PClient ID field. Print the table in landscape orientation. Close the Prospective Clients table, saving any changes. Close the database.

Job 17-2 Answer Prospective Client Requests

Skills Applied

- Opening *Access* object in appropriate views
- Sorting records in a datasheet
- Creating data access pages using the Page Wizard
- Creating queries in Design View
- Entering records into a datasheet
- Using the Input Mask Wizard
- Creating reports (with the Label Wizard)

Prospective clients often request information about trips the company offers. You will create a data access page to make answering the questions easier and help process information requests from prospective clients.

Task 1 Create a Data Access Page

Mr. Jackson has asked you to create a data access page (Web page) that is connected directly to your database. Employees can view this page in a browser. They can view, filter, and sort data from the *Access* Trip Packages table to find answers to questions quickly.

1. Open the **Star River Adventures P17** database file that you edited earlier.

2. Open the Trip Packages table and review the data. Sort the data based on the Trip Rating field to become familiar with the different types of trips offered. This table shows only the trips offered on the Star River. Trips on other rivers will be added later. Close the Trip Packages table without saving changes to the design.

3. Create a folder in which to store the HTML file that you will create in this job. Name the folder *Trip Packages*.

4. Create a data access page by using the Page Wizard. Base it on the Trip Packages table and include all of the fields. Add grouping based on the Trip Category field. Sort by Trip Weekend Rate in ascending order. Enter the title *Available River Trip Packages* and check the Theme option. Select the *Expedition* theme.

5. Add *Star River Adventures* as the main heading at the top of the page. Enter *River Trip Packages* as the subheading in the header of the page. Center the subheading and use an 18-point font.

6. View the page. Select the plus sign to display all of the trip packages. Select the minus sign to display only the trip categories. With the plus sign selected, your page should look similar to Figure 17-2 on page 263.

7. Switch to Design View and make changes as needed. Be sure the entire field name displays for each field. Make sure that all of the data displays for the fields when viewing the form. You may need to resize boxes in Design View. After you have adjusted the page, view and print the page.

8. Save the page as **Trip Packages Page** in your Trip Packages folder. (Add your name as part of the page name if your instructor has asked you to name objects in this way.)

Software Review

To create a data access page using a Wizard:

- Under Objects in the Database window, click *Pages*.

- On the Database window toolbar, click *New*.

- In the New Data Access Page dialog box, click *Page Wizard*.

- Click the name of the table, query, or view that includes the data on which you want to base your data access page.

- Click *OK*.

- Follow the directions in the Wizard dialog box.

- If the resulting page doesn't look the way you want, you can modify the page in Design View.

theme: a set of design elements and color schemes for fonts, bullets, lines, background images, and other data access page elements

Help Keywords

Data access page
Resize a control

9. Close the page. Close the database. If you are using *Internet Explorer 5.5* or higher, open the **Trip Packages Page** file in your browser and print the page. Close your browser.

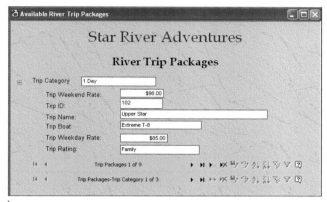

Figure 17-2 Data Access Page

Task 2 Answer Client Requests

You and Joseph need to keep track of client requests to be sure they are handled promptly. You will update the Prospective Clients table to add date fields to record when a client request is made and when that request is answered.

Joseph has received three phone calls from people interested in river trip packages. Each of these prospective clients has requested a brochure. Joseph has a form letter that he sends with brochures, but he asks you to generate mailing labels for the envelopes. You will add information for the new clients to the database table and create the mailing labels as requested.

1. Open the **Star River Adventures P17** database file that you edited earlier.

2. Open the Prospective Clients table in Design View. Insert a new field named *PClient Request Date* after the PClient ID field. Assign the data type *Date/Time* and enter the description *Prospective Client Request Date*. Use the Input Mask Wizard to define a short date input mask.

3. Insert another new field named *PClient Answer Date* after the PClient Request Date field. Assign the data type *Date/Time* and enter the description *Prospective Client Answer Date*. Use the Input Mask Wizard to define a short date input mask.

4. Save the table changes and close the table.

Update Query: a query that makes global changes to a group of records in one or more tables

5. Create a query in Design View. Add the Prospective Clients table. Select *Update Query* from the Query menu. Add the PClient Request Date and PClient Answer Date fields. Update the PClient Request to the first day of the current year (1/1/20--) and the PClient Answer Date to the current date. Run the query.

6. Save the query as *PClient Date Update Query*. Close the query.

7. Open the Prospective Clients table in Datasheet View and review the changes. Add the following new prospective clients to the Prospective Clients table. For the PClient Request and PClient Answer dates, enter the current date. Each person has requested a brochure.

026	Ms.	Marcia	Gelfer	56 Toya Lane	San Antonio	TX	78201-0056
027	Mr.	Leo	Klein	3455 Corte Cima	Thousand Oaks	CA	91360-3455
028	Dr.	Russell	Adams	3232 Fort Brown	San Antonio	TX	78201-3232

8. Print the table in landscape orientation.

9. Create a query based on the Prospective Client table. Include the following fields: PClient Title, PClient FName, PClient LName, PClient Address, PClient City, PClient State, and PClient ZIP Code.

10. Include only those records with a PClient Request date of today. Run the query. Examine the query results table to see that only the three records you just added are shown. Save the query as *PClient Address Query*. Close the query.

11. Use the Label Wizard to create mailing labels based on the PClient Address Query. Select the *Avery 5160* label. Adjust the font and color, if desired. Construct your label as shown below. Sort on the PClient LName field. Name the report *PClient Address Labels*. Choose to view the labels.

Prototype label:

```
{PClient Title} {PClient FName} {PClient LName}
{PClient Address}
{PClient City}, {PClient State} {PClient ZIP}
```

12. Print the labels report. Close the database.

Job 17-3 Create Client Tracking System

Skills Applied

- Opening database objects in the appropriate views
- Creating tables in Design View
- Using the Input Mask Wizard
- Entering and editing records using forms and Datasheet View
- Creating one-to-many relationships using the Relationships window
- Enforcing referential integrity in relationships
- Using navigation controls to move among records
- Adding a lookup field to a table using the Lookup Wizard
- Creating forms with associated subforms

Robert Jackson's department has been able to use the new Prospective Clients table for promoting Star River Adventures to interested people. Now Mr. Jackson would like to know what types of river trip packages people ask about most frequently. This information will help us with future marketing efforts.

Task 1 Create a Prospective Client Trip Table

1. Open the **Star River Adventures P17** database file that you edited earlier.

2. In Design View, create a new table named *Prospective Client Trip*. (Add your name as part of the table if your instructor has asked you to name tables in this way.) Create the fields listed below. Set all three fields as primary keys.

Field Name	Field Type	Field Size	Description
PClient ID (Primary Key)	Text	5	Prospective Client Identification Number
Trip ID (Primary Key)	Text	5	Trip Package Inquired About
Request Date (Primary Key)	Date/Time	Short Date	Date of Request

3. Use the Input Mask Wizard to define a short date input mask for the Request Date field. Save the table.

4. In Datasheet View, widen the columns to accommodate the longest entry. Add the following three records:

PClient ID	Trip ID	Request Date
022	109	Current date
010	203	Current date
023	204	Current date

Help Keywords

Relational
  Define relationships
  between tables

5. Close any open tables. Open the Relationships window. Relationships created earlier will be displayed.

6. Define a one-to-many relationship between the Prospective Client table and the Prospective Client Trip table. Relate the PClient ID in the Prospective Client table to the PClient ID in the Prospective Client Trip table. Select the *Enforce Referential Integrity* option in the Edit Relationships dialog box. Then create the relationship.

7. Define a one-to-many relationship between the Trip Packages table and the Prospective Client Trip table. Relate the Trip ID in the Trip Packages table to the Trip ID in the Prospective Client Trip table. Select the *Enforce Referential Integrity* option in the Edit Relationships dialog box. Then create the relationship.

8. The Relationships window should look similar to Figure 17-3. Print the Relationships window. Close the Relationships window, saving the changes to the layout.

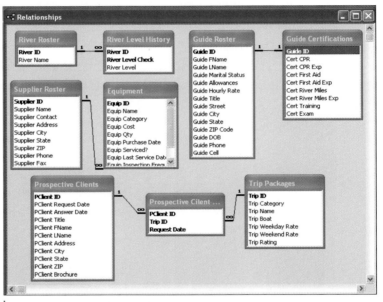

Figure 17-3 Relationships Window

9. Check your work. Open the Prospective Client table. Move to the record for Brad White. Click the plus sign by the PClient ID field. Data for Brad from the Prospective Client Trip table should appear. Click the minus sign to hide the data.

10. Open the Trip Packages table. Click the plus sign by the Trip ID field for Trip ID 109. Data for that trip from the Prospective Client Trip table should appear. Click the minus sign to hide the data. Close the database.

Task 2 Create a Subform

1. Open the **Star River Adventures P17** database file that you edited earlier. Open the Relationships window. Delete the relationship between the Prospective Client Trip table and the Trip Packages table.

2. Open the Prospective Client Trip table in Design View. Create a Lookup Field for the Trip ID field. Select the option to look up the values in a table or query. Select the *Trip Packages* table to provide the values for the lookup column. Select *Trip Category, Trip Name, Trip Boat, Trip Weekday Rate, Trip Weekend Rate,* and *Trip Rating.* Accept the default to Hide the Key column. Save the table. Close the table.

3. Open the Prospective Clients Form in Design View. Widen the form to accommodate a subform. Using the toolbox, select the *Subform/Subreport* option. Insert the subform in the lower right corner of the form, as shown in Figure 17-4.

Help Keywords

Form
   Create a subform

Figure 17-4 Form and Subform

Success Tips

The main form (Prospective Client) represents the one side and the subform (Prospective Client Trip) represents the many side of the one-to-many relationship. In other words, *one* prospective client might be interested in *many* trips.

4. Use the Subform Wizard to link the main form (Prospective Client) to the subform (Prospective Client Trip).

5. In the Subform Wizard dialog box, select *Use existing Tables and Queries* as the data to use for the subform. Select the *Prospective Client Trip* table under Tables/Queries. Select the *Trip ID* and *Request Date* fields. Choose from a list to define which fields link the main form to the subform. Name the subform *Prospective Client Trip Subform.*

6. Format the subform label for all caps and a 12-point, red font. Move the label on the subform box as needed for attractive placement. Move the form title and subtitle to center them over the form and subform fields.

7. View the form. Your form should look similar to Figure 17-4 except no data will appear in the subform fields. Save the form and subform. Close the form.

8. Open the Prospective Client form and enter the inquiries on page 268. Click in the Last Name field and use Find to locate the client. Use the drop-down list in the Trip ID subform field to select the first trip the client requested. Enter the current date in the Request Date field.

9. In the next row of the subform, enter the next trip the client requested and the current date. Repeat for all trips the client requested. Then enter data for the next client. Close the form, saving any changes.

Prospective Client	Trips
Jim Brown	1 day Sunset trip on the Adventurer T-6 1 day Lower Star on the Explorer T-8 1 day Lower Star on the Extreme T-4
Chris Merrill	All 3 day packages
Lester Barrera	All sunset trips
Bill Buchanan	All trips using the Extreme T-4 boat

10. Open the Prospective Client Trip table to review the data you entered using the form. Widen the columns to accommodate the longest entry. Save the table. Print the table.

11. Compare your printed Prospective Client Trip table with a classmate's table. Do you have the same number of trips for each client? If not, determine what the differences are and make corrections, if needed. Save and close the table.

TEAMWORK

Thinking Critically

1. How is it possible for the subform to accept the Trip ID value but list all of the details of the trip?

2. Why is this approach so helpful to the users of the form?

Job 17-4 Answer Management Requests

Skills Applied

- Opening *Access* objects in the appropriate views
- Creating Select queries using the Simple Query Wizard
- Using the AVG, SUM, and COUNT aggregate function in queries
- Creating and formatting reports in Design View and using the Report Wizard
- Adding calculated controls to a report

All members of the management team use the database to get answers to their questions. In this job, you will create and save commonly requested queries and reports so they can be conveniently accessed when needed.

Task 1 Create Queries

1. Open the **Star River Adventures P17** database file that you edited earlier.

2. Use the Simple Query Wizard to create a query based on the Prospective Clients table. Select the *PClient Title*, *PClient First Name*, and *PClient Last Name* fields. Assign the title *Prospective Clients Query*. Open the query to view the information. Print the query results. Close the query.

3. Use the Simple Query Wizard to create a query based on the Trip Packages table. Select the *Trip Category*, *Trip Weekday Rate*, and *Trip Weekend Rate*. Select a summary query. For the summary options, average both the Trip Weekday and Trip Weekend Rate fields. Use the title *Trip Packages Summary Query*.

4. Open the Trip Packages Summary Query to view the information. Adjust the column widths to display the longest item in each column. Print the query results. Close the query.

5. Create a query in Design View based on the Trip Packages table. Include the Trip Category and Trip Name fields. Include all of the records with a trip category beginning with a *3*.

6. Use the Totals row in the Trip Name column to count the number of packages that begin with a *3*. Run the query and print the results. Save the query as *3 Day Packages Query*. Close the query.

7. Create a query in Design View based on the Trip Packages, Prospective Client Trip, and Prospective Clients tables. Include the PClient FName, PClient LName, Trip Category, and Trip Name fields.

8. Sort alphabetically by PClient LName, then by Trip Category. Run the query and print the results. Save the query as *Prospective Client Trip Query*. Close the query.

Help Keywords

Wildcard
About using wildcard characters

Software Review

To view the Totals row in query Design View, select *Totals* from the View menu.

Task 2 Create Reports

1. Open the **Star River Adventures P17** database file that you edited earlier.

2. Click on the Prospective Clients table to highlight it, but do not open the table. From the Insert menu, select *Report*. Choose *AutoReport: Tabular*. The report is based on the Prospective Clients table.

3. In Design View, edit the column headings by removing *PClient* from each heading. Delete the Request Date and Answer Date fields from the report. Change the column head *FName* to *First Name* and change *LName* to *Last Name*. Redistribute and resize the fields for an attractive report. View and print the report. Save the report as *Prospective Clients*.

4. To determine how quickly the staff is responding to requests from prospective clients, create a report to show the number of days between the request date and the answer date. Use the Report Wizard and base the report on the Prospective Clients table. Include the PClient FName, PClient LName, PClient Request Date, and PClient Answer Date fields. Sort by PClient LName.

5. Select the tabular layout, portrait orientation, and *Bold* style. Use the title *Prospective Clients Response Time*. View the report.

6. In Design View, edit the column headings by removing *PClient* from each heading. Change the first column heading from *FName* to *First Name* and the second from *LName* to *Last Name*.

7. Resize the fields to make them smaller. Move the Last Name, Request Date, and Answer Date fields to the left, closer to the First Name field.

8. In the Detail section, insert a text box to the right of the Answer Date field. Delete the text box label.

9. Select the text box control. In the Properties dialog box, set the name to *Response Time*. Set the control source to =[PClient Answer Date]-[PClient Request Date]. Change the text alignment to center.

10. Use the Label tool to create a column heading *Response Time* for the new column. Format the text with the same font size and color as the other column headings.

11. Save the report. Preview and print the report. Your report should look similar to Figure 17-5 on page 271; however, the dates will be different. Note that requests that were received and answered in the same day show 0 in the Response Time column. Close the report and the database.

Help Keywords

Control source
  Control source
  property

Prospective Clients Response Time

Last Name	First Name	Request Date	Answer Date	Response Time
Acerrde	Randy	1 /1 /2003	8 /18/2003	229
Adams	Russell	8 /18/2003	8 /18/2003	0
Barrera	Lester	1 /1 /2003	8 /18/2003	229
Boblett	Joe	1 /1 /2003	8 /18/2003	229
Brinkman	Gregory	1 /1 /2003	8 /18/2003	229
Brown	Jim	1 /1 /2003	8 /18/2003	229
Buchanan	Bill	1 /1 /2003	8 /18/2003	229
Castillo	Kim	1 /1 /2003	8 /18/2003	229
Escobedo	Carrie	1 /1 /2003	8 /18/2003	229
Garza	Mario	1 /1 /2003	8 /18/2003	229
Gelfer	Marcia	8 /18/2003	8 /18/2003	0
Hurst	Dave	1 /1 /2003	8 /18/2003	229
Klein	Leo	8 /18/2003	8 /18/2003	0
Ling	Jen	1 /1 /2003	8 /18/2003	229
Lopez	Sara	1 /1 /2003	8 /18/2003	229
Lynn	Mark	1 /1 /2003	8 /18/2003	229
Merrill	Chris	1 /1 /2003	8 /18/2003	229
Miranda	Felicia	1 /1 /2003	8 /18/2003	229
Ochoa	Kristine	1 /1 /2003	8 /18/2003	229
Purst	Julie	1 /1 /2003	8 /18/2003	229
Roper	Jennifer	1 /1 /2003	8 /18/2003	229
Rowell	Barb	1 /1 /2003	8 /18/2003	229
Smart	Sue	1 /1 /2003	8 /18/2003	229
Snow	Adam	1 /1 /2003	8 /18/2003	229
Tomshowe	John	1 /1 /2003	8 /18/2003	229

Tuesday, August 19, 2003   **Page 1 of 2**

Figure 17-5 Report with Calculated Field

Job 17-5 Create River Statistics Database

Skills Applied

- Creating an *Access* database
- Opening *Access* objects in the appropriate views
- Importing *Access* tables
- Entering records

Help Keywords

Import
  Import or link data
  and objects

Software Review

To import tables from
an *Access* file:

- Open the database
  you wish to import to.

- Select *Get External
  Data* from the File
  menu.

- Select *Import*.

- Select the appropriate
  drive and folder where
  the database from
  which you want to
  import is stored.

- Double-click the
  database name.

- In the Import Objects
  dialog box, select the
  name(s) of the
  table(s) you want to
  import.

- Click *OK*.

Maria Inez, Operations Manager, would like to store statistics about the rivers on which the company offers trips. This data would be useful to the guides as they make preparations for their trips. The current database has security restrictions allowing only authorized personnel to view and edit the data. To accommodate Ms. Inez's request, you will create a stand-alone database that is accessible to the guides. Currently, only one river is listed. The guides will add the other rivers and update the river data regularly.

1. Create a blank database file named **River Stats.** Save the file to your disk or as directed by your instructor.

2. Import the River Level History and River Roster tables from the **Star River Adventures P17** database file that you edited earlier.

3. Open the Relationships window to verify the one-to-many relationship between the tables.

4. Print the Relationships window. Close the database.

Challenge: Research River Data

1. Access the Internet. Search for a Web site that provides data about river levels. Government Web sites that offer river level statistics include the U.S. Army Corps of Engineers (http://www.lrh.usace.army.mil) and the U.S. Geological Survey (http://wv.water.usgs.gov). Look for links about *water control, daily streamflow, river statistics,* or *whitewater.* The New River is in the U.S. Army Corps of Engineers Huntington District. The New River is part of the Kanawha River Basin.

2. Find the river flow (in cubic feet per second) and the river stage (depth in feet) for the New River in Thurmond, West Virginia, for the current date. Open the **River Stats** database file that you created earlier. Open the River Level History table. Enter *01* (the ID for the New River) in the River Level ID field. Enter the current date and the river statistics.

3. Save and print the River Level History table. Close the database.

Creating Graphics in Fireworks MX

Objectives

- ☐ Work with basic functions in *Fireworks MX*
- ☐ Create Graphics Interchange Format (GIF) images
- ☐ Create Joint Photographic Expert Group (JPEG) images
- ☐ Create vector images
- ☐ Animate text
- ☐ Export images from *Fireworks MX*
- ☐ Insert images in a *PowerPoint* presentation
- ☐ Work with sound and video

Summary of *Fireworks MX* and *Microsoft Office* Skills

- ✔ Add text to a path
- ✔ Animate text
- ✔ Apply live effects to text
- ✔ Copy and paste text boxes
- ✔ Create Graphics Interchange Format (GIF) images
- ✔ Create Joint Photographic Expert Group (JPEG) images
- ✔ Create text blocks
- ✔ Create vector images
- ✔ Draw objects (rectangles, circles, and other shapes)
- ✔ Duplicate frames
- ✔ Export images from *Fireworks MX*
- ✔ Feather an image
- ✔ Group and ungroup objects
- ✔ Open a *Fireworks MX* file
- ✔ Rename frames
- ✔ Rotate text using the Skew tool
- ✔ Save a file under a different name
- ✔ Set fill category, stroke, and gradient options

- ✔ Set font style, size, color, anti-aliasing, and other options for text
- ✔ Set height, width, and other options for objects
- ✔ Set the canvas size and color
- ✔ Use tools (Text, Rectangle, Circle, Ellipse, Brush, Line, Freeform, Marquee, Crop, and Skew)
- ✔ Add images to slides
- ✔ Add sound effects and video to slides
- ✔ Print handouts from slides
- ✔ Record sound and video files
- ✔ Save presentations as Web pages

ST★R River Adventures

Job 18-1 Create Image with Animated Text

Skills Applied

- Setting the canvas size and color
- Using the Text and Ellipse tools
- Setting font style, size, and color
- Setting anti-aliasing, horizontal scale, and leading options
- Applying live effects to text
- Setting options for drawn objects
- Displaying rulers, guides, and grid
- Duplicating and renaming frames
- Grouping and ungrouping objects
- Exporting images from *Fireworks MX*

Misconduct is not allowed on Star River Adventure excursions. If a customer engages in misconduct, the guide quickly reports to Star River Adventures via cell phone. The raft is docked at the nearest docking location, and the customer is removed from the excursion.

You have been asked to create an image related to misconduct for use in the presentation. You will create an image with animated text, which states that alcoholic beverages are prohibited (on river trips).

1. Open a new *Fireworks MX* document. Set the canvas size to 500 width, 500 height, and 72 resolution. Save document as **18-1 Misconduct.**

2. Change the canvas color to #003399 (dark blue).

3. Select the Text tool and draw a text box on the canvas. Select Arial Baltic for the font and change the font color to #FF0000 (red). Set 52 as the font size. Key the text shown below and apply center alignment:

   DRINKING ALCOHOLIC BEVERAGES IS PROHIBITED!

Figure 18-1 Misconduct Image

leading: the distance between adjacent lines in a paragraph

Help Keywords

Leading
    Setting leading
Shadow
    Applying shadows and
    glow

Success Tips

Remember to save your work from time to time.

Software Review

To trim the canvas:
- Select *Canvas* from the Modify menu.
- Select *Trim canvas*.

4. Select *Smooth Anti-Alias* for the anti-aliasing level if it is not selected. Highlight the text. Set the horizontal scale option to 89% and the leading option to 150%.

5. Apply effects to the text. Add an inner shadow to the text. Change the softness to 1 and the distance to 3. Sharpen the text. Set the hue to 20 and the saturation to 25.

6. Draw a circle using the Ellipse tool. Set the width of the circle to 470 and the height to 375 to create an oval.

7. Set the stroke color to #FF0000 (red) and the tip size to 21. In the stroke category, select *Air Brush*, then *Textured*.

8. Select the oval you have drawn. In the fill category, select *Linear*. Select the Fill option and choose *Black, White* under Preset.

9. Center the text in the oval as shown in Figure 18-2. Display the rulers and grid or guides, if desired, to help position the shapes. Group the text and the oval.

10. Duplicate the frame. Rename the first frame *Misconduct 1.* Rename the second frame *Misconduct 2.*

11. On the Midsconduct 2 frame, ungroup the image. Select the text and change the font color to #FFFF00 (green). Remove the inner shadow effect. Apply a drop shadow effect to the text. Set the distance to 3 and the softness to 2. Set the opacity to 80% and the angle to 243. Group the oval and the text box. The frame should appear similar to Figure 18-2 but with green text.

12. Trim the canvas. If the image does not fit the canvas, select *Fit Canvas* from the Modify menu.

13. In the Optimize panel, set *Animated GIF* for the export file format. Test your gif by previewing it in a browser. Close the browser.

14. Set the frame delay time for each frame to 75/100 seconds. Select the *Include when exporting* option. Preview again. Save the file again using the same name **18-1 Misconduct.**

15. Export the image as an animated GIF file. Use filename **18-1 Misconduct Animation.gif.** For Save as type, select *Images only*.

Figure 18-2 Misconduct Image Frame 1

Job 18-2 Create JPEG Image

Skills Applied

- Setting the canvas size and color
- Using the Text, Rectangle, Brush, Line, Freeform, and Ellipse tools
- Setting font style, size, color, and anti-aliasing options for text
- Setting options for drawn objects
- Grouping and ungrouping objects
- Adding text to a path
- Exporting images from *Fireworks MX*

Customers share in the responsibility for keeping themselves and their belongings safe on excursions with Star River Adventures. This point is emphasized in the presentation. You have been asked to create an animated image related to this topic.

Task 1 Create a Money Image

1. Open a new *Fireworks MX* document. Set the canvas size to 500 width, 500 height, and 72 resolution. Save your file as **18-2 Belongings.**

2. Select the Rectangle tool. Set the stroke color to #000000 (black) and the tip size to 1. In the fill category option, select *Linear*. In the fill option, set the color gradient on the left to #009933 (light green) and the right gradient to #FFFFFF (white).

3. Draw a rectangle shape. Format the shape with 75 as the width and 22 as the height.

4. Select the Text tool and draw a text box. Set the font style to Arial black and the font size to 14. Set the alignment to left. Set the text color to black. Enter *$10* in the text box. Place the text box on the rectangle as shown in Figure 18-3.

5. Select the Brush tool. Set the tip to 2 and the color to black. Draw several dots on the rectangle shape. Group the text, rectangle, and the dots. Copy and paste the rectangle twice and arrange them as shown in Figure 18-3. Save the file.

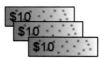

Figure 18-3 Money Image

Task 2 Create a Handbag Image

1. Open the **18-2 Belongings** file that you created earlier.

2. Select the Rounded Rectangle tool and set the stoke color to none. For the fill category, select *Linear*. For the fill, choose the copper gradient.

3. Draw a rounded rectangle shape. Set the shape width to 104 and the height to 80.

4. Select the Line tool and set the stroke color to #CC9966 (light brown). For the stroke category, select *Dark Marker*. Set the tip size to 5. Draw a straight line.

5. Select the line you have drawn; then select the Freeform tool. Set the size to 80. (Make sure the Pressure and Preview boxes are checked). Using the Freeform tool, shape the line to look like a handle of a bag. Set the width of the reshaped line to 80 and the height to 49. Place the line on and above the bag to create a handle as shown in Figure 18-4.

6. If desired, use the Ellipse tool to create a flower decoration for the handbag. Group the rectangular shape, the flower, and the handle as shown in Figure 18-4. Save the file using the same name.

Figure 18-4 Handbag Image

Task 3 Create a Camera Image

1. Open the **18-2 Belongings** file that you created earlier.

2. Select the Rounded Rectangle tool. Set the stroke color to none and change the fill color to #999999 (gray).

3. Draw a rectangle shape. Enter 72 as the width and 44 as the height for the shape.

4. Select the Ellipse tool. Set the fill color to none and the stroke color to #000000 (black). Set the tip size to 5. In the stroke category, select *1-Pixel Soft*. Draw a circle; set the width to 21 and the height to 20. Place and center the circle on the rectangle shape as shown in Figure 18-5 on page 278.

5. Select the Rectangle tool. Set the stroke color to black and the tip size to 1. Set the fill color to #000000 (black). Draw a square. Set the width to 7 and the height to 7 for the square.

6. Copy and paste the square shape twice. Place one of the square shapes at the top left corner of the rectangle shape. Place the other two squares next to each other to the right on the rectangle tool as shown in Figure 18-5 on the left.

7. Change the fill color of one of the shapes to #FF0000 (red) and the other to #FFFFFF (white), as shown. Group all of the shapes that form the camera image.

8. Arrange and group the bag, camera, and money as shown in Figure 18-5.

9. Select the Ellipse tool. Set the stroke color to none. For the fill category, select *Linear*. For the fill, choose the blue, red, yellow gradient.

mask: a method of changing the appearance of graphics, making them more creative

10. Draw a circle. Set the width to 240 and to height to 230. Place the grouped items on the circle as shown in Figure 18-5 on the left.

11. Select the grouped items and the circle. Group as a mask as shown in Figure 18-5 on the right. Save the file using the same name.

Figure 18-5 Grouped Objects

Task 4 Add a Curved Text Line

1. Open the **18-2 Belongings** file that you created earlier.

2. Select the Line tool. Set the stroke color to #FF6600 (orange) and the tip size to 1. For the stroke category option, select *1-Pixel Hard*. Draw a straight line.

3. Select the line you have drawn. Select the Freeform tool and set the size to 240. (Make sure the Pressure and Preview boxes are checked).

4. Using the Freeform tool, shape the line to look like the bottom half of a circle. Set the width of the reshaped line to 274 and the length to 103.

5. Select the Text tool. Set the font to Arial, the font size to 30, the color to #FF6600 (orange), the anti-aliasing level to Smooth Anti-Alias, and the alignment to center. Enter the following text:

```
Keep Your Belongings Safe
```

Help Keywords

Text paths
   Attaching text to a
   path

Software Review

To attach text to a line (path):

• Select the text block and the line.

• Select *Attach to Path* from the Text menu.

6. Select the reshaped line and text; then attach the text to the line. Position the text under the grouped images. Group the attached text and masked items as shown in Figure 18-6.

7. Change the canvas size to just larger than the image. Save the file using the same name. Print the image.

Figure 18-6 Objects and Text Line

8. In the Optimize panel, select JPEG–Better Quality format for the graphic. Export the image as a JPEG file using the filename **18-2 Belongings Image.jpg.** For Save as type, select *Images only.* Close the image file after exporting.

Job 18-3 Create Vector Images

Skills Applied

- Setting the canvas size and color
- Using the Rectangle, Text, and Skew tools
- Setting font style, size, and color
- Entering and rotating text
- Drawing rectangles
- Setting fill category and gradient options for drawn objects
- Setting height and width for objects
- Copying and pasting text boxes
- Grouping objects
- Exporting images from *Fireworks MX*

The difficulty level of navigating various sections of rivers varies widely. You will create a vector image related to the difficulty levels of rivers.

1. Open a new *Fireworks MX* document. Set the canvas size to 500 width, 500 height, and 72 resolution. Save the file as **18-3 Classifications.** Set the canvas color to #FFFFFF (white).

2. Select the Rectangle tool. For the fill category option, select *Solid*. For the fill category color, select #0000FF (blue). For the stroke category, select *1-Pixel Hard*. For the stroke color, select #0000FF (blue). Draw a rectangle. Set the width to 350 and the height to 250.

3. Select the Rectangle tool. For the fill category option, select *Waves*. Select the fill option and select the Preset option *Cobalt blue*. Change the settings for the middle and the right color options to white.

4. Draw a rectangle shape. Set the width to 321 and the height to 223 for the shape. Use the Pointer tool to adjust the rectangle gradient direction and length to achieve an effect similar to that shown in Figure 18-7. Center the waves rectangle over the blue rectangle. Group the two objects.

Software Review

To change the fill category for a rectangle:

- In the Property Inspector, click the down arrow for *Fill category.*

- Select the pattern you want, such as *Waves.*

Help Keywords

Fills
   Creating fills with the Gradient tool

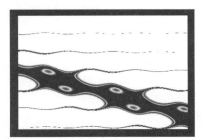

Figure 18-7 Waves Rectangle

To skew an object:

- Select the object(s).
- Select *Transform* from the Modify menu.
- Select *Skew*. (You can also use the Skew tool.)
- Drag a handle to skew the object.
- Press *Enter* to remove the handles.

5. Select the Text tool. In the Property Inspector panel, select Arial black as the font, 24 as the font size, and #FF0000 (red) as the font color. The fill color should be set to Solid.

6. Draw a text box and enter the text *Easy*. Copy and past the text box five times. Enter these words (instead of *Easy*) in the various text boxes: *Beginner*, *Intermediate*, *Advanced*, *Expert*, and *Advanced Expert*.

7. Arrange the text boxes in the order from top to bottom as shown in Figure 18-8. Select all of the text boxes. Select the Skew tool and rotate the text to a sloping angle as shown in Figure 18-8.

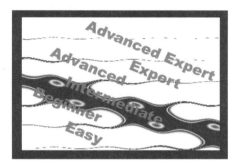

Figure 18-8 Rotated Text

Export image
Adjusting JPEG quality

8. Trim the canvas. Save the image again using the same name. Print the image.

9. Export the image as a JPEG file using the filename **18-3 Classifications Image.jpg.** For Save as type, select *Images only*. Close the image file after exporting.

Thinking Critically

1. When creating an image such as the river classifications image you created in this job, why is it important to group the text boxes before rotating the text?

2. What other techniques and tools can you use to create a background that looks like waves?

Challenge: Create Alternate Image

1. Create a different image related to river difficulty classifications. Search the Internet or other sources for an image that shows waves or a river scene to use as part of the image. Include the same text for the river classifications as used in **18-3 Classifications.** Include the heading *River Difficulty Classifications*.

2. Save the image as **18-3 Challenge.** Export the image as a JPEG file named **18-3 Challenge Image.jpg.**

Job 18-4 Feather and Crop Image

Skills Applied

- Opening a *Fireworks MX* file
- Saving a file under a different name
- Using the Marquee and Crop tools
- Feathering an image
- Exporting images from *Fireworks MX*

Customers often ask about bringing pets on excursions. For safety reasons, pets are not allowed. Exceptions may be made for "helper" pets such as guide dogs. You will edit an image to place on the presentation slide regarding pets.

1. Open the *Fireworks MX* file **Girl with Dog** from your data files. Save the file as **18-4 Girl with Dog.**

2. Use the Oval Marquee tool to draw an oval around the head and shoulders of the girl and the dog. Select *Feather* from the Select menu. Enter *30* in the Radius box and select *OK*.

3. To select the background, choose *Select Inverse* from the Select menu. Press *Delete* to delete the background. Deselect the image.

4. Use the Crop tool to remove most of the background canvas, leaving a blue rectangle around the girl and dog feathered image as shown in Figure 18-9. Save the file again using the same name. Print the image.

5. In the Optimize panel, choose *BMP 24* from the Export file format list. Export the image as a BMP file with the name **18-4 Girl with Dog2.bmp.**

Figure 18-9 Cropped Image

Help Keywords

Feather
  Feathering pixel
  selections

pixel: colored picture elements (tiny dots) that make up a bitmap image

Software Review

To crop an image:

- Select the *Crop* tool from the Tools panel.
- Drag to select the part of the image you want to keep.
- Double-click the image within the crop marks.

Job 18-5 Work with Sound, Voice, and Video Files

Skills Applied

- Downloading sound files from the Internet or other sources
- Recording sound files
- Downloading or creating video files

Help Keywords

Record
Recording sounds

Mr. Jackson has requested sound files for his presentation. He would like to include a recorded voice message to introduce the presentation. He would like to place sounds on various slides that reflect river rafting, nature, or people talking and enjoying themselves.

1. Locate sound files provided with your software or public domain sound files from the Internet. Sound files can be downloaded from Microsoft Design Gallery Live (http://dgl.microsoft.com). Select *Sounds* in the *Results should be* list. Find and download sound files as requested by Mr. Jackson.

2. Record sound using the *Sound Recorder* program or other means available to you. Record the message shown below. Save the file as **18-5 Welcome Message.**

Welcome to Star River Adventures! This presentation will provide you with important information about safety, proper attire, your responsibilities, and river classifications. We hope you enjoy the presentation and your trip with Star River Adventures.

Challenge: Find or Create Video for Presentation

Option 1. Search the Internet for video files related to rafting or water safety. Download a video file for use in the presentation. Be sure to observe any copyright restrictions for video files you find on the Internet.

Option 2. Record a short video related to some topic in the presentation. For example, you might record a video showing the proper way to wear a safety jacket (life jacket). Save the video in a format that can be used with the presentation, such as an AVI file.

Job 18-6 Add Images and Sounds to Presentation

Skills Applied

- Adding images to slides
- Adding sound effects and video to slides
- Printing handouts from slides
- Saving presentations as Web pages

Now that you have created the media Mr. Jackson requested, you will insert image and sound files into the presentation.

1. Open the *PowerPoint* file **Welcome** found in your data files. Save the file as **18-6 Welcome** with your other solution files.

2. On Slide 1, insert the sound file you created, **18-5 Welcome Message.** Set the file to play once automatically when the slide displays. Drag the sound icon off the slide so it does not appear when the show is run.

3. If you downloaded or created a video file, insert the file on the appropriate slide in the presentation.

4. Insert the images you created for the presentation on the following slides:

Slide 3	**18-1 Misconduct Animation.gif**
Slide 4	**18-2 Belongings Image.jpg**
Slide 6	**18-4 Girl with Dog2.bmp**
Slide 10	**18-3 Classifications Image.jpg**

5. Insert the sound file you downloaded on the appropriate slide. For example, you might use a sound file of thunder, high wind, or a rainstorm on Slide 5. Set the file to play once when the slide is accessed. Drag the sound icon off the slide.

6. Add clip art or other images to other slides as desired. For example, you might add an image of a safety jacket (life vest) to Slide 7.

7. Ask a classmate to review your slide show as you review his or her show. Discuss the two shows and offer comments for improvement. Make changes as needed and save the file again using the same name.

8. Print the slides as handouts, four per page in black and white.

9. Save the file as a Web page. Name the file **18-6 Welcome Online.** Preview the slide show in your browser. Make adjustments, if needed, and save the file again using the same name.

Creating an Intranet with FrontPage

Objectives

- ☐ View and modify the diagram of a Web site in *FrontPage*
- ☐ Modify content of Web pages
- ☐ Insert and modify graphics on Web pages
- ☐ Create hyperlinks to other sites
- ☐ Develop site navigation
- ☐ Apply a theme to a Web site
- ☐ Publish a Web site

Summary of *Microsoft Office* Skills

- ✔ Create and Preview Web pages
- ✔ Open, view, and rename Web pages
- ✔ Insert text and images
- ✔ Apply text and paragraph formats
- ✔ Insert hyperlinks
- ✔ Apply Web themes
- ✔ Edit graphic elements
- ✔ Create image maps
- ✔ Use *FrontPage* views
- ✔ Manage Web structures
- ✔ Organize Web files
- ✔ Publish a Web page

STAR
River
Adventures

Job 19-1 Update Intranet Structure

Skills Applied

- Opening pages and viewing pages using *FrontPage* views
- Managing files for *FrontPage* Webs
- Deleting pages from a Web

intranet: a privately maintained computer network that can be accessed only by authorized individuals, such as members or employees of an organization

Mr. Newland has asked you to work on a company intranet begun by another employee. The intranet will allow employees to stay informed about changes made in the company and to give input on new ventures. The intranet should have a consistent design throughout all pages and be easy to navigate. Keep in mind that this site will be accessed by employees only. The following pages have been planned for the intranet:

- **Home.** This page will welcome employees to the intranet and list events scheduled for employees.
- **News and Information.** On this page, employees can learn the latest information about the company and read Mr. Newland's comments.
- **New Frontiers.** On this page, ideas for new excursions and other company ventures can be posted.
- **Customer Corner.** On this page, comments from customers will be shown and employees can send suggestions about customer service.
- **Nature Watch.** On this page, guides can access links to get up-to-date weather or river information to help them prepare for their trips.

1. Locate the folder **SRA Intranet** found in your data files. Copy this folder to the location where you save files for this class. Rename the folder **P19 SRA Intranet.**

2. Start *FrontPage* and open the Web **P19 SRA Intranet** folder. Most of the basic elements needed for the intranet are present in the file. Four of the pages described earlier are included.

3. Click *Navigation* on the View bar to open Navigation view. This view shows a diagram of the pages in the Web, as shown in Figure 19-1.

Help Keywords

Open Web
 Open a Web site

Software Review

To open a Web:
- Select *Open Web* from the File menu.
- Locate the Web folder name and select it.
- Select *Open*.

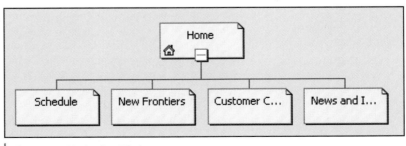

Figure 19-1 Navigation Window

4. Mr. Newland has decided that events scheduled for employees will be listed on the Home page. The Schedule page will not be needed. Delete the Schedule page.

5. The revised structure of your intranet should appear as shown in Figure 19-2. Print the Navigation window. Close the Web.

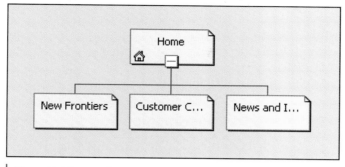

Figure 19-2 Intranet Structure

Thinking Critically

1. The Star River Adventures intranet shown in Figure 19-2 uses a structure that allows all pages to be accessed from all other pages. What other type of structure might be used for the Star River Adventures intranet pages?

2. What are the advantages and disadvantages of the other structure you identified in Step 1?

Job 19-2 Update Intranet Design Elements

Skills Applied

- Using *FrontPage* views
- Inserting graphics into pages
- Editing graphics on one or more pages
- Applying text formats to pages

Task 1   Add a Logo Graphic

1. Open the Web **P19 SRA Intranet** that you saved earlier. Click *Navigation* on the View bar.

2. Double-click the Home page to open it for editing. Choose the *Normal* tab if it is not already selected.

3. Insert the graphic file **StarLogo3** from your data files at the top left of the page (in the top border). See Figure 19-3.

4. Change the size of the logo image to 200 pixels wide by 69 pixels high. Make the alignment for the image left. Because the Shared Borders option is set to All Pages, the image will appear on all of the pages in the Web.

Help Keywords

Graphic
  Add a graphic to a
  Web page

Success Tips

Keep your logo small so it will not interfere with the way the page is displayed in a browser.

Figure 19-3 Home Page with Logo

5. Open each of the other three pages in the Web to verify that the logo appears on all of the pages.

6. Select *Save All* from the File menu to save your changes to all pages. Remember that you are saving an entire folder, not an individual file. Close the Web or continue to the next task.

Task 2 Change Fonts and Add Images

1. Open the Web **P19 SRA Intranet** that you saved earlier. Click *Navigation* on the View bar.

2. Change font styles or colors as desired on all pages to alter the design of the intranet. Make the use of font sizes and colors consistent on all pages.

3. Insert images pertaining to Star River Adventures on the intranet pages. Use clip art or photos available with your software or images you find on the Internet. For example, you might insert photos to represent the people whose comments appear on the Customer Corner page. You might insert rafting clip art or photos on the New Frontiers page. You might insert holiday clip art by the luncheon announcement on the Home page. Be sure to follow copyright restrictions for images from the Internet.

4. Click *Save All* from the File menu to save your changes to all pages. Close the Web or continue to the next task.

Task 3 Evaluate an Intranet Design

1. Open the Web **P19 SRA Intranet** that you saved earlier. Select *Preview in Browser* from the File menu. Open the **index.htm** file to display the Home page.

2. Ask a classmate to review your intranet pages as you review his or her pages. Consider the design and function of the intranet.

   - Do the links take you logically from page to page?
   - Are the fonts easy to read and in appropriate sizes?
   - Are the images used (photos or clip art) appropriately, and are they sized and placed in an attractive way?

3. Discuss the two intranets, offering helpful suggestions to improve the design. Make changes to your intranet pages using the suggestions offered by your classmate.

4. Save all of the files. Print all four pages of the intranet. Close the Web.

Job 19-3 Create Image Map and Add Content

Skills Applied

- Using *FrontPage* views
- Creating image maps
- Adding hyperlinks to pages
- Copying text from another application to *FrontPage*

Mr. Newland requests that the company logo on each page be a link to the intranet's Home page. You will create an image map and a link using the logo. You also need to add comments from Mr. Newland to the News and Information page.

Task 1 Create a Hot Spot

1. Open the Web **P19 SRA Intranet** that you saved earlier. Click *Navigation* on the View bar.
2. Double-click the Home page to open it for editing. Choose the *Normal* tab if it is not already selected.
3. Create a hot spot on the logo image to use as a link. Link the image to the Home page (**index.htm**).
4. Test your hot spot in the Preview window for each page in the intranet.
5. Save all of the pages. Your instructor may wish to test your hot spot to check your work. Close the Web or continue to the next task.

Task 2 Add Content to an Intranet Page

1. Open the Web **P19 SRA Intranet** that you saved earlier. Click *Navigation* on the View bar. Double-click the News and Information page to open it for editing. Choose the *Normal* tab if it is not already selected.
2. Delete the text line. *[Comments from Mr. Newland will appear here.]* Open the *Word* data file **News.** Copy the text from this file into the intranet page under the heading *A Word from Mr. Newland.* Format the text to be consistent with other pages.
3. Save all of the files. Print the News and Information page. Close the Web.

Help Keywords

Image map
    Add a hot spot to a
    graphic

image map: a graphic with
one or more hot spots

Software Review

To add a graphical hot
spot to a graphic:

- Click the graphic to
  select it.
- On the Pictures
  toolbar, click a
  Hotspot button for the
  shape you want.
- On the graphic, draw
  a shape for the hot
  spot.
- In the Insert Hyperlink
  dialog box, enter the
  link information.
- Select *OK*.

Job 19-4 Create New Pages and Site Navigation

Skills Applied

- Using *FrontPage* views
- Creating blank pages
- Renaming pages
- Entering text on pages
- Applying text formats to pages
- Adding hyperlinks to pages
- Managing the navigation structure of Webs

Navigation is important to the design of your intranet. The basic design has pages that link from the Home page of the intranet. You will add a page and link from the News and Information page.

Software Review

To add a new page to a Web:

- In Navigation view, right-click the page you wish to add to.
- Select *New*.
- Select *Page*.

Task 1 Create Nature Watch Page

1. Open the Web **P19 SRA Intranet** that you saved earlier. Click *Navigation* on the View bar.

2. In Navigation view, right-click on the News and Information page. Select *New* and then *Page*.

3. Your intranet diagram should now appear similar to Figure 19-4.

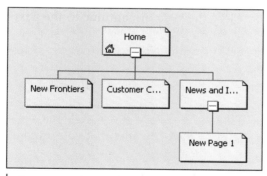

Figure 19-4 Diagram with New Page 1

4. Change the title of New Page 1 to *Nature Watch*. Change the filename for the file to **naturewatch.htm.**

5. Open the News and Information page in Normal view for editing. Enter the text *Nature Watch Page* above the heading *A Word from Mr. Newland*. Make the text *Nature Watch Page* a hyperlink to the Nature Watch page.

6. Switch to Preview view and test the link. Save all pages.

7. Add the following content to the Nature Watch page.

Weather

Current information and weather forecasts can be found at these sites:

The Weather Channel
NOAA National Weather Service

River Levels

Current information and historical data on river levels can be found at these sites:

USGS Water Resources of WV Real Time Data
US Army Corps of Engineers Huntington District Water Control

---

8. Create hyperlinks for the weather and river information sites as follows:

Site Name	Link to URL
The Weather Channel	http://www.weather.com
NOAA National Weather Service	http://www.nws.noaa.gov
USGS Water Resources of WV Real Time Data	http://wv.usgs.gov/wrt/
US Army Corps of Engineers Huntington District Water Control	http://www.lrh-wc.usace.army.mil/wc/whitewater.html

9. Test the links in Preview view. The URLs listed were correct when this text was published; however, URLs can change. If a URL is no longer correct, identify the correct URL for the site and use that URL.

10. Save all pages. Print the Nature Watch page. Close the Web or continue to the next task.

Help Keywords

Navigation
Create a navigation
structure

Task 2 Create a Hazards Page

1. Open the Web **P19 SRA Intranet** that you saved earlier. Click *Navigation* on the View bar.

2. In Navigation view, right-click on the Nature Watch page. Select *New* and then *Page*. Your intranet diagram should now appear similar to Figure 19-5 on page 293.

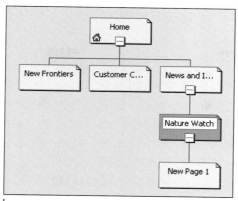

Figure 19-5 Updated Diagram

3. Change the title of New Page 1 to *Hazards*. Change the filename for the file to **hazards.htm.**

4. Open the Hazards page in Normal view for editing. Enter the following text on the page:

Reporting Hazards

Please send an email to <u>Webmaster.StarRiver@trophe.com</u> to report any new river hazards you encounter on an excursion. Include *River Hazard* in the subject line of the message. Provide complete information about the nature and location of the hazard.

Recently Reported Hazards

[Information on recently reported hazards will appear here.]

---

5. Save all pages. Print the Hazards page. Close the Web or continue to the next task.

Task 3 Create a Navigation Bar

You need to be able to navigate easily from the Nature Watch page and the Hazards pages. To make this possible, you will create a navigation bar on both pages.

1. Open the Web **P19 SRA Intranet** that you saved earlier. Double-click the Nature Watch page in the Navigation view diagram to open it for editing. Insert a blank line about the Weather heading. Position the cursor on the blank line. Change the style to Normal.

2. Select *Navigation* from the Insert menu. In the right column select *Bar based on navigation structure*. Click *Next* to continue. Choose *Use Page's Theme* and click *Next* again. Choose horizontal orientation and click *Finish*.

3. In the Link Bar Properties dialog box, select the *Parent page* option and make sure the *Child level* option is selected. Click *OK*. You should now have navigation from the Nature Watch page to the Hazards page and the News and Information page. See Figure 19-6 on page 294. Check your pages in Preview view to verify this.

4. Open the Hazards page for editing. Insert a blank line about the Reporting Hazards heading. Position the cursor on the blank line. Change the style to Normal.

5. Repeat Steps 2 and 3 to create a navigation bar on the page. The bar on this page will contain only an [Up] link.

6. Save all pages. Print the Hazards page and the Nature Watch page. Close the Web.

Navigation Bar ——

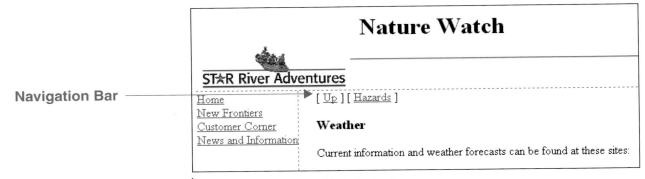

Figure 19-6 Intranet Page with Navigation Bar

Job 19-5 Update Links and Apply Theme

Skills Applied

- Using *FrontPage* views
- Adding hyperlinks to pages
- Applying themes to entire Webs

Your work on the intranet is progressing well. Tasks that remain to be completed include updating an email link and choosing a theme design for the pages.

Task 1 Update Email Link

Help Keywords

Hyperlink
  Create a hyperlink

Software Review

To edit a hyperlink:

- Right-click the text or graphic that is a hyperlink.
- Select *Hyperlink Properties*.
- Make changes as desired for text to display and address.
- Click *OK*.

The Home page of the intranet provides a link for emailing problems, comments, or questions regarding the intranet. Currently, a placeholder "Email name" is used for the email address. You will update this link.

1. Open the Web **P19 SRA Intranet** that you saved earlier. Click *Navigation* on the View bar. Open the Home page for editing.

2. Right-click the hyperlink *Email name* at the bottom of the page. Select *Hyperlink Properties* from the list.

3. In the Edit Hyperlink dialog box, enter *Webmaster* in the Text to display box. In the Email address box, enter *mailto:Webmaster.StarRiver@trophe.com*. (Mail sent to this address will return an "undeliverable" message. Your instructor may give you another address to use.) Select *OK*.

4. On the Home page, change the sentence to read:

   ```
   For problems or questions regarding this Web,
   contact the SRA Webmaster.
   ```

5. Your link should now be visible on all pages. Save all pages. Close the Web or continue to the next task.

Task 2 Apply a Theme

theme: a unified set of design elements and color schemes that can be applied to Web pages

Help Keywords

Theme
  Apply a theme

1. Open the Web **P19 SRA Intranet** that you saved earlier. Click *Navigation* on the View bar.

2. Now that the intranet is almost completed, you can add a theme to the entire project. From the Format menu, select *Theme*. Apply the theme to the whole project so all pages are consistent throughout.

3. Scroll through the themes and select one that is appropriate for Star River Adventures. Keep in mind the overall company image and any graphics you may have added to the intranet pages. A sample page with a theme applied is shown in Figure 19-7 on page 296.

4. Preview your pages and make any final adjustments that are needed. For example, check the spelling on all pages and read carefully to find all errors. You may wish to change the width of tables or cells to make some pages display more attractively. You may wish to adjust the size of the company logo or other images you have placed on pages.

5. Save all pages. Print all pages of the intranet. Close the Web.

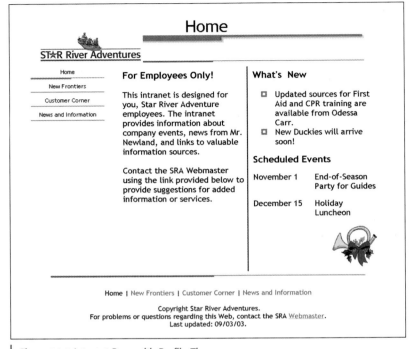

Figure 19-7 Intranet Page with Profile Theme

Challenge: Modify an Intranet

Option 1. Mr. Newland may require frequent changes to the intranet content. Create a version of your intranet using frames to allow pages to open within a single page.

Option 2. Employees have requested the ability to post information and questions on the site in real time. Create an additional page for the intranet where a bulletin board will show comments made by employees.

Job 19-6 Publish Intranet

Skills Applied

- Using *FrontPage* views
- Publishing Webs

protocol: rules that organize the execution of a function

Once all of the pages for an intranet are complete, the files can be posted to a company intranet site. *FrontPage* can be used to post and update an intranet site. Another option for publishing to the Internet is to use an FTP (File Transfer Protocol) program. Several FTP programs are available on the Internet as freeware or shareware.

If you instructor has provided you with a Web address to which you may publish your site, complete the steps in this job. If not, simply read the steps to review the process of publishing an intranet.

1. In *FrontPage*, open the Web **P19 SRA Intranet** that you saved earlier.

2. To publish your intranet, select *Publish Web* from the File menu. The Publish Destination dialog box appears as shown in Figure 19-8.

3. Enter the Web address of the server where your intranet will be published (provided by your instructor) and select *OK*. The server or Web space must support *FrontPage* to use this function.

4. Access your online intranet and review the pages to make sure all links work properly and pages display correctly.

Help Keywords

Publish
   Publish a Web site

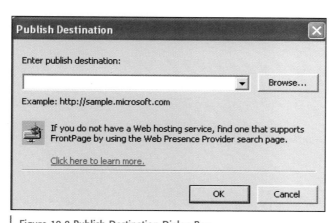

Figure 19-8 Publish Destination Dialog Box

Mr. Newland and several managers will attend the National Outfitting and Adventure Trade Show in Las Vegas, Nevada, during October 15-18. The annual show is an opportunity for the company to gain national exposure. It also allows the attendees to learn about the latest equipment and events related to whitewater rafting.

At this show, Mr. Newland and the managers are able to meet representatives from travel agencies throughout the United States. These agents can arrange trips through Star River Adventures.

This show is an important event for Star River Adventures. The company has budgeted money for several expenses related to the show. These expenses include:

- Travel
- Entertainment of potential clients
- Exhibit space rental
- Displays
- Brochures and handouts
- Media presentations

Several employees, including you, will be asked to assist in preparing for this event.

You have worked in Marketing and Sales, Finance and Accounting, and Operations as you completed Parts 1-3 of this simulation. In this part, you will work for Mr. Newland and other managers as you complete tasks related to various departments. You must use your creativity and communication, decision-making, and critical-thinking skills as you complete the jobs, which have fewer detailed instructions than those in previous projects. You must also apply and integrate skills you have practiced in other assignments as you complete this capstone project.

Preparing for a Trade Show

Objectives

- ☐ Prepare travel expense requests and summary worksheets
- ☐ Compose memos and letters
- ☐ Create letters using mail merge and an *Access* data table
- ☐ Create a new database
- ☐ Create database tables, queries, and reports
- ☐ Create presentations and brochures
- ☐ Record sound files
- ☐ Create *Excel* charts and integrate with *Word* documents

Summary of *Microsoft Office* Skills

- ✔ Create workbooks using templates
- ✔ Save workbooks using different names and file formats
- ✔ Preview and print worksheets and workbooks
- ✔ Enter and edit cell data, including text, numbers, and formulas
- ✔ Manage workbook files and folders
- ✔ Insert and delete worksheets
- ✔ Modify worksheet names and positions
- ✔ Modify row and column formats
- ✔ Apply and modify cell formats
- ✔ Create and revise formulas
- ✔ Create, modify, position, and print charts
- ✔ Modify paragraph formats
- ✔ Apply and modify text formats
- ✔ Set and modify tabs
- ✔ Create and modify a header and footer
- ✔ Insert images and graphics
- ✔ Preview and print documents, envelopes, and labels
- ✔ Merge letters with an *Access* data source
- ✔ Create documents using templates
- ✔ Apply paragraph styles

- ✔ Insert, cut, copy, and paste special text
- ✔ Correct spelling and grammar usage
- ✔ Apply and modify column settings
- ✔ Create *Access* databases
- ✔ Import data to *Access*
- ✔ Create and modify tables
- ✔ Sort records
- ✔ Create queries
- ✔ Create and format reports
- ✔ Open database objects in multiple views
- ✔ Enter, edit, and delete records
- ✔ Create and display forms
- ✔ Create presentations
- ✔ Add slides to presentations
- ✔ Insert, format, and modify text on slides
- ✔ Add tables, charts, clip art, and bitmap images to slides
- ✔ Add OfficeArt elements to slides
- ✔ Apply slide transitions
- ✔ Apply animation schemes
- ✔ Add sound to slides
- ✔ Print handouts of slides
- ✔ Publish presentations to the Web

Job 20-1 Prepare Requests for Travel

Skills Applied

- Creating a workbook from a template
- Using Save As to store workbooks to different locations or names
- Printing a worksheet
- Applying paragraph formats
- Setting and modifying tabs
- Creating and modifying a document header
- Adding images to a document
- Printing a document

Mr. Newland has provided you with information to complete requests for travel for employees attending a trade show in Las Vegas.

1. Open and print the data file **Travel Requests Email.** This document contains Mr. Newland's notes and instructions regarding the travel arrangements.

2. Complete the request for travel forms as requested by Mr. Newland. Use the file **Request for Travel Template** found in your data files. Complete all three sections of the form. Use September 15 of the current year as the date the requests are prepared and processed.

Help Keywords

Copy
Copy sheets

3. Most of the information on the request for travel forms will be the same for all individuals. After completing the first form, copy the worksheet and update it for the next employee. Repeat this process to create a worksheet for each individual. Rename each sheet using the employee's last name. Save the workbook as **20-1 Travel Requests.** Print all of the request for travel forms.

Success Tips

Review the proper format for a memo in the Reference Guide on pages 314–315.

4. Write a memo from you to the managers who will attend the trade show, summarizing the travel arrangements Mr. Newland has made. Include the information listed below. Allow one hour and fifteen minutes travel time to and from the airport.

   - Trade show name
   - Departure times
   - Specific travel arrangements made
   - Anticipated time schedule

5. Insert the company logo in the memo in a header, using the data file **StarLogo2.** Right-align the image.

6. Save your memo as **20-1 Memo.** Print the memo.

Job 20-2 Create Contacts Database

Skills Applied

- Creating an *Access* database
- Importing structured data into *Access* tables
- Sorting records in a datasheet
- Completing an entire mail merge process for form letters
- Creating Select queries
- Creating and formatting *Access* reports

Robert Jackson has a list of travel agents and vendors who will likely attend the National Outfitting and Adventure Trade Show. He has asked you to create a database for these contacts so the data can be sorted and queried more easily.

Task 1 Create a New Database

1. Open the *Excel* file **Contacts List** found in your data files. Review the type of data in this file. Close the file.

2. In *Access*, create a new database file named **P20 Contacts.** Import the data from the *Excel* file **Contacts List** as a new table into the **P20 Contacts** database file. Name the new table *Contacts from Jackson.*

3. Open the Contacts from Jackson table. Sort the table in ascending order by ZIP Code. Print the table. Save and close the table. Close the database.

Task 2 Create Promotional Letters

Companies attending trade shows often mail cards or letters to people who will be attending the show. These letters usually invite attendees to stop by the company's booth or to attend presentations. You have been asked to create such a letter for Mr. Jackson.

1. In *Word*, write a letter to be sent to each of Mr. Jackson's contacts. Assume the letter will be printed on letterhead paper. Date the letter September 15 of the current year. Leave the address and salutation information blank for now.

2. Writing as Mr. Jackson, include these points in the letter body:

   - Thank the person for his or her previous interest in Star River Adventures.
   - Mention that you enjoyed talking with him or her at last year's National Outfitting and Adventure Trade Show. Say that you are excited about this year's show and hope to see him or her there.
   - Invite him or her to stop by the Star River Adventures booth to learn about new trips the company offers.
   - Mention that you are enclosing a brochure about Star River Adventures.
   - Ask him or her to let you know if you can provide any information about Star River Adventures before the show.

3. Use an appropriate complimentary close. Use Mr. Jackson's full name and title in the signature block. Use your reference initials and an enclosure notation.

Success Tips

Add your name as part of the database elements you create if your instructor has asked you to name files and objects in this way.

Help Keywords

Import
   Import or link data
   and objects

Success Tips

Ask a classmate to review your letter and offer suggestions for improvement before merging the letters.

Help Keywords

Merge
  Create and print form
  letters

4. You will merge this letter with the database table Contacts from Jackson. Insert appropriate mail merge codes for the letter address and salutation. Sort the recipients list so the merged letters will be in ascending order by ZIP Code. Save the letter as **20-2 Letter.**

5. Merge the letter you created with the database table Contacts from Jackson in the **P20 Contacts** database. Save the merged letters as **20-2 Merged Letters.** Print the letters.

Task 3 Create Queries and Reports

Mr. Jackson has requested a report showing selected information from the database.

Help Keywords

Query
  Create a Select or
  Crosstab query

1. Open the **P20 Contacts** database file that you created earlier.

2. Create a query based on the Contacts from Jackson table. The query results should include the title, first name, last name, company name, city, and state for all records. Run the query. Save the query as *Report Query*. Close the query.

3. Create a report based on the Report Query. Name the report *NOATS Contacts from Jackson*. Include all fields from the query. Sort the data by company name.

4. Open the report in Design View and make any adjustments needed for an attractive report. Print the report. Close the database.

Job 20-3 Prepare Brochure

Skills Applied

- Creating a document from a template
- Applying columns and modifying text alignment
- Applying paragraph styles and formats
- Adding images to documents
- Copying and pasting text
- Using Spelling and Grammar checks

Mr. Newland wants a brochure prepared that will be sent to various vendors and travel agents. The brochures will also be distributed at the National Outfitting and Adventure Trade Show. He has asked you to organize a team of employees to prepare the brochure.

> **Success Tips**
>
> Open the *Word* file **4-4 Brochure** that you created earlier to review a trifold brochure format.

1. Create a brochure in three-column format to be printed on both sides of a sheet in landscape orientation. The brochure will be a trifold similar to the one you created in Project 4. You may wish to use a brochure template to set up the document.

2. Include the following information in the brochure:

   - The company name and logo (use the data file **StarLogo1**)
   - The company address and phone number
   - A brief description of where the trips take place
   - A brief description of excursions and special events
   - A brief section about the company's emphasis on safety
   - Operation dates and recommended attire
   - Other information you think will create interest in Star River Adventures

3. Work with two or three classmates to write the articles for the brochure. Use the introduction to the textbook and the various jobs you completed in other projects to find information you can use or adapt for the brochure articles. Give each article an appropriate title.

4. The brochure will be printed in color. Include images such as photos, clip art, or *PowerPoint* slides related to rafting, safety, or special events.

5. Save your completed document as **20-3 Brochure.** Print the brochure. Work with your classmates again to proofread and correct the brochure. Print a final copy of the brochure.

TEAMWORK

Job 20-4 Create Presentations

Skills Applied

- Creating presentations from a blank presentation
- Adding slides to presentations
- Adding text to slides
- Creating tables on slides
- Adding clip art and other images to slides
- Adding OfficeArt elements to slides
- Applying transition effects
- Applying animation to slides
- Adding sound effects to slides
- Printing handouts
- Saving presentations in HTML format

kiosk: unmanned booths or stands, often containing computers or monitors, placed in public places to provide information

Task 1 Create a Kiosk Presentation

Mr. Newland wants you to prepare a presentation that will be displayed at a kiosk at the company's exhibition area at the trade show. He has sketched out the presentation and provided general guidelines for each slide. You may be able to use graphics and pictures from shows you created earlier. You can also copy and paste slides from earlier presentations, if appropriate.

1. Open the *Word* data file **Kiosk Show.** This document contains Mr. Newland's notes and instructions for the slide.

2. Create a presentation as directed by Mr. Newland. Add appropriate transitions to all slides.

3. Have the slides display automatically, allowing enough time for viewers to read the content of each slide. Set up the slide show to loop continuously.

TEAMWORK

4. Ask a classmate to evaluate your slide show and make suggestions for improving it. Make any needed changes. Save the file as **20-4 Kiosk Show.** Print the show as handouts, four per page in black and white.

5. Save the presentation as a Web page. Use *Star River Adventures* as the page title. Name the Web file **20-4 Kiosk Web Page.** View the Web file in a browser. Make changes, if needed, after viewing the file.

Task 2 Prepare Mr. Newland's Presentation

Mr. Newland has asked you to prepare a slide show for his presentation at the National Outfitting and Adventure Trade Show. The slides will support his presentation by providing visual images of the main points to appeal to the audience.

Mr. Newland's session is scheduled for 45 minutes. He estimates the introduction by the chair of the session will take about five minutes. He will leave 10 to 15 minutes for a question-and-answer session. A good guide to use for the number of slides needed for a presentation is about one slide for every two minutes.

1. Open and print the data file **Changing Business.** This file contains Mr. Newland's notes and instructions for the slide show. Create the slides as requested by Mr. Newland.

2. Add appropriate slide transitions. Add the following footer to appear on all slides: © *Star River Adventures.*

3. Save the presentation as **20-4 Changing Business.** Print handouts four per page in black and white.

Help Keywords

Footer
  Add headers and
  footers

Success Tips

Enter the footer on the slide master where you can access the Insert, Symbol command for the copyright symbol.

Challenge: Research Travel Costs

Mr. Newland wants you to make sure he has chosen the least expensive flights for employees traveling to the trade show.

1. Access the Internet. Search for the best price for airline tickets for the party traveling to the trade show. They can leave any time after 9 a.m. on October 15. They can return any time after 1 p.m. on October 18. Mr. Newland wants to be back at Star River Adventures no later than 11 p.m., so consider the driving time when choosing flights.

2. Write a short memo explaining your recommendations to Mr. Newland for the airline, the price, and the schedule you recommend. Save your memo as **20-4 Challenge Memo.** Attach a printout showing the flight schedule and price you recommend, if possible.

Job 20-5 Complete Follow-up Reports

Skills Applied

- Locating and opening existing workbooks
- Entering and editing text and numbers in cells
- Inserting and copying sheets in a workbook
- Formatting worksheet tabs
- Formatting cells
- Modifying alignment
- Creating formulas using functions
- Creating, formatting, and printing charts

The employees have returned from the National Outfitting and Adventure Trade Show. You have been asked to check their expense reports and create a worksheet summarizing travel expenses for the show.

1. Individuals who attended the National Outfitting and Adventure Trade Show have sent you their expense reports (data files **Newland 10-19.xls, Jackson 10-19.xls, Inez 10-19.xls, Abraham 10-19.xls,** and **Collins 10-19.xls**). Open and print each expense report.

2. Check each expense report to see that the Advance Received amount is equal to the Amount available for advance on the employee's request for travel form that you created before the trip. Make corrections on the travel expense reports if needed.

3. On September 20, Mr. Newland decided to pay the registration for all employees in advance. Check each expense report to see that the registration amount is shown for Other Expense Paid in Advance. Make corrections on the travel expense reports if needed.

4. Check each expense report to see that the proper amount is shown for Airfare Paid in Advance. Make corrections on the travel expense reports if needed.

5. Save the corrected forms in the folder with your other solutions for this project. Print any reports that you corrected.

6. Open a new workbook. Save the workbook as **20-5 NOATS Worksheet.** Copy the five expense reports for those who attended the trade show, each to a separate sheet into **NOAST Workbook.** Name each sheet with the last name of the individual.

7. Add a new sheet to the NOAST Workbook. Name the sheet *Summary.* Enter the information provided by Mr. Newland (shown in Figure 20-1 on page 308) into the Summary sheet. Use your own judgment for formatting the worksheet.

8. Enter formulas in the appropriate cells to calculate the summary amounts. For example, the Airfare amount should be the total airfare for the five employees who attended the show. For the Per Diem amount, enter the amount paid, not the number of per diem hours. Save the workbook again using the same name. Print the Summary sheet.

Help Keywords

Sheet
Move or copy sheets

Help Keywords

Formula
Create a formula

9. Prepare a pie chart that compares total expenses for the trade show in each of the three categories: Transportation, Lodging and Meals, and Miscellaneous. Place the chart on a separate sheet in the workbook. Save the workbook again using the same name. Print the chart.

STAR RIVER ADVENTURES
205 Riverview Drive
Sutton, WV 26601-1311

Travel Expense Report Summary
National Outfitters and Adventure Trade Show

Transportation
Personal Auto
Airfare
Auto Rental
Taxi
Other
     Total Transportation

Lodging and Meals
Per Diem
Hotel
Other
     Total Lodging and Meals

Miscellaneous Expenses
Entertainment
Rentals
Phone or FAX
Copying and Printing
Registration
Other
     Total Miscellaneous

Figure 20-1 Notes from Mr. Newland

Job 20-6 Prepare Follow-up Correspondence

Skills Applied

- Applying character formats
- Setting and modifying tabs
- Adding images to a document
- Opening *Access* objects in the appropriate views
- Creating an *Access* table by copying a table
- Entering and deleting records in a database
- Creating AutoForms
- Completing an entire mail merge process for form letters

Mr. Newland has asked you to prepare a memo regarding travel expenses for the employees who attended the trade show. He has also asked that you write letters to travel agencies that indicated an interest in booking excursions with Star River Adventures at the trade show.

Task 1 Prepare Memo to Employees

Success Tips

Review using a distribution list in a memo in the Reference Guide on pages 314–315.

1. Prepare a memo from Mr. Newland to be sent to those individuals who attended the trade show. The memo is from Mr. Newland on October 20 of the current year. Use *Distribution List* in the To heading and list the employees at the end of the memo. Use an appropriate subject line.

2. In the body of the memo, thank the employees for their hard work. Mention how beneficial the show was to Star River Adventures because of the many important contacts made.

3. Use Paste Special to paste a copy of the pie chart in the memo as a picture. Refer to the chart in the text of the memo and congratulate employees on keeping travel costs low.

4. Save the document as **20-6 Memo.** Print the memo.

Task 2 Prepare Letter to Travel Agents

1. Prepare a follow-up letter from Tommy Newland to the travel agencies. Assume the letter will be printed on letterhead paper. Use October 20 of the current year as the letter date. Leave the letter address and salutation blank for now.

2. In the body of the letter:
   - Thank the person for his or her interest in the company.
   - State that we feel confident we can develop a business arrangement with the travel agency that will be beneficial to the agency and to Star River Adventures.
   - Mention that we will provide clients with a first-rate, quality excursion at a competitive price.
   - Indicate that a representative from Star River Adventures will contact this person in the near future to discuss the type of services we can provide.

3. Include an appropriate complimentary close. Use Mr. Newland's full name and title in the signature block. Save the letter as **20-6 Letter.**

4. Open the **P20 Contacts** database file you created earlier. Create a copy of the Contacts from Jackson table. Name the new table *Contacts from Newland*. Delete all of the records in the new table.

5. Open and print the *Word* file **Travel Agents** from your data files. This file contains information collected from travel agents at the trade show. Use these source documents to enter data into the Contacts from Newland database table. You may wish to create an AutoForm based on the Contacts from Newland table to make data entry easier. Save and close the database.

6. Open the file **20-6 Letter** that you created earlier. You will merge this letter with the database table Contacts from Newland. Insert appropriate mail merge codes for the letter address and salutation. Save the letter again using the same name.

7. Merge the letter you created with the database table Contacts from Newland in the **P20 Contacts** database. Save the merged letters as **20-6 Merged Letters.** Print the letters.

Thinking Critically

In Mr. Newland's letter, he indicated that someone will contact each travel agent. He has asked you to provide information from the P20 Contacts database that would be helpful to the employee placing the call. What information from the database do you think you should provide? What type of database object(s) will you use to provide the data?

Appendix A

Reference Guide

Business Letter

Formatting Tips

Format: Use block format with open punctuation.

Margins: Use default side margins. Position the dateline at approximately 2″ from the top of the page, leaving about .5″ below the letterhead.

Header: Use a header on the second and succeeding pages of letters that require more than one page. The header should include the recipient's name, Page #, and the date. See a sample header on the interoffice memo example on page 315.

ST★R River Adventures

205 Riverview Drive Sutton, WV 26601-1311

Dateline	January 15, 20--
Letter Address	Mrs. Ruby Lewis, Manager Kindred Printing Company 1234 Helpful Road Huntington, WV 25507-0103
Salutation	Dear Mrs. Lewis
Body	Thank you for shipping our recent brochure order promptly. I have checked the number of boxes we received. One box is missing from the order, and one box is damaged. The damage to the box is extensive, and the contents are unusable. This box is labeled *Box 4 of 5.* Your salesperson, Vivian Harrison, is scheduled to visit us on Tuesday of next week. We will hold the box and its contents for her to inspect. Box 2 of 5 is the missing box. After checking the contents of the other boxes, it appears the missing box contained all of the Upper Gauley Rafting Special brochures we ordered. We will expect the replacement to arrive within one week, as you assured me in our phone conversation.
Complimentary Close	Sincerely *Joe Coward*
Name and Title	Joe Coward, Administrative Assistant
Reference Initials	xx
Enclosure Notation	Enclosures: Photocopies of four packing slips
Copy Notation	c Robert Jackson, Manager, Marketing and Sales

Interoffice Memorandum

Formatting Tips

Memos are used for communications within a company.

Margins: Begin the first heading approximately 2″ from the top of the page. (Press **Enter** to position the cursor at approximately 2″.) Use default or 1″ side margins on all pages. Leave at least a 1″ bottom margin.

Headings: Key the introduction lines double-spaced in bold and all caps and followed by colons. Align the text following the heading words.

Approximately 2″

Default or 1″ side margins

Align words after headings

TO: Managers (See Distribution List)

FROM: Tommy Newland

DATE: January 20, 20--

SUBJECT: Employee Parking

Joyce Forde will assess the parking needs of employees working in the main headquarters of Star River Adventures. An evaluation of the cost and benefits of available solutions will follow this assessment of the parking problem.

Joyce will begin the task by surveying the parking needs of current employees. Two sample surveys that she will use in developing her review are attached. She will create a questionnaire that will determine the following factors:

- The number of employees who regularly drive to work
- The average cost of parking per employee
- The average distance from headquarters that the employees park
- Safety concerns with present parking situations

Joyce will need to determine any increase expected in the number of employees at Star River Adventures. Also, she will evaluate the number of visitors to be accommodated in any projected parking plan.

Using the results of the survey, Joyce will determine the parking needs of Star River Adventures employees. If sufficient demand is determined, an appropriate range of available solutions will be identified. Eric Collins will need to analyze the following:

- Will the company absorb the entire cost of the parking solution and provide the parking spaces as an employee benefit?

At least 1″ bottom margin

Interoffice Memorandum Page 2

Formatting Tips

Heading: Key a heading on the second and all following pages to include the name of the recipient, the date, and the page number. Use a 1″ top margin.

Attachment: Use an Attachment notation to indicate that something is attached (staple or paper-clipped) to the memo.

Distribution List: Indicates the recipients of the memo when there are several. Indent the list of names .5″ from the left margin. Indicate in the *TO:* line that there is a distribution list.

Header

Default
or 1"
side
margins

Managers
Page 2
January 20, 20--

1" or default top margin

• Will employees be charged a monthly parking fee to offset the cost of providing a parking facility?

• Is the empty lot on 5th and Elm Streets of adequate size to handle our entire parking needs, or will the purchase of additional land be required?

Joyce should complete the assessment of the current parking situation by the first of next month. A report outlining the current parking situation, along with suggested solutions and costs, should be completed by Eric by the end of next month.

xx

Attachments: Two Sample Surveys

Distribution List:
    Eric Collins
    Maria Inez
    Robert Jackson

At least 1" bottom margin

Email

What Is Email?

Electronic mail, or email, is the first and still most popular use of the Internet. Email involves posting (sending) messages from one computer to another over a network. Speed is an advantage of using email. While first-class mail takes days to arrive and "overnight" mail takes up to 24 hours, email is routinely delivered in less than five minutes.

Email may be sent to one person or to a group. Copies of electronic files may be attached to email, enabling the receiver to view and use the files on his or her computer. Email saves postages and delivery fees as well as time.

Email Procedures

If you have access to an email system, follow your instructor's directions for addressing and routing an email message. If you do not have access to an email system, you can simulate creating email in a *Word* document as shown in the illustration below.

Email Etiquette

As you write email, remember to present yourself professionally. Your correspondence is a reflection on you and Star River Adventures. Follow these guidelines:

- Do not key a message in all caps. In email, all caps indicate shouting.
- Run the spell checker and proofread carefully before you send an email.
- Be courteous and professional.
- Remember that your email message is recorded and may be viewed by people other than the person to whom you sent it.

Email	
To:	josephcoward@trophe.com
cc:	
Subject:	Rough Draft Letter
Attachment:	Trip Request Reply.doc
Message:	An edited copy of a letter explaining why Star River Adventures cannot grant a request for a free rafting trip is attached. Please prepare the final letter for my signature. Thanks. Robert Jackson

Report Title Page

Formatting Tips

Margins: Use default or 1″ side margins. Position the report title approximately 2″ from the top of the page.

Spacing: Center the text lines horizontally. Space evenly between parts. (Leave approximately 1.5″ between parts, and then adjust if necessary.) Single-space titles that have more than one line.

Title: Use all caps and bold for the title. Use the same format for the title as that used for the main title of the report. For example, use Arial, bold, 16 point or use the *Title* style.

Page number: Do not number the title page.

Approximately 2″

POLICY MANUAL

Default or 1″ side margins
Center all lines horizontally

Prepared for
Star River Adventures Employees

Prepared by
Joseph Coward, Administrative Assistant

Current Date

Report Table of Contents

Formatting Tips

Margins: Position the title approximately 2″ from the top of the page. Use default or 1″ side margins. Leave at least a 1″ bottom margin.

Headings: Center the title horizontally in all caps. Use the same format for the title as that used for the main title of the report. For example, use Arial, bold, 16 point. Use the side headings (from the body of the report) to create the entries. Set a leader tab at the right margin for the page numbers or generate the entries automatically. (See Success Tips at the left.)

Page number: Include a lowercase Roman numeral as the page number centered at the bottom of the page. (Begin counting with the title page even though it has no number printed on the page.)

Approximately 2"

Default or 1" side margins

TABLE OF CONTENTS

At least 1" bottom margin

ii

Unbound Report

Formatting Tips

Margins: Position the title approximately 2″ from the top of the page on the first page of the body of an unbound report and for the Reference or Bibliography page. (Press the **Enter** key until you see approximately 2″ on the status bar.) Use a 1″ top margin for all other pages. Use default or 1″ side margins. Leave at least 1″ for the bottom margin.

Spacing: Single-space paragraphs with a double space between paragraphs. Single-space bulleted and numbered lists and indent them .5″. Double-space between the items in the lists if any item is more than one line long.

Page numbers: Place page numbers in the upper right corner of all pages in the body of the report except the first page. Place the page number in a header.

Headings: Center the title in a sans serif font using bold 16 point or use the *Title* style. Place the first-level side headings at the left margin in a sans serif font using bold 16 point or use the *Heading 1* style. Place the second-level side headings at the left margin in a sans serif font using bold, italic, 14 point or use the *Heading 2* style.

Unbound Report Page 1

Approximately 2"

Default or 1" side margins

Title centered in ALL CAPS

POLICY MANUAL

Introduction

Purpose

The policies included in this policy manual were developed during the past 20-plus years of Star River Adventures' operation. All employees are expected to read, understand, and follow these policies as they pertain to their particular job assignments. Please review this manual on a regular basis to refresh your memory concerning its contents. **THIS POLICY MANUAL IS NOT A CONTRACT.** You are an employee "at-will."

Keep in mind that this is a fluid document and will change. As changes are made, they will be posted on the company Web site and on the staff bulletin boards. The manual is reviewed and reprinted in its entirety on an annual basis.

Revisions

Any part of the manual may be revised or deleted at any time. A current copy of the manual, including all revisions, will be available at the front desk.

Quality Policy

The most important thing to know about Star River Adventures is that it is a service business. The safety and enjoyment of our customers is our main company concern. All aspects of our customers' experiences, which are under our control, must meet with the customers' satisfaction.

Mission Statement

Star River Adventures is focused on the customer. We plan professionally guided whitewater events that range from gentle, tranquil raft day trips down one of our scenic streams to wild and wet excursions that will challenge even the expert rafter. Whatever the adventure, safety is always our number one concern. Many amenities are available with our excursions, such as sleepovers at various sites, camping, bicycle tours, hiking, food services, and a variety of other special events.

At least 1" bottom margin

Unbound Report Page 2

1" top margin

Default or 1" side margins

Our mission at Star River Adventures is to:

- Offer the adventures that customers envision in a safe and exciting environ-ment.

- Provide the best value for the customer's dollar.

- Make customers feel as though they are members of the Star River Adventures family.

- Have customers return to Star River Adventures because they have experi-enced excellent service at a fair price.

Facilities and Equipment

Exceptional service includes providing clean, attractive, organized facilities and equipment to our guests (and each other). Staff should:

- Always park in designated areas. The areas with easiest access to facilities are reserved for our guests.

- Clean up litter. Do not contribute to litter. Do not ignore a problem because "It is not my job."

- Return all equipment to the appropriate locations. Report damaged equipment to the equipment manager.

Company Safety Philosophy

Star River Adventures believes that the safety of both the guests and employees is our first priority. Safe operating procedures result in the protection of both monetary and human value, with the human value being recognized by the employer and the community as having the greater value. Observe these principles concerning safety:

- Establishing and complying with safe work procedures will prevent injuries and accidents from happening.

- The first consideration in all workplace actions is the prevention of bodily injury and the safeguarding of health. To prevent injury and maintain health, it is essential that employees be in good enough physical condition to do their assigned jobs.

- The written safety plan, provided in this manual, represents Star River Adventures' proactive safety position. It is the responsibility of all Star River Adventures employees to communicate and follow established safety practices.

At least 1" bottom margin

Bibliography

Formatting Tips

Margins: Position the title approximately 2″ from the top of the page. Use default or 1″ side margins. Leave at least 1″ bottom margin.

Spacing: Single-space entries with a double space between them. Use a .5″ hanging indent for entries.

Heading: Center the title in all caps and bold. If the bibliography is part of a report, use the same format for the title as that used for the main title of the report. For example, use Arial, bold, 16 point or use the *Title* style.

Success Tips

- Arrange entries alphabetically by authors' last names. If no author is given (as for a Web page), use the title.
- Disregard the words *A* or *The* at the beginning of a title when alphabetizing.

Approximately 2″

Default or 1″ side margins

Title centered in ALL CAPS

BIBLIOGRAPHY

Cleary, M. J., et al. "Tell Them Why." *America Tomorrow*, September 1999.

Harris, Paul, and Sara Riggs. "Five Steps to Effective Group Leadership." *Psychology In Action*, July 2001, 16-17.

Howard, Kyle, and Beatrice Stone. "Having Fun in the Great Outdoors." *Outdoor Adventure Journal*, August 2003.

"The International Scale of River Difficulty." American Whitewater, <http://www.americanwhitewater.org/archive/safety/.htm>, (June 25, 2003).

Smith, Linda. "Difficult Customers and How to Help Them." *Salesmanship Quarterly*, Spring 2002, 4-8.

At least 1″ bottom margin

Agenda

Formatting Tips

Margins: Use default or 1″ side margins. Position the title approximately 2″ from the top of the page.

Headings: Key the name of the meeting or event in bold, all caps and use center alignment. Center the date in bold under the main title. Double-space and center *Agenda* in bold.

Spacing: Single-space items on the agenda, double-spacing between items. Use leaders and align names at the right.

Default or 1"
side margins

Approximately 2"

PARKING REPORT MEETING
February 14, 20--

Agenda

1. Call to order .... Tommy Newland

2. Progress report on employee parking .... Joyce Forde
      Cost estimates .... Eric Collins
      Employee benefits .... Maria Inez

3. New business
      Buses .... Maria Inez
      Photocopier .... Robert Jackson

4. Adjournment

At least 1" bottom margin

Proofreading Tips

To be acceptable, your final copy must be free of errors. Before printing documents, carefully proofread all copy on the screen.

Begin proofreading by using the software's spell-checking utility. Make all necessary corrections. If your software marks spelling errors as you key, scroll through the document to be sure that all errors marked by the software have been corrected.

Use the full-page view to check each page for formatting and style errors. In this view, you can easily identify the following errors:

- Inconsistent paragraph indentations
- Incorrect margins
- Inappropriate line spacing
- Inconsistent heading styles
- Incorrect vertical placement
- General appearance

After correcting errors onscreen, print the document and carefully proofread each page. Use a ruler or the straight edge of a piece of paper to keep your place and to avoid skipping lines while you proofread. Clearly indicate all corrections with a colored pencil, using the standard proofreaders' marks shown on page 325.

Read all of the text to identify content errors, incorrect punctuation, and repeated or omitted words. (These are errors that the spell checker does not find.) Be careful to read and check headings at this time.

Check each page carefully for typographical, spacing, and word-division errors. (Tip: Read each line from right to left. This will help you concentrate on individual words.) Proofread unfamiliar words letter by letter.

Carefully compare the document you produce against the original text. If the text is unusually complex, work with a partner who reads from the original while you check your work.

Make final corrections to the document file. Run the spelling and grammar checker one last time before printing a final copy.

Proofreaders' Marks

Mark	Meaning	Example
#	Add horizontal space	I sincerely hope you enjoy your rafting trip.
~~	Bold	September 8 or September 8
≡	Capitalize	our goal is to maintain these relationships.
◡	Close up	Data base Software Update
℮	Delete	Teamwork is is crucial to our success.
∧	Insert	Please submit quarterly report before the meeting.
⊙	Insert a period	We offer several exciting trips
stet	Let it stand; ignore correction	Our staff will help you plan your entire adventure. stet
lc	Lowercase	Internet Connection lc
⌐	Move left	Star River Adventures is located in Sutton, West Virginia. We plan and conduct events throughout the state.
⌐	Move right	Star River Adventures is located in Sutton, West Virginia. We plan and conduct events throughout the state.
⌂	Move up	Star River Adventures is located in Sutton, West Virginia. We plan and conduct events throughout the state.
⌴	Move down	Star River Adventures is located in Sutton, West Virginia. We plan and conduct events throughout the state.
¶	Paragraph	for an individual, a family, or another group. Star River Adventures is located in Sutton, West Virginia
SP	Spell out	Star River Adventures is located in Sutton, WV. SP
∼ tr	Transpose	Our trips allow you to gently raft down streams. tr
___	Underline or italic	She is the author of the book See the Customer Without Rose Colored Glasses.

Appendix B

Computer Concepts

Introduction

Computers have been around for many years. Only in the last 15 to 20 years have they become a part of our everyday life. In the following section, you will learn about the history of computers, the parts of a computer system, and some common uses of computers.

Years ago there were no calculators, no Internet, and nothing that even looked like a modern computer. The need for quicker ways of doing calculations began to grow. At first, machines were developed that could do very simple calculations. Progress was slow, but eventually more complicated machines were built that could do calculations such as adding, subtracting, multiplying, and dividing. These machines could complete several calculations at the same time.

The punch card system for computing was introduced around 1886. This system used electricity and a punch card system for calculating large amounts of information. This was a big step in the growth of computers.

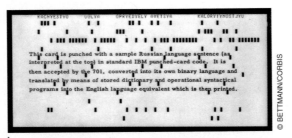

Figure B-1 Punch cards were used in early computer systems.

Early computers were very large. Some computers covered 1,800 square feet and were as tall as most ceilings. Generally, these machines were limited to the basic operations of addition, subtraction, division, and multiplication. They could perform these functions at speeds thousands of times faster than by hand. This was a tremendous leap forward in the building of computers as we know them today. However, these machines were still very limited in what they could do. Early computers were not like the desktop systems used today. Most early machines had many mechanical parts and weighed tons instead of pounds. To change the tasks the machine could perform, the machine had to be rewired.

© JERRY COOKE/CORBIS

Figure B-2 Early computers had to be rewired to change their functions.

By 1945, the world started to see practical uses for computers. Interest grew in designing and building computers. By 1947, early computers were able to calculate and store information many times faster than any other human device available at that time. Once this happened, the computer became a useful machine and the design of computers moved forward.

With the introduction of computer memory (a way to store information), computers became even more useful. People started building smaller computers, and the demands for computers increased. By the 1970s, computers were available as desktop systems. However, they were still limited in what they could do.

© HOT IDEAS/INDEX STOCK IMAGERY

Figure B-3 Example of Early Computers

From the mid-1970s to today, companies made giant leaps in the advancement of computer systems. Processors became faster, memory increased, and operating systems were developed. As the technology advanced so did the rising need for computers in everyday life. Doctors, lawyers, businesspeople, teachers, students, researchers, artists, and many other people use computers today. The demand for faster processing and new features continues to grow.

Computer System Components

Computer components fall into one of two categories: **hardware** and **software.** Hardware is any physical component or device of a computer system. Software is a program that contains instructions for the computer hardware. Software is also commonly called programs or applications.

Hardware

Computer hardware varies in size and function. Many types of hardware are found in computer systems. As technology changes, more types of hardware are developed. Several types of hardware are discussed in the following paragraphs.

Central Processing Unit

A computer's **central processing unit** (CPU) is the "brains" of the computer. The CPU interprets and carries out the instructions contained in the software. The computer case that contains the CPU also usually contains other hardware, such as a hard drive, a floppy drive, a CD/DVD drive, and various other components that make the computer work. Some of these other components are discussed later.

© ERIC KAMP/INDEX STOCK IMAGERY

Figure B-4 A computer's CPU is housed in the computer case.

Input Devices

Input devices give the computer data or instructions. Some common input devices are described below.

- A keyboard allows users to type information.
- A scanner allows users to scan images or text into the computer.
- A mouse allows users to move the pointer onscreen and choose commands or options.
- A touch screen gives users direct interaction with the screen.

These are not the only input devices used, but they are the most common ones. Microphones for inputting audio, hand tracking devices that work like a mouse, and video cameras are other input devices.

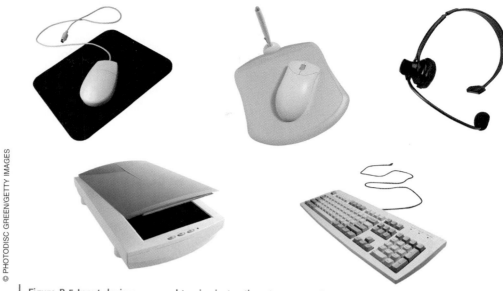

© PHOTODISC GREEN/GETTY IMAGES

Figure B-5 Input devices are used to give instructions to a computer.

Output Devices

Output devices deliver information from the computer. Some examples of output devices are listed below.

- Printers create information as text or images on paper.
- Monitors allow users to view information from the computer.
- Speakers produce sound from the computer.
- Projectors display information similar to a monitor but usually in a large-screen format.

© BILL ARON/PHOTO EDIT

Figure B-6 A monitor is a typical output device.

Storage Devices

Storage devices save information from the computer and keep it to be used later. Examples of storage devices and media include:

- CD-ROM and DVD. These discs hold information digitally. A laser inside the computer drive burns the information onto the surface of the disc. The information can be retrieved later.
- Floppy disk. This disk contains magnetic media and holds small amounts of information. Its name comes from the fact that the disc itself is somewhat flexible. Bending is not recommended, though, because it can damage the disk.
- Zip® disk. This type of floppy disk is mounted in a sturdy cartridge and holds much more information than a standard floppy disk. This disk also allows users to read and write data more quickly than with a standard floppy.
- USB flash memory card. This device is relatively new and holds information digitally on a portable microchip.
- Hard drive. This device stores and retrieves digital data from a magnetic surface. A hard disk can store much more data than a floppy disk and access and transmit the data faster. A hard drive can be an internal or external device. It can contain the operating system for the computer as well as data stored by the user.

© PHOTODISC GREEN/GETTY IMAGES

Figure B-7 Storage devices are an important part of a computer system.

Software

Software is a program that tells the computer what tasks to accomplish and how. Examples of software include the following:

- Games with graphics and animation
- Word processors that allow typing of documents
- Databases that store information in organized forms
- Graphics programs used to create images
- Desktop publishing programs used to design layouts for books or magazines
- Audio software for editing or enhancing sound files
- Animation software for building and changing three-dimensional objects

Like hardware, new and more powerful software is developed as technologies change and evolve. The two basic forms of software are **operating systems** and **applications.**

Operating system (OS) software tells the computer how to function and work with other software and hardware. Practically all computer systems have an OS.

Examples of OSs you may be familiar with are *DOS, Microsoft Windows®, (Apple) OS X,* and *Linux.*

Application software works with the OS to accomplish tasks such as word processing, graphics display, and technical drawing. Application software varies greatly in function. Some examples of application software you may be familiar with are *Microsoft Word, Adobe Acrobat®, Windows Media® Player,* and *Apple QuickTime.*

Computer Networks

A **computer network** is a group of linked computers. These computers can communicate and may be able to share hard drives, printers, scanners, and other equipment or software. A network can connect computers in small or large geographic areas. The **Internet** is a computer network that spans the globe. Many smaller networks are connected to the Internet.

The **World Wide Web** is a part of the Internet. This part of the Internet consists of computers that support documents created in HTML (HyperText Markup Language) format. This format allows documents to contain graphics, audio, video, and links to other documents. HTML documents are accessed using programs called Web browsers. *Internet Explorer* and *Netscape® Navigator* are popular Web browsers.

Figure B-8 Microsoft's *Internet Explorer* is a popular Web browser.

Types of Networks

A network that is confined to a small area is often called a **LAN** (local area network). Many companies have local area networks that allow employees to share data and work cooperatively. A network that covers a large area may be called a **WAN** (wide area network). Usually, a user is required to enter certain information to gain access to a network. This process is called "logging in." A login procedure usually includes entering a password. Passwords help keep the network more secure by ensuring that the users who access the network have permission to do so.

An **intranet** is a privately maintained computer network that can be accessed only by authorized persons, such as members or employees of an organization. An intranet often looks and operates like a Web site.

Communications

Communications among computers can involve several different technologies. Many communications systems work using the Internet. Computers on the Internet have an **IP address** (Internet Protocol address) that lets them communicate with each other. The Internet allows access to vast amounts of information. The Internet can be used for research, games, entertainment, and many other activities.

There are many ways to connect to the Internet. An **ISP** (Internet Service Provider) is a company that sells a connection or access to the Internet. These companies offer their service for a fee, usually charged monthly.

A **modem** is a device (usually inside the computer case) that uses a telephone line to dial out to an Internet Service Provider or to another computer. Once a connection to the Internet is made, a user can browse through the files offered and send or receive data.

An **Ethernet connection** is similar to a modem connection except that it allows much faster connections and does not dial out. An Ethernet connection is constantly connected. This type of connection is the primary connection used for companies or large networked systems.

A **wireless connection** to the Internet uses radio waves to receive data. This works kind of like a car radio that receives music. The connection also sends or transmits data. This connection requires an access point, a device that connects to the Internet and then creates a wireless connection to the computer system. This system is more commonly used with laptop computers but is sometimes used with desktop systems. The computer also must have the required equipment to use this system.

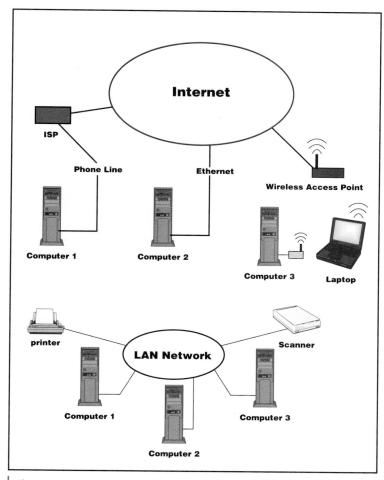

Figure B-9 Computers may be connected in local or wide area networks.

The *Microsoft Windows* Environment

This section will explore the *Microsoft Windows* operating system environment. Microsoft built *Windows* as a way to use and operate the computer with a graphical user interface (GUI). A GUI allows users to operate a computer system by using graphics rather than by typing commands. Different versions of *Windows* have been designed over the years. A recent version is called *Windows XP*. Illustrations in this section are from *Windows XP*.

Parts of the *Windows* Environment

The **desktop** in *Windows* is an onscreen work area in which windows, icons, menus, and dialog boxes appear. **Icons** are small pictures that represent files, folders, or programs. You can double-click a program icon on the desktop to open the program.

The desktop contains a **taskbar,** usually located at the bottom of the screen. The taskbar contains a Start button used to access programs and documents. The taskbar may also contain icons and buttons for programs that are running.

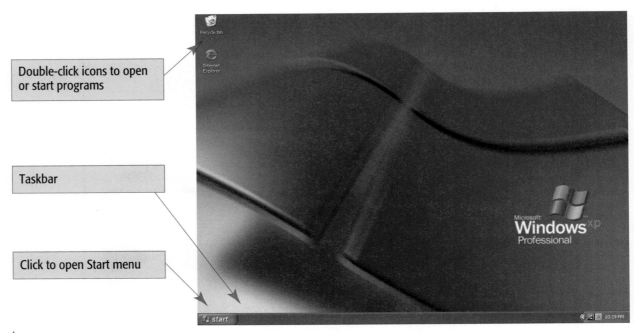

Double-click icons to open or start programs

Taskbar

Click to open Start menu

Figure B-10 *Windows XP* Desktop

Windows are frames that open on the screen where programs and processes may be run. Several windows may be open at once. Windows may be resized, moved, closed, minimized to a taskbar button, or maximized to use the entire screen.

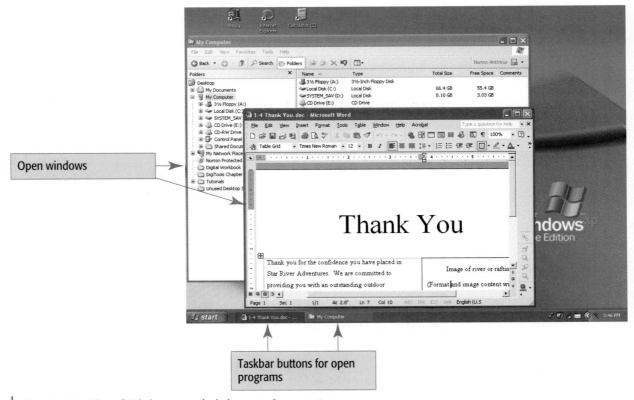

Open windows

Taskbar buttons for open programs

Figure B-11 In *Microsoft Windows*, several windows may be open at once.

Using Windows

Clicking the *Windows* Start button opens a menu that shows icons and names for different functions and programs. The All Programs option shows installed programs on your system. You can select a program from the list to open it.

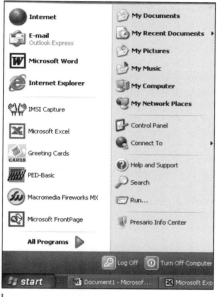

Figure B-12 Start Menu

When you have applications open, you can see their names on buttons on the taskbar. Clicking on the button brings that window to the front or minimizes the window. Minimizing a window does not close it, but hides it, leaving its name on the taskbar.

Figure B-13 Taskbar Buttons

You can maximize a window so it uses the entire screen. When the window is maximized from the taskbar, it goes back to the size it was before it was minimized. The Minimize and Maximize buttons in the upper right corner of the window can also be used to minimize and maximize windows. The Maximize button also makes the window full-screen when the window is already open. The Close button closes the window or exits the program you are running.

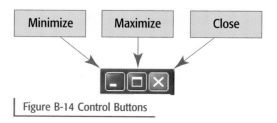

Figure B-14 Control Buttons

The window for an application program typically has a **title bar** at the top. The title bar gives the program name and may contain an icon that represents the program. Application programs usually contain a **menu bar** located near the top or side of the window. The menu bar provides access to program features and commands. The program may also have a **toolbar.** A toolbar typically contains buttons with icons or text that allow users quick access to program commands and features. The menu bar and toolbar have different commands depending on the program you are using.

Figure B-15 Menu and toolbar options will vary with the program.

A document may contain more information than can be displayed on the screen at one time. **Scroll bars** are used to display different parts of a document or program on the screen. Scroll bars may be located at the right or bottom of a window.

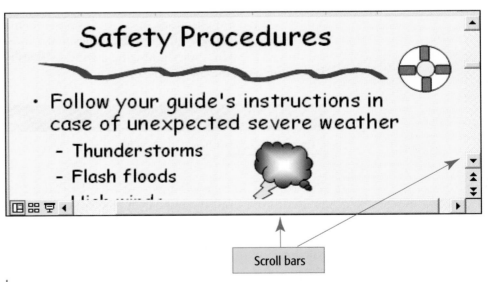

Figure B-16 Scroll Bars

Windows can be moved or resized on the screen. To move a window that is not maximized, click on a blank area of the title bar and drag the window to the desired location. To resize a window, move the mouse to the lower right-hand corner of the window until the cursor turns into an arrow. Click and drag in the direction you want to resize the window. The arrows on page 339 show what aspect of the window you are changing.

Size up, down, left, and right

 Size left to right

 Size up and down

Using the Taskbar

The taskbar in *Windows* can be used to do several things. The taskbar shows the open windows or applications and, as mentioned earlier, can be used to minimize, maximize, or close windows. To access a menu of options, right-click on the taskbar. Some of the menu options are discussed below.

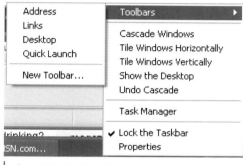

Figure B-17 Taskbar Popup Menu

The Toolbars option allows you to add a button to your taskbar that, when clicked, displays the information listed. For example, assume you selected Desktop from the menu. A button would display on the taskbar. When clicked, the button would show in a menu form all of the files and icons on the desktop. This would allow quick and easy navigation of your desktop even if it was covered by several open windows.

You can also build your own toolbars using the New Toolbar option. You can place this toolbar in different areas of the screen for easy navigation.

Quick Launch adds a section to your existing taskbar where you can place often-used programs so there is no need to open the Start menu. To start the program, simply click the icon from the Quick Launch menu.

The Cascade Windows option arranges the open windows on the screen one on top of the other. A portion of each window is displayed, allowing you to see what the window is. The Tile Windows option places the open windows side by side or top to bottom for easy viewing. The Show the Desktop option displays the desktop and hides all open windows in the taskbar.

Using Menus

Menus in *Windows* programs are helpful tools that let you access features and commands of the program. Options on the menu vary from program to program. Some options, such as Open and Save, are in most programs. A drop-down menu of options may appear when you click on one of the main menu options.

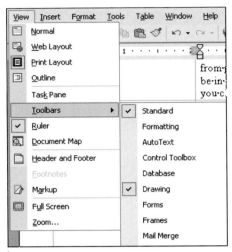

Figure B-18 View Drop-Down Menu

Grayed-out options on a menu, such as *Footnotes* in Figure B-18, are not available for use at that particular time. An option that has a check mark next to it, such as *Ruler* in Figure B-18, can be clicked to deselect it or to turn the function off. Selecting (clicking) the option will turn it on. An arrow means there is a submenu for that option. In the example in Figure B-18, the *Toolbars* option has a submenu that appears when you roll the mouse over this option.

Using Dialog Boxes

Dialog boxes are like windows except their purpose is usually to gather or display information. A dialog box usually disappears after you enter information or indicate that you have read information, such as by clicking OK. Menu options followed by an ellipsis (...) usually open a dialog box. A typical dialog box is shown in Figure B-19 on page 341.

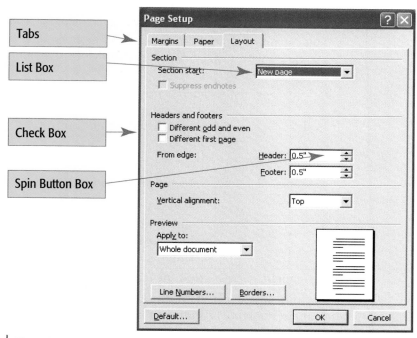

Figure B-19 Page Setup Dialog Box

The dialog box in Figure B-19 has many typical dialog box elements. Across the top of this box are **tabs.** The tabs allow you to see the title of the information you may want to look at. You can click a tab to display the information for that tab.

Near the top of the dialog box in Figure B-19 is a **list box.** A list box has more than one option that may be selected. The current selection is shown with a down arrow beside it. When you click on this list box arrow, the other choices are displayed. You select the option you want. Another similar box is the **spin button box.** This box looks like the list box, but it has two arrows beside it. Clicking the up or down arrow scrolls through the choices for the box.

In Figure B-19, **check boxes** are shown beside the header and footer options. Check boxes are like switches that turn a function on or off. If the box is checked, the function is on. If the box is blank, the function is off.

You may also see a **radio button** in some dialog boxes. A radio button works like a check box. The difference is that a radio button is round rather than square and is used when only one choice can be selected from among several options. This means that if you choose one option, the rest are unchecked.

Buttons on a dialog box execute commands or open related dialog boxes. In Figure B-19, the Borders button opens the Borders and Shading dialog box.

Mouse Terms

You must understand how to use a mouse to use *Windows* effectively. Terms associated with using a mouse are shown in the table below.

Mouse Terms	
Click	Press the mouse button (usually the left mouse button unless specified).
Right-click	Press the right mouse button.
Double-click	Quickly press the mouse button twice in a row.
Point	Move the mouse until the arrow points to an object.
Drag	Point to an object and then hold down the mouse button while moving the mouse, dragging the object with the pointer.
Highlight	Roll the mouse over menu items or click on an item.
Scroll (applies only to a wheel mouse)	Turn the small wheel in between the left and right mouse buttons to scroll up or down in *Windows* and some programs.

Windows File Management

Files are instructions or data in one form or another that computers use. There are two basic file types: program files and data files. Program files tell the computer how to function. Data files contain information needed by program files.

These files can be stored alone or in **folders.** Folders are just what they sound like. A folder holds information and can have other folders contained in it. Folders on a computer serve the same purpose as paper file folders. They help organize files into a logical order. The files contained in folders or by themselves have individual **filenames.** Filenames are simply titles that identify files.

Saving, Opening, and Deleting Files

Files can be named when they are saved, and the names can be changed later. There are several ways to change a file name or **rename** a file. For example, to rename a file when using *Windows Explorer*:

- Right-click the name of the file you wish to rename.
- Choose Rename from the pop-up menu.
- Key a new name for the file.
- Press Enter.

To open files in *Windows,* you can often double-click the filename to open it. To open a file in an application program such as *Microsoft Word*:

- Select *File* from the menu bar.
- Select *Open* from the list of options.
- Navigate to the folder that contains the file.
- Select the file you wish to open.
- Click *Open.*

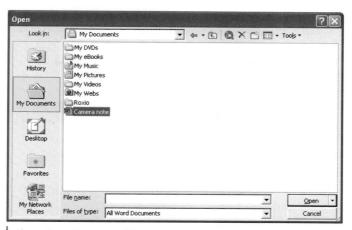

Figure B-20 The Open Dialog Box

To delete a file, you can drag it to the **Recycle Bin** on the desktop. The Recycle Bin icon looks like a trash can. You can also right-click the file and choose *Delete* from the menu.

File Navigation

File navigation in *Windows* has been streamlined to work efficiently. There are various ways to navigate files or file structures.

The My Computer window for the *Windows Explorer* program can be accessed using the *Windows XP* Start menu. (In earlier versions of *Windows* click *Start, Programs, Windows Explorer* or *Start, Programs, Accessories, Windows Explorer*.)

Selecting My Computer opens a window that shows all drives available to the computer system. Double-clicking a folder or drive in this view allows further viewing of files contained within that drive or folder. The My Computer window is shown in Figure B-21. *Windows XP* views look slightly different than earlier versions of *Windows*, but they have the same functionality.

Figure B-21 My Computer Window

Windows allows you to view your files in different ways. To change the view of your files, select *View* on the menu bar. From the choices, select the view you wish to use, such as *Icons* or *List*. The List view is shown in Figure B-21. The Icons view is shown in Figure B-22.

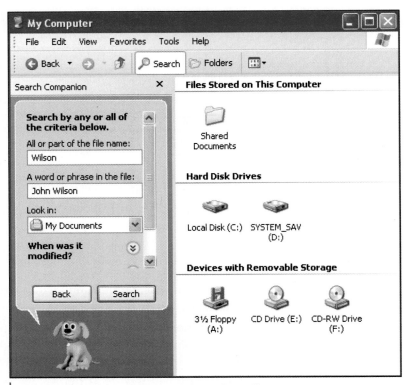

Figure B-22 The Search feature can help you locate files.

You may have trouble locating a file because you forget the folder name in which you placed the file or you forget the exact filename. You can use the Search option to find files quickly within drives or folders. To use the Search feature, click the *Search* button on the toolbar. Enter all or part of a filename or enter a word or phrase found in the file. Indicate which drives or folders to search in and click *Search*.

Figure B-23 Clicking a drive name displays its contents.

You can choose to display drives, folders, and files in two panels of a *Windows Explorer* window. To do so, click the *Folders* button on the toolbar. In the left panel, a tree or navigation structure is displayed. There are plus and minus signs beside some of the items in this panel. Clicking on a plus sign **expands** the file structure, showing the subfolders for that drive or folder. Clicking the minus sign **collapses** the navigation back to the folder you clicked.

When you click the name of a drive or folder in the left panel, the files or folders within are displayed in the right panel. In Figure B-23, the contents of Drive A are displayed.

Creating New Folders

You may need to create new folders in which to store files. To create a new folder in *Windows Explorer*:

- Select the drive or folder in which you want the new folder to appear.
- Select *New* from the File menu.
- Select *Folder*.
- Key a name for the folder and press **Enter**.

The default name New Folder will be replaced with the name you keyed. If you click off of the folder without keying a name, the name will remain New Folder.

You can also create a new folder on the desktop. To do so, right-click an empty area of the desktop. Select *New* and then *Folder* from the menu. A new folder with the default name New Folder will appear. You can type a different name for the new folder as described earlier.

Figure B-24 New Folder

Copying Files

You may wish to copy a file to a different drive or folder. To do so in *Windows Explorer*:

- Locate the file you wish to copy and select it.
- Select *Copy* from the Edit menu.
- Navigate to the drive or folder where you wish to place a copy of the file.
- Select *Paste* from the Edit menu.

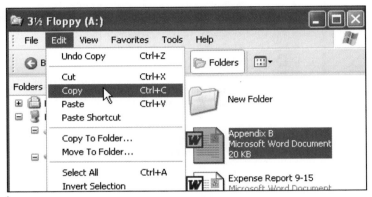

Figure B-25 The Copy and Paste commands are found on the Edit menu.

If you paste a file to the same folder from which you copied it, "Copy of" will appear at the beginning of the filename for the new file. You can rename the copied file using a different filename.

Appendix C

Keyboarding Skill Building

Writing 1

1. Key one 3' writing on both paragraphs.
2. Key one 5' writing on both paragraphs.

The icon indicates that the difficulty level of the writing is average.

   all letters

	gwam	3'	5'

Most people are afraid to stand up and speak before a group.   4 | 2 | 39

The ability to make presentations is a skill that is required for   9 | 5 | 41

success in business.   The job is easy if you do your homework   13 | 8 | 44

and if you develop confidence in yourself.   Always plan a presen-   17 | 10 | 46

tation carefully; organize your material, and then rehearse the   21 | 13 | 49

speech several times.   The first time you get up is the hardest;   26 | 15 | 51

it gets easier each time.   Experience helps to make you feel   30 | 18 | 54

more comfortable.   31 | 19 | 55

A quality presentation can be made even better with the use   35 | 21 | 57

of visuals to enhance the spoken word.   Neat, well-prepared   39 | 24 | 60

visuals that are used in an effective manner help the audience   43 | 26 | 62

to focus attention on the important points you want to communi-   48 | 29 | 65

cate.   They can also serve as cues to the next point you wish to   52 | 31 | 67

present; these cues make you less dependent on your notes.   Good   56 | 34 | 70

visuals are uncluttered, attractive, and easy to read.   60 | 36 | 72

gwam 3' | 1 | 2 | 3 | 4 | 5 |
5' | 1 | 2 | 3 |

The writings in Appendix C, Keyboarding Skill Building, are taken from *Extended Drills and Timed Writings, College Keyboarding, 14th Edition,* by VanHuss, Duncan, Forde, and Woo, Copyright 1998 by South-Western Educational Publishing, Cincinnati, Ohio.

Writing 2

1. Key two 1' writings on each paragraph.
2. Key one 3' writing on both paragraphs.

The icon indicates that the difficulty level of the writing is easy.

 all letters and figures

gwam 3'

Will you order a book on travel (#478XZ) from the red cata-	4 | 36
log on my desk? The book costs $25, or $20 when 4 or more books	8 | 41
are ordered at a time--this can save us 20%. I am sure you will	13 | 45
like the chapter "On the Road"; it is quite good!	16 | 48
Do write on the form the full name and order number of each	20 | 52
book we wish to order, and send an extra $1.25 with the order--	24 | 56
this is used to pay for shipping the books. A bill is now sub-	28 | 61
ject to 6/10, net 30. Can't we order 4 books by 9/30?	32 | 65

gwam 3' | 1 | 2 | 3 | 4 | 5 |

Writing 3

1. Key one 3' writing on both paragraphs.
2. Key one 5' writing on both paragraphs.

 all letters and figures

gwam   3' 5'

A conversion table is a real convenience for making changes	4 | 2 | 54
between a U.S. and a metric weight or measure. To determine the	8 | 5 | 57
metric value of 6,783 feet, 129 miles, or some similar measure,	13 | 8 | 59
simply multiply feet by 30, yards by 0.9, and miles by 1.6 to	17 | 10 | 62
get centimeters, meters, and kilometers. Use the same procedure	21 | 13 | 64
if you know the metric value; that is, just multiply meters by	25 | 15 | 67
1.1 to get yards, by 3.3 to get feet, or by 0.6 to get miles.	29 | 18 | 69
Volume changes are made by multiplying the number of cups by	34 | 20 | 72
0.24, pints by 0.47, quarts by 0.95, and gallons by 3.8 to	37 | 22 | 74
determine liters. Or, multiply the number of liters by 3.1,	42 | 25 | 77
1.06, or 0.26 to determine the quantity of pints, quarts, or	46 | 27 | 79
gallons.	46 | 28 | 80
Conversions of area (size) and weight are easily determined	50 | 30 | 82
by the same process. For making changes in area, multiply square	55 | 33 | 84
centimeters by 0.16 to get square inches. Square meters are	59 | 35 | 87
changed to square yards if they are multiplied by 1.2, and square	63 | 38 | 90
kilometers become square miles if multiplied by 0.4. If you want	68 | 41 | 92
to obtain square meters, multiply square feet by 0.09 and square	72 | 43 | 95
yards by 0.8. The same rules apply to obtain a weight value;	76 | 46 | 97
that is, approximately 0.035 ounce is the same as one gram	80 | 48 | 100
(28 grams in an ounce), and about 2.2 pounds make a kilogram	84 | 50 | 102
(or 0.45 kilogram makes a pound).	86 | 52 | 103

gwam 3' | 1 | 2 | 3 | 4 | 5 |
    5' | 1 | 2 | 3 |

Writing 4

1. Key one 1' writing on the paragraph.
2. Key two 2' writings on the paragraph.

 all letters   *gwam* 1' | 2'

Good human relation skills are needed at every level. A   11 | 6 | 61
first-line supervisor has the greatest need for technical skills.   25 | 12 | 68
He or she must be able to train workers, explain procedures, and   38 | 19 | 74
solve the problems of one work group. Since he or she works with   51 | 26 | 81
only one group, conceptual skills are not as necessary at this   64 | 32 | 84
level. Supervisors at higher levels work with a number of   75 | 38 | 93
groups, and conceptual skills become far more critical. Techni-   88 | 44 | 100
cal skills are not as essential at higher levels because each   101 | 50 | 106
group has a supervisor who knows how to do the job.   111 | 55 | 111

gwam 1' | 1 | 2 | 3 | 4 | 5 | 6 | 7 | 8 | 9 | 10 | 11 | 12 | 13 |
2' | 1 | 2 | 3 | 4 | 5 | 6 | 7 |

Writing 5

1. Key two 1' writings on each paragraph.
2. Key one 3' writing on both paragraphs.
3. Key one 5' writing on both paragraphs.

 all letters   *gwam* 1' | 3' | 5'

Who is a creative person? Many people think creative people   12 | 4 | 2
are born that way. If a person really wants to, she or he can   25 | 8 | 5
increase her or his creative abilities. To do so requires chal-   37 | 13 | 8
lenging the status quo. A high percentage of what every person   50 | 17 | 10
does is routine work. Routine work is done in the same way over   63 | 21 | 13
and over. Habits are formed by doing the same thing repeatedly;   76 | 25 | 15
they are not easily changed because they become very comfortable.   90 | 30 | 18

The first step in becoming more creative is analyzing the   12 | 34 | 20
mental locks that inhibit creativity. Most people have been   24 | 38 | 23
conditioned to be practical or to use judgment and not to be   36 | 42 | 25
foolish. The next step is to overcome those mental locks and   48 | 46 | 28
dare to be different. When the telephone was invented, most   61 | 50 | 30
people could not envision any practical use for it. Today, most   74 | 54 | 33
people cannot imagine what it would be like not to have a tele-   86 | 59 | 35
phone. The third step is to generate as many ideas as possible.   99 | 63 | 38
People quickly throw out some of their clever ideas because they   112 | 67 | 40
do not seem to be realistic. If an idea is not practical for one   126 | 72 | 43
situation, think how it might be used in other circumstances.   138 | 76 | 46

gwam 1' | 1 | 2 | 3 | 4 | 5 | 6 | 7 | 8 | 9 | 10 | 11 | 12 | 13 |
3' | 1 | 2 | 3 | 4 | 5 |
5' | 1 | 2 | 3 |

Writing 6

1. Key one 1' writing on the paragraph.
2. Key two 2' writings on the paragraph.

 all letters

	gwam	1'	2'

Power is a fascinating concept. Power is simply the ability 12 | 6 | 62
to act or to get others to act. Many people define power as 24 | 12 | 68
using one's position to exploit or to manipulate others. Power 37 | 19 | 75
can be used to exploit or to manipulate, but that view of power 50 | 25 | 81
is somewhat narrow. Each person in an organization has or can 63 | 31 | 87
acquire power. The amount of power and the source of that power 76 | 38 | 94
will vary widely. Persons in positions of high rank and persons 89 | 44 | 100
who perform jobs that make significant contributions to the 101 | 50 | 106
profits of a company are said to be in "power" positions. 112 | 56 | 112

gwam 1' | 1 | 2 | 3 | 4 | 5 | 6 | 7 | 8 | 9 | 10 | 11 | 12 | 13 |
2' | 1 | 2 | 3 | 4 | 5 | 6 | 7 |

Writing 7

1. Key two 1' writings on each paragraph.
2. Key one 3' writing on both paragraphs.
3. Key one 5' writing on both paragraphs.

 all letters

	gwam	1'	3'	5'

If you choose to succeed in business, one skill you must 11 | 4 | 2
acquire is the ability to ask questions effectively. Asking 24 | 8 | 5
questions that produce the desired results is both an art and a 36 | 12 | 7
science. You can master the science of asking questions by ana- 49 | 16 | 10
lyzing each situation and learning to pose the right type of 61 | 21 | 12
question. The art of asking questions involves the way you pose 74 | 25 | 15
questions rather than what you ask. If you are not diplomatic, 87 | 29 | 17
you may make the other person defensive. 95 | 32 | 19

Most of the information you seek from others is either fact 12 | 36 | 21
or opinion. Factual questions are easy to ask, and they rarely 25 | 40 | 24
produce emotional reactions. Questions of opinion may be just 37 | 44 | 27
the opposite. They are hard to ask, and they may produce emo- 50 | 48 | 29
tional reactions. Closed-ended questions are excellent when 62 | 52 | 31
seeking facts because they get the facts quickly and they enable 75 | 57 | 34
you to control the kind of answers you get. Open-ended questions 88 | 61 | 37
are best when seeking opinion because they let the respondent 101 | 65 | 39
give the kind of answers he or she wants to give. 111 | 69 | 41

gwam 1' | 1 | 2 | 3 | 4 | 5 | 6 | 7 | 8 | 9 | 10 | 11 | 12 | 13 |
3' | 1 | 2 | 3 | 4 | 5 |
5' | 1 | 2 | 3 |

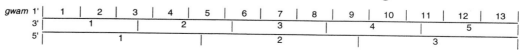

Writing 8

1. Key one 1' writing on the paragraph.
2. Key two 2' writings on the paragraph.

 all letters   *gwam* 1' | 2'

	1'	2'
According to a number of recent studies, taking time for	11	6	59
leisure, relaxation, and recreation is extremely important. This	25	12	66
fact has taken on new significance in the last ten years as the	37	19	72
pressures which face a person in daily life have also increased.	51	25	79
While automation has, no doubt, taken much of the drudgery out of	64	32	85
many of the routine tasks that people do, quite a few people find	77	39	92
that they have to solve complex problems and make major decisions	90	45	99
to survive in society's maze. Relaxation from this stress can be	103	52	105
vital to a person.	107	54	107

gwam 1' | 1 | 2 | 3 | 4 | 5 | 6 | 7 | 8 | 9 | 10 | 11 | 12 | 13 |
      2' | 1 | 2 | 3 | 4 | 5 | 6 | 7 |

Writing 9

1. Key two 1' writings on each paragraph.
2. Key one 3' writing on both paragraphs.
3. Key one 5' writing on both paragraphs.

 all letters   *gwam* 1' | 3' | 5'

	1'	3'	5'
Do employees have the right to privacy? The use of a drug	12	4	2
test, a lie-detector test, or a computer to check the performance	25	8	5
of employees raises a number of questions about privacy in the	38	13	8
workplace. The issues are complex, and they are often settled in	51	17	10
court by a jury. Why would a company agree to invade the privacy	64	21	13
of its workers? Absenteeism, turnover, theft, and liability are	77	26	15
the reasons given most often. These problems cost billions of	90	30	18
dollars each year, and many believe that something must be done	102	34	21
to control the costs.	107	36	21
Employees who use drugs or steal from their organizations	12	39	24
obviously have reason to fear the tests. An excellent question	24	44	26
is, why are employees who do not use drugs or steal so concerned?	38	48	29
Fear of abuse is the principal reason cited. Many employees	50	52	31
question the accuracy of the tests that are administered. They	63	57	34
realize that they could lose their jobs on the basis of false	75	61	36
information. Many object as a matter of principle. They believe	88	65	39
that the right to privacy is the right of all citizens who live	101	69	42
in this country.	104	70	42

gwam 1' | 1 | 2 | 3 | 4 | 5 | 6 | 7 | 8 | 9 | 10 | 11 | 12 | 13 |
      3' | 1 | 2 | 3 | 4 | 5 |
      5' | 1 | 2 | 3 |

Writing 10

1. Key one 1' writing on the paragraph.
2. Key two 2' writings on the paragraph.

 all letters

	gwam	1'	2'
Dressing well does not mean you must select only the most	12	6	62
expensive high-quality clothing. Many experts say you should	24	12	68
favor styles which not only make you feel good when wearing them	37	19	74
but also flatter your figure. Selecting clothes by these stan-	50	25	81
dards usually will produce a desirable result for most people.	62	31	87
However, just because you like something and it looks good on you	76	38	94
does not ensure it can be categorized as high fashion. Follow	88	44	100
your instincts, but also be aware that there are rules for dress-	101	51	106
ing just as there are rules for other areas of life.	112	56	112

gwam 1' | 1 | 2 | 3 | 4 | 5 | 6 | 7 | 8 | 9 | 10 | 11 | 12 | 13 |
2' | 1 | 2 | 3 | 4 | 5 | 6 | 7 |

Writing 11

1. Key one 3' writing on both paragraphs.
2. Key one 5' writing on both paragraphs.

A **all letters**

	gwam	3'	5'
Many white-collar workers spend a significant amount of time	4	78	2
in meetings. Meetings can be very expensive and may or may not	8	83	5
be very effective. Time and travel expenses are the major fac-	13	88	8
tors that influence the cost of a meeting. Each leader in charge	17	91	10
of a meeting should be required to estimate the cost of the meet-	21	96	13
ing and to attempt to assess objectively if the benefits of the	26	100	15
meeting justify the cost of it. Meetings that cannot be justi-	30	104	18
fied due to the cost should be eliminated or made cost effective.	34	108	20
How can meetings be made more beneficial? A key step is to	38	112	23
determine if a meeting is the best way to convey the information.	43	117	26
A telephone call or memo may be just as effective. If a meeting	47	121	28
is essential, then it should be planned and organized carefully	51	125	31
to derive maximum benefit from the time invested. An agenda	55	129	33
should be distributed prior to the meeting so that participants	59	134	36
can be prepared for discussion. The agenda should specify the	64	138	38
starting and ending times of the meeting as well as the time	68	142	41
allotted for each item to be discussed. Good leadership during	72	146	43
the meeting is also very critical.	74	148	45

gwam 3' | 1 | 2 | 3 | 4 | 5 |
5' | 1 | 2 | 3 |

Writing 12

1. Key one 1' writing on the paragraph.
2. Key two 2' writings on the paragraph.

 all letters

	gwam	1'	2'
The vast quantities of information available to a person		11	6	60
today have placed greater demands on each one of us to improve		24	12	66
our levels of productivity. The fact that information is so much		37	19	73
easier to access now than it was just five or six years ago has		50	25	80
sharpened the competition that exists in many of the areas which		63	32	86
touch our lives daily, such as work. Information is of little		76	38	92
value if people are not productive in the way they handle and		88	44	98
disperse it. To increase information flow and output, first zero		101	51	105
in on improving communication skills.		108	54	108

gwam 1' | 1 | 2 | 3 | 4 | 5 | 6 | 7 | 8 | 9 | 10 | 11 | 12 | 13 |
2' | 1 | 2 | 3 | 4 | 5 | 6 | 7 |

Writing 13

1. Key two 1' writings on each paragraph.
2. Key one 3' writing on both paragraphs.
3. Key one 5' writing on both paragraphs.

 all letters

	gwam	1'	3'	5'
Most people consider an office a safe place of employment,		12	4	2
and generally offices are safe. However, an office can have some		25	8	5
hazards; and accidents do happen in offices. Usually, accidents		38	13	8
in an office can be prevented by using common sense and paying a		51	17	10
little extra attention to detail. The most frequent accidents		64	21	13
are small cuts from paper. Other ways in which an individual can		77	26	15
get hurt are to slip on a wet floor, fall over an object, or fall		90	30	18
off of a chair or stepstool.		96	32	19
Office workers can also be victims of crime. Theft is one		12	36	22
of the most common crimes in the office. The things that are		24	40	24
taken most often are money, clothes, and office supplies. More		37	44	27
serious crimes involving bodily harm can also occur in offices.		50	49	29
Many companies use security guards to protect workers and prop-		63	53	32
erty. Another way to prevent crime in offices is to limit access		76	57	34
to the offices. Visitors must sign in and receive badges before		89	62	37
they can go into the office area. In some cases, workers are		101	66	39
asked to wear badges as well.		107	68	41

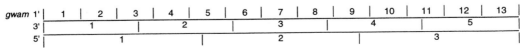

gwam 1' | 1 | 2 | 3 | 4 | 5 | 6 | 7 | 8 | 9 | 10 | 11 | 12 | 13 |
3' | 1 | 2 | 3 | 4 | 5 |
5' | 1 | 2 | 3 |

Writing 14

1. Key two 1'
writings on the
paragraph.
2. Key one 2' writing
on the paragraph.

 all letters

	gwam 2'
When you go to a job interview, the first few minutes are	6 | 69
the most important. The interviewer's first impressions of you	12 | 76
will be more detailed than what you have written on your resume.	19 | 82
Remember, smile sincerely, have a hearty handshake, dress prop-	25 | 89
erly, and exhibit a pleasant personality. Look confident and be	32 | 95
positive about what you, as an employee, have to offer the orga-	38 | 102
nization. Be careful that you do not give the impression that	44 | 108
you are interested only in what you can get from the firm. If	51 | 114
you can also articulate your answers to the interview questions,	57 | 121
you will have a better chance of having an offer extended to you.	64 | 127

gwam 2' | 1 | 2 | 3 | 4 | 5 | 6 | 7 |

Writing 15

1. Key two 1'
writings on each
paragraph.
2. Key one 3' writing
on both paragraphs.
3. Key one 5' writing
on both paragraphs.

 all letters

	gwam	1'	3'	5'
A great deal of research has been done to determine why		11	4	2
individuals remember certain advertisements but do not remember		24	8	5
others. Basically, research suggests that advertisements first		37	12	7
must get people's attention. This may not be so easy. If you		49	17	10
have been looking for a good set of golf clubs and you see an		62	21	12
advertisement in the newspaper for a particular set of golf		74	25	15
clubs, you may stop to read the ad. On the other hand, if you		86	29	17
are looking for a new automobile, chances are you will pass right		100	33	20
over the advertisement for golf clubs. Scientists explain this		112	38	23
by saying that individuals have to be primed, or made ready, for		125	42	25
a message in order to pay attention to it.		134	45	27
Once an ad gets attention, it then must convey a message.		12	49	29
In order to convey a message, it needs to be clear, easy to		24	53	32
understand, and easy to remember. The advertisement should also		37	57	34
focus on the product--the characteristics and images that are		49	61	37
quite likely to appeal to the market it is trying to reach.		61	65	39
Developing a message that best summarizes the advantage of a		74	69	42
product is not easy; however, the success of a product may well		86	73	44
rest on the message that is projected.		94	76	46

gwam 1' | 1 | 2 | 3 | 4 | 5 | 6 | 7 | 8 | 9 | 10 | 11 | 12 | 13 |
3' | 1 | 2 | 3 | 4 | 5 |
5' | 1 | 2 | 3 |

Writing 16

1. Key one 1' writing on the paragraph.
2. Key two 2' writings on the paragraph.

 all letters

	gwam	1'	2'
Small business is, no doubt, the backbone of our country and	12	6	54
plays an extremely important role for our citizens. Small busi-	25	13	61
ness has been quite important in building a healthy economy,	37	19	67
especially during economic lows. As a matter of fact, well over	50	25	73
half of all new jobs that come open each year are those offered	63	32	80
by firms with twenty or fewer workers. People entering the world	76	38	86
of work should note the differences between small and large busi-	89	45	93
nesses in terms of their own choices.	97	48	97

gwam 1' | 1 | 2 | 3 | 4 | 5 | 6 | 7 | 8 | 9 | 10 | 11 | 12 | 13 |
2' | 1 | 2 | 3 | 4 | 5 | 6 | 7 |

Writing 17

1. Key two 1' writings on each paragraph.
2. Key one 3' writing on both paragraphs.
3. Key one 5' writing on both paragraphs.

 all letters

	gwam	1'	3'	5'
Students who desire a career in business can benefit from	12	4	2
learning how to use word processing software. In many business	24	8	5
positions, workers spend a major amount of time writing various	37	12	7
types of business communications. The best writers are often	50	17	10
those who have learned how to edit their work properly. Editing	63	21	13
is amazingly easy when word processing is used. Copy can be	75	25	15
added, deleted, or replaced; or it can be moved from one place to	88	29	18
another. Changes can be made before a final copy is printed.	101	34	20
Even if the copy has already been printed, it is easy to make the	114	38	23
needed changes and print a corrected copy.	122	41	24
The important point to remember is that editing does not re-	12	45	27
quire an entire document to be rekeyed when word processing is	25	49	29
used. Keying is limited just to the changes that must be made.	38	53	32
The types of changes that can be made in a document are not lim-	50	58	35
ited to correcting content and mechanical errors. The format of	63	62	37
a document can also be changed during the editing process. A few	77	66	40
simple format changes can give a complex document a very dif-	89	70	42
ferent appearance.	92	72	43

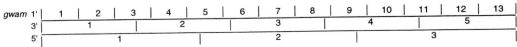

gwam 1' | 1 | 2 | 3 | 4 | 5 | 6 | 7 | 8 | 9 | 10 | 11 | 12 | 13 |
3' | 1 | 2 | 3 | 4 | 5 |
5' | 1 | 2 | 3 |

Writing 18

1. Key one 1' writing on the paragraph.
2. Key two 2' writings on the paragraph.

 all letters

	gwam	1'	2'
The good use of basic management skills by an office worker	12	6	62
is vital to an employer. Basic, but essential, work management	25	12	69
skills include the ability to plan, organize, and control.	37	18	75
Besides these important skills, one should develop leadership	49	25	81
skills and a good attitude. Most of these skills may not be job	63	31	88
specific; but, without exception, they do contribute to the pro-	75	37	94
ductivity of an office and to quality work. The success of an	88	44	100
office job may not be how much one knows about a job, but how	100	50	106
effectively one applies the basic skills to the work to be done.	113	56	113

gwam 1' | 1 | 2 | 3 | 4 | 5 | 6 | 7 | 8 | 9 | 10 | 11 | 12 | 13 |
2' | 1 | 2 | 3 | 4 | 5 | 6 | 7 |

Writing 19

1. Key two 1' writings on each paragraph.
2. Key one 3' writing on all paragraphs.
3. Key one 5' writing on all paragraphs.

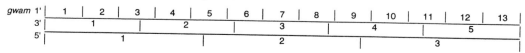 all letters

	gwam	1'	3'	5'
Traffic jams, deadlines, problems at work, and squabbles at	12	4	2
home are some ways in which tension is created. When our tension	25	8	5
is about to reach the boiling point, what do people usually tell	38	13	8
us? In most cases, they urge us to relax. But relaxing is not	51	17	10
always easy to accomplish. We frequently think we cannot find	64	21	13
the time for this important part of our daily activity.	75	25	15
To understand how relaxation works for us, we must realize	12	29	17
how the stress of contemporary existence works. People are	24	33	20
developed for survival in a challenging world. The human body	36	37	22
reacts to a crisis by getting ready for action. Whether we are	49	41	25
preparing for a timed writing or for an encounter in a dark	61	45	27
street, our muscles tighten and our blood pressure goes up.	73	49	30
After years of this type of response, we often find it difficult	86	54	32
to relax when we want to.	91	55	33
Now think about the feeling which is the opposite of this	12	59	36
turmoil. The pulse slows down, the breath comes slowly and	24	63	38
calmly, and the tension leaves the body. This is total relax-	36	67	40
ation. And if it sounds good, consider how good it must actually	49	72	43
feel. Our bodies are already prepared to relax; it is an ability	52	76	46
all individuals have within themselves. What we have to practice	76	81	48
is how to use this response.	81	82	49

gwam 1' | 1 | 2 | 3 | 4 | 5 | 6 | 7 | 8 | 9 | 10 | 11 | 12 | 13 |
3' | 1 | 2 | 3 | 4 | 5 |
5' | 1 | 2 | 3 |

Appendix D

Directory of Jobs and Files

Directory of Jobs and Files

Project	Job Nos.	Data Files	Solution Files	File Types
1	1-1 to 1-7	Return to Work Policy B.doc StarLogo1.bmp WhitewaterNewRiver-def01.tif	1-1 Request.doc 1-1 Baskets.doc 1-1 Request Envelope.doc 1-1 Baskets Envelope.doc 1-2 List.doc 1-2 Challenge List.doc 1-3 Petty Cash.doc 1-4 Stickers.doc 1-4 Thank You.doc 1-5 Manual.doc 1-6 River Classifications.doc 1-7 Injury Follow-up.doc	*Word* BMP graphic TIF graphic
2	2-1 to 2-6	None	2-1 Org Chart.doc 2-2 Description Bus Driver.doc 2-2 Description Admin Assistant.doc 2-2 Description Reservationist.doc 2-3 Tents.doc 2-4 Rafting Sheet.doc 2-5 Manual.doc 2-6 Guide Application.doc 2-6 Regulations.doc	*Word*
3	3-1 to 3-6	Roster.xls Scouts.doc Scouts Letter.doc	3-1 Meals.doc 3-1 Meals Form.doc 3-1 Meals for 1742.doc 3-2 Meeting Agenda.doc 3-2 Agenda Newland.doc 3-2 Agenda for Notes.doc 3-2 February Minutes.doc 3-2 Scouts Agenda.doc 3-2 Scouts Agenda Jackson.doc 3-2 Scouts Agenda for Notes.doc 3-3 Checklist.doc 3-3 Checklist Online.htm 3-3 Signup Sheet.doc 3-3 Signup Sheet Online.htm 3-4 Employee List Setup.doc 3-4 Employee List Merged.doc 3-4 Employee Directory Setup.doc 3-4 Employee Directory Merged.doc 3-4 Employee Directory Booklet.doc 3-5 Scouts Troops.doc 3-5 Scouts Letter Setup.doc 3-5 Scouts Letter Merged.doc 3-5 Scouts Labels Setup.doc 3-5 Scouts Labels Merged.doc 3-6 Manual.doc	*Excel* *Word* HTML

Project	Job Nos.	Data Files	Solution Files	File Types
4	4-1 to 4-5	Letterhead.doc P4 Employees.mdb Email from Newland.doc Special Use Request.doc Classified.xls River Classifications.doc Printed Form.doc Brochure Text.doc	4-1 Student Fax Cover Sheet.dot 4-1 Letterhead Setup.doc 4-1 Letterhead Merged.doc 4-1 Notepad Setup 1.doc 4-1 Notepad Merged 1.doc 4-1 Notepad Setup 2.doc 4-1 Notepad Merged 2.doc 4-2 River Classifications.doc 4-2 Request Form Printed.doc 4-2 Request Form Onscreen.doc 4-2 Request Form Challenge.htm 4-3 Fax.doc 4-3 Special Use Request.ppt 4-4 Brochure.doc 4-5 Manual.doc	*Word* *Access* *Excel* *HTML* *PowerPoint*
5	5-1 to 5-5	Gift Certificates.xls Certificate Template.dot Preparing Gift Certificates.htm Jackson Itinerary.doc February Articles.doc Newsletter List.doc April Articles.doc Trip 800.doc Trip Packages.mdb Spring Season.doc Mothers Day.doc Styles.doc Logaul01.tif Logaul02.tif Sittop01.tif Oaraft02.tif Brochure Page 2.doc Distances.doc	5-1 Certificate Record.xls 5-1 Certificate Template G.dot 5-1 G Certificates Issued.doc 5-1 S Certificate Template.dot 5-1 S Certificates Issued.doc 5-2 NWRAC Itinerary.doc 5-2 AMA Itinerary.doc 5-3 February Newsletter.doc 5-3 April Newsletter.doc 5-4 February Newsletter.htm 5-4 Trip 800.htm 5-4 Spring Season.htm 5-4 Mothers Day.htm 5-5 Brochure.doc 5-5 Challenge Brochure.doc	*Excel* *Word* HTML *Access* TIF graphic
6	6-1 to 6-5	Office Documents.ppt Request.doc Reading List Memo.doc Manual.ppt Training.doc New River.bmp	6-1 Office Documents.ppt 6-2 Slide Capture.doc 6-2 Sorter Capture.doc 6-2 Handouts.doc 6-2 Office Documents.ppt 6-2 Office Documents Timed.ppt 6-3 Template.pot 6-4 Manual.ppt 6-5 Athlete's Foot.ppt 6-5 Athlete's Foot Online.htm 6-5 Challenge.htm Reading List Memo.doc Request.doc	*PowerPoint* *Word* BMP graphic HTML
7	7-1 to 7-6	Monthly Payroll.xls Biweekly Payroll.xls Star River Adventures P7.mdb	7-1 Payroll.xls 7-1 Challenge Payroll.xls 7-2 Payroll.xls 7-3 Payroll.xls 7-4 Payroll.xls 7-5 Payroll.xls 7-6 Payroll.xls 7-6 Challenge Payroll.xls 7-6 Challenge Memo.doc	*Excel* *Access* *Word*

Project	Job Nos.	Data Files	Solution Files	File Types
8	8-1 to 8-6	Expenditures.xls Budget Summary.xls	8-1 Budget.xls 8-2 Budget.xls 8-2 Challenge Budget.xls 8-3 Budget.xls 8-4 Budget.xls 8-5 Budget.xls 8-6 Report.doc	*Excel* *Word*
9	9-1 to 9-6	Jackson Travel Request.xls Inez Travel Request.xls Gauley.bmp Inez Expense Report.xls	9-1 Request for Travel Template.xlt 9-2 Carr Travel Request.xls 9-2 Jackson Travel Request.xls 9-2 Inez Travel Request.xls 9-3 Application.doc 9-3 Presentation.ppt 9-3 Challenge Application.htm 9-4 Expense Report Template.xlt 9-5 Jackson Expense Report.xls 9-6 Inez Updated Report.xls 9-6 Inez Memo.doc	*Excel* *BMP graphic* *Word* *PowerPoint* *HTML*
10	10-1 to 10-6	Pricing Report.doc New River Trip.doc Gauley List.xls	10-1 Pricing.xls 10-2 Pricing.xls 10-3 Pricing.xls 10-3 Pricing Report.doc 10-4 Pricing.xls 10-5 New River Discovery Show.ppt 10-5 Challenge Show.ppt 10-6 Gauley List.xls 10-6 Gauley List Challenge.xls	*Word* *Excel* *PowerPoint*
11	11-1 to 11-6	Evaluation Form.doc New River Excursion Data.xls Evaluation Report.doc	11-1 Evaluation Form.doc 11-2 Evaluation Analysis.xls 11-3 New River Data.xls 11-4 New River Data.xls 11-5 New River Data.xls 11-6 Evaluation Report.doc 11-6 Challenge.xls 11-6 Challenge Memo.doc	*Word* *Excel*
12	12-1 to 12-6	May Balance Sheet.doc June Balance Sheet.doc	12-1 Balance Sheet Template.xlt 12-2 May Balance Sheet.xls 12-2 Balance Sheet Template.xlt 12-3 June Balance Sheet.xls 12-3 June Balance Sheet Online.htm 12-3 Sample Email Solution.doc 12-4 2nd Quarter Income Statement.xls 12-4 2nd Quarter Income Statement Online.htm 12-4 Income Statement Template.xlt 12-5 1st Quarter Income Statement.xls 12-5 1st Quarter Income Statement Online.htm 12-6 May Chart.xls 12-6 June Chart.xls 12-6 2nd Quarter Chart.xls 12-6 Comparison Chart.xls	*Word* *Excel* *HTML*

Project	Job Nos.	Data Files	Solution Files	File Types
13	13-1 to 13-6	July 4 Text.doc July 4 Sound.wav Register Text.doc Registration Form.xls Events Text.doc Clothing Text.doc Forms Text.doc	13-1 July 4.ppt 13-2 Register.ppt 13-2 Registration Form.xlt 13-2 Dorazio.xls 13-3 Events.ppt 13-4 Clothing.ppt 13-5 Forms.ppt 13-5 Information Form.doc 13-6 July 4.ppt 13-6 July 4 Online.htm	*Word* WAV sound *Excel* *PowerPoint* HTML
14	14-1 to 14-5	Star River Adventures P14.mdb	Star River Adventures P14 Key J14-1 T1.mdb Star River Adventures P14 Key J14-1 T2.mdb Star River Adventures P14 Key J14-2 T1.mdb Star River Adventures P14 Key J14-2 T2.mdb Star River Adventures P14 Key J14-2 T3.mdb Star River Adventures P14 Key J14-3.mdb Star River Adventures P14 Key J14-4.mdb 14-4 Letter.doc 14-4 Merged Letters.doc 14-4 Challenge Letter.doc 14-4 Challenge Merged.doc	*Access* *Word*
15	15-1 to 15-6	Star River Adventures P15.mdb Equipment.doc	Star River Adventures P15 Key J15-1.mdb Star River Adventures P15 Key J15-2.mdb Star River Adventures P15 Key J15-3.mdb Star River Adventures P15 Key J15-4.mdb Star River Adventures P15 Key J15-5.mdb Star River Adventures P15 Key J15-6.mdb 15-6 Memo1.doc 15-6 Memo2.doc	*Access* *Word*
16	16-1 to 16-5	Star River Adventures P16.mdb WV Scouts Attendees.xls Sutton Junior Boaters.doc WV Act.doc	SRA Event Management P16 Key J16-1.mdb SRA Event Management P16 Key J16-2.mdb SRA Event Management P16 Key J16-3.mdb Star River Adventures P16 Key J16-3.mdb 16-4 Events by Event Type Report.html SRA Event Management P16 Key J16-4.mdb 16-5 WV Whitewater Act.ppt	*Access* *Excel* *Word* HTML *PowerPoint*
17	17-1 to 17-5	P17 Star River Adventures.mdb New Clients.doc	Star River Adventures P17 Key J17-1.mdb Star River Adventures P17 Key J17-2.mdb Trip Packages Page.htm Star River Adventures P17 Key J17-3.mdb Star River Adventures P17 Key J17-4.mdb River Stats P17 Key J17-5.mdb	*Access* *Word* PDF HTML

Project	Job Nos.	Data Files	Solution Files	File Types
18	18-1 to 18-6	Girl with Dog.png Welcome.ppt	18-1 Misconduct.png 18-1 Misconduct Animation.gif 18-2 Belongings.png 18-2 Belongings Image.jpg 18-3 Classifications.png 18-3 Classifications Image.jpg 18-3 Challenge.png 18-3 Challenge Image.jpg 18-4 Girl with Dog.png 18-4 Girl with Dog2.bmp 18-5 Welcome Message.wav 18-6 Welcome.ppt 18-6 Welcome Online.htm	*Fireworks MX* *PowerPoint* GIF graphic JPEG graphic BMP graphic WAV sound HTML
19	19-1 to 19-6	News.doc StarLogo3.gif SRA Intranet (Web folder)	P19 SRA Intranet Key J19-1 (Web folder) P19 SRA Intranet Key J19-2 (Web folder) P19 SRA Intranet Key J19-3 (Web folder) P19 SRA Intranet Key J19-4 (Web folder) P19 SRA Intranet Key J19-5 (Web folder)	*Word* GIF graphic JPEG graphic HTML Web folder
20	20-1 to 20-6	Travel Requests Email.doc Request for Travel Template.xlt StarLogo2.bmp Contacts List.xls StarLogo1.bmp Kiosk Show.doc Changing Business.doc Newland 10-19.xls Jackson 10-19.xls Inez 10-19.xls Abraham 10-19.xls Collins 10-19.xls Travel Agents.doc	20-1 Travel Requests.xls 20-1 Memo.doc P20 Contacts.mdb 20-2 Letter.doc 20-2 Merged Letters.doc 20-3 Brochure.doc Kiosk1.wav 20-4 Kiosk Show.ppt 20-4 Kiosk Web Page.htm 20-4 Changing Business.ppt 20-5 Inez 10-19.doc 20-5 Newland 10-19.xls 20-5 NOATS Worksheet.xls 20-6 Memo.doc 20-6 Letter.doc 20-6 Merged Letters.doc	*Word* *Excel* BMP graphic *Access* WAV sound *PowerPoint* HTML

Appendix E

Microsoft Office Certification Correlation

Access 2003 Specialist		
	Skill Sets and Skills	**Project Numbers**
AC03S-1	**Structuring Databases**	
AC03S-1-1	Create Access databases	16, 17, 20
AC03S-1-2	Create and modify tables	14, 17
AC03S-1-3	Define and create field types	17
AC03S-1-4	Modify field properties	14, 15, 17
AC03S-1-5	Create and modify one-to-many relationships	14, 15, 17
AC03S-1-6	Enforce referential integrity	14, 15, 17
AC03S-1-7	Create and modify queries	14, 17
AC03S-1-8	Create forms	14, 20
AC03S-1-9	Add and modify form controls and properties	N/A
AC03S-1-10	Create reports	14, 16, 17, 20
AC03S-1-11	Add and modify report control properties	N/A
AC03S-1-12	Create a data access page	N/A
AC03S-2	**Entering Data**	
AC03S-2-1	Enter, edit, and delete records	16, 20
AC03S-2-2	Find and move among records	16
AC03S-2-3	Import data to Access	3, 4, 5, 16, 17, 20
AC03S-3	**Organizing Data**	
AC03S-3-1	Create and modify calculated fields and aggregate functions	N/A
AC03S-3-2	Modify form layout	N/A
AC03S-3-3	Modify report layout and page setup	N/A
AC03S-3-4	Format datasheets	N/A
AC03S-3-5	Sort records	15, 17, 20
AC03S-3-6	Filter records	17
AC03S-4	**Managing Databases**	
AC03S-4-1	Identify and modify object dependencies	N/A
AC03S-4-2	View objects and object data in other views	20
AC03S-4-3	Print database objects and data	N/A
AC03S-4-4	Export data from Access	14, 16, 20
AC03S-4-5	Back up a database	N/A
AC03S-4-6	Compact and repair databases	N/A

Excel 2003 Specialist

	Skill Sets and Skills	Project Numbers
XL03S-1	**Creating Data and Content**	
XL03S-1-1	Enter and edit cell content	7, 8, 9, 10, 11, 12, 20
XL03S-1-2	Navigate to specific cell content	N/A
XL03S-1-3	Locate, select, and insert supporting information	N/A
XL03S-1-4	Insert, position, and size graphics	8, 9
XL03S-2	**Analyzing Data**	
XL03S-2-1	Filter lists using AutoFilter	N/A
XL03S-2-2	Sort lists	N/A
XL03S-2-3	Insert and modify formulas	20
XL03S-2-4	Use statistical, date and time, financial, and logical functions	8, 9, 11
XL03S-2-5	Create, modify, and position diagrams and charts based on worksheet data	8, 11, 20
XL03S-3	**Formatting Data and Content**	
XL03S-3-1	Apply and modify cell formats	8, 9, 10, 11, 12, 13, 20
XL03S-3-2	Apply and modify cell styles	9, 10
XL03S-3-3	Modify row and column formats	9, 10, 11, 20
XL03S-3-4	Format worksheets	N/A
XL03S-4	**Collaborating**	
XL03S-4-1	Insert, view, and edit comments	10
XL03S-5	**Managing Workbooks**	
XL03S-5-1	Create new workbooks from templates	20
XL03S-5-2	Insert, delete, and move cells	8, 9, 10, 11, 12
XL03S-5-3	Create and modify hyperlinks	9, 12
XL03S-5-4	Organize worksheets	10
XL03S-5-5	Preview data in other views	N/A
XL03S-5-6	Customize Window layout	N/A
XL03S-5-9	Organize workbooks using file folders	20
XL03S-5-10	Save data in appropriate formats for different uses	N/A

Excel 2003 Expert

	Skill Sets and Skills	Project Numbers
XL03E-1	**Organizing and Analyzing Data**	
XL03E-1-1	Use subtotals	N/A
XL03E-1-2	Define and apply advanced filters	N/A
XL03E-1-3	Group and outline data	N/A
XL03E-1-4	Use data validation	N/A
XL03E-1-5	Create and modify list ranges	N/A
XL03E-1-6	Add, show, close, edit, merge, and summarize scenarios	N/A
XL03E-1-7	Perform data analysis using automated tools	N/A
XL03E-1-8	Create PivotTable and PivotChart reports	N/A
XL03E-1-9	Use Lookup and Reference functions	N/A
XL03E-1-10	Use Database functions	N/A
XL03E-1-11	Trace formula precedents, dependents, and errors	N/A
XL03E-1-12	Locate invalid data and formulas	N/A
XL03E-1-13	Watch and evaluate formulas	N/A
XL03E-1-14	Define, modify, and use named ranges	N/A
XL03E-1-15	Structure workbooks using XML	N/A
XL03E-2	**Formatting Data and Content**	
XL03E-2-1	Create and modify custom data formats	N/A
XL03E-2-2	Use conditional formatting	N/A
XL03E-2-3	Format and resize graphics	N/A
XL03E-2-4	Format charts and diagrams	N/A
XL03E-3	**Collaborating**	
XL03E-3-1	Protect cells, worksheets, and workbooks	N/A
XL03E-3-2	Apply workbook security settings	N/A
XL03E-3-3	Share workbooks	N/A
XL03E-3-4	Merge workbooks	N/A
XL03E-3-5	Track, accept, and reject changes to workbooks	N/A
XL03E-4	**Managing Data and Workbooks**	
XL03E-4-1	Import data to Excel	3, 4, 7, 8, 10, 11
XL03E-4-2	Export data from Excel	7, 8, 10, 11
XL03E-4-3	Publish and edit Web worksheets and workbooks	N/A
XL03E-4-4	Create and edit templates	N/A
XL03E-4-5	Consolidate data	N/A
XL03E-4-6	Define and modify workbook properties	N/A
XL03E-5	**Customizing Excel**	
XL03E-5-1	Customize toolbars and menus	N/A
XL03E-5-2	Create, edit, and run macros	N/A
XL03E-5-3	Modify Excel default settings	N/A

PowerPoint 2003		
	Skill Sets and Skills	**Project Numbers**
PP03S-1	**Creating Content**	
PP03S-1-1	Create new presentations from templates	N/A
PP03S-1-2	Insert and edit text-based content	6, 9, 13, 20
PP03S-1-3	Insert tables, charts, and diagrams	6, 9, 20
PP03S-1-4	Insert pictures, shapes, and graphics	6, 9, 20
PP03S-1-5	Insert objects	N/A
PP03S-2	**Formatting Content**	
PP03S-2-1	Format text-based content	6, 9, 13, 20
PP03S-2-2	Format pictures, shapes, and graphics	6
PP03S-2-3	Format slides	6
PP03S-2-4	Apply animation schemes	6, 10, 13, 16, 18, 20
PP03S-2-5	Apply slide transitions	6, 9, 13, 16, 20
PP03S-2-6	Customize slide templates	6
PP03S-2-7	Work with masters	6, 9
PP03S-3	**Collaborating**	
PP03S-3-1	Track, accept, and reject changes in a presentation	N/A
PP03S-3-2	Add, edit, and delete comments in a presentation	N/A
PP03S-3-3	Compare and merge presentations	N/A
PP03S-4	**Managing and Delivering Presentations**	
PP03S-4-1	Organize a presentation	N/A
PP03S-4-2	Set up slide shows for delivery	6, 9, 10, 13, 16
PP03S-4-3	Rehearse timing	6
PP03S-4-4	Deliver presentations	6, 10, 13
PP03S-4-5	Prepare presentations for remote delivery	N/A
PP03S-4-6	Save and publish presentations	6, 13, 20
PP03S-4-7	Print slides, outlines, handouts, and speaker notes	6, 10, 13, 16, 18, 20
PP03S-4-8	Export a presentation to another *Microsoft Office* program	13, 16

Word 2003 Specialist		
	Skill Sets and Skills	**Project Numbers**
WW03S-1	**Creating Content**	
WW03S-1-1	Insert and edit text, symbols, and special characters	1, 2, 3, 4, 5, 20
WW03S-1-2	Insert frequently used and pre-defined text	N/A
WW03S-1-3	Navigate to specific content	N/A
WW03S-1-4	Insert, position, and size graphics	1, 3, 4, 5, 20
WW03S-1-5	Create and modify diagrams and charts	2, 20
WW03S-2	**Organizing Content**	
WW03S-2-1	Insert and modify tables	1, 3, 4, 5
WW03S-2-2	Create bulleted lists, numbered lists, and outlines	1
WW03S-2-3	Insert and modify hyperlinks	5
WW03S-3	**Formatting Content**	
WW03S-3-1	Format text	N/A
WW03S-3-2	Format paragraphs	2, 5
WW03S-3-3	Apply and format columns	2
WW03S-3-4	Insert and modify content in headers and footers	1, 3, 4, 5, 20
WW03S-3-5	Modify document layout and page setup	1, 2, 3, 4, 5
WW03S-4	**Collaborating**	
WW03S-4-1	Circulate documents for review	N/A
WW03S-4-2	Compare and merge documents	3, 4
WW03S-4-3	Insert, view, and edit comments	3
WW03S-4-4	Track, accept, and reject proposed changes	3
WW03S-5	**Formatting and Managing Documents**	
WW03S-5-1	Create new documents using templates	3, 4, 5, 20
WW03S-5-2	Review and modify document properties	N/A
WW03S-5-3	Organize documents using file folders	N/A
WW03S-5-4	Save documents in appropriate formats for different uses	2, 3, 4, 5
WW03S-5-5	Print documents, envelopes, and labels	1, 2, 3, 4, 5, 20
WW03S-5-6	Preview documents and Web pages	2, 3, 4, 20
WW03S-5-7	Change and organize document views and windows	N/A

Word 2003 Expert

	Skill Sets and Skills	Project Numbers
WW03E-1	**Formatting Content**	
WW03E-1-1	Create custom styles for text, tables, and lists	4
WW03E-1-2	Control pagination	2
WW03E-1-3	Format, position, and resize graphics using advanced layout features	2
WW03E-1-4	Insert and modify objects	N/A
WW03E-1-5	Create and modify diagrams and charts using data from other sources	2
WW03E-2	**Organizing Content**	
WW03E-2-1	Sort content in lists and tables	1
WW03E-2-2	Perform calculations in tables	1, 8
WW03E-2-3	Modify table formats	1, 2, 3, 4, 5
WW03E-2-4	Summarize document content using automated tools	N/A
WW03E-2-5	Use automated tools for document navigation	N/A
WW03E-2-6	Merge letters with other data sources	3, 4, 20
WW03E-2-7	Merge labels with other data sources	7
WW03E-2-8	Structure documents using XML	N/A
WW03E-3	**Formatting Documents**	
WW03E-3-1	Create and modify forms	4
WW03E-3-2	Create and modify document background	N/A
WW03E-3-3	Create and modify document indexes and tables	N/A
WW03E-3-4	Insert and modify endnotes, footnotes, captions, and cross-references	4
WW03E-3-5	Create and manage master documents and subdocuments	2
WW03E-4	**Collaborating**	
WW03E-4-1	Modify track changes options	N/A
WW03E-4-2	Publish and edit Web documents	3, 4, 5
WW03E-4-3	Manage document versions	N/A
WW03E-4-4	Protect and restrict forms and documents	N/A
WW03E-4-5	Attach digital signatures to documents	N/A
WW03E-4-6	Customize document properties	N/A
WW03E-5	**Customizing Word**	
WW03E-5-1	Create, edit, and run macros	N/A
WW03E-5-2	Customize menus and toolbars	N/A
WW03E-5-3	Modify Word default settings	N/A

Access Core 2002		
Skill Sets and Skills		**Project Numbers**
AC2002-1	**Creating and Using Databases**	
AC2002-1-1	Create Access databases	16, 17, 20
AC2002-1-2	Open database objects in multiple views	14, 15, 16, 17, 20
AC2002-1-3	Move among records	15, 16, 17
AC2002-1-4	Format datasheets	14, 16, 17
AC2002-2	**Creating and Modifying Tables**	
AC2002-2-1	Create and modify tables	14, 15, 17, 20
AC2002-2-2	Add a pre-defined input mask to a field	15, 17
AC2002-2-3	Create lookup fields	15, 16, 17
AC2002-2-4	Modify field properties	14, 15, 16, 17
AC2002-3	**Creating and Modifying Queries**	
AC2002-3-1	Create and modify Select queries	14, 15, 17
AC2002-3-2	Add calculated fields to Select queries	14, 15, 17
AC2002-4	**Creating and Modifying Forms**	
AC2002-4-1	Create and display forms	14, 15, 16, 17, 20
AC2002-4-2	Modify form properties	14, 15, 16, 17
AC2002-5	**Viewing and Organizing Information**	
AC2002-5-1	Enter, edit, and delete records	14, 15, 16, 17, 20
AC2002-5-2	Create queries	14, 15, 17, 20
AC2002-5-3	Sort records	14, 15, 17, 20
AC2002-5-4	Filter records	17
AC2002-6	**Defining Relationships**	
AC2002-6-1	Create one-to-many relationships	14, 15, 17
AC2002-6-2	Enforce referential integrity	14, 15, 17
AC2002-7	**Producing Reports**	
AC2002-7-1	Create and format reports	16, 17, 20
AC2002-7-2	Add calculated controls to reports	17
AC2002-7-3	Preview and print reports	14, 16, 17
AC2002-8	**Integrating with Other Applications**	
AC2002-8-1	Import data to Access	4, 5, 16, 17, 20
AC2002-8-2	Export data from Access	14, 16, 20
AC2002-8-3	Create a simple data access page	N/A

Access Expert 2002	
Skill Sets and Skills	**Project Numbers**
AC2002E-1 **Creating and Modifying Tables**	
AC2002E-1-1 Use data validation	N/A
AC2002E-1-2 Link tables	16
AC2002E-1-3 Create lookup fields and modify lookup field properties	15
AC2002E-1-4 Create and modify input masks	N/A
AC2002E-2 **Creating and Modifying Forms**	
AC2002E-2-1 Create a form in Design View	N/A
AC2002E-2-2 Create a Switchboard and set startup options	N/A
AC2002E-2-3 Add Subform controls to Access forms	N/A
AC2002E-3 **Refining Queries**	
AC2002E-3-1 Specify multiple query criteria	N/A
AC2002E-3-2 Create and apply advanced filters	N/A
AC2002E-3-3 Create and run parameter queries	N/A
AC2002E-3-4 Create and run action queries	N/A
AC2002E-3-5 Use aggregate functions in queries	N/A
AC2002E-4 **Producing Reports**	
AC2002E-4-1 Create and modify reports	N/A
AC2002E-4-2 Add Subreport controls to Access reports	N/A
AC2002E-4-3 Sort and group data in reports	N/A
AC2002E-5 **Defining Relationships**	
AC2002E-5-1 Establish one-to-many relationships	N/A
AC2002E-5-2 Establish many-to-many relationships	N/A
AC2002E-6 **Operating Access on the Web**	
AC2002E-6-1 Create and modify a data access page	N/A
AC2002E-6-2 Save PivotTables and PivotCharts views to data access pages	N/A
AC2002E-7 **Using Access Tools**	
AC2002E-7-1 Import XML documents into Access	N/A
AC2002E-7-2 Export Access data to XML documents	N/A
AC2002E-7-3 Encrypt and decrypt databases	N/A
AC2002E-7-4 Compact and repair databases	N/A
AC2002E-7-5 Assign database security	N/A
AC2002E-7-6 Replicate a database	N/A
AC2002E-8 **Creating Database Applications**	
AC2002E-8-1 Create Access modules	N/A
AC2002E-8-2 Use the Database Splitter	N/A
AC2002E-8-3 Create an MDE file	N/A

Excel Core 2002

	Skill Sets and Skills	Project Numbers
EX2002-1	**Working with Cells and Cell Data**	
EX2002-1-1	Insert, delete, and move cells	7, 8, 9, 10, 11, 12
EX2002-1-2	Enter and edit cell data including text, numbers, and formulas	7, 8, 9, 10, 11, 12, 20
EX2002-1-3	Check spelling	7, 8, 9, 10, 11, 12
EX2002-1-4	Find and replace cell data and formats	7
EX2002-1-5	Work with a subset of data by filtering lists	10
EX2002-2	**Managing Workbooks**	
EX2002-2-1	Manage workbook files and folders	7, 8, 9, 10, 11, 12, 20
EX2002-2-2	Save workbooks using different names and file formats	7, 8, 9, 10, 11, 12, 20
EX2002-3	**Formatting and Printing Worksheets**	
EX2002-3-1	Apply and modify cell formats	7, 8, 9, 10, 11, 12, 20
EX2002-3-2	Modify row and column settings	7, 8, 9, 10, 11
EX2002-3-3	Modify row and column formats	7, 9, 10, 11, 20
EX2002-3-4	Apply styles	10, 13
EX2002-3-5	Use automated tools to format worksheets	7, 9
EX2002-3-6	Modify Page Setup options for worksheets	7, 8, 9, 10, 11
EX2002-3-7	Preview and print worksheets and workbooks	7, 8, 9, 10, 11, 12, 20
EX2002-4	**Modifying Workbooks**	
EX2002-4-1	Insert and delete worksheets	7, 8, 10, 11, 12, 20
EX2002-4-2	Modify worksheet names and positions	7, 8, 10, 11, 12, 20
EX2002-4-3	Use 3-D references	7, 8
EX2002-5	**Creating and Revising Formulas**	
EX2002-5-1	Create and revise formulas	7, 8, 9, 10, 12, 20
EX2002-5-2	Use statistical, date and time, financial, and logical functions in formulas	7, 8, 9, 11, 12
EX2002-6	**Creating and Modifying Graphics**	
EX2002-6-1	Create, modify, position, and print charts	8, 9, 11, 12, 20
EX2002-6-2	Create, modify, and position graphics	9, 10, 12
EX2002-7	**Workgroup Collaboration**	
EX2002-7-1	Convert worksheets into Web pages	9, 12
EX2002-7-2	Create hyperlinks	9, 12
EX2002-7-3	View and edit comments	10, 12

Excel Expert 2002

	Skill Sets and Skills	Project Numbers
EX2002E-1	**Importing and Exporting Data**	
EX2002E-1-1	Import data to Excel	3, 4, 7, 8, 10, 11
EX2002E-1-2	Export data from Excel	7, 8, 10, 11
EX2002E-1-3	Publish worksheets and workbooks to the Web	N/A
EX2002E-2	**Managing Workbooks**	
EX2002E-2-1	Create, edit, and apply templates	9, 20
EX2002E-2-2	Create workspaces	N/A
EX2002E-2-3	Use Data Consolidation	N/A
EX2002E-3	**Formatting Numbers**	
EX2002E-3-1	Create and apply custom number formats	N/A
EX2002E-3-2	Use conditional formats	N/A
EX2002E-4	**Working with Ranges**	
EX2002E-4-1	Use named ranges in formulas	11
EX2002E-4-2	Use Lookup and Reference functions	N/A
EX2002E-5	**Customizing Excel**	
EX2002E-5-1	Customize toolbars and menus	N/A
EX2002E-5-2	Create, edit, and run macros	12
EX2002E-6	**Auditing Worksheets**	
EX2002E-6-1	Audit formulas	N/A
EX2002E-6-2	Locate and resolve errors	N/A
EX2002E-6-3	Identify dependencies in formulas	N/A
EX2002E-7	**Summarizing Data**	
EX2002E-7-1	Use subtotals with lists and ranges	N/A
EX2002E-7-2	Define and apply filters	N/A
EX2002E-7-3	Add group and outline criteria to ranges	N/A
EX2002E-7-4	Use data validation	N/A
EX2002E-7-5	Retrieve external data and create queries	N/A
EX2002E-7-6	Create Extensible Markup Language (XML) Web queries	N/A
EX2002E-8	**Analyzing Data**	
EX2002E-8-1	Create PivotTables, PivotCharts, and PivotTable/PivotChart Reports	N/A
EX2002E-8-2	Forecast values with *what-if* analysis	N/A
EX2002E-8-3	Create and display scenarios	N/A
EX2002E-9	**Workgroup Collaboration**	
EX2002E-9-1	Modify passwords, protections, and properties	N/A
EX2002E-9-2	Create a shared workbook	N/A
EX2002E-9-3	Track, accept, and reject changes to workbooks	N/A
EX2002E-9-4	Merge workbooks	N/A

PowerPoint 2002	
Skill Sets and Skills	**Project Numbers**
PP2002-1	**Creating Presentations**
PP2002-1-1	Create presentations (manually and using automated tools) · 6, 9, 10, 13, 16, 20
PP2002-1-2	Add slides to and delete slides from presentations · 6, 9, 10, 13, 16, 20
PP2002-1-3	Modify headers and footers in the Slide Master · 6, 9, 16
PP2002-2	**Inserting and Modifying Text**
PP2002-2-1	Import text from Word · 4
PP2002-2-2	Insert, format, and modify text · 9, 10, 13, 16, 20
PP2002-3	**Inserting and Modifying Visual Elements**
PP2002-3-1	Add tables, charts, clip art, and bitmap images to slides · 6, 13, 16, 20
PP2002-3-2	Customize slide backgrounds · 6
PP2002-3-3	Add OfficeArt elements to slides · 6, 9, 20
PP2002-3-4	Apply custom formats to tables · 13
PP2002-4	**Modifying Presentation Formats**
PP2002-4-1	Apply formats to presentations · 6, 13
PP2002-4-2	Apply animation schemes · 6, 13, 16, 20
PP2002-4-3	Apply slide transitions · 6, 10, 13, 16, 20
PP2002-4-4	Customize slide formats · 6
PP2002-4-5	Customize slide templates · N/A
PP2002-4-6	Manage a Slide Master · 6, 9
PP2002-4-7	Rehearse timing · 6
PP2002-4-8	Rearrange slides · 6, 9
PP2002-4-9	Modify slide layout · 6, 13, 16
PP2002-4-10	Add links to a presentation · 6, 9, 10, 13
PP2002-5	**Printing Presentations**
PP2002-5-1	Preview and print slides, outlines, handouts, and speaker notes · 6, 10, 13, 16, 20
PP2002-6	**Working with Data from Other Sources**
PP2002-6-1	Import Excel charts to slides · 10
PP2002-6-2	Add sound and video to slides · 13, 20
PP2002-6-3	Insert Word tables on slides · N/A
PP2002-6-4	Export a presentation as an outline · 18
PP2002-7	**Managing and Delivering Presentations**
PP2002-7-1	Set up slide shows · 6, 9, 10, 13, 16
PP2002-7-2	Manage files and folders for presentations · 10, 13
PP2002-7-3	Work with embedded fonts · N/A
PP2002-7-4	Publish presentations to the Web · 6
PP2002-7-5	Use Pack and Go · N/A

PP2002-8	Workgroup Collaboration	
PP2002-8-1	Set up a review cycle	N/A
PP2002-8-2	Schedule and deliver presentation broadcasts	N/A
PP2002-8-3	Publish presentations to the Web	6, 20

Word Core 2002		
	Skill Sets and Skills	**Project Numbers**
W2002-1	**Inserting and Modifying Text**	
W2002-1-1	Insert, modify, and move text and symbols	2, 3, 4, 5
W2002-1-2	Apply and modify text formats	2, 19, 20
W2002-1-3	Correct spelling and grammar usage	1, 2, 3, 4, 5, 20
W2002-1-4	Apply font and text effects	3
W2002-1-5	Enter and format date and time	1, 3, 4
W2002-1-6	Apply character styles	1, 10
W2002-2	**Creating and Modifying Paragraphs**	
W2002-2-1	Modify paragraph formats	1, 3, 4, 5, 6, 14, 20
W2002-2-2	Set and modify tabs	1, 2, 3, 5, 20
W2002-2-3	Apply bullet, outline, and numbering format to paragraphs	1, 2, 4
W2002-2-4	Apply paragraph styles	1, 2, 3, 4, 5, 20
W2002-3	**Formatting Documents**	
W2002-3-1	Create and modify a header and footer	1, 3, 5, 20
W2002-3-2	Apply and modify column settings	2, 3, 20
W2002-3-3	Modify document layout and Page Setup options	1, 2, 3, 4, 5
W2002-3-4	Create and modify tables	1, 2, 3, 4, 5
W2002-3-5	Preview and print documents, envelopes, and labels	1, 2, 3, 4, 5, 20
W2002-4	**Managing Documents**	
W2002-4-1	Manage files and folders for documents	1, 2, 3, 4, 5
W2002-4-2	Create documents using templates	3, 4, 5, 20
W2002-4-3	Save documents using different names and file formats	1, 2, 3, 4, 5
W2002-5	**Working with Graphics**	
W2002-5-1	Insert images and graphics	1, 2, 3, 4, 5, 20
W2002-5-2	Create and modify diagrams and charts	2
W2002-6	**Workgroup Collaboration**	
W2002-6-1	Compare and merge documents	3, 4
W2002-6-2	Insert, view, and edit comments	3
W2002-6-3	Convert documents into Web pages	4, 5, 20

Word Expert 2002		
	Skill Sets and Skills	**Project Numbers**
W2002E-1	**Customizing Paragraphs**	
W2002E-1-1	Control pagination	1, 2, 4
W2002E-1-2	Sort paragraphs in lists and tables	1
W2002E-2	**Formatting Documents**	
W2002E-2-1	Create and format document sections	4
W2002E-2-2	Create and apply character and paragraph styles	4, 5
W2002E-2-3	Create and update document indexes and tables of contents, figures, and authorities	N/A
W2002E-2-4	Create cross references	N/A
W2002E-2-5	Add and revise endnotes and footnotes	N/A
W2002E-2-6	Create and manage master documents and subdocuments	N/A
W2002E-2-7	Move within documents	N/A
W2002E-2-8	Create and modify forms using various form controls	4
W2002E-2-9	Create forms and prepare forms for distribution	4
W2002E-3	**Customizing Tables**	
W2002E-3-1	Use Excel data in tables	4, 5
W2002E-3-2	Perform calculations in Word tables	1
W2002E-4	**Creating and Modifying Graphics**	
W2002E-4-1	Create, modify, and position graphics	2, 3, 4, 5
W2002E-4-2	Create and modify charts using data from other applications	N/A
W2002E-4-3	Align text and graphics	N/A
W2002E-5	**Customizing Word**	
W2002E-5-1	Create, edit, and run macros	N/A
W2002E-5-2	Customize menus and toolbars	N/A
W2002E-6	**Workgroup Collaboration**	
W2002E-6-1	Track, accept, and reject changes to documents	N/A
W2002E-6-2	Merge input from several reviewers	N/A
W2002E-6-3	Insert and modify hyperlinks to other documents and Web pages	N/A
W2002E-6-4	Create and edit Web documents in Word	N/A
W2002E-6-5	Create document versions	N/A
W2002E-6-6	Protect documents	N/A
W2002E-6-7	Define and modify default file locations for workgroup templates	N/A
W2002E-6-8	Attach digital signatures to documents	N/A

W2002E-7	Using Mail Merge	
W2002E-7-1	Merge letters with a Word, Excel, or Access data source	3, 4, 20
W2002E-7-2	Merge labels with a Word, Excel, or Access data source	3
W2002E-7-3	Use Outlook data as mail merge data source	N/A

Index